Corpus-Based Approaches
to Metaphor and Metonymy

Corpus-Based Approaches to Metaphor and Metonymy

edited by
Anatol Stefanowitsch
Stefan Th. Gries

Mouton de Gruyter
Berlin · New York

Mouton de Gruyter (formerly Mouton, The Hague)
is a Division of Walter de Gruyter GmbH & Co. KG, Berlin.

The hardcover edition was published in 2006 as volume 171
of the series *Trends in Linguistics. Studies and Monographs.*

♾ Printed on acid-free paper which falls within the guidelines
of the ANSI to ensure permanence and durability.

The Library of Congress has cataloged the hardcover edition as follows:

Corpus-based approaches to metaphor and metonymy / edited by
Anatol Stefanowitsch, Stefan Th. Gries.
    p. cm. − (Trends in linguistics. Studies and monographs ; 171)
Includes bibliographical references and index.
ISBN-13: 978-3-11-018604-8 (alk. paper)
ISBN-10: 3-11-018604-7 (alk. paper)
    1. Metaphor − Data processing.   2. Metonyms − Data processing.
3. Cognitive Grammar − Data processing.   I. Stefanowitsch, Anatol,
1970−   II. Gries, Stefan Thomas, 1970−   III. Series.
    P301.5.M48C677   2006
    808.00285−dc22
                                                                  2006002353

ISBN 978-3-11-019827-0

Bibliographic information published by the Deutsche Nationalbibliothek

The Deutsche Nationalbibliothek lists this publication in the Deutsche
Nationalbibliografie; detailed bibliographic data are available in the Internet
at http://dnb.d-nb.de.

© Copyright 2006, 2007 by Walter de Gruyter GmbH & Co. KG, D-10785 Berlin
All rights reserved, including those of translation into foreign languages. No part of this
book may be reproduced or transmitted in any form or by any means, electronic or mechanical, including photocopy, recording or any information storage and retrieval system, without permission in writing from the publisher.
Cover design: Martin Zech, Bremen.
Typesetting: OLD-Media, Neckarsteinach.
Printed in Germany.

Table of contents

Corpus-based approaches to metaphor and metonymy *Anatol Stefanowitsch*	1
Metaphoricity is gradable *Patrick Hanks*	17
A corpus-based study of metaphors for speech activity in British English *Elena Semino*	36
Words and their metaphors: A corpus-based approach. *Anatol Stefanowitsch*	63
The grammar of linguistic metaphors *Alice Deignan*	106
Keeping and eye on the data: Metonymies and their patterns *Martin Hilpert*	123
Metonymic proper names: A corpus-based account *Katja Markert and Malvina Nissim*	152
On groutnolls and nog-heads: A case study of the interaction between culture and cognition in intelligence metaphors *Kathryn Allan*	175
Sense and sensibility: Rational thought versus emotion in metaphorical language. *Päivi-Koivisto-Alanko and Heli Tissari*	191
A corpus-based analysis of context effects on metaphor comprehension *James H. Martin*	214
Of critical importance: Using electronic text corpora to study metaphor in business media discourse. *Veronika Koller*	237
Metaphors, motifs and similes across discourse types: Corpus-Assisted Discourse Studies (CADS) at work *Alan Partington*	267

Author index 305
Subject index 308
Index of domains and mappings 311

Corpus-based approaches to metaphor and metonymy

Anatol Stefanowitsch

1. Introduction

It is probably fair to say that over the past fifteen years, corpus-based methods have established themselves as the major empirical paradigm in linguistics. They have been insightfully applied to research issues pertaining to all levels of linguistic structure (although there is a certain dominance of studies dealing with lexis and grammar) and to many aspects of language use.

The field of metaphor and metonymy research, which has received a huge impetus by the emergence of the theory of conceptual mappings (Lakoff and Johnson 1980, cf. also Lakoff 1987, Johnson 1987, Lakoff and Turner 1989, Lakoff 1993), is lagging slightly behind with respect to this trend, but recently, a number of researchers have begun to remedy this situation by laying the methodological foundations for a strong emphasis on authentic data and the empirical verification of many of the fascinating theoretical claims in the field. In the following, I will attempt to give a brief overview over this work (including, but not limited to the papers in this volume), focusing on methodological problems and possible solutions as well as the most important results of corpus-based research into metaphor and metonymy to date.

2. Extracting metaphors and metonymies from corpora

The first problem that any corpus-based analysis faces is that of identifying and extracting the relevant data from the corpus. This is a simple task in investigations of lexical items or fixed expressions (which can be retrieved directly), and a somewhat more complex though still reasonably straightforward task in investigations of many grammatical phenomena (which can be retrieved by making use of the part-of-speech tagging or the grammatical annotation available in at least some relatively large corpora or by automatic or semi-automatic on-the-fly parsing). However, in the case of metaphor and metonymy, retrieving the relevant data is, at first glance, almost impossible for the simple reason that conceptual mappings are not linked to particular linguistic forms. There are various conceivable types of semantic annotation that could help solve this problem, but none of the currently available large corpora contain any semantic annotation (and this true even more so of corpora assembled by researchers in the context of specific research questions). Thus, the vast majority of corpus-based research on conceptual mappings cannot rely on annotated corpora. Consequently, a number of strategies for extracting linguistic expressions manifesting conceptual mappings from non-annotated corpora have been proposed, in particular, the following three (*searching* is here used as a cover term for traditional concordancing and automatic or semi-automatic annotation/extraction):

(i) *Manual searching.* Early text-based studies of metaphor rely on a procedure where the researcher carefully reads through the corpus extracting all metaphors he or she comes across (see Semino and Masci 1996, Jäkel 1995, 1997 for examples of this approach, and esp. Jäkel 1997: 145ff. for a justification of this method as compared to genuinely corpus-based methods). The manual extraction of metaphors has a number of problems, not the least of which is that it drastically limits the potential size of the corpus. In addition, it shares a number of additional problems with the manual annotation of metaphors, discussed in detail in Section 4 below.

(ii) *Searching for source domain vocabulary.* Metaphorical and metonymic expressions always contain lexical items from their source domain (this is what makes them non-literal in the first place). Thus, it is a reasonable strategy to begin an investigation by selecting a potential source domain (i.e., a semantic domain or field that is known to play a role in metaphorical or metonymic expressions. In a first step, the researcher can then search for individual lexical items from this domain (cf. Deignan 1999a, b, this volume, Hanks 2004, this volume, Hilpert, this volume) or whole sets of such items (cf. Partington 1997, 2003, this volume, Koller, this volume, Markert and Nissim 2002b, this volume). The choice of items can be based on *a priori* decisions (cf. Deignan, this volume, Koller, this volume, Hilpert, this volume), it can be based on existing exhaustive lists (cf. Markert and Nissim, this volume), or it can be based on a preceding keyword analysis of texts dealing with target-domain topics (cf. the six-step procedure presented by Partington, this volume, based on Partington 1997, 2003). The search for these items can then be exhaustive (i.e., all occurrences of the item(s) in question are retrieved, cf. Deignan, this volume, Hilpert, this volume, Koller, this volume), or it can be limited to particular contexts that are considered to be promising (cf. Hanks, 2004, this volume) or relevant to the research question (Stefanowitsch 2005). In a second step, the researcher then identifies the target domains in which these items occur, and thus, the metaphorical or metonymic mappings in which they participate. How and on the basis of what criteria this identification proceeds is, of course, a non-trivial matter (cf. Section 4 below).

(iii) *Searching for target domain vocabulary*. Often, research on conceptual mappings is concerned with particular target domains and the conceptual mappings that structure it. In these cases, the source-domain oriented approach described in the preceding section cannot be fruitfully applied, since it requires *a priori* knowledge of the source domains that are likely to be found in the target domain. While Partington's *keywords*-based method goes some way towards solving this issue, it comes with two caveats. First, it requires the existence of large bodies of representative and relatively monothematic texts dealing with the target domain; thus, it can be fruitfully applied in the case of target domains like ECONOMICS, SPORTS, or POLITICS, but it is less clear how it could be applied with target domains like EMOTIONS, MENTAL ACTIVITY, PERCEPTION, etc.). Second, it will identify only those source domains that are associated with particular words whose frequencies are sufficiently inflated in the target-domain texts to achieve keyword status; thus, it will not identify metaphorical expressions exhaustively or systematically. A number of researchers have suggested an alternative strategy for investigating target domains (Koivisto-Alanko 2000, Tissari 2003, Stefanowitsch, 2004, this volume, Koivisto-Alanko and Tissari, this volume). They begin by selecting and searching for lexical items referring directly to target-domain concepts. In a second step, the researcher then identifies those cases where these words are embedded in metaphorical expressions and thus, the metaphorical mappings occurring in the target domain (it is not clear whether this method can be applied to the investigation of metonymy). Clearly, this method will only identify a subset of metaphorical expressions, namely those that contain target-domain vocabulary. For example, it will identify *His pent-up anger* WELLED UP *inside him*, but not *We got a* RISE *out of him* (both from Lakoff 1987: 384). There is initial evidence, however, that this subset of expressions, referred to by Stefanowitsch (2004, this volume) as *metaphor-*

ical patterns, is representative; it seems to identify all mappings posited in the literature as well as additional ones (Stefanowitsch, this volume).

(iv) *Searching for sentences containing lexical items from both the source domain and the target domain.* The two methods described above can be combined, i.e., the researcher can search for sentences (or other parsing units deemed suitable) containing both source and target domain vocabulary; this is especially useful for automatic annotation/extraction (Martin, this volume). This method requires exhaustive lists of source and target domain vocabulary as well as corpora that are annotated for clause and/or sentence boundaries (alternatively, they must be preprocessed accordingly). Given these preconditions, the annotation and extraction itself is a relatively easy task. Like the other two methods, this one is not perfect. First, manual post-editing is required to get rid of false hits due to, for example, homographs or the literal use of both source and target domain vocabulary in a single sentence (note, however, that this post-editing presumably takes less time than the completely manual annotation required by the previously discussed strategies). Recall will also not be perfect, since it is probably impossible to list source and target domain vocabulary exhaustively, and thus specific lexical items will be missing on the lists; however, a human annotator in the methods described above will almost certainly also miss examples, so this is not really a disadvantage specific to this method. Third, this method can only be used straightforwardly to identify expressions manifesting conceptual mappings that are known in advance (although more exploratory extensions are imaginable, given word lists for many different potential source and target domains). Finally, this method, like the one discussed in (ii) above, will only capture those metaphorical expressions that Stefanowitsch (2004, this volume) refers to as *metaphorical patterns*. However, these disadvantages are counterbalanced by the fact that the method allows fast annotation of vast amounts of text, far beyond what a human annotator could achieve in a reasonable time frame. Thus, it is surprising that it has not, so far, been used more widely.

(v) *Searching for metaphors based on 'markers of metaphor'.* An intriguing possibility for the automatic retrieval of metaphors is indicated by Goatly (1997, Ch. 6). Goatly discusses a wide variety of explicit linguistic devices that may signal the presence of a metaphor, including, for example, metalinguistic expressions referring to non-literalness, such as *metaphorically/figuratively speaking* or *so to speak*, general metalanguage about semantics, such as *in more than one sense*, 'mimetic terms' like *image, likeness* or *picture*, intensifiers like *literally, actually, veritable*, etc., and even orthographic devices like quotation marks (see Goatly 1997: 174–175 for an overview). Although it certainly seems to be a promising strategy to extract metaphors on the basis of such markers, no major study so far has applied this method systematically. It should also be noted that an initial evaluation of the method casts some doubt on its utility: Wallington, Barnden, Barnden, Ferguson and Glasbey (2003) find that Goatly's markers do not in fact consistently signal the presence of metaphorical expressions.

Returning to the possibilities potentially offered by semantically annotated corpora, there are two types of annotation that are particularly promising, and that augment the set of possible research strategies:

(vi) *Extraction from a corpus annotated for semantic fields/domains.* The strategies described in (i)–(iii) can all be adapted, in principle, to corpora that are (comprehensively or selectively) annotated for semantic fields/domains. Extending strategy (i), the researcher can specify a potential source domain and search directly for all lexical items belonging to that source domain (instead of specifying sets of source-domain lexemes that will always be incomplete). An example for this strategy is the work by Semino (2005, this volume), which makes use of a corpus annotated for expressions reporting speech activity. In corpora that are exhaustively annotated, of course, extensions of the strategies in (ii) and (iii) are also possible, i.e., the researcher could specify and search for a potential target domain or for parsing units containing both potential source and target domains. Of course, as mentioned above, the necessary corpora are not currently widely available. Even where they are, however, researchers face an additional problem: semantically annotated corpora may not be consistent with respect to the semantic fields that they assign words to; unless the annotation scheme is informed by considerations of metaphor and metonymy analysis, these semantic fields may simply be assigned on the basis of the target domain. For example, the verb *rise* may be annotated as belonging to the semantic field of QUANTITY in *Inflation rose to an all-time high* and to the semantic field of MOTION in *The plane rose to a height of thirty thousand feet* (cf. Castellón et al. 2004 for a defense of precisely this strategy). In a corpus thus annotated, expressions manifesting conceptual mappings could not be identified on the basis of the annotation. A more general problem of annotated corpora is, of course, that the researcher has to rely on the annotation (this is also true for studies based on thesauri, for example, Allan, this volume).

(vii) *Extraction from a corpus annotated for conceptual mappings.* Large corpora annotated for conceptual mappings would be a valuable resource for metaphor research. If such corpora were available, the task of extracting conceptual mappings would become trivial. Of course, in order to create such corpora, the task of annotating metaphorical mappings appropriately in the first place becomes the problem – this problem will be discussed in more detail in Section 4 below.

3. Results of the corpus-based approaches

So far, the results of corpus-based approaches to metaphor and metonymy clearly demonstrate its usefulness: relevant data can be examined more exhaustively and more systematically than with more introspective/opportunistic methods, and this has led to a number of potential reassessments of previous analyses, touching on some of the central claims of the conceptual theory of metaphor.

In addition, the focus on the cognitive or conceptual nature of metaphor and metonymy has led to a certain neglect of detailed, bottom-up analysis, and, in consequence, to a disregard of many aspects of the *linguistic* nature of metaphor. Concerning these, there is a whole range of issues that are slowly beginning to be addressed in a systematic way.

3.1. The nature of particular conceptual mappings

A corpus-based analysis of conceptual mappings is faced with and must account for a much broader range of data than introspective/opportunistic approaches. In many cases, this richness of the data inevitably leads to new insights. It may, for example, necessitate a reanalysis of the way that a mapping is best defined, as Semino (this volume) shows when she reanalyzes ARGUMENT IS WAR as ANTAGONISTIC COMMUNICATION IS PHYSICAL CONFLICT. An attempt at exhaustiveness also requires the researcher to deal with the issue that linguistic expressions may exhibit different degrees of metaphoricity or metonymicity (cf. Hanks, this volume, cf. also Hilpert, this volume, Partington, this volume, Stefanowitsch, this volume).

3.2. The importance of particular conceptual mappings

The inherently quantitative nature of corpus data also puts the apparently monolithic importance of some frequently discussed mappings into perspective. For example, Semino (this volume) finds that the two textbook cases of communication metaphors, the ARGUMENT-AS-WAR metaphor and the CONDUIT metaphor, account for just under 50 per cent of all communication metaphors; Stefanowitsch (this volume) reports very similar proportions for previously postulated metaphors in the domain of EMOTIONS. For metonymy, Markert and Nissim (this volume) as well as Hilpert (this volume) also find mappings that are not discussed in the previous literature at all.

Of course, the use of frequency data concerning conceptual mappings is not limited to general assessments of the importance of a given mapping; it can also serve as a basis for determining which mappings are most strongly associated with a particular target domain (see Koivisto-Alanko and Tissari, this volume) or a particular subdomain within a target domain (see Stefanowitsch, this volume).

Finally, corpus data allow us in principle to assess the systematicity of conceptual mappings. For example, Deignan (1999b) finds that often only one of a pair of antonymous source domain adjectives (such as *hot* and *cold*) can be mapped onto a given target domain, and Stefanowitsch (this volume) notes that target domains that are plausibly thought of as opposites are not necessarily significantly associated with source domains that are thought of as opposites (for example, while the source domain LIGHT plays a central role in the target domain HAPPINESS, the source domain DARKNESS plays a relatively minor role in the target domain SADNESS).

Source-domain oriented studies and target-domain oriented studies often complement each other in the investigation of these aspects of conceptual mappings. For example, while source-domain oriented studies often reveal a much broader set of target-domains for any given source item than we might have expected on the basis of introspective data, target-domain oriented studies constrain this range by allowing us to identify those mappings and source domains that are significantly associated with a given target domain.

3.3. Structural properties of expressions instantiating conceptual mappings

One of the most intriguing insights gained from corpus-based approaches to metaphor and metonymy is that there are often formal differences between literal and non-literal uses or between different non-literal uses of a lexical item.

For example, Deignan finds that metaphorical (and metonymic) uses of lexical items frequently prefer a different word class than literal uses (1995, 1999a, this volume). Also, literal and non-literal uses are often associated with different colligates or different grammatical patterns (for metaphor, see Deignan 1999, Hanks 2004, this volume; for metonymy cf. Hilpert, this volume, Markert and Nissim 2002c). Deignan (this volume) even finds that different metaphorical uses of the same source-domain item may prefer different inflectional forms.

Sometimes, these differences can be accounted for by a careful application of the principles of the Conceptual Theory of Metaphor. For example, Deignan (this volume) shows that singular *flame* is typically used in positively construed target domains, while plural *flames* is typically used in negatively construed target domains. She argues that this is due to the fact that the topology of the source domain is preserved in the mapping; a single flame is naturally associated with positive situations (as in the case of the *Olympic flame*), while more than one flame is naturally associated with negative situations (such as uncontrollable fires).

At other times, it seems as though we simply have to accept that there are item-specific differences regarding the participation of source-domain vocabulary in conceptual mappings; such differences are often simply a consequence of conventionalization (lexicalization, grammaticalization, etc.), which naturally leads to the emergence of unique formal properties for different uses of a lexical item (cf. Deignan, this volume, Hanks 2004, this volume, Hilpert, this volume). Hilpert hints at the possibility that such unique properties may play an important role in processing metonymic expressions, in that they potentially allow the hearer to side-step a lengthy inferencing process. Clearly, this possibility is worthy of further investigation.

3.4. Textual properties of conceptual mappings

Corpus-based approaches to conceptual mappings also allow the researcher to investigate a range of textual and contextual properties of metaphor and metonymy that cannot be captured by introspective/opportunistic methods at all.

In the simplest case, this concerns the importance of conceptual mappings in general or of particular conceptual mappings in particular genres (cf. Koller, this volume, who investigates the type-token ratio of selected metaphorical mappings to assess how varied a given genre is in terms of the metaphors employed to structure it) or in target-domain related discourses (cf. Partington's (1997, this volume) method for identifying important metaphors in a given discourse area). Thus, while the ubiquity of metaphor and metonymy in everyday language use is an article of faith in the Conceptual Theory of Metaphor, corpus-based studies allow the researcher to put such claims to the test for the first time.

Of course, the corpus-based investigation of metaphors in a given genre or discourse does not stop at the assessment of their general frequency. There is a tradition of text-based metaphor analysis within the Conceptual Theory of Metaphor that precedes strictly corpus-based approaches and that deals with the ideological, social, communicative and cultural functions of metaphor (cf. e.g. Semino and Masci 1996 for the discourse domain POLITICS, Jäkel 1997 for ECONOMY and MENTAL ACTIVITY). This type of detailed qualitative analysis based on manual extraction can be aided and fruitfully complemented by corpus-based methods (cf. Deignan 2000, 2003, Partington 1997, 2003, Cameron 2003, Musolff 2003, Charteris-Black 2004, Koller, 2002, 2003, this volume). In this context, the potential intertextuality of metaphorical expressions is an interesting research area that has hardly been touched upon (cf. Hanks, this volume), as are pragmatic properties of metaphorical expressions (cf. Goatly 1997, Cameron and Deignan 2003).

Finally, corpus-based studies open up completely novel ways of investigating contextually determined processing effects: Martin (this volume) finds that the occurrence of a given metaphor increases the likelihood that the same metaphor will be used again in the immediately subsequent discourse, while lowering the likelihood that the source domain will be referred to literally. The importance of such findings for psycholinguistic models of metaphor processing can hardly be overestimated.

3.5. Cross-linguistic and diachronic differences

The reliance on introspection has also led to a certain lack of attention to cross-linguistic and diachronic issues. This is very unfortunate. The existence of general mappings can often be postulated on the basis of introspective data, and in some cases such mappings may even be plausibly assumed to recur in different speech communities across space or time (cf. Lakoff 1993). However, a plausible assumption cannot replace empirical investigation – many mappings do differ across speech communities (Allan, this volume, Koivisto-Alanko and Tissari, this volume), and it is impossible to determine this based on introspection. Moreover, even if certain mappings do recur, the precise way in which they are instantiated differs both across languages (cf. e.g. Charteris-Black and Ennis 2001, Chun 2002, Chung et al. 2003, Stefanowitsch 2004) and across time (cf. e.g. Koivisto-Alanko 2000, Tissari 2003, Koivisto-Alanko and Tissari, this volume, Allan, this volume).

There are many questions concerning this variation to which currently only preliminary answers (and often not even these) exist. For example, what are the preconditions that must hold for particular mappings to manifest themselves at any given point in time or in any given speech community? When do metaphorical mappings 'fail' to manifest themselves, or to become conventional? Deignan (2003) plausibly claims that this depends on the degree of importance that a culture assigns to particular domains, i.e. that culturally salient domains are more likely to serve as input for metaphorical mappings; as the importance of certain domains changes, this may be reflected in changing metaphors (cf. Koivisto-Alanko and Tissari's (this volume) brief discussion of the emergence of the WIT AS INSTRUMENT/TOOL/WEAPON mapping in Early Modern English). In addition, Allan (this volume) suggests that conventional associations of certain source concepts to certain target domains preclude their becoming associated with other cognitively plausible but incompatible target domains (cf. also Hanks, this volume, for discussion).

4. Metaphor identification and annotation

As was mentioned above, corpora that are manually annotated for (expressions manifesting) conceptual mappings would be an invaluable resource for corpus-based research.

An appropriate annotation scheme must define (i) a reliable procedure for discovering instances of the phenomenon in question, (ii) the attributes that are considered relevant for each instance and the set of values that each of these attributes can take as well as guidelines as to how these values are to be assigned, and (iii) an annotation format. Let us briefly consider each of these aspects in turn.

(i) *Metaphor/metonymy identification.* In virtually all studies of metaphor, whether corpus-based or not, metaphors are identified and categorized based on more-or-less explicit commonsensical intuitions of the part of the researcher (this includes most of the studies in this volume). This strategy may be unproblematic for very clear-cut cases, but an exhaustive annotation (and, of course, any potentially exhaustive retrieval) will confront the researcher with many cases that are not clear cut. In these cases, a maximally explicit procedure must be set up, justified on theoretical grounds, and tested for inter-rater reliability. Suggestions for such procedures exist (for metaphor, cf. Steen 2001, 2002a, Crisp et al. 2002; for metonymy, cf. Markert and Nissim 2002a), but so far, they stand relatively isolated, and have not received the intensive theoretical discussion they deserve, nor the broad empirical testing needed to determine whether they can be reliably applied (although initial small-scale studies are promising, cf. Steen and Semino 2001, Steen 2002b, Markert and Nissim 2002b, this volume).

(ii) *Relevant attributes for metaphor and metonymy.* Relevant attributes seem to include minimally the source domain and the target domain, sometimes as individual attributes, sometimes jointly as a single attribute. Various additional attributes have been suggested, for example, degree of metaphoricity or metonymicity (Markert and Nissim 2002b, Semino and Steen 2001), degree of conventionality (Wallington, Barnden, Buchlovsky, Fellows and Glasbey (2003)), the certainty an annotator feels about annotating something as metaphorical (Wallington, Barnden, Buchlovsky, Fellows and Glasbey (2003)), the inter-rater reliability of specific annotation decisions, or various aspects concerning the complexity of a mapping (Semino and Steen 2001), or the reason for using a metaphor (Trausan-Matu et al. 2001). Such attributes are, of course, defined with respect to particular theoretical frameworks or research questions; only time will tell what attributes are needed and which of them have a broader relevance.

(iii) *Annotation formats.* From a theoretical perspective, nothing at all hinges on the specific format chosen for representing attributes and their values, but there are at least three arguments for ensuring compliance to SGML (*Standard Generalized Markup Language*) (as in the case of Semino and Steen 2001), or even better, to the subset of SGML known as XML (*Extensible Markup Language*) (as in Trausan-Matu et al's (2001) and Wallington, Barnden, Buchlovsky, Fellows and Glasbey's (2003) annotation schemes for metaphor or Markert and Nissim's (2002a, b, this volume) annotation scheme for metonymies. First, these markup languages are de facto standards in corpus annotation; second, they are open formats, and thus ensure portability across platforms and applications (cf. Markert and Nissim

2002b, this volume); third, they are extremely flexible with respect to the content that can be encoded, and are thus ideally suited to a situation where there is no agreement yet – and possibly never will be – concerning what aspects of the phenomenon under investigation are to be annotated, and how. Finally, of course, SGML/XML annotation keeps text files comparatively human-readable as compared to many proprietary formats (especially if a stand-off format is used, i.e. if the embedded markup contains nothing more than an index number while the actual markup information is placed at the end of the file, as in Wallington, Barnden, Buchlovsky, Fellows and Glasbey (2003)).

5. Conclusion

Corpus-based research into the linguistic and cognitive nature of conceptual mappings is still very much in its initial stages. Many methodological issues have to be (and are being) sorted out, and potential research issues have to be identified and tackled systematically and exhaustively.

Nevertheless, the research record so far is impressive. The corpus-based approach has uncovered a wealth of intriguing facts about conceptual mappings that was not known beforehand, and, indeed, that could not have been learned from the traditional, introspective approach. The next decade will no doubt see a continuation of this process of discovery. In addition, corpus-based approaches to metaphorical mappings face two major tasks. First, many of the results are provisional, awaiting more stringent quantification and statistical evaluation. There are studies that point the way to such procedures, and, of course, there is a wealth of literature on statistical methods both within the field of language studies and outside that is just waiting to be discovered by metaphor researchers. The growing awareness in the corpus-linguistic community concerning the importance of strict quantification and sophisticated statistical methods will undoubtedly ensure that these methods will find their way into the relevant research. Second, while many of the facts uncovered by corpus-based approaches to conceptual mappings can be and are being integrated into a broader theoretical discussion, others are not. In those cases where the results are provisional, this is presumably a good thing, since there is not much point in building theories of conceptual mappings on tentative results. However, in those cases where the results seem solid, it is desirable that corpus-oriented researchers propagate their results yet more emphatically even where they call into question received wisdom. Corpus-oriented researchers are generally very self-confident with respect to their methods; they should increasingly show the same self-confidence with respect to the theoretical relevance of their results.

References

Allan, Kathryn
    This volume On groutnolls and nog-heads: a case study of the interaction between culture and cognition in intelligence metaphors.

Cameron, Lynne
    2003 *Metaphor in Educational Discourse*. London: Continuum.

Cameron, Lynne and Alice Deignan
    2003 Combining large and small corpora to investigate tuning devices around metaphor in spoken discourse. *Metaphor and Symbol* 18: 149–160.

Castellón, Irene, Glòria Vàquez, Ana Fernández, Elisabeth Comelles, Victoria Arranz and David Farwell
    2004 Interlingual annotation of the Catalan dataset. Unpublished manuscript.

Charteris-Black, Jonathan and Timothy Ennis
    2001 A comparative study of metaphor in Spanish and English financial reporting. *English for Specific Purposes* 20: 249–266.

Charteris-Black, Jonathan
    2004 *Corpus Approaches to Critical Metaphor Analysis*. Basingstoke: Palgrave Macmillan.

Chun, Lan
    2002 A cognitive approach to *Up/Down* metaphors in English and *Shang/Xia* metaphors in Chinese. In: Bengt Altenberg and Sylviane Granger (eds.), *Lexis in Contrast. Corpus-Based Approaches*, 151–174. Amsterdam and Philadelphia: John Benjamins.

Chung Siaw-Fong, Kathleen Ahrens and Ya-hui Sung
    2003 STOCK MARKETS AS OCEAN WATER: A corpus-based, comparative study of Mandarin Chinese, English and Spanish. *Proceedings of the 17th Pacific Asia Conference on Language, Information and Computation (PACLIC)*, Singapore, 124–133.

Crisp, Peter, John Heywood, and Gerard J. Steen
    2002 Metaphor identification and analysis, classification and quantification. *Language and Literature* 11: 55–69.

Deignan, Alice
    1999a Corpus-based research into metaphor. In: Lynne Cameron and Graham Low (eds.), *Researching and Applying Metaphor*, 177–199. Cambridge: Cambridge University Press.
    1999b Metaphorical polysemy and paradigmatic relations: A corpus study. *Word* 50: 319–337.

2000 Persuasive uses of metaphor in discourse about business and the economy. In: Chris Heffer and Helen Sauntson (eds.), *Words in Context: A Tribute to John Sinclair on his Retirement*, 156–68. Birmingham: University of Birmingham.
2003 Metaphorical expressions and culture: An indirect link. *Metaphor and Symbol* 18: 255–271.
This volume The grammar of linguistic metaphors.
Goatly, Andrew
1997 *The Language of Metaphors*. London: Routledge.
Hanks, Patrick
2004 The syntagmatics of metaphor and idiom. *International Journal of Lexicography* 17: 245–274.
This volume Metaphoricity is gradable.
Heywood, John, Elena Semino and Mick Short
2002 Linguistic metaphor identification in two extracts from novels. *Language and Literature* 11: 35–54.
Hilpert, Martin
This volume Keeping an eye on the data: metonymies and their patterns.
Jäkel, Olaf
1995 The metaphorical concept of mind: 'Mental activity is manipulation'. In: John R. Taylor and Robert E. MacLaury (eds.), *Language and the Cognitive Construal of the World*, 197–229. Berlin and New York: Mouton de Gruyter.
1997 *Metaphern in abstrakten Diskurs-Domänen*. Frankfurt a.M.: Lang.
Johnson, Mark
1987 *The Body in the Mind*. Chicago and London: The University of Chicago Press.
Koivisto-Alanko, Päivi
2000 *Abstract Words in Abstract Worlds: Directionality and Prototypical Structure in the Semantic Change in English Nouns of Cognition*. Helsinki: Société Néophilologique.
Koivisto-Alanko, Päivi and Heli Tissari
This volume Sense and sensibility: Rational thought versus emotion in metaphorical language.
Koller, Veronika
2002 'A shotgun wedding': Co-occurence of war and marriage metaphors in mergers and acquisitions discourse. *Metaphor and Symbol* 17: 179–203.
2003 Metaphor clusters, metaphor chains: Analyzing the multifunctionality of metaphor in text. *Metaphorik.de* 5: 115–134. Available online at <http://www.metaphorik.de/05/koller.pdf>.
This volume Of critical importance: Using electronic text corpora to study metaphor in business media discourse.
Lakoff, George and Mark Johnson
1980 *Metaphors We Live By*. Chicago and London: The University of Chicago Press.
Lakoff, George, and Mark Turner

1989 *More than Cool Reason*. Chicago and London: The University of Chicago Press.

Lakoff, George
1987 *Women, fire, and dangerous things*. Chicago: The University of Chicago Press.
1993 The contemporary theory of metaphor. In: Andrew Ortony (ed.), *Metaphor and thought*. Second edition, 202–251. Cambridge: Cambridge University Press.

Markert, Katja and Malvina Nissim
2002a Annotation scheme for metonymies (AS1). Unpublished manuscript, University of Edinburgh. Available online at <http://www.ltg.ed.ac.uk/~malvi/mascara>.
2002b Towards a corpus annotated for metonymies: the case of location names. *Proceedings of the 3rd International Conference on Language Resources and Evaluation*, 1385–1392. Las Palmas, Canary Islands.
2002c Metonymy resolution as a classification task. *Proceedings of the 2002 Conference on Empirical Methods in Natural Language Processing*, 204–213. Philadelphia, PA, 6–7 July 2002.
This volume Metonymic proper names: a corpus-based account.

Martin, James H.
1994 Metabank: A knowledge-base of metaphoric language conventions. *Computational Intelligence* 10: 134–149.
This volume A corpus-based analysis of context effects on metaphor comprehension.

Musolff, Andreas
2003 Ideological functions of metaphor: The conceptual metaphors of *health* and *illness* in public discourse. In: René. Dirven, Roslyn Frank and Martin Pütz (eds.), *Cognitive Models in Language and Thought: Ideology, Metaphor and Meanings*, 327–352. Berlin and New York: Mouton de Gruyter.

Partington, Alan
1997 *Patterns and meaning*. Amsterdam and Philadelphia: Benjamins.
2003 *The Linguistics of Political Argument: Spin-doctor and the Wolf-pack at the White House*. London: Routledge.
This volume Metaphors, motifs and similes across discourse types: Corpus-Assisted Discourse Studies (CADS) at work.

Semino, Elena
2005 The metaphorical construction of complex domains: the case of speech activity in English. *Metaphor and Symbol* 20: 35–70.
This volume A corpus-based study of metaphors for speech activity in British English

Semino, Elena and Gerard J. Steen
2001 A method for annotating metaphors in corpora. In: John Barnden, Mark Lee, and Katja Markert (eds.), *Proceedings of the Workshop on Corpus-based and Processing Approaches to Figurative Language*, 59–66. Lancaster: University Centre for Computer Corpus Research on Language.

Semino, Elena and Michaela Masci
 1996 Politics in football: metaphor in the discourse of Silvio Berlusconi in Italy. *Discourse and Society* 7: 243–269.

Steen, Gerard J.
 2002a Towards a procedure for metaphor identification. *Language and Literature* 11: 17–34.
 2002b Identifying metaphor in language: A cognitive approach. *Style* 36: 386–407.
 2001 A reliable procedure for metaphor identification. In: John Barnden, Mark Lee, and Katja Markert (eds.), *Proceedings of the Workshop on Corpus-based and Processing Aproaches to Figurative Language*, 67–75. Lancaster: University Centre for Computer Corpus Research on Language.

Stefanowitsch, Anatol
 2004 HAPPINESS in English and German: A metaphorical-pattern analysis. In Michel Achard and Suzanne Kemmer (eds.), *Language, Culture, and Mind*, 137–149. Stanford: CSLI.
 2005 A corpus-based approach to the function of metaphor. *International Journal of Corpus Linguistics* 10: 161–198.
 In preparation A corpus-based approach to the productivity of metaphorical mappings.
 This volume Words and their metaphors: A corpus-based approach.

Tissari, Heli
 2003 *LOVEscapes: Changes in prototypical senses and cognitive metaphors since 1500*. Helsinki: Société Néophilologique.

Trausan-Matu, Stefan, Adrian Novischi, Stefano Cerri, Daniele Maraschi
 2001 Personalised metaphor processing in texts on the web for learning a foreign language. *Proceedings of RILW 2001*, 205–212.

Wallington, Alan, John A. Barnden, Marina A. Barnden, Fiona J. Ferguson and Sheila R. Glasbey
 2003 Metaphoricity signals: A corpus-based investigation. *Technical Report CSRP-03-05*. The University of Birmingham, School of Computer Science.

Wallington, Alan., John A. Barnden, Peter Buchlovsky, Louise Fellows, Sheila R. Glasbey
 2003 Metaphor annotation: A systematic study, *Technical Report CSRP-03-4*. The University of Birmingham, School of Computer Science.

Metaphoricity is gradable*

Patrick Hanks

Abstract

The relationship between metaphor and literal meaning is often discussed in terms that imply that the distinction is absolute: a statement either is a metaphor or it is not. This paper adduces evidence in support of analysis of metaphors by reference to stereotypical usage, and concludes that some metaphors are more metaphorical than others. At the present time, sharply defined boundaries of categories in linguistics are being questioned in the light of empirical evidence, and metaphor is no exception. Theories that invoke partial or full matching to 'best examples' of categories – norms or prototypes – seem to explain linguistic phenomena more adequately than theories that invoke necessary conditions and sharp distinctions. The question then arises, how to handle fuzzy sets, to which an empirically well-founded theory of metaphor can itself offer useful answers. Two detailed case studies are offered as a contribution to the study of metaphor in this context. Against those who argue that metaphor is merely a diachronic phenomenon, the paper shows that metaphor is a useful synchronic, empirical semantic classification, although its boundaries are fuzzy and a distinction must be made between dynamic metaphors (ad-hoc coinages) and conventional metaphors.

1. Introduction

In Hanks (2004) I proposed that the distinction between conventional metaphors and literal meanings is less important than the distinction between dynamic metaphors and conventional metaphors. Dynamic metaphors are coined ad hoc to express some new insight; conventional metaphors are just one more kind of normal use of language. I pointed out that at least some metaphors are associated with particular sets of syntagmatic realizations, which contrast with the patterns of other, more literal uses of the same words (cf. also Deignan, this volume). In that paper, I showed that one of the most basic ways of realizing a metaphor in English involves use of a partitive or quantifying *of* construction. The metaphoricity here is conventional, i.e. it represents a normal (though secondary) use of the words concerned. In literal contexts, *storm* denotes a kind of atmo-

---

* This work was supported by the Wolfgang Paul Prize awarded to Christiane Fellbaum by the Zukunftsinvestitionsprogram of the Alexander von Humboldt Foundation. I am grateful to Christiane Fellbaum for comments on an earlier draft of this paper.

spheric phenomenon; *torrent, mountain, lake,* and *oasis* denote kinds of geographical locations. But all these words have regular secondary patterns of use which (unlike other kinds of secondary meaning) can be usefully classed as metaphorical. They activate what Max Black (1962) called 'resonance' between the literal meaning potentials of two words. *A storm of protest, a torrent of abuse, a mountain of paperwork, a lake of blood, an oasis of sanity* are conventional metaphorical patterns, which can be recognized in corpora and contrasted with other uses of these words that are not metaphorical. When the metaphor is dynamic (i.e. when it is coined ad hoc, e.g. "*a storm of stars across the heavens*"), we can say that the conventional partitive *of,* signalling a metaphor, is being exploited dynamically. Needless to say, the word *of* has many other uses besides signalling a metaphor and there are, of course, many other ways of forming metaphors beside using a partitive *of.* However, metaphorical use of *of* features quite prominently in English, and it provides a good starting point for an investigation of syntagmatic aspects of metaphor.

2. Are metaphors secondary meanings of words?

There is a strong folk notion of metaphor as a semantic entity that is intuitively satisfying, though people still argue over its definition. It is hard to define metaphor, but easy to point to examples of text fragments that almost everyone agrees are metaphorical. To take one example, Max Black (1962) cites Wallace Stevens's metaphor "Society is a sea." Everyone knows that this is a metaphor, with the exception of a few hardy systemic linguists who deny the very existence of metaphor or who assert that metaphor is nothing more than a diachronic concept. If there is general agreement that at least some metaphors can be easily recognized in text, then it is up to linguistic theoreticians to say what conditions determine metaphoricity.

More difficult to pin down is the truth-conditional view that all metaphors are false, like lies, and that metaphor therefore has nothing to do with semantics[1]. Davidson (1980) says: "Metaphors mean what the words, in their most literal interpretation, mean, and nothing more. [...] The central mistake [...] is the idea that a metaphor has, in addition to its literal sense

---

1. Metaphorical interpretations are relegated by Davidson from semantics to pragmatics. To do this is to overload the semantic notion of literal meaning with conditions that very few normal discourse utterances fulfill.

or meaning, another sense or meaning." He asserts or takes it for granted that words have literal meaning. The present paper, developing a theme first mentioned by Fillmore (1975), denies that words, strictly speaking, have meaning at all. It takes the view expressed in the Theory of Norms and Exploitations (TNE; Pustejovsky and Hanks 2002, Hanks 2004, Hanks forthcoming) that words only have meanings when they are put into context. In isolation, they have meaning potentials, which are composed of any number of rather fuzzy semantic components, some or all of which are activated when the word is used (Hanks 1994). The term 'literal meaning of a word' is nevertheless useful, provided that not too much theoretical weight is put on it. It can be regarded as a shorthand term for those aspects of a word's meaning potential that are activated when it is used in its most normal contexts. Thanks to the availability of large corpora and statistical tests such as Mutual Information (MI; see Church and Hanks 1989), normal contexts can now be measured. It is therefore possible to say that conventional metaphors are secondary senses insofar as they activate only certain elements of the meaning potential of at least one of the words involved.

Not all secondary senses (uses) of words are metaphors: indeed, very few are. According to dictionaries, the word *realization*, for example, has three main senses: 1) a sudden or growing awareness of something; 2) the act of fulfilling or achieving some plan or concept; 3) the act of converting an asset into money. As far as I know, no one has ever proposed that any of these senses is a metaphorical exploitation of either of the other two; indeed it would seem bizarre to attempt to do so. Truth conditionalists claim that there is a basic, underlying meaning 'to make real', uniting all three senses, and may then argue that the way the word is actually used is a matter of pragmatics not semantics, but this seems unhelpful when it comes to understanding the meaning of words in texts.

There is a vast literature on metaphor, but the writers do not always state clearly what they think a metaphor is. A standard view, following Black (1962) and Lakoff and Johnson (1980), is that metaphor is an interaction between two concepts which enables us to interpret the one in terms of the other. Thus, a *storm of protest* is not only a lot of protest, but a lot of protest perceived in terms of a violent atmospheric disturbance. Lakoff and Johnson's basic thesis about metaphor is that its function is to enable us to interpret concepts (especially abstract concepts) in terms of familiar, everyday cognitive experiences. This is broadly satisfactory, though we might be tempted to substitute 'perceptual experiences' for 'cognitive experiences', and common sense forces us to acknowledge that the 'everyday experience' in question is that of the language community at large, not each individual. (Even people who have never visited an oasis know what oasis is supposed to be like, stereotypically, and can use and interpret metaphors that exploit this literal notion.)

3. Which words are used to make metaphors, and how?

Not all words can be used metaphorically. It is hard to imagine what a metaphorical use of the noun *idea* or the verb *imagine* would be like, and even harder to think of one involving nouns such as *alteration* or *quantity*. Abstract nouns are not normally (if ever) used to make metaphors. A first shot at distinguishing word uses that are conventional metaphors from other secondary senses would take account of at least the following parameters:

(i) *Semantic class.* Particularly productive sources of metaphor are nouns denoting types of physical location (*mountain, desert, jungle, sea, ocean, torrent*), including types of locations whose physical existence is debatable (*heaven, hell*), and nouns and verbs denoting certain types of event (*storm, attack, drown, burn*). An empirically well-founded classification of the nouns, adjectives, and verbs of a language according to the degree of their participation in metaphorical constructions would be a valuable addition to the literature (cf. also Stefanowitsch, this volume).

(ii) *Salient cognitive (or perceptual) features.* Words that are readily used to make metaphors usually denote some class of entities with at least one striking salient cognitive feature – in particular the way that it strikes human perceptions: mountains are high, deserts are dry, jungles are impenetrable, seas and oceans are vast expanses; heaven is nice, hell is nasty; storms are violent, attacks are damaging, drowning is slow death, burning is quick destruction, orgies are unrestrained. This salient cognitive feature is often the focus for a cluster of contributory but less salient features.

(iii) *Resonance.* Unlike other secondary senses, secondary senses that are classed as metaphors 'resonate' (see Black 1962) with some other term (the primary subject) in the immediate context in a text. The reader interprets the primary subject in the light of the salient features of the secondary subject.

(iv) *Collocations.* Resonance is not restricted to the term that explicitly realizes the secondary subject. Terms that collocate significantly with the secondary subject may also be activated, to create a veritable symphony of resonance, whether or not they are explicitly present in the text. This seems to be the foundation of extended metaphors, as well as a good reason for objecting to the dissonance of mixed metaphors.

(v) *Register and domain.* It may be that words normally used in a highly technical register are rarely used metaphorically. Thus, there is no evidence that *appendicitis*, a medical term, is ever used metaphorically, whereas *pain in the gut* is. But terms change register over time. Often, once a technical term has been accepted into the general register, it becomes available for metaphorical exploitation. An interesting contrast in this respect is presented by the cognate pair of English words *orgy* and *orgasm*. *Orgy*, whose basic meaning is "a wild party, especially one involving excessive drinking and indiscriminate sexual activity" (NODE), is often used metaphorically, as in (1) and (2) below. On the other hand, there are no metaphorical uses of *orgasm* in BNC. (The adjective *orgasmic* is a different matter: it is often used as a kind of vague intensifier, as in (3), which comes from a text referring to shoes). No doubt it is theoretically *possible* to use *orgasm* in a metaphorical way, but the point is that it is not *normal* to do so. This is because the word is still generally perceived as a technical term belonging to the domain of physiology, even though nowadays it is in regular general use.

(1) an *orgy* of denunciations and evasions of responsibility.
(2) a veritable *orgy* of statistical analysis.
(3) an airy whirl of *orgasmic* delight.

(vi) *Frequency.* Metaphorical uses cannot be too frequent. Frequency breeds literalness. Note that the reference here is to absolute frequency, not to comparative frequency within uses of the word in question. A *torrent of abuse* may still be perceived as metaphorical, even though this particular pattern (torrent + of + [[Language]]) is no less common than the use to denote raging flow of water in a watercourse. This perception of metaphoricity is possible because the word itself is comparatively infrequent.

The details of these parameters are not yet worked out, and it must be acknowledged that some cases are undecidable. Consider the word *area*, for example. Is the use of *area* in (5) a metaphorical exploitation of its 'normal' or 'literal' use as in (4), or should these be categorized as two separate senses? Certainly, it is possible and maybe even helpful to perceive a group of research activities in terms of a district or neighbourhood, which argues in favour of the metaphor view, but against that, the use of *area* to denote an abstract domain is very well established, very frequent, and so the cognitive salience of the resonance is very weak:

(4) Both youths stated that they were from the Nottingham area.
(5) This therefore appears to be a very fruitful area for research.

4. Gradability

The argument in this paper is that some metaphors are more metaphorical than others.

In the most metaphorical cases, the secondary subject shares fewest properties with the primary subject. Therefore, the reader or hearer has to work correspondingly harder to create a relevant interpretation. At the other extreme, the more shared properties there are, the weaker the metaphoricity. Let us look at an example. In (6) the primary subject, *railway tracks*, shares the property of physical location with the secondary subject, *desert*, so that resonance between the two is more readily established than in (7) and (8), where the primary subject is an abstract quality. Thus, (7) and (8) are more metaphorcial than (6). The semantic resonance of (7) and (8) is greater than in (6), because of the greater semantic distance between the two concepts:

(6) A desert, that's what it is – a *desert* of railway tracks.
(7) ... seeking to bring some awareness of spirituality to those mostly brought up in a spiritual *desert*.
(8) I walked in a *desert* of barren obsession.

In (8), resonance is amplified by the metaphorical use of the verb *walk* and by the explicit application of the adjective *barren* to the primary subject, *obsession*, even though in English at large *barren* is more associated with *desert* (there are 8 hits for 'barren+desert' in BNC) than with *obsession* (only this one hit in BNC).

Metaphorical interpretation evidently does not depend on semantic frequency or preference matching. Thus, it seems intuitively obvious that example (8) is a metaphor about someone's state of mind, not a statement about the physical condition of a particular desert location. However, it contains three terms associated with physical locations and only one associated with an abstract quality, so why do we not conclude that the noun *obsession* is being used metaphorically? The most plausible answer is that abstract nouns such as *obsession* cannot be used metaphorically.

5. Case study 1: *Sea*

There are 11,565 occurrences of *sea* in the British National Corpus. Within this vast mass of data, I tried to find examples that, prima facie, are clearly metaphorical, both by random spot checking and by systematic searching for known idiomatic patterns. The random spot checks were not very successful. I read thousands of lines without seeing a single metaphor. Systematic searches, looking for particular structures, e.g. *a sea of N* and *N PREP ... sea*, were more productive.

BNC contains 301 metaphorical uses of the construction '*a sea of [NP]*'. It is well known (see e.g. Sinclair 1991) that, in the pattern *N1 of N2*, where N1 is a partitive noun or a quantifier, it is not the semantic head. This is true of traditional partitive constructions such as *a piece of wood* and *a slice of bacon* and traditional quantifiers such as *a lot of nonsense* and *a great deal of hope*. Is it also true of metaphorical partitives and quantifiers such as *a torrent of abuse* and *a sea of faces*? In most cases, the answer seems to be yes. Faces and people can *watch* something, but seas don't. Hands in a classroom can *shoot up*, but seas don't. You can *shake hands with* people, but not with a sea. Therefore, the head noun (semantically) of (9), (10), and (11) is not *sea*, but *faces, hands,* and *people* respectively:

(9) She glanced up with dread and peered into the *sea of faces* that was watching her with curiosity.
(10) "How many people think this project ought to be stopped right now before it goes any further?" Immediately a *sea of hands* shot up.
(11) He ... leaped down into the crowd and shook hands with *the sea of people* almost engulfing him.

An apparent exception is (12), where one might expect 'burned' rather than 'drowned':

(12) ... drowned in the surrounding *sea of fire*.

However, (12) is not as clear-cut as at first sight appears. On closer examination, we find that it is in a discussion of a disaster on a North Sea oil platform, in which the oil spilling into the surrounding sea caught fire. So the sea of fire here is literal – or maybe it would be more correct to say that a standard metaphor is being reverse-exploited to form a literal meaning. This property of fuzziness, once believed to be a defect of natural language, is now seen as an essential design feature, enabling speakers to capture precisely the right degree of vagueness and indeterminacy that is relevant, as well as to maintain discourse fluency.

The noun in the N2 slot is not only the head of the phrase but also the primary subject of the metaphor. The noun in the N1 position (in this case *sea*) is being used metaphorically and, in Max Black's phrase, 'resonates' with the primary subject. A wide range of semantic categories of N2 are found resonating with *sea*. These include mass substances (in particular, *mud* and *blood*), physical objects (in particular, *people, faces, heads,* and *hats*), abstract nouns, and even events. The selected examples in Appendix 1 (20% of the total hits) are arranged in order of metaphoricity, with a view to showing the gradability of the metaphor. The semantic feature of *sea* that is exploited systematically in these metaphors is its vastness. All these metaphors share the property of being perceived as a vast expanse of something that is not salt water, and not necessarily liquid. (The expanse may in reality be quite small – it's the perception that matters.) If N2 denotes a liquid, the metaphor is less metaphorical than otherwise, because of course the sea, too, is liquid. In addition to being liquids, *mud, blood,* and *mutton broth* share with the literal sea the property of being liquids and mass substances, though in each case the "vast expanse" is a considerable overstatement compared with real seas such as the Baltic, the Caribbean, or the Caspian. Exaggeration is a typical feature of metaphor: the secondary subject (*sea*) is, as it were, perceived from a far distance.

When the primary subject denotes an abstract entity or an event, the metaphoricity is greater, because there are no shared features other than a postulated (and usually exaggerated) vast expanse. It is also noteworthy that the metaphor is extended much more often (with words and phrases such as *drown, adrift, swim, fish, boats, turn turtle, go down with all hands, anchor, plunge in, sail*) in the most highly metaphorical uses than in the less metaphorical ones. Some extended metaphors continue to be exploited for many sentences after the initial resonance has been established. More work will be needed to establish whether this inverse relationship between extended metaphors and high degree of metaphoricity is systematic in the language.

This is as good a place as any to mention the intertextuality of metaphor. Metaphors do not merely exploit the literal semantics of two terms:

they also exploit references to key phrases in the artistic literature of the language. Some metaphors coined by poets and other writers become established points of reference for subsequent users of the language. The phrases "the sea of faith" and "a sunless sea" in the examples in Appendix 1 exploit the whole tenor of the poems, by Matthew Arnold and Samuel Taylor Coleridge respectively, in which these phrases were first used.

In addition to these metaphorical uses of 'sea of', there are three occurrences in BNC (13–15) of the expression 'a sea of water'. This apparently pleonastic expression deserves closer examination. It is what Hanks (1999) calls a "nearly literal metaphor":

(13) this would be very expensive: a mere K537,000 had been allocated for capital expenditure – "just a drop in *a sea of water*".
(14) The idea ... was to trap German forces with Americans in front and *a sea of water* behind them.
(15) But he floated into the midst of *a sea of water* stretching as far as he could discern on every side around him.

Example (13) is merely a variant wording of the idiom 'a drop in the ocean'; the context clearly has nothing to do with water. In (14) and (15), the sea of water does indeed contain water, but with this difference: a sea (literal meaning) is a permanent location. In (14) and (15), the sea is temporary, the result of flood water (in (14), it is the intended result of a bombing raid on a dam in wartime). This corresponds precisely to the semantics of the metaphor 'a torrent of water', as in (16) and (17):

(16) They hung on until the battering ceased, then ran, slithering in the sluicing *torrent of water* until they reached the hatch that led below decks.
(17) A *torrent of flood water* swept through a North Wales hospital last night when a freak rain storm brought havoc to parts of North Wales.

In each case, the *torrent of water* is not where it ought to be: in a watercourse. The semantics of the literal meaning of both words (*sea* and *torrent*) requires that the denotatum must a) contain water and b) be in a particular location. Displacement of the LOCATION component allows the writer to exploit the WIDE EXPANSE component of *sea* and the FORCEFUL FLOW component of *torrent*, but then if the expanse or flow really does consist of water, it seems to be necessary to re-state this explicitly in order to indicate that some other semantic component or property is being set aside in order that the word may be exploited metaphorically.

6. Metaphor, phraseology, and idioms

Before leaving *sea*, we can take a look at another conventional phrase in which this word participates, which will serve to illustrate the relationship between metaphor, phraseology, and idioms. There are 763 occurrences of the expression *at sea* in BNC. The vast majority of them denote, quite literally, the situation of being a ship (or people on board a ship) somewhere far from land. The conventionality of the phraseology is important and not open to a reductionist interpretation: the preposition *at* is not being used in any of its conventional senses. A more logical compositional expression would be *on the sea*. This phrasing is indeed found, but not with the same meaning. *At sea* is used to denote the location of a ship or of people as sailors or voyagers; *on the sea* is used much more narrowly, typically to denote a physically contiguous relationship between a physical object (which may, of course be a ship) and the surface of the sea. The second thing to notice about the conventional expression *at sea* is the absence of a determiner. *At the sea* is also found, though rather rarely; but again, with a different meaning. *At the sea* denotes the situation of people on land beside the sea: it is synonymous with *at the seaside*.

The distinctions discussed in the previous paragraph have nothing to do with metaphor, for metaphor is defined as a resonant semantic relationship between a primary subject and a secondary subject, and there is no resonance between the sea and the people or things that are at the seaside, on the sea. The previous paragraph is about phraseology, not metaphor. However, *at sea* may be different. Should it be classified as an idiom? This is to some extent a matter of taste. Typical, best-example idioms (for example, *keep one's head above water*) are frozen phrases that were originally metaphors (even when, as in the case of the much-quoted example *kick the bucket*, the original metaphor is lost, obscure, or disputed). There is nothing metaphorical about the most normal uses of *at sea*, so it is best to class it as a phraseological phenomenon rather than as an idiom.

The expression *at sea* has, however, given rise to an idiom, the canonical form of which is *all at sea*. In this form (with *all*) it never means voyaging on the ocean. It means baffled or confused. Why is this classified as an idiom, not phraseology? The main reason is that it is an expression consisting of more than one word, having a canonical form, and expressing a fixed meaning that is not compositional. No doubt the idiom arose as a result of the bewildering technical complexity of sailing ships and nautical jargon that confronted landlubbers needing to make a voyage, or pressed into naval service, in times gone by, but it is not necessary to know this to understand the meaning of the expression. It is an idiom, not a conventional metaphor, because its meaning is fixed and does not depend on resonance between primary and secondary subjects. The fact that the resonance just alluded to is *historical* is a reason for classifying it as an idiom, not a metaphor. If the resonance were still active at the present day, it would be more tempting to classify it as a metaphor.

The canonical form of the idiom (which occurs 15 times in BNC[2]) tells only part of the story. Automatic recognition of the idiom in text would require a sophisticated procedure for recognition of at least seven alternations (14 tokens) on the canonical form: *completely at sea* ($\times$ 5), *totally at sea* ($\times$ 2), *utterly at sea, rather at sea* ($\times$ 2), *quite at sea* ($\times$ 2), *a bit at sea, somewhat at sea.* Unfortunately for lexicographers, there is a further alternation, in which the quantifier *all* is omitted altogether, as in the last four lines of Appendix 2. This results in a local ambiguity that cannot be resolved by analysis of the immediate context. Is a person who is "at sea" located in a ship out on the ocean, or is he or she baffled and confused? A combination of genre classification and wider context generally serves to resolve the ambiguity. For example, the Indian batsmen ("the Indian batting" – a metonym) mentioned in the very last line of Appendix 2 are most unlikely to be on board a ship. In fact, this fragment comes from a newspaper report of a cricket match, a fact that resolves the ambiguity before it even arises. The psycholinguistic claim that all meanings of a word or phrase are activated in the mind of a reader or hearer and then the right one is selected seems questionable, therefore. More probably, the wrong meanings simply lie dormant and are not activated at all: i.e. no reader of a report on a cricket match suddenly starts thinking of ships at sea when the context requires that the text should say how well or badly the cricketers performed.

---

2. Figures obtained from automatic processing of this phrase in BNC are, unfortunately, distorted by the fact that a racehorse called All At Sea is mentioned frequently in some of BNC's newspaper texts.

7. Case study 2: *Oasis*

Only half of all uses of *oasis* are literal. How can such a statement be made, and how can it be justified? If half of all uses are non-literal, then should they not be classified by all right-thinking empirical linguists as separate literal senses in their own right? This is indeed the position taken by many dictionaries (e.g. *Collins English Dictionary:* see below) and by some linguists (e.g. John Sinclair (p.c.)). However, it is unsatisfactory because such uses do not constitute a coherent unity of their own. The *New Oxford Dictionary of English* takes a different view, and explicitly uses the label *figurative* to denote secondary senses that have the status of conventional metaphors.

> **oasis** ... **1.** a fertile patch in a desert occurring where the water table approaches or reaches the ground surface. **2.** a refuge; haven ... (*Collins English Dictionary* (1979))

> **oasis** ... a fertile spot in a desert, where water is found.
> – *figurative.* a pleasant or peaceful area or period in the midst of a difficult, troubled, or hectic place: *an oasis of calm in the centre of the city.*
> (*New Oxford Dictionary of English* (1998))

No doubt because it has great resonance, 'Oasis' is a popular name for hotels, sports and leisure centres, and other buildings. It is also found in trade names, in particular the name of a kind of water-absorbent silicon foam used by florists. All of these uses must first be cleared out of the way before analysis can begin. All of these uses have been ignored. Headlines and mentions are likewise set on one side. The remaining 240 uses of *oasis* in BNC were analysed in some detail.

The Wasps statistical analyser (Kilgarriff and Tugwell 2001; http://wasps.itri.bton.ac.uk/) shows very few significant collocations with an MI score greater than 9 for this word in BNC. The ones that exist are as follows:

> oasis in ... desert ($\times$ 13; MI score 20.8)
> oasis of calm ($\times$ 7; MI score 14.1)
> oasis of greenery ($\times$ 3; MI score 9.6)

These are highly suggestive of the semantic properties of this word. The fact (if it is a fact) that, in reality, many oases are noisy, smelly places full of honking car, roaring trucks, careering buses, grumbling camels, and shouting people is irrelevant. As far as the conventions of English are concerned, oases are calm and green.

There is a cline of metaphoricity in the usage of this word, which (I claim) is typical of all words that are frequently used to make metaphors. At one extreme, about 50% of the collocates (in particular place names and contrastive use with *desert*) make it clear that oasis is a referring expression referring to a location in a desert where water and vegetation are found (the 'literal' sense). The resonance of this use is indicated by further collocations (albeit not statistically significant ones) with words such as *peace, calm, cool, lush, luxurious, green, pool, water, trees, palm trees*, etc. (The calm and charming unity of these resonances is sadly shattered by occasional collocation with terms of warfare in British English texts referring to World War II.)

Related to this use are other uses of *oasis*, where it is also a referring expression denoting a location, but now not a location in a (literal) desert, but rather a location in an area regarded figuratively as a wasteland or desert:

(18) An *oasis* of calm in the centre of Leeds.
(19) one of several splendid *oases* of green in the city.
(20) Stoke Mandeville station is a little *oasis*; clean and bright and friendly.

Examples (18) and (19) are metaphorical because, although cities are regularly referred to (explicitly or, as here, by implication) as deserts, they are not deserts. They do not have any of the basic attributes of deserts: they are not, for example, hot, sandy, arid, or uninhabited. In these examples, the resonance is extended to terms that may or may not actually be present in the text, but which are significant collocates: *desert, calm,* and *greenery*. This is achieved by the strong statistical association of these words with *oasis*.

In several such metaphors, the 'of' structure singles out a property of *oasis* (its 'formal' to use Pustejovsky's (1995) term: *calm, serenity*, and *greenery* in examples (21–24)) as a basis for contrastive resonance with some other term or concept: *the hurly-burly, the crowded pavements of the city centre, the bustling city,* or *the ceaseless grind and roar* of traffic, as the case may be:

(21) … where people can escape *the hurly-burly* to an *oasis of calm* and do what they like best.

(22) Visitors to the city may easily fail to chance upon Portugal Place, which remains an *oasis of timeless calm* only a few paces from *the crowded pavements* of the city centre.
(23) Here the lush and peaceful courtyard with two ancient wells is an oasis of *serenity* amidst *the bustling city.*
(24) Campden Hill Square lay in its midday calm, an *urban oasis of greenery and Georgian elegance* rising from *the ceaseless grind and roar of Holland Park Avenue.*

At the other extreme of the metaphoricity cline are uses where the oasis in question denotes an abstract entity:

(25) These brief *oases of super-wealth* were a direct result of exploitation of the developing world.
(26) It's about *oases of control* where there should be none.
(27) These Sundays were the *oases of human contact* in the desert of my loneliness.
(28) ... Kenya, a country previously regarded as an *oasis of economic success* in east Africa.
(29) She now regards her job as an *oasis in a desert of coping* with Harry's lack of direction.

These uses are highly metaphorical, because uses of *super-wealth, control, human contact, economic success,* and *job* have no features in common with the normal use and meaning potential of *oasis*.

As in the case of *sea, torrent, jungle* and many other words denoting types of location, there is a wide variety of semantic types (in between the two extremes) fulfilling the N2 roles grammatically:

(30) a little *oasis of bottles*, coffee pot and cheeseboard [on a dinner table].
(31) He lowered his tongue and lips to the tiny *oasis of moisture.*
(32) an *oasis of life* in the solar system.

It is also worth pointing out that although oases are typically found in hot deserts, this is not a necessary condition. There are also Antarctic oases, as in (33):

(33) Shumskiy (1957) defines Antarctic oases as substantial ice-free areas separated from an ice-sheet by an ablation zone, and kept free from snow by ablation due to low albedo and radiation.

People who believe in the Aristotelian doctrine of essences would probably claim that this is a literal use of *oasis*. The argument goes roughly as follows: the 'essential property' of an oasis is that it is a type of fertile location surrounded by a barren area. Heat, palm trees, a calm atmosphere, human habitation, etc., are merely 'accidental properties'. If the oasis in the Antarctic is fertile and the surrounding area is barren, then it is literally an oasis: it doesn't matter whether the barren area is barren because of snow and ice or because of sand, nor whether the weather is cold or hot. People who believe in prototype theory, on the other hand, would claim that prototypical oases are not only fertile and surrounded by barrenness, but also hot and lush and calm and inhabited by humans. Therefore, in the prototype theorist's view, an Antarctic oasis is a much less literal oasis that a Saharan one.

The lexicographer's dilemma is how to represent these facts. In a theoretical analysis, the problem can be solved by distinguishing typical literal meanings (oases in hot deserts) from possible literal meaning (oases in any kind of wasteland). But in a dictionary, the lexicographer has to decide whether to treat an expression as an idiom, with its own entry (however this may be arranged alphabetically) or as a metaphor, entered as a secondary sense.

8. Conclusion

This paper took as a theoretical basis for exploration Max Black's idea that metaphor depends on 'resonance' between at least two concepts, in which one (the primary subject) is interpreted in terms of the other (the secondary subject). It argues that resonance can be measured by studying actual uses of metaphors in corpora, and it proposes that there is more resonance (i.e. more metaphoricity) when two concepts share fewer semantic properties. Some metaphors are more metaphorical than others. The prototypical oasis is in a hot desert, but there are also Antarctic oases, which are not prototypical and may or may not be classified as literal oases; an oasis in a big city is more metaphorical than an oasis in the Antarctic; an oasis in the mind is more metaphorical than either. The resonance is amplified and extended when other, related terms and concepts (significant collocates) are brought into play, and may even resonate with terms that are not explicitly realized in the text: for example, the citations mentioning oases in a city environment assign the role of the desert to the city, although in such cases the word *desert* is rarely explicitly present. Collocates that are significantly associated with the secondary subject seem to be destined inevitably to participate in secondary resonance of this kind.

The notion of semantic resonance is, of course, itself a metaphor, but rather that shunning it, we should embrace it, as many writers have done, as the only effective way of explaining this linguistic phenomenon. Furthermore, if words only have meaning in context and if the notion of literal meaning must be replaced by (or interpreted through) the notion of normal use, then metaphorical resonance has an important, and as yet unexplored, role to play in the interpretation of non-normal uses.

Many words, for example abstract nouns, are not used metaphorically at all. Those that *are* used metaphorically are normally realized as such in an apparently limited set of syntagmatic patterns, the full details of which remain to be elaborated. This paper has mentioned only a few of the syntagmatic patterns in which metaphors occur. It is already clear that different syntagmatic patterns are associated with different words used metaphorically.

Finally, we noted that, while metaphors are distinguished from normal, literal phraseology by their semantic resonance, on the other hand they are distinguished from idioms because the resonance of idioms is (in most cases) only historical.

Appendix 1: Selected examples of *sea of [NP]* arranged by degree of metaphoricity

sea of [[Substance]] (76 hits)

s incomplete entrance steps and the	**sea of**	mud and rubble that surrounds theliving in
squalor, surrounded by a	**sea of**	mud, because a council ca n't reho
enty five she has to wade through a	**sea of**	mud to get to her council home at
f 1857 which had been put down in a	**sea of**	blood. Hang without mercy, hang
further and further into a boiling	**sea of**	mutton broth. In the kitchen, with
shores of an island surrounded by a	**sea of**	acid. At the island's summit is t
houses we passed were floating in a	**sea of**	snow. There was so much snow that
most wonderful I can recall, as the	**sea of**	cloud broke up only on gaining the
ation or drowned in the surrounding	**sea of**	fire. Such disasters with heavy lo
rying to find her children. It's a	**sea of**	fire. Everyone has gone. Children
te flowers like tiny sails amidst a	**sea of**	dark green glossy foliage. Spikes
lms reaching gigantically above the	**sea of**	foliage. She heard her name again,
ntry to Crane Beach wound through a	**sea of**	sugar cane in undulating waves ten
left onto it, through an undulating	**sea of**	purple heather up to Golden Height
re like coral reefs looming above a	**sea of**	hostile jungle. Kefalov bulged lik
e a sensation like drowning under a	**sea of**	the sweetest, stickiest honey. Sev
ng there, surrounded by a veritable	**sea of**	paper; memoranda, notes, bills, le

Metaphoricity is gradable   33

sea of [N-PLURAL[PhysObj]] (121 hits)

he platform, she looked down upon a	**sea of**	faces, rows and rows of black-stoc
time out she had seen nothing but a	**sea of**	faces, so hard had she been concen
azing how welcome they were in that	**sea of**	faces. And they too seemed glad to
d up with dread and peered into the	**sea of**	faces that was watching her with c
ht his eye, waved at him across the	**sea of**	heads, abandoned him to the tide:
see him, bobbing his way through a	**sea of**	heads. As soon as she saw him look
go home # Clasper looked out at the	**sea of**	open mouths which chorused against
it goes any further." Immediately a	**sea of**	hands shot up, waving, and Gerrard
acher 's questions are greeted by a	**sea of**	waving hands and shouts of the tea
the Princess of Wales. There was a	**sea of**	dinner-jacketed dignitaries and a
al observer team, Ortega parted the	**sea of**	cameramen and journalists and appr
nto focus, one is aware of a rising	**sea of**	people and their vehicles which de
is fine this even creates a waving	**sea of**	people; many bidding, many just en
the crowd and shook hands with the	**sea of**	people almost engulfing him. The b
ly along the island 's roads amid a	**sea of**	obese Americans on mopeds. Can it
o hear him; the crowd was a bobbing	**sea of**	black and white cowboy hats. The f
ts of old clothes. The square was a	**sea of**	flat caps, all tilted upwards towa
in the open under a gaily-coloured	**sea of**	umbrellas. The Queen also stood br
d buses blast their way through the	**sea of**	bicycles by liberal use of their h
ossom, and over in Tingle 's Wood a	**sea of**	bluebells rose out of the morning
orm that was surrounded by a frothy	**sea of**	pink and white azalea plants. She
grant disappeared into a bottomless	**sea of**	cigarettes and beer with hardly en
command modules jutting out over a	**sea of**	computer screens and flashing ligh
plunged irretrievably into the vast	**sea of**	photographs for raw material. Down

sea of [[Colour | Light]] (19 hits)

ine # St Patrick 's Cathedral was a	**sea of**	blue for the funeral. It was a Pol
p, mild winters. The gardens were a	**sea of**	dripping green, the roses and late
football 's Premier Division amid a	**sea of**	red and white yesterday. Middlesbr
pionship, when Twickenham became a	**sea of**	gold and black and when London bec
airo. We found the courtyard a wide	**sea of**	light. At midday we climbed the mi
on and a high wind. The night was a	**sea of**	darkness and the unknown. The wind

sea of [[Abstract]] (50 hits)

Claudia was drowning in a	**sea of**	sensations so strong that she want
ir brightest students drowning in a	**sea of**	output. The second stage in the ha
In the end we are all drowned in a	**sea of**	schmaltz. Warner Home Video, 15, &
cro-economists would be adrift in a	**sea of**	unorganized data # Samuelson and N
y Unix boxes each year. Adrift in a	**sea of**	virtual reality # Little more than
ed not only to be able to swim in a	**sea of**	uncertainty but also to resist pan
swam like a blind earless fish in a	**sea of**	sedation, where there was no time
urring in an island set in a leaden	**sea of**	even greater misery, in a world wh
burnt my boats, turned turtle in a	**sea of**	heartbreak or gone down with all h
ines provide an anchor in the rough	**sea of**	life, who does not switch his alle
eone who had plunged fully into the	**sea of**	life than with someone who had sto

ore tipping them over into an angry	**sea of**	debt. Making your fortune while yo
ts, after many hours in the sunless	**sea of**	bafflement, apology and flopsweat,
annel, thought of Sophocles and the	**sea of**	faith that had since receded. I th
hich its comparative isolation in a	**sea of**	illiteracy gives it in earlier epo
ell him his secrets, get rid of the	**sea of**	misery he felt bathing his body, d
se receded, leaving them alone in a	**sea of**	passion. His fingers dispensed wit
released, leaving her rocking on a	**sea of**	pleasure of such width and depth t
ation like islands of richness in a	**sea of**	poverty. Moreover, by adopting too
hance and drifted into the Sargasso	**sea of**	EFL work. Yet here I was, in sedat

sea of [N-PLURAL[Event]] (16 hits)

mic historians are cast adrift in a	**sea of**	events: they possess the potential
were like a peaceful island in the	**sea of**	activity that constituted the cent
d flick her tail and swim away in a	**sea of**	lies – or seeing her pop like a b
ingleton chuckled. All sailing on a	**sea of**	Italian misadventures." End of She
e 'islands of conscious power' in a	**sea of**	market transactions. This idea of
, you would not only wade through a	**sea of**	wrongs, but through hell itself, t
an nature above that which it is, a	**sea of**	flowings and ebbings, and of all m
dom was preferable to the deep blue	**sea of**	reform. Even in 1856, however, the
ve avoided that almost overwhelming	**sea of**	troubles which resulted from harml

Appendix 2: Selected uses of the idiom *all at sea* and its variants

class structure, but seemed all	**at sea**	with his Bond spoof, Modesty Blaise
us man, Sean. You 've got me all	**at sea**	indeed # Contraband, Michael. That 's
reak caught the home defence all	**at sea**,	giving the visitors the lead. Hindhe
ever, when you find yourself all	**at sea**,	you may wonder whether you 've chose
rowers left the competition all	**at sea**	in South Africa recently. At a regatt
ke this lad, who clearly was all	**at sea**	and did n't know how to light the fla
swept United away. They were all	**at sea**	as Neil Matthews took aim and fired i
ssed by spin and Graeme Hick all	**at sea**	whenever Merv Hughes targeted his che
the Swedish second seed was all	**at sea**	in the 32-minute opening set, losing
heir chances and ended up at all	**at sea**.	Blackpool are riding high in Divisio
hed from the world or completely	**at sea**.	Later comes a point of being unable
ubcultures he will be completely	**at sea**	outside his own milieu unless he take
ay leave our students completely	**at sea**.	TASK 7 Here is another chapter openi
hich hearing folk are completely	**at sea**	in their ideas about what is right an
17. He appeared to be completely	**at sea**	again when I asked why primary school
nd 's biographers would be quite	**at sea**	if the editors had not marshalled, de
# I 'm so bad at names and quite	**at sea**	about your relationship # She # told
ut these new lps find him rather	**at sea**.	Most often he falters by trying to s
ient about the office and rather	**at sea**	about the home. I, she thought discon
enient benchmarks, I 'm somewhat	**at sea**.	It 's a little like describing the t
cise rigid control or be totally	**at sea**	in the house. It can take a long time
indergarten teacher felt totally	**at sea**	in the deferential hierarchy of Bucki
nce 's distress she felt utterly	**at sea**	and did n't know how to help her. She
band 's consent. So we are a bit	**at sea**.	I do n't suppose you know of anyone
experience and find ourselves '	**at sea**',	not knowing what to do. The existen

uld have been the poorer." "I'm **at sea**, Mr Wycliffe." "Then let me be more
For our emotions, too, can be **at sea** unless the authority of God's word
Indian batting, though, was often **at sea**, and their selectors will have much

References

Black, Max
    1962   *Models and Metaphors.* Cornell University Press.
Church, Kenneth W. and Patrick Hanks
    1990   Word association norms, mutual information, and lexicography. *Computational Linguistics* 16: 22–29.
Davidson, Donald
    1978   What Metaphors Mean. *Critical Inquiry* 5: 31–47.
Deignan, Alice
    This volume The grammar of linguistic metaphors
Fillmore, Charles J.
    1975   An alternative to checklist theories of meaning. *Papers from the First Annual Meeting of the Berkeley Linguistics Society*, 123–131.
Hanks, Patrick
    1994   Linguistic norms and pragmatic exploitations, or Why lexicographers need prototype theory and vice versa. In: Ferenc Kiefer, Gabor Kiss and Julia Pajzs (eds.), *Papers in Computational Lexicography: Complex '94*, 89–113. Research Institute for Linguistics, Hungarian Academy of Sciences.
    1999   How to tell a meaning from a metaphor. Paper presented to the *Dictionary Society of North America*, University of California at Berkeley.
    2004   The syntagmatics of metaphor. *International Journal of Lexicography* 17: 245–274.
    Forthcoming *Norms and Exploitations.* Cambridge, MA: MIT Press.
Kilgarriff, Adam and David Tugwell
    2001   Word sketch: extraction and display of significant collocations for lexicography. *Proceedings of the workshop on Collocation: Computational Extraction, Analysis and Exploitation*, 32–38. ACL, Toulouse.
Lakoff, George, and Mark Johnson
    1980   *Metaphors We Live By.* Chicago: The University of Chicago Press.
Pustejovsky, James
    1995   *The Generative Lexicon.* Cambridge, MA: MIT Press.
Pustejovsky, James and Patrick Hanks
    2001   *Tutorial on Very Large Lexical Databases.* Toulouse: ACL.
Sinclair, John
    1991   *Corpus, Concordance, Collocation.* Oxford University Press.
Stefanowitsch, Anatol
    This volume Words and their metaphors: a corpus-based approach.

A corpus-based study of metaphors for speech activity in British English

Elena Semino

Abstract

In this paper I present the findings of a corpus-based study of metaphorical expressions used to refer to verbal activity in written British English narratives. The corpus contains a quarter-of-a-million words of fictional and non-fictional written narratives, and was annotated for speech, thought and writing presentation categories at Lancaster University. The availability of the annotated corpus makes it possible to concordance different categories of speech, thought or writing presentation, and therefore easily provides more, and more varied, representative examples of the relevant phenomena than have been available to scholars so far.

This paper focuses particularly on the category known as Narrator's Representation of Speech Acts (NRSA) (e.g. *Traditionalists have accused the authors of heresy...* and *He blasted critics in his party who want him to buy victory ...*). I provide the relative proportions of literal and metaphorical NRSAs in the corpus as a whole and in each of its main sections. I then present a provisional categorization of the metaphorical examples on the basis of the relevant source domains, and discuss the implications of my findings for existing accounts of metaphors for communication in English. I finish by showing how most of the metaphorical NRSAs in the corpus can be explained in terms of a coherent scenario whereby verbal communication is conventionally constructed in terms of actions and positions within a physical, concrete scenario.

1. Introduction

Over the last few decades, research on metaphor has been dominated by the exploration of the relationship between language and thought, from a variety of perspectives (e.g. Glucksberg 2001; Lakoff and Johnson 1980, 1999; Ortony 1979, 1993; Sperber and Wilson 1986, 1995). In particular, cognitive metaphor theorists from Reddy (1979) and Lakoff and Johnson (1980) onwards have argued that the presence of systematic patterns of metaphorical expressions in language is evidence of the existence of metaphorical thought, and particularly of conventional conceptual metaphors – systematic sets of correspondences across different domains in conceptual structure.

While Cognitive Metaphor theory has arguably become the dominant paradigm in current metaphor research, however, concerns have been expressed over the absence of an explicit and reliable methodology for the extrapolation of conceptual metaphors from linguistic data (e.g. Cameron 1999, 2003: 239–241; Heywood *et al.* 2002; Low 1999, 2003; Steen 1999). More specifically, some recent studies have cast doubt on the validity of some earlier claims on particular conceptual metaphors, and have arrived at partly different conclusions on the basis of a re-analysis of the available linguistic evidence (e.g. Grady 1997a, 1997b, 1998; Ritchie 2003).

The increasing availability of large electronic corpora (for English in particular) provides new opportunities for investigating metaphorical expressions in naturally-occurring discourse, as shown by a number of recent studies (e.g. Boers 1999, Cameron and Deignan 2003, Deignan 1999, 2000; Peters and Wilks 2003, Semino 2002, Semino *et al.* 2004, and the contributions to this volume). Corpora enable researchers to study linguistic patterns on a large scale, and can therefore provide the basis for more reliable hypotheses about possible underlying conceptual metaphors.

In this paper I present the results of a study of metaphorical expressions referring to speech activity in a corpus of contemporary written British English. I focus particularly on the kinds of expressions that have so far been explained in relation to (i) Lakoff and Johnson's (1980) ARGUMENT IS WAR conceptual metaphor, and (ii) Reddy's (1979) CONDUIT metaphor, which Grady (1997, 1998) recently 'decomposed' into a set of what he calls 'primary' metaphors. In each case, the analysis of my data results in some adjustments to current formulations of conceptual metaphors for communication. More specifically, I will show that Lakoff and Johnson's ARGUMENT IS WAR only accounts for *some* of the expressions which construct verbal conflict in terms of physical conflict, and that it should therefore be replaced by a more general conceptual metaphor, which I refer to as ANTAGONISTIC COMMUNICATION IS PHYSICAL CONFLICT (see also Ritchie 2003). Similarly, I will show that my data contains a wider range of expressions than were considered by both Reddy (1979) and Grady (1998), and I will therefore propose some revisions to their formulations of some of the main conceptual metaphors for communication in English. I will finish by considering how the particular metaphorical patterns I discuss in this chapter relate to other frequent metaphorical patterns I have identified in my data.

2. The corpus data

This study is based on a corpus of (late) 20th century written British English, which was constructed by a team working at Lancaster University in the 1990s (see Wynne *et al.* 1998, Semino *et al.* 1999, Semino and Short 2004). It contains 120 text samples of approximately 2,000 words each, for a total of 258,348 words. The corpus is equally divided into three main genre sections, namely: prose fiction (87,709 words), newspaper news reports (83,603 words), and biography and autobiography (87,036 words). Each of the three genre sections was in turn equally divided into a 'popular' and a 'serious' sub-section (e.g. tabloid vs. broadsheet newspapers, and popular vs highbrow fiction; see Semino *et al.* 1999 and Semino and Short 2004: 21–22 for our criteria in implementing this distinction).

The corpus was constructed in order to study the forms, functions and patterns of speech, thought, and writing presentation (SW&TP) in fictional and non-fictional text-types that could broadly be defined as 'narrative'. The whole corpus was therefore manually annotated for categories of SW&TP, such as Direct Speech, Free Indirect Thought, and so on. I do not have the space here to describe the annotation system we applied to the corpus (but see Wynne *et al.* 1998 and Semino and Short 2004: 26 ff. for a detailed discussion). What is relevant for the purposes of this study is that it is possible to search the corpus automatically in order to obtain concordances for each of the categories of SW&TP included within the annotation system. Here I will focus on one particular speech presentation category: the Narrator's Representation of Speech Acts (NRSA).

2.1. The Narrator's Representation of Speech Acts (NRSA) in the corpus

The NRSA category was originally introduced in Leech and Short (1981) in order to capture those expressions which report one or more utterances by referring to their (supposed) illocutionary force or speech act value (see Austin 1962, Searle 1979). Below is a prototypical example from the popular newspaper section of corpus:

(1) During the 16-hour siege he had demanded a helicopter (The Daily Mirror, 29/4/1996)

Typically, NRSAs consist of a verb referring to a speech act (e.g. 'demand' in example 1), and a noun phrase or prepositional phrase giving some indication of the content of the relevant utterance (e.g. 'a helicopter' in example 1). NRSAs can also be realized by noun phrases where the head noun refer to a speech act, as in: 'demands for an overhaul of the constitution'. In practice, however, during the annotation of the corpus the NRSA tag was also applied to expressions that do not refer to illocutionary force in the strictest sense, but to speech activity more generally (see Ballmer and Brennenstuhl 1981[1]). The main *formal* criterion for the application of the NRSA tag was that the relevant stretch of text included no grammatical separation between a reporting clause and a reported clause, since this structure is typical of the category of Indirect Speech presentation (e.g. the Indirect Speech tag was applied to the italicized part of the sentence: 'Hundreds of protesters and politicians gathered in central Moscow, *demanding that Russia halt the invasion*') (see Semino and Short 2004: 53).

For the purposes of this study, I considered a concordance containing 985 instances of NRSA.[2] In analysing the concordance, I identified individual instances of NRSA as metaphorical when:
(i) one or more of the lexical items that, in context, refer to speech activity have a more basic sense that is not to do with verbal communication, and
(ii) the speech activity sense of the relevant expressions can be said to be related to the more basic sense via a cross-domain mapping where the target is verbal communication and the source is a different domain that is not to do with verbal communication.

Consider the following extract, again from the popular newspaper section of the corpus (NB: in giving quotations from the corpus, I italicize the relevant metaphorically used words, for the sake of clarity):

(2) And he *blasted* critics in his party who want him to buy victory. (*The Daily Star*, 13/5/1996)

This sentence is part of an extended report of what the then UK Chancellor of the Exchequer (Kenneth Clarke) said in an interview. In this sentence the verb 'blast' is used to refer to the force of one or more utterances in which Clarke forcefully countered the criticisms of those who believed that he could ensure a new electoral victory for the Conservative

---

1. In their 'Speech Act classification' (which includes 4,800 English verbs) Balmer and Brennenstuhl (1981) do not restrict themselves to verbs that have performative uses, but include 'any kind of (aspect of) speech activity designating verb' (Ballmer and Brennenstuhl 1981: 16). This, they argue, results in 'a more relevant class of expressions with respect to linguistic behaviour than the "performative" verbs' (Ballmer and Brennenstuhl 1981: 16).
2. This figure is lower than the total figure for NRSA in the corpus given in Semino and Short (2004: 67), since I excluded all borderline cases of NRSA and all cases where instances of NRSA occurred within another category of SW&TP.

government by reducing income tax. However, the verb 'blast' has a more basic sense that is not to do with verbal communication, but with damaging or destroying physical entities, usually via an explosion caused by a bomb or other weapon. The speech act sense of 'blast' (which is conventional in British English) can be explained in term of a mapping from the domain typically associated with the basic sense of 'blast' (WAR or, more generally, (ARMED) PHYSICAL CONFLICT) to the domain of verbal communication. This helps to explains why the use of 'blast' in reference to communication suggests a very negative attitude and strong criticism. I will return to this example below.

According to my analysis, 214 out of the total 985 instances of NRSAs in my concordance involve metaphorical references to speech acts or speech activity, amounting to approximately 22 per cent of the total. Overall, NRSA is not equally distributed within the corpus: the press section has 470 instances, the (auto)biography section has 361, and the fiction section only 154 (see Semino and Short 2004: 73 for a discussion of these differences among our three text-types). However, the proportion of metaphorical NRSAs is very similar across the three genres: 22 per cent for the newspaper section, 17 per cent for the fiction section, and 23 per cent for the (auto)biography section.

The majority of metaphorical NRSAs in the corpus involve the metaphorical use of verbs, as in the case of 'blast' in example 2. In other cases, speech acts are referred to via the heads of noun phrases (e.g. 'In an astonishing *attack* on Mr Major' referring to somebody's utterances), or via the combination of a metaphorically used verb with a direct object that refers to a type of text or speech act (e.g. 'Kenneth Clarke [...] *has delivered* a defiant message to').

In the rest of this chapter, I will focus particularly on the examples in my NRSA concordance that can be related to ARGUMENT IS WAR or to the CONDUIT metaphor.

3. ARGUMENT IS WAR

The conceptual metaphor ARGUMENT IS WAR was initially proposed by Lakoff and Johnson (1980) in *Metaphors We Live By* on the basis of conventional metaphorical expressions such as 'Your claims are *indefensible*', 'His criticism were *right on target*' and 'I've never *won* an argument with him'. The pervasiveness of expressions such as these led Lakoff and Johnson to conclude that, in English, 'ARGUMENT is partially structured, understood, performed, and talked about in terms of WAR' (Lakoff and Johnson 1980: 5).

Lakoff and Johnson place ARGUMENT IS WAR within the category of 'structural metaphors', which 'allow us [...] to structure one highly delineated concept in terms of another' (Lakoff and Johnson 1980: 61). Structural metaphors, they argue, 'are grounded in systematic correlations in experience' (Lakoff and Johnson 1980: 61). In the case of ARGUMENT IS WAR, they see a correlation between verbal arguments and physical fights, which are common both among animals and among humans, and which humans 'have institutionalized [...] in a number of ways, one of them being war' (Lakoff and Johnson 1980: 62). More recently, Kövecses (2002) has argued that the experiential basis of metaphors such as ARGUMENT IS WAR can be identified in the fact that the source domain (WAR) is the origin or 'root' of the target (ARGUMENT). In the case of ARGUMENT IS WAR, Kövecses argues, the root is cultural (as opposed to biological), since 'the verbal institution of arguments has evolved historically from the physical domain of fighting'(Kövecses 2002: 74).

In a recent paper, Ritchie (2003) has questioned the validity of ARGUMENT IS WAR as formulated by Lakoff and Johnson (1980). He points out that many of the metaphorical expressions which have been seen as linguistic realizations of ARGUMENT IS WAR can also be related to other potential source domains, such as sports, or games like chess and bridge. Ritchie therefore argues that 'conceptual metaphors such as ARGUMENT IS WAR often emerge from a field of interrelated concepts, all available for metaphorical application to each other, as well as to external concepts such as business and politics' (Ritchie 2003: 126). In the case of the metaphorical construction of arguments, Ritchie proposes that the relevant source domain is best seen as a complex conceptual field including different types of conflict, ranging from games through fisticuffs to all-out war (Ritchie 2003: 135). Ritchie therefore argues that the fact that this complex conceptual field is conventionally mapped onto the target domain of arguments has a clear experiential basis: although most (American) native speakers of English do not have first-hand experience of war, they do have direct experience of many types of less extreme physical conflict, such as scuffles among children, physical contests, sports and games.

I will now show how an analysis of my corpus data partly supports Ritchie's critique, and I will propose a reformulation of ARGUMENT IS WAR to account more systematically for the linguistic evidence at my disposal.

3.1. ARGUMENT IS WAR revisited

My NRSA concordance contains a group of examples that are very similar to those cited by Lakoff and Johnson (1980) as evidence for ARGUMENT IS WAR. The use of the verb 'blast' in example (2) above belongs to this group, as do the verb 'flare' (in 'questions flaring'), the noun 'flak' (in 'flak over fat cat pay') and the italicized expressions in the examples below:

(3) The Americans [...] were now *bombarding* the security man at the front gate with questions about just which building was the actual home of the Benny Hill Show (John Smith, *The Benny Hill Story*, 1988: 96)
(4) amid renewed backbench *sniping at* the Blair style of leadership (*The Guardian*, 13/5/1996)
(5) [O]nce again we were *firing* questions (*The Daily Mirror*, 13/5/1996)

There is some formal variation among these examples. First, the expression that metaphorically refers to speech activity may be a verb (e.g. 'bombarding ... with questions') or a noun (e.g. 'flak over fat cat pay'). Second, the reference to speech activity may be achieved entirely via a metaphorical expression (e.g. 'blasting' in example 2), or via the combination of a metaphorically used verb with a noun referring (literally) to a speech act, which may, in turn, be (part of) the grammatical subject (e.g. 'questions flaring'), the direct object (e.g. 'firing questions'), or a prepositional phrase functioning as an adverbial (e.g. 'bombarding ... with questions').

In spite of these formal differences, the above expressions may, at first sight, be seen as prototypical linguistic realisations of the conceptual metaphor ARGUMENT IS WAR. On closer look, however, some difficulties arise. While some of these examples refer to the expression of (critical) views in arguments or controversies (e.g. 'he blasted critics'), others refer to persistent and forceful communicative behaviour which does not necessarily occur within an argument (e.g. 'bombarding ... with questions'). Moreover, in their literal senses, these expressions do not relate exclusively to the domain of war in the sense of organised military conflict among countries, but rather to the wider domain of armed violence, which also includes, for example, the activities of terrorist organisations and of armed criminals generally.

Similar issues arise from a consideration of the use of the verbs 'attack' and 'defend' in reference to speech activities, as in the examples below:

(6) Last night M Delors *attacked* M Balladur's idea of a "Europe of circles" in which each member country could progress at its own speed. (*The Daily Telegraph*, 12/12/1994)
(7) The Chancellor also *defended* his stand on a European single currency. (*The Daily Star*, 13/5/1996)

While both 'attack' and 'defend' can be applied literally in relation to war, their literal senses also apply more generally to contexts involving (unarmed) physical aggression and violence (e.g. 'Police attacked at acid house parties' and 'Michael told the Old Bailey he had tried to defend his brother Lee, 13, before his father turned on him' from the *British National Corpus*, hereafter the *BNC*).

My NRSA concordance also contains a further group of expression which present speech activities in terms of low-level physical aggression that does not normally involve the use of weapons. These expressions include the noun 'bust-up' when used in relation to a verbal argument, and the italicized verbs in the examples below:

(8) Crime victims *hit out* yesterday over plans to give thugs a five-star Christmas in jail. (*The Sun*, 5/12/1994)
(9) Both presenters have been *slammed* for fluffing their lines (*The News of the World*, 11/12/1994)
(10) He *rapped* his decision to remove the whip from eight MPs who voted against the Euro-cash bill last week. (*The Daily Star*, 5/12/1994)

The italicized expressions in all three examples have basic physical senses to do with the delivery of blows against physical entities, including, in some cases, people. More specifically, the physical sense of 'hit out' relates to the action of delivering repeated blows against someone or something in uncontrolled fashion, either to attack or to defend oneself (e.g. 'If you are convinced that he or she is going to hurt you and you can't escape, you may even hit out as they come forward', from the *BNC*). In contrast, the physical sense of 'slam' normally involves the delivery of a single blow to a concrete object (e.g. 'Jamie backed away, laughing, and slammed the door shut behind him', from the *BNC*), while the physical sense of 'rap' relates to multiple, but more gentle, blows to an object, or, in a more restricted sense, somebody else's knuckles (e.g. 'He told his teacher he had lost it on the way to school, and Mr Watson promptly rapped his knuckles with a ruler for his carelessness', from the *BNC*). In my data all three verbs are used to refer metaphorically to the expression of critical views in relation to somebody else's decisions or behaviour.

On the basis of the analysis of my data, I would therefore suggest that Lakoff and Johnson's formulation of ARGUMENT IS WAR is too restricted, both in terms of the source and the target domain. As far as the source domain is concerned, my examples do not (or not only) relate to the domain of WAR, but to the more general domain of physical conflict. This general domain includes a large variety of forms of violence and aggression, from the delivery of blows with one's bare hands to the deployment of the kind of weaponry that is typically used in armed conflict between countries. As far as the target domain is concerned, some of my examples do relate to arguments (even though not necessarily face-to-face), but others relate more generally to critical, forceful, or antagonistic communicative behaviour, which may not be part of an argument as such (e.g. 'bombarding ... with questions' in example 3), or which may not necessarily receive a reply from the addressee (e.g. 'Both presenters have been slammed ...' in example 9). My proposal, therefore, is that the expressions discussed in this section are better seen as realizations of a more general conceptual metaphor, which may be referred to as ANTAGONISTIC COMMUNICATION IS PHYSICAL CONFLICT.

Clearly, my findings are broadly compatible with Ritchie's (2003) proposal, and specifically with his account of the experiential basis of the metaphorical construction of verbal conflict as physical conflict: while war is not necessarily part of everybody's first-hand experience, almost everybody has some direct experience of physical conflict of a more general nature, especially in childhood. This does not deny, of course, that war is a salient part of the complex domain of physical conflict, and that it functions as the specific source of some metaphorical expressions relating to arguments. Indeed, as I mentioned earlier, Lakoff and Johnson's (1980: 62) discussion of the background to ARGUMENT IS WAR contains very similar points, but their formulation of the relevant conceptual metaphor does not properly account for the linguistic evidence, and tends to force a narrow interpretation of expressions that do not necessarily relate specifically either to (metaphorical) war or to (literal) arguments.

My concordance contains 27 instances of NRSA that can be seen as realizations of the metaphor ANTAGONISTIC COMMUNICATION IS PHYSICAL CONFLICT. Not surprisingly, the majority of these examples (22 out of 27) occur in news reports, which tend to be concerned with controversies and debates on topical issues, both of a private and of a public nature. More specifically, the expressions that most clearly relate to war or armed violence occur in the popular sub-sections of the corpus. All metaphorical uses of 'blast', 'slam', 'flak' and 'rap' within NRSAs occur in tabloid newspapers, as does the expression 'firing questions'. In addition, the expressions 'questions flaring' and 'bombard with questions' were found in popular (auto)biographies. My impression is that in these cases the metaphorical use of these expressions does not necessarily project the notion of extreme and destructive violence onto the target, but rather has the kind of hyperbolic, sensationalist, and in some cases humorous effects that are normally associated with popular reporting. In all cases, however, the various expressions that evoke physical conflict are used metaphorically to refer to negative, critical or forceful speech activity, whose targets are other people, their views, or the utterances or texts they have produced.

4. The CONDUIT metaphor

In one of the first studies in cognitive metaphor theory, Reddy (1979) famously argued that, in English, communication is frequently talked about as a process involving the manipulation and exchange of physical objects, as in 'You have to *put each concept into* words very carefully' and 'Try to *get* your *thoughts across* better' (Reddy 1979: 166–167; original italics). On the basis of the analysis of a large set of similar examples, Reddy concluded that speakers of English share a dominant metaphorical conceptualization of communication in terms of the transfer of objects, which he labelled 'the conduit metaphor'. Within this metaphor, Reddy argued, language 'functions like a conduit, transferring thoughts bodily from one person to another' (Reddy 1979: 170). Speakers and writers 'insert thoughts or feelings in the words'; words containing the thoughts and feelings are transferred to the addressee(s); and finally listeners or readers 'extract the thoughts and feelings again from the words' (Reddy 1979: 170). On the basis of his data, Reddy estimated that the conduit metaphor accounts for as many as 70 per cent of the expressions commonly used in English to talk about communication.

In *Metaphors we Live By*, Lakoff and Johnson (1980: 10–12 *et passim*) describe what they call the 'CONDUIT metaphor' as a cross-domain mapping consisting of the following main correspondences:

IDEAS (OR MEANINGS) ARE OBJECTS
LINGUISTIC EXPRESSIONS ARE CONTAINERS
COMMUNICATION IS SENDING (Lakoff and Johnson 1980: 10)

This formulation of the CONDUIT metaphor has since become the most widely accepted account of the dominant way in which speakers of English talk and think about communication (e.g. Taylor 2002: 490 and Kövecses 2002: 73–74). More recently, however, Grady (1997a, 1997b 1998, 1999) has questioned the validity of the CONDUIT metaphor alongside that of many other well-established formulations of conceptual metaphors, for the following reasons: first, it lacks a clear experiential basis; second, it does not explain why some prominent elements of the source domain are not conventionally mapped onto the target (e.g. the notion of opening or sealing packages is not conventionally projected from the domain of the transfer of objects to the domain of communication); and third, it does not account for why many expressions that have been associated with the CONDUIT metaphor are in fact conventionally used in relation to other domains of experience as well (e.g. 'The detective couldn't *get* much information *out of* the partial shoeprint (Grady 1998: 209, italics in original)).

Grady (1997a, 1998) has proposed an alternative account of the data Reddy (1979) and Lakoff and Johnson (1980) analysed, based on the notion of 'primary metaphors'. Primary metaphors are defined as simple, basic mappings that have a strong experiential basis and that combine to produce many different complex metaphors (see also Grady 1997b, 1999). More specifically, Grady suggests that the linguistic data from which the CONDUIT metaphor was extrapolated is best accounted for in terms of a small set of primary metaphors, which also account for the use of similar expressions in relation to other target domains. Grady's (1998) proposed primary metaphors are listed below (NB: each primary metaphor is followed by two of Grady's own linguistic examples, one relating to communication and one relating to other areas of experience. The italics in all examples are Grady's own):

CONSTITUENTS ARE CONTENTS
'She *packs* a tremendous number of ideas *into* each carefully worded statement.'
'Our agenda is *packed* with events.' (Grady 1998: 211)

ACHIEVING A PURPOSE IS ACQUIRING A DESIRED OBJECT
'I have to struggle to *get* any meaning at all *out of* the sentence.'
'I finally *got/found/landed* a good job.' (Grady 1998: 212–213)

INFORMATION IS CONTENTS
'I couldn't *get* the necessary information *out of* that book.'
'Tree rings *contain* the story of the region.' (Grady 1998: 214)

BECOMING ACCESSIBLE IS EMERGING
'Close reading reveals altogether uncharacteristic feelings in the story.'
'Salt brings out the natural flavor of meat.' (Grady 1998: 214–215)

TRANSMISSION OF ENERGY IS TRANSFER
'Your concepts *came across* beautifully.'
'This action should *send* the appropriate message *to* the Serbs.' Grady 1998: 215)

RMs [I.E. IDEAS, THOUGHTS, FEELINGS, ETC.] ARE POSSESSIONS/LEARNING IS ACQUIRING
'This paper has *given* me new insights into equi.'
'I *have* a much better understanding of tax law now than I did before I took that course.' (Grady 1998: 216)

Although these primary metaphors are separate from one another, they are mutually compatible, and combine to form a coherent picture of (some aspects of) communication, which Grady (1998) summarises as follows:
- Large linguistic structures *contain* the smaller structures of which they are composed; writers/speakers *insert* these smaller structures (CONSTITUENTS ARE CONTENTS).
- Linguistic forms *contain* meaning (BECOMING ACCESSIBLE IS EMERGING).
- Meaning is *transferred* from one person to another via communication (TRANSMISSION OF ENERGY IS TRANSFER);
- Readers/listeners may *acquire* RMs by interacting with linguistic forms (ACHIEVING A PURPOSE IS ACQUIRING A DESIRED OBJECT, RMs ARE POSSESSIONS). (Grady 1998: 217)

At the end of this chapter, I will propose a broader scenario on the basis of the analysis of my corpus data. It is important to bear in mind, however, that, as Grady himself (1998: 216) acknowledges, the CONDUIT metaphor and the primary metaphors mentioned above account for the metaphorical structuring of *some aspects* of linguistic communication, namely the process whereby meanings, ideas, thoughts, feelings, etc. (i.e. what Reddy calls 'Repertoire Members', or RMs) are expressed and communicated via language. The more interactive, interpersonal and social aspects of verbal communication, are constructed via other metaphors, including ARGUMENT IS WAR (and my own reformulation of it).

4.1. The *CONDUIT* metaphor revisited

In discussing the expressions that Reddy accounted for via the CONDUIT metaphor, I will follow Grady (1998) in distinguishing between different metaphorical patterns.

4.1.1. *Expressions relating to transfer*

My corpus data contains 45 expressions of the kind that led Reddy (1979) to formulate the CONDUIT metaphor. Two typical examples are given below:

(11) Don Quarrie has *given* me helpful advice on sprints (Fatima Whitbread with Adrianne Blue, *Fatima*, 1988: 152)
(12) Kenneth Clarke, the Chancellor of the Exchequer, has *delivered* a defiant message to restless Tory backbenchers ... (*The Observer*, 13/5/1996)

Both 'give' and 'deliver' have basic physical senses which relate to the transfer of concrete objects in the physical world. Examples 11 and 12 show that both verbs also have conventional metaphorical senses whereby the performance of speech acts and the production of texts/utterances are constructed in terms of the transfer of physical objects from one person (the speaker) to others (the addressees). A number of other verbs are used metaphorically in the corpus in the same way (although not as frequently as 'give' and 'deliver'), including: 'issue' (e.g. 'issue a warning'), 'leave' (e.g. 'leave a message'), 'offer' (e.g. 'offer concessions'), 'pass on'(e.g. 'pass on news'), 'send' (e.g. 'send a message'), and 'throw' (e.g. 'throw questions').[3]

---

3. As these examples show, the metaphorical expressions relating to transfer tend to be light-verb constructions involving conventional metaphorical uses of verbs that are delexicalised to varying degrees. I have, however, followed Cameron (2003: 72–3) in analysing these delexicalised verbs as metaphorically used in my data because it is possible in each case to identify a basic, physical sense which can function as source for the conventional metaphorical senses to do with communication. For example, although the verb 'give' is highly delexicalised and has a wide range of metaphorical senses (e.g. 'give way', 'give attention', 'give a party'), it nonetheless still has a physical sense to do with the transfer of concrete objects that can be regarded as basic and primary (e.g. 'She gave me her watch').

Within Grady's reformulation of the CONDUIT metaphor (1997a: 25ff, 1998), these expressions are seen as realizations of the primary metaphor TRANSMISSION OF ENERGY IS TRANSFER (OF OBJECTS). According to Grady, this metaphor has a solid experiential grounding, since communication literally involves the transfer of some sort of physical entity (e.g. acoustic signals in spoken communication, physical objects in traditional written communication, electric signals in email communication, and so on).

However, in Reddy's and Grady's data the range of communicative phenomena that are presented as being transferred in expressions of this kind is limited to (i) the contents of an utterance/text (e.g. 'give evidence', 'pass on news') and (ii) what Reddy called 'Repertoire Members' or RMs (e.g. 'give views'). In my data, the range of such phenomena also includes (iii) text-types (e.g. 'send a message') and (iv) speech acts (e.g. 'give advice', 'issue a warning'). All of these phenomena can therefore be metaphorically constructed as objects that are either physically transferred from the addresser to the addressee (e.g. 'give encouragement', 'deliver an appeal') or made available within the communication space so that others can pick them up (e.g. 'issue a command', 'leave a message'). Grady's primary metaphor TRANSMISSION OF ENERGY IS TRANSFER (OF OBJECTS) therefore also involves a general ontological metaphor whereby RMs as well as utterances, their contents and their speech act values are constructed as physical entities (although not necessarily as possessions in the way suggested by Grady 1997a, 1998).

My NRSA concordance contains 45 examples which present speech activity in terms of physical transfer. This constitutes the largest group of metaphorical NRSAs in the corpus, amounting to 21 per cent of the total. I will now turn to the second largest group of examples, which includes a range of expressions that present speech activity in terms of visibility and emergence. In Reddy's terms, these expressions would also count as realizations of the CONDUIT metaphor.

4.1.2. Expressions relating to visibility

Within Reddy's (1979) formulation of the CONDUIT metaphor, meanings correspond to objects, and linguistics expressions correspond to containers. Hence, the process of expressing meanings is conceptualized as putting objects into containers, and the process of understanding is conceptualized as the emergence of objects from containers. This, according to Reddy, explains the conventional use of 'reveal' in relation to communication, as in: 'Closer reading *reveals* altogether uncharacteristic feelings *in* the story' (Reddy 1979: 193; also quoted, with italics, in Grady 1998: 215).

Within Grady's (1998) approach, this kind of expression is explained in relation to two primary metaphors: INFORMATION IS CONTENTS and BECOMING ACCESSIBLE IS EMERGING. According to Grady, the latter metaphor, which motivates the former, is grounded in our physical and sensorial experience:

> There are numerous linguistic examples which reflect a metaphoric association between perceptibility and location outside a container. The motivation for such a metaphor could not be more natural, of course, since perceptibility is literally correlated with location out in the open in so many cases. (Grady 1998: 214)

Grady's (1997a: 296) list of primary metaphors includes two separate metaphors which construct perceptual/cognitive accessibility in terms of location of an object outside a container: PERCEPTIBLE IS 'OUT' (e.g. 'Heat brings *out* the flavor in the soup') and ACCESSIBLE TO AWARENESS IS 'OUT' (e.g. 'The facts in the case will *come out* sooner or later'). In addition, Grady (1997a: 297) also proposes the primary metaphor ACCESSIBLE TO PERCEPTION/AWARENESS IS 'UP' (e.g. 'Why did you have to *bring that up* again?'), which, he argues, is based on 'the correlation between being in a higher position – e.g., at eye level, or out from under an obstruction – and being perceptible' (Grady 1997a: 297).

My NRSA concordance contains a range of examples where the expression and comprehension of meaning in verbal communication is metaphorically presented in terms of visibility and emergence. There are, however, three different patterns, which differ with respect to how exactly meanings are metaphorically presented as being made perceptible to addressees. I will discuss each of these three patterns in turn.

Expressions relating to emergence and movement into view. The corpus contains 16 metaphorical NRSAs which can be seen as realizations of Grady's primary metaphors ACCESSIBLE TO AWARENESS IS 'OUT' or BECOMING ACCESSIBLE IS EMERGING. However, these expressions suggest a somewhat more complex picture than that proposed by Grady. Consider the following examples:

(13) But her mouth motored on and what *came out* was simply, and childishly, rude. (Sara Maitland, *Three Times Table*, 1990: 143)

(14) The last meeting was with Tony Newton who, though clearly nervous, just about managed to *get out* the agreed line. (Margaret Thatcher, *The Downing Street Years*, 1993: 855)

In their physical senses, both 'come out' and 'get out' relate to movement out of a container or a bounded space. However, here it is not the words or the text that are constructed as containers, as is the case in both Reddy's and Grady's examples. Rather, the speakers themselves are implicitly constructed as containers from which meanings and feelings emerge via language. More precisely, in example (13), the contents of the speaker's utterances are presented as the agent of a movement out of the speaker's mouth; in example (14), the speaker is presented as forcing particular meanings out of himself. Examples such as these, therefore, appear to realise both ACCESSIBLE TO AWARENESS IS 'OUT'/BECOMING ACCESSIBLE IS EMERGING and THE BODY IS A CONTAINER.[4]

Not all of the metaphorical NRSAs that relate to visibility or emergence contain explicit or implicit references to movement out of containers, however. My concordance also contains one instance of the use of 'bring up' in the sense of 'mention' that was noticed by Grady, as well as examples such as the following:

(15) Objections were *raised* to this positively Moorish practice; (Salman Rushdie, *The Moor's Last Sigh*, 1995: 75)
(16) I *put forward* the view [...] that [...] (Kenneth Baker, *The Turbulent Years*, 1993: 394)

Example (15) is one of five cases in the corpus where the verb 'raise' is used in reference to verbal activity, with subjects/direct objects referring either to speech acts or to what Reddy calls RMs ('doubts', 'alarm', 'questions'). Since the physical sense of 'raise' suggests movement from below upwards, its use in my examples can be seen as a realization of Grady's primary metaphor ACCESSIBLE TO PERCEPTION/AWARENESS IS 'UP'.

In example (16), on the other hand, 'put forward' is used with a direct object referring to RMs in order to refer to the verbal expressions of particular opinions. Unlike what I noted for 'raise' and 'get out', however, the relevant physical sense of 'put forward' does not refer to movement upwards or our of a container, but rather suggests movement towards the addressee. This metaphorical use of 'put forward' can nonetheless also be

---

4. The corpus also contains an instance of the expression 'trot out a tale', which also presents the production of discourse as the emergence of an object from a container, where the container is the speaker. It is also interesting to notice the use of the prepositional adverb 'out' in the common expression 'spell something out' (in the sense of 'explain'), which is also represented in the corpus. Here the verb 'spell' metonymically refers to verbal activity, while the prepositional adverb 'out' suggests emergence from a container.

explained in relation to visual experience, given that moving an entity towards somebody normally ensures that the entity is within their field of vision. The expression 'float a suggestion', which is also contained in the corpus, can be explained in a similar way: the physical notion of 'floating' involves both movement with the current (and hence, possibly, towards the addressee) and permanence on the surface of the water (and hence visibility).

Overall, the analysis of my NRSA concordance confirms the correlation, noted by Grady, Lakoff and Johnson and others, between (1) knowledge and vision and (2) the expression of meaning and emergence/movement into view. However, the corpus data shows that the metaphorical construction of communication as emergence may not just involve movement upwards or out of a container, but also movement forwards towards the addressee. This could be explained in terms of a metaphor along the lines of ACCESSIBLE TO AWARENESS/CONSIDERATION IS 'IN FRONT' (see also, for example, expressions such as 'We must *face* the facts' and 'The defence establishment is *faced with* a dual problem' from the *BNC*), which has a similar experiential basis as Grady's ACCESSIBLE TO AWARENESS IS 'OUT' and ACCESSIBLE TO AWARENSS IS 'UP': in visual experience, there is a correlation between having an object in front of us and being able to perceive its properties. At a more general level, all these expressions can be related to KNOWING/UNDERSTANDING IS SEEING, which, according to Grady (1997a: 296) has as a corollary CONSIDERING IS LOOKING AT. On the basis of my examples, I could suggest the converse corollary, namely ACCESSIBLE TO AWARENESS/CONSIDERATION IS VISIBLE. On the basis of these conceptual metaphors, it is therefore possible to explain why communication can be metaphorically presented in terms of different types of movements into view.

Expressions relating to pointing. A further set of metaphorical NRSAs in the corpus refer to verbal activity in terms of the physical action of pointing:

(17) Officials at the Department of Energy still wanted to commission Pressurised Water Reactors which were an American development, *pointing to* the success of the French nuclear industry (Jad Adams, *Tony Benn*, 1992: 442)

(18) In Parliament he was one of a phalanx of Labour MPs [...] *pointing out* the involvement of the armed forces in supplying facilities used in the policing of mining communities; (Jad Adams, *Tony Benn*, 1992: 439)

In these examples, the verbs 'point to' and 'point out' are used to refer metaphorically to the action of mentioning something that is relevant to and supports the speakers' argument. The expression 'point out' in example (18) includes both a metaphorical reference to the physical act of pointing and the notion of emergence from containers in the prepositional adverb 'out'. In both cases, verbal communication is constructed in terms of a physical scenario where speakers make meanings/ideas/facts accessible not by moving them into the addressee's field of vision but by indicating their existence and position to the addressee. Within this scenario, meanings are therefore constructed as physical entities that are potentially visible but that may not be noticed by the addressee without the speaker's intervention. My NRSA concordance contains six such expressions, amounting to just under three per cent of all metaphorical NRSAs in my concordance.

In Grady's (1997a: 296) terms, these expressions can explained via the primary metaphor CONSIDERING IS LOOKING AT, which is realized by expressions such as 'We'll be taking a good, long *look* at him as a suspect in this case' (Grady 1997a: 296). However, in my examples the focus is not on the addressee's actions, but rather on what the speaker/writer does in order to enable the addressee to 'look at' and 'see' the meanings that he or she is trying to convey. As a consequence, these examples would best be captured by a conceptual metaphor along the lines of ENABLING KNOWLEDGE/ CONSIDERATION IS POINTING, which can also explain metaphorical expressions that do not relate to verbal communication such as 'The evidence clearly points to her guilt'. This metaphor is also closely related to KNOWING IS SEEING, as well as to Grady's EXISTENCE IS VISIBILITY. The latter is a primary metaphor that Grady (1997a: 284) proposes in order to explain examples such as 'The dodo *disappeared* in the 1600s' and 'Rap music first *appeared* in the late 70s'. As Grady puts it, this metaphor is based on 'the correlation between our awareness of objects (i.e. knowledge of their existence) and their presence within our field of vision' (Grady 1997a: 284). This correlation helps to explain why the use of 'point out' and 'point to' in my examples suggests that whatever is being pointed out/to is presented as 'true': in basic, perceptual experience, if something can be pointed out/to, it can also be seen, and if it can be seen, it exists.

Expressions relating to visual representation. In addition to expressions that construct communication in terms of the process of enabling vision, the NRSA concordance also contains six examples where speech activity is metaphorically referred to via expressions which have basic senses to do with visual representation. Consider the examples below:

(19) Churchill *outlined* the same ideas to Eden (Clive Pointing, *Churchill*, 1994: 736)
(20) Kenneth Clarke, the Chancellor of the Exchequer, has delivered a defiant message to restless Tory backbenchers, *portraying* himself as a staunch defender of the welfare state. (*The Observer*, 13/5/1996)
(21) [...] in the hope that John Major will be unable at the next election to *represent* Labour's plans as an attack on the national identity (*The Guardian*, 5/12/1994)

In (19) the speaker's expression of a general summary of his ideas is metaphorically presented in terms of the provision of an outline, i.e. a visual representation that shows the outer edges or shape of the represented objects, rather than the details. In (20) the verbal expression of a particular opinion on something (in this case the speaker himself) is metaphorically presented in terms of visual portrayal. Similarly, in (21) a potential future criticism of a proposal by the Labour party is metaphorically presented in terms of visual representation. In each case, what is involved is a highly conventional metaphorical sense of verbs whose basic senses relate to the process of producing a visual representation of physical entities. In some cases, however, these verbs can be applied not just to the use of words (spoken or written) to express one's opinions, but to the communication of meaning or information more generally, as in the following examples from the *BNC*:

(22) Table 18 *outlines* these limitations.
(23) the film does not *portray* its hero as homosexual, merely a little strange
(24) these numbers, which *represent* people who have put themselves forward for testing, are underestimates

All of these examples may be explained in terms of an underlying metaphor where the source domain is visual representation and the target is communication in the broadest possible sense, i.e. including informing, suggesting, explaining, or generally enabling the construction of particular meanings. This metaphor, which could be referred to as ENABLING KNOWLEDGE/CONSIDERATION IS PROVIDING A VISUAL REPRESENTATION, is clearly closely connected with KNOWING IS SEEING and the other visual metaphors I have discussed so far.

Overall, the expressions discussed in the whole of this section construct communication in terms of enabling visual perception in a number of different ways, namely by:
(i) moving an entity out of a container, upwards, or towards the addressee;
(ii) physically pointing at something that is potentially visible but may not be seen or noticed by the addressee;
(iii) creating visual images that the addressee can see.

Cumulatively, the different types of expressions relating to visibility and emergence discussed in this section account for 28 NRSAs in my data, corresponding to 13 per cent of all metaphorical NRSAs. This represents the second largest group, after expressions to do with the transfer of objects, which, as I mentioned earlier, account for 21 per cent of the metaphorical NRSAs in my concordance. Added together, therefore, the different types of expressions that Reddy would have subsumed under the CONDUIT metaphor represent 34 per cent of metaphorical NRSAs in my data and just over seven per cent of all the NRSA instances I analysed. Although this is a substantial proportion of metaphorical NRSAs in my concordance, it is considerably less than Reddy's estimate that 70 per cent of all commonly used expressions for communication in English are realizations of the CONDUIT metaphor.

Overall, my analysis also supports Grady's idea that Reddy's CONDUIT metaphor attempts to account for several different patterns of metaphorical expressions, which are best explained in terms of a set of partly independent primary metaphors.

5. Conclusions

My corpus-based analysis of metaphorical references to speech activity in written British English has allowed me to assess the validity of current formulations of conceptual metaphors for communication, and to propose some adjustments to them. I have argued that the range of expressions which have traditionally been seen as realizations of ARGUMENT IS WAR are better accounted for by a more general conceptual metaphor, which I have expressed as ANTAGONISTIC COMMUNICATION IS PHYSICAL CONFLICT. I have also found evidence in favour of Grady's reformulation of Reddy's CONDUIT metaphor in terms of a set of primary metaphors, but I have suggested some additions to Grady's proposed primary metaphors in the light of my data.

In this chapter I have also provided some information about the frequency of different metaphorical patterns in my corpus, and cast some doubts on Reddy's (1979) claim about the pervasiveness of linguistic realizations of the CONDUIT metaphor in English. As shown in Table 1, the realizations of ANTAGONISTIC COMMUNICATION IS PHYSICAL CONFLICT account for just under 13 per cent of all metaphorical NRSAs in my concordance (and for approximately three per cent of all the NRSAs I analysed); the expressions which present speech activity in terms of the transfer of objects account for 21 per cent of metaphorical NRSAs (and for 4.5 per cent of the total); and the expressions which present speech activity in terms of enabling vision account for 13 per cent of metaphorical NRSAs (and for just under three per cent of the total). Cumulatively, therefore, the patterns I have discussed in this chapter represent approximately 47 per cent of the metaphorical NRSAs in my data.

The remainder of the data includes a number of further patterns that I cannot discuss in detail here (but see Semino 2005). These patterns are formed by the following types of expressions:
- expressions which present speech activity in terms of movement (e.g. 'John Major also *joined* the condolences in a message to Mr Howard.')
- expressions which present speech activity in terms of physical proximity (e.g. 'Afterwards Mr Milosevic [...] *backed* the proposals')
- expressions which present speech activity in terms of physical support (e.g. 'Mr Milosevic *supported* the plan then, but made little headway in persuading the Bosnian Serbs.')
- expressions which present speech activity in terms of physical pressure (e.g. 'The UN's military commanders, led by General Sir Michael Rose, have *pressed for* an end to Nato's aerial presence over Bosnia')
- expressions involving the verb 'make', which present speech activity in terms of the construction of physical object (e.g. 'Churchill made his first post-war appeal for European union in a speech in Zurich on 19 September 1946.')

Table 1 shows that, in combination with the groups of expressions I have focus on in this chapter, these patterns account for approximately 75 per cent of all metaphorical NRSAs in my data (i.e. 161 of the 214 NRSAs that I analysed as metaphorical out of the 985 occurrences included in the concordance from the corpus). The remainder of the data consists of expressions that do not appear to be part of larger metaphorical patterns relating to communication (e.g. 'crack jokes', 'have a go at').

Table 1. Number of occurrences of expressions belonging to different metaphorical patterns (and percentages of all metaphorical NRSAs).

Metaphors	Overall numbers (and percentage of met. NRSAs in concordance)
TRANSFER	45 (21.0%)
VISIBILITY	28 (13.0%)
'MAKE'	27 (12.6%)
PHYSICAL CONFLICT	27 (12.6%)
MOVEMENT	14 (6.5%)
PHYSICAL PROXIMITY	9 (4.2%)
PHYSICAL PRESSURE	7 (3.1%)
PHYSICAL SUPPORT	4 (1.8%)
OTHER	53 (24.8%)
Total	214 (100.0%)

Overall, therefore, the analysis of my data suggests that speech activity is metaphorically constructed in British English by means of a wide range of expressions, which relate to a wide range of different source domains. As is the case with many complex and abstract target domains, speech activity is also mostly constructed via source domains that, in Kövecses's (2000b) terms, have a wide 'scope', i.e. they contribute to structure a wide range of target domains. In Grady's 'primary metaphor' approach, this is reflected in the fact that the same primary metaphors can account for metaphorical expressions that apply to different target domains: for example, the primary metaphor ASSISTANCE IS SUPPORT accounts both for metaphorical expressions that refer to verbal activity (e.g. 'six months earlier he *supported* the very same regime in a letter to a fellow MP') and for metaphorical expressions that relate to a wide range of social and interpersonal relationships (e.g. 'Bill Clinton won the US Presidential race, *supported* by wife Hillary' and 'Louise came up for the funeral and stayed on for three weeks to give moral *support*', from the *BNC*). Each particular source domain has the function of constructing a particular aspect or dimension of the complex target domain of speech activity. For example, the source domain of PHYSICAL CONFLICT relates particularly to disagreement, criticism or forcefulness in communication, while the source domains of SEEING/VISIBILITY/EMERGENCE relate to how speech activity results in knowledge or understanding.

The analysis has also shown that in my data speech activity is overwhelmingly presented by means of expressions that have basic senses to do with actions and interactions in physical, concrete experience. Although different linguistic expressions can be related to different source domains, the patterns I have identified collectively suggest a conceptualisation of communication in terms of a single coherent scenario, namely a physical space containing entities corresponding to the interactants, their speech acts, their utterances/texts, their views/ideas, etc. Within this space:

- interactants can move in or out, towards or away from other participants, speech acts, conversational goals (e.g. 'join the condolences');
- interactants can be positioned in different ways in relation to each other (e.g. 'back');
- interactants can come into physical contact with each other in different ways, i.e. with or without pressure (e.g. 'press', 'support') or engaging in different types of physical conflict (e.g. 'rap', 'hit out', 'bombard with questions');
- texts/utterances, their contents, or their illocutionary force can become visually accessible to the addressee via different types of movement (e.g. 'came out', 'raise doubts'), via pointing (e.g. 'point to'), or via visual representation (e.g. 'outline');
- speech acts and texts/utterances are physical objects that can be constructed ('make a plea') and transferred from addressers to addressees (e.g. 'give an order', 'deliver a speech').

I am not suggesting that this scenario above 'exists' as a single conceptualization in the minds of any, let alone all, speakers of English. What I am suggesting is that the main patterns I have identified in my data seem to indicate that speech activity is conceptualised in English in terms of a range of physical actions and interactions which, at a general level, are compatible with each other and can be integrated into a single scenario.

The overall scenario I have proposed is significantly different from Grady's (1998), largely because of the nature and quantity of my data. While Grady's scenario (quoted in 4 above) accounts particularly for how meanings are linguistically communicated to others, my own analysis has been concerned with the metaphorical conceptualization of the performance of speech acts and speech activity more generally, and has included metaphorical references to goals and attitudes in communication.

I would argue that the adoption of a corpus methodology has enabled me to arrive at results that are more exhaustive and reliable than those obtained on the basis of introspection and/or the random collection of examples. First, my data was obtained from a balanced and representative quarter-of-a-million word corpus of (late) 20th century written British narrative texts (see Semino and Short 2004: 24–26 for a discussion of the different degrees of representativeness of different sections of the corpus). Second, the fact that the corpus was annotated for forms of SW&TP provided me with a fairly large number of relevant examples (985 references to speech acts/activity, of which 214 were analysed as metaphorical). Third, I systematically used a larger corpus (the 100-million word *British National Corpus*) in order to provide examples of other (not speech-related) uses of the expressions under analysis (see Cameron and Deignan 2003 and Semino 2002 for a similar combination of smaller and larger corpora in metaphor research). All this has enabled me to notice a larger and richer variety of metaphorical linguistic patterns for speech activity than had been observed before.

Insofar as the examination of conventional linguistic patterns is (one of) the main source(s) of evidence in cognitive linguistics, corpus-based analysis places the extrapolation of conceptual metaphors from linguistic data on a much firmer empirical footing than has been the case in the past (see, for example, Low 2003 for a critique of recent applications of cognitive metaphor theory in applied linguistics). On the other hand, however, much caution is still necessary in moving from the analysis of linguistic patterns to claims about the conceptual structure of language speakers. A study such as the present one can only claim to arrive at more reliable generalizations on linguistic patterns in authentic discourse, which in turn lead to better, more plausible hypotheses about the potential cross-domain conceptual mappings that might explain those linguistic patterns. Indeed, the conceptual metaphors that I have discussed in this chapter are best seen, in my view, as hypotheses about conventional cross-domain mappings in the minds of (some) speakers of English. Further analysis of relevant linguistic data may lead to adjustments to these hypotheses, which then need to be tested via empirical psychological research in order to verify their validity as claims about the conceptual structure of (different groups of) English speakers.

References

Austin, John L.
   1962   *How to Do Things with Words*. Oxford: Oxford University Press.
Ballmer, Thomas and Waltraud Brennenstuhl
   1981   *Speech Act Classification: A Study in the Lexical Analysis of English Speech Activity Verbs*. Berlin: Springer.
Boers, Frank
   1999   When a bodily source domain becomes prominent: the joy of counting metaphors in the socio-economic domain. In: Raymond W. Gibbs and Gerard J.

Steen (eds.), *Metaphor in Cognitive Linguistics*, 47–56. Amsterdam: John Benjamins.

Cameron, Lynne
- 1999 Operationalising 'metaphor' for applied linguistic research. In: Lynne Cameron and Graham Low (eds), *Researching and Applying Metaphor*, 3–28. Cambridge: Cambridge University Press.
- 2003 *Metaphor in Educational Discourse*. London: Continuum.

Cameron, Lynne and Alice Deignan
- 2003 Combining large and small corpora to investigate tuning devices around metaphor in spoken discourse. *Metaphor and Symbol* 18: 149–160.

Deignan, Alice
- 1999 Corpus-based research into metaphor. In: Lynne Cameron and Graham Low (eds), *Researching and Applying Metaphor*, 177–199. Cambridge: Cambridge University Press.
- 2000 Persuasive uses of metaphor in discourse about business and the economy. In Chris Heffer and Helen Sauntson (eds.), *Words in Context: A Tribute to John Sinclair on his Retirement*, 156–168. Birmingham: ELR.

Glucksberg, Sam
- 2001 *Understanding Figurative Language*. New York: Oxford University Press.

Grady, Joseph
- 1997a *Foundations of meaning: primary metaphors and primary scenes*. Ph.D. dissertation. University of California, Berkeley.
- 1997b THEORIES ARE BUILDINGS revisited. *Cognitive Linguistics* 8: 267–290.
- 1998 The 'Conduit' metaphor revisited: A reassessment of metaphors for communication. In: Jean-Pierre Koenig (ed.), *Discourse and Cognition: Bridging the Gap*, 205–218. Stanford, CA.: CSLI Publications.
- 1999 A typology of motivation for conceptual metaphor: correlation vs. resemblance". In: Raymond W. Gibbs and Gerard J. Steen (eds), *Metaphor in Cognitive Linguistics*, 79–100. Amsterdam: John Benjamins.

Heywood, John, Elena Semino and Mick Short
- 2002 Linguistic metaphor identificati on in two extracts from novels". *Language and Literature* 11: 35–54.

Kövecses, Zoltan
- 2000 The scope of metaphor. In: Antonio Barcelona (ed.), *Metaphor and Metonymy at the Crossroads: A Cognitive Perspective*, 79–92. Berlin: Mouton de Gruyter.
- 2002 *Metaphor: A Practical Introduction*. Oxford and New York: Oxford University Press.

Lakoff, George
- 1993 The contemporary theory of metaphor. In: Andrew Ortony (ed.), *Metaphor and Thought*. Second edition, 202–251. Cambridge: Cambridge University Press.

Lakoff, George and Mark Johnson
- 1980 *Metaphors We Live By*. Chicago: The University of Chicago Press.

Lakoff George and Mark Johnson
- 1999 *Philosophy in the Flesh: The Embodied Mind and its Challenge to Western Thought*. New York: Basic Books.

Leech, Geoffrey N. and Michael H. Short
  1981   *Style in Fiction*. London: Longman.
Low, Graham
  1999   Validating metaphor research projects. In: Lynne Cameron and Graham Low (eds), *Researching and Applying Metaphor*, 48–65. Cambridge: Cambridge University Press.
  2003   Validating metaphoric models in applied linguistics. *Metaphor and Symbol* 18: 239–254
Ortony, Andrew (Ed.)
  1979   *Metaphor and Thought*. First edition. Cambridge: Cambridge University Press.
  1993   *Metaphor and Thought*. Second edition. Cambridge: Cambridge University Press.
Peters, Wim and Yorick Wilks
  2003   Data-driven detection of figurative language use in electronic language resources. *Metaphor and Symbol* 18: 161–173.
Reddy, Michael J.
  1979   The conduit metaphor: a case of frame conflict in our language about language". In Andrew Ortony (ed.), *Metaphor and Thought*. Second edition, 164–201. Cambridge: Cambridge University Press.
Ritchie, David
  2003   ARGUMENT IS WAR – Or is it a game of chess? Multiple meanings in the analysis of implicit metaphors. *Metaphor and Symbol* 18: 125–146.
Searle, John R.
  1979   *Expression and Meaning*. Cambridge: Cambridge University Press.
Semino, Elena
  2002   A sturdy baby or a derailing train? Metaphorical representations of the euro in British and Italian newspapers. *Text* 22: 107–139.
  2005   The metaphorical construction of complex domains: the case of speech activity in English. *Metaphor and Symbol* 20: 35–70.
Semino, Elena, John Heywood and Mick Short
  2004   Methodological problems in the analysis of metaphors in a corpus of conversations about cancer. *Journal of Pragmatics* 36: 1271–1294.
Semino, Elena, Mick Short and Martin Wynne
  1999   Hypothetical words and thoughts in contemporary British narratives. *Narrative* 7: 307–334.
Semino, Elena and Mick Short
  2004   *Corpus Stylistics: Speech, Writing and Thought Presentation in a Corpus of English Writing*. London: Routledge.
Sperber, Dan and Deidre Wilson
  1986   *Relevance: Communication and Cognition*, Oxford: Blackwell.
  1995   *Relevance: Communication and Cognition*. Second edition. Oxford: Blackwell.
Steen, Gerard J.
  1999   From linguistic to conceptual metaphor in five steps. In: Raymond W. Gibbs and Gerard J. Steen (eds), *Metaphor in Cognitive Linguistics*, 57–77. Amsterdam: John Benjamins.

Taylor, John R.
   2002   *Cognitive Grammar.* Oxford: Oxford University Press.
Wynne, Martin, Mick Short, and Elena Semino
   1998   A corpus-based investigation of speech, thought and writing presentation in English narrative texts. In Anette Renouf (ed.), *Explorations in Corpus Linguistics,* 231–245. Amsterdam: Rodopi.

Words and their metaphors: A corpus-based approach

Anatol Stefanowitsch

Abstract

In this paper, I propose and demonstrate a corpus-based approach to the investigation of metaphorical target domains based on retrieving representative lexical items from the target domain and identifying the metaphorical expressions associated with them. I show that this approach is superior in terms of data coverage compared to the traditional method of eclectically collecting citations or gathering data from introspection. In addition to its superior coverage, a corpus-based approach allows us to quantify the frequency of individual metaphors, and I show how central metaphors can be identified on the basis of such quantitative data. Finally, I argue that a focus on metaphors associated with individual lexical items opens up the possibility of investigating the interaction between metaphor and lexical semantics.

1. Introduction

Over the past twenty-five years, the study of metaphor has been at the core of the research program now known as *cognitive linguistics*, a development that began with the publication of Lakoff and Johnson's 1980 monograph *Metaphors We Live By*. Like other theories before it, Lakoff and Johnson's 'conceptual theory of metaphor' draws a distinction between *metaphorical concepts* (or *conceptual metaphors*) and *metaphorical expressions*. Conceptual metaphors are general mental mappings from a (typically concrete) source domain to a (typically abstract) target domain, while metaphorical expressions are individual linguistic items instantiating these mappings.[1] For example, the metaphorical expressions in (1) are analyzed as instantiating the general metaphorical concept ANGER IS FIRE:

(1) a. Those are *inflammatory* remarks.
    b. He was *breathing fire*.
    c. He was *consumed* by his anger. (Lakoff 1987: 388)

---

1. Cf. Black's (1962, 1992[1979]) distinction between *metaphor(ical) statements* and *metaphor themes*, where the latter are understood as 'projections' of 'secondary subjects' onto 'primary subjects'; cf. also Weinrich's (1976: 299ff.) notions of *image donor* (*Bildspender*) and *image recipient* (*Bildempfänger*)).

Crucially, the conceptual theory of metaphor differs from many previous approaches in that it is primarily a theory of metaphorical cognition rather than metaphorical language. Metaphorical mappings such as ANGER IS FIRE are seen as instances of a psychological process of "understanding and experiencing one kind of thing in terms of another" (Lakoff and Johnson 1980: 5), and thus as a fundamentally non-linguistic phenomenon: "What constitutes [a] metaphor is not any particular word or expression. It is the ontological mapping across conceptual domains" (Lakoff 1993: 208).

Consequently, cognitive metaphor research has focused on uncovering general mappings rather than exhaustively describing the specific linguistic expressions instantiating these mappings. Studies are mostly based on introspection or eclectic collections of individual citations. This may not be a major problem if our aim is merely to establish the *existence* of a particular mapping, but it causes at least two problems if our aim is the systematic characterization of a specific mapping, source or target domain: first, it is impossible to decide at what point we have exhaustively charted the relevant metaphors; second, it is impossible to quantify the results in order to determine the importance of a given metaphor in a given language. In other words, it is difficult to establish a firm empirical basis for studying conceptual metaphor from a linguistic perspective.

At first glance, corpus linguistics does not seem to be an ideal candidate to remedy these methodological shortcomings. The principal way in which corpora are accessed is via word forms (more precisely, orthographic strings), and since metaphorical mappings are not generally associated with particular word forms (or particular linguistic items in general), they cannot easily be retrieved automatically. Take the expressions in (1) above: there is no search string that would retrieve all of them.

However, several strategies have been proposed to deal with this problem (see Stefanowitsch, this volume, for an overview). This paper presents one such strategy in detail and compares it systematically to the traditional way of collecting data introspectively or by amassing individual citations eclectically. The basic idea behind this method is fairly straightforward: we choose a lexical item referring to the target domain under investigation and extract (a sample of) its occurrences in the corpus. In this sample, we then identify all metaphorical expressions that the search word is a part of and group them into coherent groups representing general mappings. This general approach has been used by some researchers in previous work but it has, to my knowledge, never been investigated whether the metaphorical mappings identified in this way actually represent the complete inventory of metaphorical mappings occurring in the target domain in question. My first aim in this paper is therefore to demonstrate that this method is equal or superior to the introspective method with regard to the identification of metaphors (Section 3). I use metaphorical expressions associated with the target domain of basic emotions as a test case, specifically, the words *anger*, *fear*, *joy*, *sadness*, and *disgust*. My second aim is to point out several avenues of research opened up by the possibility of quantifying the frequency of occurrence of metaphorical mappings. I show how the frequency of occurrence of a given metaphorical mapping with a given lexical item can be used to identify mappings that are significantly associated with particular target words/concepts (Section 4), and I investigate differences in the metaphorical behavior of antonyms and near-synonyms, showing that the reliance on representative lexical items is a methodological advantage that allows us to uncover subtle differences between lexical items from the same target domain (Section 5).

2. Metaphorical pattern analysis

The method presented here is not as simple as the short characterization above suggests: as mentioned, conceptual metaphors are not tied to specific lexical items, and in particular, they do not all contain lexical items from the target domain. In fact, we can distinguish two broad types of metaphorical expressions on formal grounds: those that contain target-domain items and those that do not. Consider the following textbook examples; while those in (2a–c) all contain lexical items from both the source domain (*indefensible*, *target*, *shoot down*) and the target domain (*claim*, *criticism*, *argument*), the examples in (3a–c) contain source-domain items only:

(2) ARGUMENT IS WAR (Lakoff and Johnson 1980: 4)
   SD WAR
   TD ARGUMENT (i.e. DISCUSSION)
   a. Your *claims* are indefensible.
   b. His *criticisms* were right on target.
   c. He shot down all of my *arguments*.

(3) LOVE IS WAR (Lakoff and Johnson 1980: 49)
    SD WAR
    TD LOVE
    a. He is known for his many rapid conquests.
    b. He fled from her advances.
    c. He is slowly gaining ground with her.

The fact that some metaphorical expressions contain both source and target domain lexemes has sometimes been used as a means of identifying metaphors, but as far as I can tell, little or no attention has been drawn to the fact that such expressions constitute a specific subclass of metaphorical expressions, a subclass that I will refer to as a *metaphorical pattern* and that I will define as follows:

> A metaphorical pattern is a multi-word expression from a given source domain (SD) into which one or more specific lexical item from a given target domain (TD) have been inserted.

Expressions like those in (2a–c) above, then, are metaphorical patterns, while those in (3a–c) are not. Crucially, metaphorical patterns provide a basis for target-domain oriented studies on the basis of corpus data: we can retrieve a large number of instances of a target domain item (such as *claim*, *criticism*, *argument*, etc.) from a corpus and exhaustively identify the metaphorical patterns that it occurs with. Obviously, this kind of procedure, which I will refer to as *metaphorical pattern analysis* (MPA) will capture only a subset of metaphorical expressions – those manifesting themselves as metaphorical patterns for specific lexical items – but I will show that this potential drawback is outweighed by the advantages that this method offers.

First, and perhaps most importantly, MPA allows us to quantify the importance of any given metaphorical pattern for particular (sets of) lexical items. If we choose the lexical items wisely, this should also enable us to make generalizations concerning the importance of the conceptual metaphors underlying these patterns.[2] The fact that statements derived from MPA pertain to particular target domain lexemes rather than to the target domain in general may be regarded as a drawback in terms of generality by some, but note that it also provides an advantage. For metaphorical expressions that do *not* constitute metaphorical patterns, it is often difficult to determine which precise target-domain we are in fact dealing with – for

---

2. Its commitment to quantification and exhaustive data extraction place MPA in the methodological framework of *quantitative corpus linguistics* (as discussed, for example, in Stefanowitsch and Gries 2005).

example, do the metaphorical expressions in (3) really involve the target domain LOVE, or do they involve target domains such as DESIRE, LUST, ADORATION, etc.? Presumably, this depends to some degree on the context in which they are used, but some uncertainty always remains. Metaphorical patterns do not present us with such uncertainty, as the target domain is spelled out explicitly by the target domain lexis.

Second, related to the point just made, metaphorical patterns do not merely instantiate general mappings between two semantic domains. In addition, they establish specific paradigmatic relations between target domain lexical items and the source domain items that would be expected in their place in a non-metaphorical use. For example, the metaphorical pattern in (2c) above establishes such a relation between the word *argument* and the word(s) that would occur in the same pattern (*shoot down NP*) if used in a source-domain contexts (words like *(fighter) plane* or *missile*):

(4) He shot down all of my *arguments.*
    TD DISCUSSION: *argument*
    SD WAR: He shot down my planes/missiles/...
    General mapping: DISCUSSION IS WAR
    Specific relation: *argument* ≈ *plane/missile*

Thus, we get not only the general mapping DISCUSSION IS WAR from this pattern, but also the more specific ARGUMENTS ARE MISSILES. Metaphorical expressions that do not constitute metaphorical patterns do not establish such specific relations. As an example, take following expression:

(5) He is known for his many rapid *conquests.* (= 3a)
    TD LOVE: Ø (does not provide lexical items)
    SD WAR: He is known for his many conquests
    General mapping: LOVE IS WAR
    Specific relation: Ø

Here, the word *conquest* is the only word that evokes the source domain WAR, while the target domain LOVE is not evoked by any lexical item at all. Thus, no specific relation is established between the source domain item *conquest* and potential target domain expressions such as *lover*. This does not mean that there is no connection between these two expressions, but this connection is not explicit in the expression in (5). In contrast, explicit relations between source and target domain items established by paradigmatic relations in metaphorical patterns allow us to investigate the correspondences between source and target domain at a level of detail not usually found in studies of metaphor.

Third, metaphorical patterns may have different degrees of conventionality – there are cases, where a target domain item is much more likely to occur than source domain items, and in very conventionalized cases, it may be almost impossible to insert a source domain item into the pattern. An example of the first kind is the expression *wealth of NP* – source domain items like *money* or *possessions* may occur in it, as shown in (6), but they do so much less frequently than target domain items like *information, experience, ideas, knowledge*, etc.:

(6) He has a wealth of *ideas*.
    TD IDEAS: *ideas*
    SD MONEY: Now that the weather's cold, she says she's lost those customers along with a wealth of money. (Source 1)

An example of the second kind is *elucidate NP*, which occurs with source domain items extremely rarely (if at all), and which sounds unacceptable to most speakers when it does:[3]

(7) Could you elucidate your *remarks*.
    TD IDEAS: *remark*
    SD LIGHT: ?? Sunlight elucidated the room.

The relative frequency of source and target domain items in a given metaphorical pattern may be used to determine the degree to which the pattern in question is transparently motivated by a metaphorical mapping, and the relative frequency of source and target domain items in a coherent *set of* metaphorical patterns may be used to assess the degree to which the metaphorical mapping underlying them can be regarded as productive, i.e. as a candidate for a truly *conceptual* metaphor. For the purposes of this paper, I will accept as metaphorical patterns all metaphorical expressions that can in principle occur with source domain items in the relevant slots.

---

3. An extensive web search yields examples like *Meg [...] flipped the light switch, the lights began to elucidate the room slowly* (Source 2), but it is unclear whether these are cases of natural language use or rather failed attempts at literary style. The OED suggests that *elucidate* originally had literal uses, but does not any longer; its meaning is given as "to render lucid; now only *fig.*" (*OED*, s.v. elucidate). However, the first citation (from 1568) is already metaphorical, and no literal citations are given at all.

Fourth, there may be more than two domains (and thus, more than one metaphor) involved in a metaphorical pattern:

(8) His eyes were filled with *anger*.
TD1 EMOTIONS: *anger*
TD2 ORGANS: *eyes*
SD CONTAINERS/LIQUIDS: The container was filled with liquid.
General mappings: EMOTIONS ARE LIQUIDS
ORGANS ARE CONTAINERS
Specific relations: *anger* ≈ *liquid*, *eye* ≈ *container*

Presumably, metaphorical mappings are not freely combinable, and the investigation of metaphorical patterns that simultaneously instantiate two mappings could uncover the principles determining their combinability.

Finally, metaphorical pattern analysis provides us with a standard of comparison for cross-linguistic research, which is otherwise difficult to establish: since MPA focuses on individual lexical items (or sets of such items) from a given target domain, cross-linguistic studies can use translation equivalents of these items as their *tertium comparationis* (cf. the study of the English words *happiness* and *joy* and their German translation equivalents *Glück* and *Freude* presented in Stefanowitsch 2004).

Of course, not all issues raised here can be discussed in the present paper. I will therefore focus on three issues that seem most fundamental in justifying MPA as a viable method for the investigation of metaphor: first, how good is the match between the metaphorical mappings identified for a given domain via MPA as compared to those identified via the introspective method; second, what is gained from quantifying the results of MPA; and third, to what degree is the lexeme-specificity of the mappings identified via MPA a disadvantage or an advantage?

The first issue primarily concerns the descriptive adequacy of the method, and my main aim will be to show that MPA can indeed identify mappings more systematically and more exhaustively than non-corpus-based approaches. The second issue is mainly a methodological one, but its repercussions for a theory of metaphor should not be underestimated. If metaphorical expressions can in fact be seen as manifestations of general cognitive models or principles of conceptualization, then a statistical assessment of the importance of a given mapping yields crucial information about the relative importance of the corresponding cognitive model (for example, its entrenchment in the sense of Langacker 1987). The third issue, like the first one, is partly concerned with descriptive adequacy, as the lexeme-specificity of MPA can be regarded as a disadvantage only if it leads to an impoverished data set; if the data set is not impoverished by the focus on individual lexical items, then MPA is, in the worst case, descriptively equivalent to the introspective method. In addition, though, there is a theoretically interesting aspect to this issue: if metaphorical mappings interact with individual lexical items such that there are differences, for example, between near synonyms or antonyms, then the existence and nature of these differences must be accounted for.

3. Metaphorical pattern analysis and the introspective method compared

In order to compare the results of a study based on metaphorical pattern analysis with those yielded by the traditional introspective method, we need to choose a target domain that (i) has vocabulary associated with it that is uncontroversially representative of the domain in question, and that (ii) has been investigated sufficiently intensively using the introspective method. The domain that I have chosen for the following case studies is that of (BASIC) EMOTIONS, which meets both criteria: there are target domain items like *anger, happiness*, etc. that are undeniably representative of their respective (sub)domains, and there are a vast number of studies exclusively dedicated to investigating metaphors of emotion (cf. e.g. the contributions in Niemeier and Dirven 1997 and Athanasiadou and Tabaskowska 1998).

I chose a paper by Zoltán Kövecses entitled *Are there any emotion-specific metaphors* (Kövecses 1998) as representative of the kinds of results that are routinely achieved by the introspective method of data collection. In the first part of his paper, Kövecses summarizes the descriptive results of his own research and that of his colleagues on emotion metaphors. He explicitly suggests that this summary paints a complete picture of the metaphors found with each of the emotion concepts he looks at (Kövecses 1998: 128), and since he is one of the most prolific researchers on emotion metaphors (cf. e.g. Kövecses 1986, 1989, 2002), there is good reason to assume that his work is representative of the method in general. Choosing this paper has an additional advantage: the theoretical question Kövecses deals with in the second part of it – the question whether there are metaphorical mappings that are specific to individual emotion concepts – is a perfect context for assessing the usefulness of quantification.

Köveces deals with nine emotion concepts that are frequently found in the psychological literature on 'basic emotions': ANGER, FEAR, HAPPI-

NESS, SADNESS, LOVE, LUST/SEXUAL DESIRE, PRIDE, SHAME, and SURPRISE. For this paper, I chose the five emotions that are mentioned most frequently in the psychological literature, and that can thus be seen as generally agreed upon to be basic, universal emotions (cf. Ortony and T. Turner 1990 for an overview): ANGER, DISGUST, FEAR, HAPPINESS, and SADNESS (four out of these five overlap with Kövecses' set). Obviously, each of these emotions has a set of semantically similar lexical items associated with it (e.g. *anger, fury, rage, wrath*, etc. for ANGER). Since metaphorical pattern analysis is by definition lexeme-specific, a representative lexical item had to be chosen for each emotion. I took raw frequency as an indicator of representativity, and chose the most frequent emotion term for each of the five emotions. These were the words also used above as labels for the concepts: *anger, disgust, fear, joy,* and *sadness*. For HAPPINESS, I chose the word *happiness* in addition, in order to be able to compare near synonyms referring to the 'same' emotion. I then retrieved a random sample of 1000 hits for each lexical item from the *British National Corpus* (*disgust* and *sadness* occurred less than 1000 times; in these cases, I retrieved all occurrences).

3.1. ANGER

The metaphorical target domain ANGER has been investigated in detail in the cognitive linguistics literature (cf. the detailed accounts in Kövecses 1986 and Lakoff 1987: 380ff., cf. also Gibbs 1994 and Ungerer and Schmid 1996: 131ff.). Kövecses (1998) summarizes this research by positing the following twelve metaphorical mappings for the concept ANGER:

(9) ANGER/BEING ANGRY IS
    a. HOT FLUID IN A CONTAINER *She is boiling with anger*
    b. FIRE *Oh boy, was I burned up!*
    c. INSANITY *The man was insane with rage*
    d. AN OPPONENT IN A STRUGGLE *I was struggling with my anger*
    e. A CAPTIVE ANIMAL *He unleashed his anger*
    f. A BURDEN *He carries his anger around with him*
    g. AGGRESSIVE ANIMAL BEHAVIOR *Don't snarl at me!*
    h. TRESPASSING (cause of anger) *Here I draw the line*
    i. PHYSICAL ANNOYANCE *He's a pain in the neck*
    j. A NATURAL FORCE *It was a stormy meeting*
    k. BEING A FUNCTIONING MACHINE *That really got him going*

1. A SUPERIOR   *His actions were completely governed by anger*
(Kövecses 1998: 129)

There are several general issues here that must be dealt with before we can turn to a detailed comparison of these results with those yielded by metaphorical pattern analysis.

First of all, note that some of Kövecses' examples include target domain expressions (and are thus metaphorical patterns in the sense discussed above), namely (9a, c, d, e, f, l), while others do not, namely (9b, g, h, i, j, k). The latter demonstrate quite clearly the difficulty of determining which precise target-domain we are in fact dealing with. While the connection of example (9b) to the domain ANGER is relatively uncontroversial, things are less straightforward in the other cases. The claim that they refer to ANGER is not immediately obvious – example (9h) seems better analyzed as referring to (UN)ACCEPTABLE BEHAVIOR, (9g) to AGGRESSIVENESS, (9i) to a feeling of INCONVENIENCE, and example (9j, k) to ANIMATED BEHAVIOR. While unacceptable behavior, aggressiveness, inconvenience, and animated behavior *may* of course be related to feelings of anger, they do not *have* to be. This does not mean, of course, that the metaphors posited to account for these examples do not exist – the choice of examples may simply be unfortunate. It also does not mean that such examples cannot in principle be analyzed in a satisfactory way – the fact that it is possible to contest the claim that they refer to ANGER shows that it is possible to argue about their meaning and presumably to come to some agreement. However, the problems in interpreting these examples are not trivial, and they should be addressed in a principled way.

Second, note that in those examples that do include target-domain expressions, the expressions *anger* and *rage* are both treated as referring to ANGER, i.e., they are not lexeme-specific in the sense of metaphorical pattern analysis. Of course, this is not a problem for the introspective approach unless it can be shown that such near synonyms do not participate in the same metaphorical mappings. Since this issue will be the topic of Section 5, I will ignore it for now and simply accept that all of Kövecses' examples refer to ANGER.

Third, it is often unclear how a particular example should be analyzed, i.e. at what level of generality a conceptual metaphor should be posited (this is true for any kind of metaphor analysis, not just the introspective method). For example, it is unclear why example (9i), *He's a pain in the neck*, is categorized as an example for ANGER IS A PHYSICAL ANNOYANCE rather than simply ANGER IS PAIN. Such decisions often result from an attempt to categorize examples that are felt to be similar under a single mapping. In this case, Lakoff (1987: 395), who originally posited this mapping, gives additional examples like *Get off my back* and *You're getting under my skin*. In the context of these examples, the analysis of (9i) makes more sense. Still, in my analysis I will try to be somewhat stricter in judging which examples should be grouped together, except where I follow Kövecses' categories for expository reasons.

Let us now turn to the question whether metaphorical pattern analysis is potentially able to identify metaphorical mappings exhaustively. In a first step, this requires us to show that metaphorical pattern analysis can identify all the metaphors that Kövecses has identified using the introspective method. There were 1443 metaphorical patterns in the sample investigated. Table 1a shows all of these that manifest one of the mappings in (9) above together with their frequency of occurrence in the sample (i.e., their frequency per thousand examples of the word *anger*). The patterns are presented in a form that is somewhat abstracted from the actual citations: verbs are shown in the infinitive, slots for participants are shown as X or Y, and similar patterns are collapsed into compact form using slashes for alternatives and parentheses for optional elements.

Note that only two of the mappings did not manifest themselves as metaphorical patterns: BEING ANGRY IS BEING A FUNCTIONING MACHINE and CAUSING ANGER IS TRESPASSING. This would be a problem for MPA if these were central cases of ANGER metaphors. However, this is not the case: these are two of the mappings that seem questionable anyway. In other words, MPA compares very well to the introspective method when it comes to identifying metaphorical mappings. Conversely, however, all examples in Table 1a taken together account for a mere 14.3 percent of all metaphorical patterns identified via MPA, which suggests that the introspective method misses the majority of metaphorical expressions for the domain of ANGER. This seemingly poor performance is to a large part due to the fact that Kövecses excludes from consideration very general metaphors, that "apply to all emotion concepts" (Kövecses 1998: 133); he seems to have in mind primarily those metaphors that Lakoff (1993) refers to as EVENT STRUCTURE metaphors, i.e. general metaphorical systems for verbalizing "notions like states, changes, processes, actions, causes, purposes, and means" (Lakoff 1993: 220). There are two major metaphorical event structure systems: the location system, where change is conceptualized as "the motion of the thing-changing to a new location from an old one" (Lakoff 1993: 225), and the object system, where change is con-

Table 1a. Metaphorical patterns manifesting ANGER metaphors posited in the literature

ANGER/BEING ANGRY IS	N
HOT FLUID IN A CONTAINER *boiling/simmering anger, anger boil (up)/simmer (inside X/beneath surface), anger seethe through X, anger boil over (into action), anger reach boiling point, X boil/seethe with anger, X keep lid on anger, X vent anger (against Y), X give vent to anger, seething of anger*	26
FIRE *burning/flaring/searing anger, X burn/smoulder/spark with anger, X fan/fuel/spark/stoke (Y's) anger, resentment burn into anger, anger blaze into hatred, anger burn inside X, anger spark/flare (in X's eyes), anger scorch X, anger rekindle X's eye, flare/flame(s) of anger, presence of anger in fire, X's eyes blaze/be ablaze with anger*	35
INSANITY *frenzy of anger*	2
AN OPPONENT IN A STRUGGLE *X fight against/down/off anger, X wrestle with anger, X overcome/placate/suppress/withstand anger, X protect Y from anger, X confront/deal with/encounter anger, X shrink away from anger, X control anger, X keep anger under control, X be overcome with anger, X be victim of anger, X fear anger, X lose Y to anger, anger overcome/have hold of X, anger be destructive/powerful, (un)controlled/repressed/suppressed anger, emotion overcome anger, emotion protect X from anger, struggle between anger and emotion, anger war with emotion, anger overcome emotion, conspiracy of emotion and anger, anger injure X*	47
A CAPTIVE ANIMAL *anger be loosed, X unleash/let loose/release anger, X lock away/domesticate anger*	22
A BURDEN *X carry anger, weight of anger*	2
AGGRESSIVE ANIMAL BEHAVIOR *X's hackles rise in anger, savage/fierce anger*	4
TRESPASSING —	0
PHYSICAL ANNOYANCE (I.E. PAIN) *fit of anger, X be seized with anger, X's face contort with anger, X's face be(come) contorted/distorted with anger, X throb away with anger, X mitigate anger, X wince in face of anger*	14
A NATURAL FORCE *climate of anger, flood/surge/wave of anger, anger surge, anger roil in(side) of X, anger sweep X beyond EMOTION, anger wash over/through X, anger subside/ebb away, X let anger unroll like wave, X staunch anger, haven from anger*	17
BEING A FUNCTIONING MACHINE —	0
A SUPERIOR *anger rule the day*	1
Total	170

ceptualized as "the motion of an object to, or away from, the thing changing" (ibid.); a specific subcase of the latter is what we might call the possession system, where "the object in motion is conceptualized as a possession and the thing-changing as a possessor". Evidence for both major systems can be found in the sample investigated here. There are 121 examples where ANGER is conceptualized as a location, and experiencers as existing in, moving or being moved into or out of this location (*X act in anger, X run away from anger, X goad Y into anger*, etc.), i.e., the location system accounts for 10.2 percent of the metaphorical expressions in the sample. The object system and the possession system are instantiated 666 times in the sample, and thus constitute the majority of metaphorical expressions (56.15%). In this system, being angry can be conceptualized as possessing an object (e.g. *X's anger, X have anger*), and causing anger can be conceptualized as transferring an object (e.g. *X bring/pass on/share anger*); more generally, anger can be conceptualized as a moving object (*anger return, anger follow its course, anger sweep through X, anger be gone from X*), as a moved object (*X direct/target anger at Y, X divert anger into action*), and as an object in some location (*anger in(side) X, there be anger about X, X do sth. with anger*, etc.). Within the ANGER-AS-OBJECT system, the intensity of the anger can be conceptualized as physical size or quantity (*enormous/great/mounting anger, much/more anger*, etc.).

The two event-structure systems thus account for 787 cases, i.e. for 66.36 percent of all metaphorical expressions with *anger*. This shows that these metaphors play a central role in the conceptualization of emotions, and that excluding them from consideration is therefore a risky strategy (note that Lakoff does discuss some of these metaphors, e.g. Lakoff 1987: 397, 406). I will show in Section 5 that different emotion terms can differ significantly with respect to their participation in such general metaphors and that the analysis of such differences can yield important insights into the interaction between lexical semantics and metaphorical mappings.

Even ignoring these very general metaphors, however, the introspective method misses a fifth of the metaphorical expressions from the domain ANGER (20.03%). Table 1b shows all additional metaphorical mappings instantiated at least four times.

To be fair, the first three mappings in Table 1b, are discussed in Lakoff (1987: 387ff.). Clearly the two relatively general metaphors ANGER IS A SUBSTANCE/LIQUID (IN A CONTAINER) and ANGER IS HEAT also account for the mappings ANGER IS A HOT LIQUID IN A CONTAINER (which is a combination of the two, ANGER IS FIRE (which is a specific case of ANGER IS HEAT), and most examples of ANGER IS A NATURAL FORCE (which are specific cases

Table 1b. More ANGER metaphors identified via metaphorical pattern analysis

ANGER/BEING ANGRY IS	N
A SUBSTANCE IN A CONTAINER (UNDER PRESSURE) *X fill with anger, X be full of/filled with anger, X keep lid on/contain anger, held-in/pent-up anger, X be unable to contain anger, buildup of anger, anger build (up) (inside X), pent-up/explosive/volcanic anger, outlet for anger, burst/explosion/outburst of anger, anger have volcanic eruptions, anger blow up/burst out/erupt/explode (into action), X erupt/burst (out) with anger*	49
A LIQUID *anger well up, anger seep into X('s voice),, anger bubble inside X, anger well/spill over, anger pour from eyes, anger pour out of X, X channel anger (against Y), anger evaporate, anger drain from X('s face), source of anger, spurt of anger*	16
HEAT/COLD *anger have lava flow, X flush/be flushed with anger, anger flush cheek, hot anger, anger be/grow hot, anger be heated reaction, anger grow/turn cold, anger melt away*	17
A MIXED OR PURE SUBSTANCE *mixture/mingling/combination of anger and EMOTION, X combine anger with EMOTION, anger be pure, EMOTION be mixed/mingled with anger, trace of anger, combined anger, X diffuse anger*	17
LIGHT *flash/flicker/white glow of anger, blinding/scarlet anger, anger flicker across face, anger flash/glow in X's eyes, anger light X's eyes, X's eyes be alight/bright/brilliant with anger, X's eyes flash/glint/glitter with-anger*	29
DARKNESS *black gloom of anger, dark/dull anger, anger eclipse EMOTION, eyes be dark with anger, eyes flash dark with anger, face darken with anger, face be black/dark with anger, features be darkly contorted with anger*	10
HIGH/LOW (INTENSITY) *level of anger, anger rise (in X), anger drop, anger arise/come arising from X, rising/high anger, level/height of anger, X get up Y's anger*	21
A SLEEPING ORGANISM *X rouse anger, X arouse anger (in Y)*	10
A DISEASE *bouts of anger, festering/impotent/paralysing anger, anger reemerge as cancer, X purge (X-self of) anger, X be apoplectic/sick with anger, X suffer anger*	11
GORGE *anger rise into X's mouth, bitter anger, bitter with anger, X bite back/swallow anger, X strangle on anger*	7
A SHARP OBJECT *sharp anger, pinpoint of anger, spike of anger, hook of anger, blunted anger, anger clip X's words*	5
A PLANT *anger be rooted in X, anger stem from EMOTION, anger grow*	4
Total	196

of ANGER IS A LIQUID). Taken together, these mappings account for 158 expressions in the sample, and thus form the largest single group after the object metaphor (13.3%).

The next mapping in Table 1b, ANGER IS A MIXED/PURE SUBSTANCE, could have partly been subsumed under the ANGER IS A LIQUID mapping, since some of the source-domain items used, e.g. *mixture* or *trace*, often refer to liquids. However, this strategy would have backgrounded the similarity between *mixture* and *combination*; note that MPA is essentially a bottom-up procedure, and decisions about which expressions should be grouped together must be guided by the richness of the corpus data.

The next mapping, ANGER IS LIGHT, is not mentioned in the literature (although it could conceivably be related to ANGER IS FIRE, since fire gives off light); interestingly, the opposite mapping, ANGER IS DARKNESS, is also found. Unlike in the case of HEAT, the two opposites here do not encode the opposite ends of a scale: there are no examples where *dark anger* refers to a less intensive (or less intensively experienced) anger (although *dull anger* is conceivably interpreted in this way). Instead, ANGER IS DARKNESS seems to highlight a different dimension of anger than ANGER IS LIGHT. While the latter is similar to the experiential aspects also picked out by ANGER IS FIRE, i.e. the experience of a heightened energetic state, the former makes reference to an assessment of emotions as positive or negative, where POSITIVE EMOTIONS ARE LIGHT and NEGATIVE EMOTIONS ARE DARKNESS (a mapping also found, for example, with *fear* and *happiness*, cf. below). The next mapping, INTENSITY OF ANGER IS HEIGHT could be the kind of general mapping discussed in the context of the event-structure metaphors above, i.e. a specific instance of a general metaphor MORE IS UP/ LESS IS DOWN. I have included it because the domain HEIGHT sometimes structures the domain EMOTIONS directly (as in the case of HAPPY IS UP, cf. Section 3.3 below), and it is important to distinguish these two cases and to determine which mapping occurs with a given emotion.

The next four mappings are not discussed in the literature at all, though presumably ANGER IS A SLEEPING ORGANISM could be analyzed as belonging to the ANGER IS A FIERCE ANIMAL mapping, and ANGER IS GORGE is subsumed under ANGER IS A HEATED FLUID IN A CONTAINER by Lakoff (1987: 384). Finally, ANGER IS A PLANT is explicitly ignored by Kövecses on the basis that it can be used with any emotion; however, the same is potentially true of any metaphor and I see no grounds for this kind of *a priori* judgment (see further Section 4 below).

Taken together, the mappings in Table 1b account for 16.5 percent, bringing the coverage to 97.22 percent. The remaining 2.8 percent of the sample instantiate a variety of infrequent metaphors such as ANGER IS A BALLOON (*X pierce Y's anger, X deflate Y's anger*), ANGER IS HARD (*anger turn hard*), ANGER IS BLOOD (*anger pump through body*).

3.2. Fear

Kövecses (1998) lists the following eleven metaphorical mappings for the concept FEAR:

(10) FEAR/BEING AFRAID IS
    a. FLUID IN A CONTAINER   *The sight filled her with fear*
    b. A VICIOUS ENEMY   *Fear slowly crept up on him*
    c. A TORMENTOR   *My mother was tormented by fear*
    d. A SUPERNATURAL BEING   *He was haunted by fear*
    e. ILLNESS   *Jill was sick with fright*
    f. INSANITY   *Jack was insane with fear*
    g. AN INCOMPLETE OBJECT   *I was beside myself*
    h. AN OPPONENT IN A STRUGGLE   *Fear took hold of me*
    i. A BURDEN   *Fear weighed heavily on them*
    j. A NATURAL FORCE   *She was engulfed by panic*
    k. A SUPERIOR   *His actions were dictated by fear*
    (Kövecses 1998: 128–129)

Again, some of these mappings seem questionable. First, it is not clear why FEAR IS A VICIOUS ENEMY and FEAR IS A TORMENTOR are posited as separate mappings rather than being subsumed under something like FEAR IS AN ENEMY, together with FEAR IS AN OPPONENT IN A STRUGGLE. Second, the mapping in (10g), FEAR IS AN INCOMPLETE OBJECT, does not account in any straightforward way for the example *I was beside myself*, which seems to refer to an out-of-body situation rather than an incomplete object; nor is it clear why *I was beside myself* is categorized as referring to fear at all. In fact, the expression can refer to any strong emotion and there is no reason to assume that it is even particularly frequent with *fear*.[4]

---

4. This is confirmed by a web search using *Google*. In 200 random examples of the string [*beside myself with*], the ten most frequent emotion terms that occur with this expression are *joy* (14.5%), *anger* (9.5%), *glee* (9%), *grief* (8%), *excitement* (7%), *worry* (6%), *anticipation* (3%), *fury* (3%), and – in tenth place – *fear* (2.5%). Thus, it is doubtful that there is a strong connection between the expression *I was beside myself* and the emotion concept FEAR.

The sample of 1000 occurrences of *fear* yielded 886 metaphorical patterns. Table 2a lists those that instantiate one of the mappings in (8).

Table 2a. Metaphorical patterns manifesting FEAR metaphors posited in the literature

FEAR/BEING AFRAID IS	N
FLUID IN A CONTAINER *fear permeate X, fear well up inside X*	2
AN ENEMY/OPPONENT *overwhelming/powerful fear, fear grip X('s stomach), fear choke/take hold of/torment X, fear overcome X, fear occupy X's mind, fear exert constraining effect, fear bruise X's eyes, fear drive X away, X be seized/occupied by fear, X give way to y, X (be) victim of fear, X attack/combat/counteract/deal with/tackle fear, X banish/conquer/curb/hold down/overcome/push back fear, X be defense against fear*	35
A SUPERNATURAL BEING *fear haunt/take possession of fear*	4
ILLNESS *unhealthy/sick fear, X suffer from fear, X feel sick with fear, X suffer from fear, X' belly churn with fear, X recover from fear, X be immobilized with fear, fear create mental paralysis, X (be) dead of fear*	9
INSANITY *irrational fear*	1
AN INCOMPLETE OBJECT —	0
A BURDEN —	0
A NATURAL FORCE *wave of fear*	2
A SUPERIOR *fear dominate X('s life), fear spur X, fear dictate/govern X's action, fear keep X in line, fear constrict X('s actions), X be driven by fear, X become free of fear*	13
Total	66

With two exceptions, all of the metaphors identified via the introspective method are also found by MPA. The first exception, FEAR IS AN INCOMPLETE OBJECT, is unproblematic: the existence of this mapping was doubtful anyway, and the MPA essentially confirms these doubts. The second exception, the complete absence of FEAR IS A BURDEN, does present a problem, since WEIGHT is a source domain that would intuitively be expected to occur in the target domain FEAR. There are two reasons why this mapping could be absent from the sample: either it never manifests itself as a metaphorical pattern, or it does not do so frequently enough to occur in a sample of 1000 hits. The first possibility would be a serious problem for MPA, as it would suggest that there are metaphors that cannot be identified via this method; the second possibility would simply be a relatively trivial sampling problem. In order to determine which of these possibilities applies in the present case, I created a complete concordance of the word *fear* on the basis of the BNC and searched specifically for metaphorical patterns instantiating the mapping FEAR IS A HEAVY OBJECT. Eight metaphorical patterns were found in the concordance of 7145 lines (*fear be a burden, burdened by fear, heavy with fear, outweighed by fear, X weigh Y's fear, EMOTION outweigh X's fear*), i.e. the mapping manifests itself on average 1.12 times per 1000 occurrences of the word *fear*). Thus, the fact that it was not found in the sample used here is not a fundamental problem of MPA but simply of the relatively small sample size chosen here.

Taken together, the mappings in Table 2a account for 7.4 percent of all metaphorical patterns found with *fear*. Again, the vast majority of cases missed by the introspective method consists of patterns instantiating the object metaphor (486 cases, or 51.35%) or the location metaphor (173 cases, or 19.5%). However, this again leaves around a fifth of all metaphors (18.2%) unaccounted for (more than twice the number it actually identifies!). The most frequent of these are shown in Table 2b.

The mappings in Table 2b account for 12 percent of all metaphors, bringing the total coverage up to 93.79 percent. The remainder is made up of infrequent metaphors such as FEAR IS METAL (*metal fear*) and FEAR IS A SLEEPING ORGANISM (*X raise/arouse fear*).

3.3. HAPPINESS

Kövecses (1998) lists the following fifteen metaphorical mappings for the concept HAPPINESS:

(11) HAPPINESS/BEING HAPPY IS
    a. UP   *We had to cheer him up*
    b. BEING OFF THE GROUND   *I am six feet off the ground*
    c. BEING IN HEAVEN   *That was heaven on earth*
    d. LIGHT   *Lighten up*
    e. VITALITY   *He was alive with joy*
    f. WARM   *That warmed my spirits*
    g. HEALTH   *It made me feel great*
    h. AN ANIMAL THAT LIVES WELL   *He was happy as a pig in shit*
    i. A PLEASURABLE PHYS. SENSATION   *I was tickled pink*
    j. FLUID IN A CONTAINER   *He was overflowing with joy*
    k. CAPTIVE ANIMAL   *His feelings of happiness*

Table 2b. More FEAR metaphors identified via metaphorical pattern analysis

FEAR/BEING AFRAID IS	N
LIQUID *source of fear, trickling/undercurrent of fear, sap of fear, X secrete fear, fear pour out, fear evaporate, expression dissolve into fear, X tap into fear*	10
A SUBSTANCE IN A CONTAINER (UNDER PRESSURE) *X('s heart) be(come) filled with fear, X be full of/contain fear, X fill Y with fear, X put fear into Y, fear fill X, fear pour out, pent_up fear*	15
MIX *tinge of fear, mixture of fear and EMOTION, EMOTION be combined/mixed with fear, relief be mixed with fear, X blend fear and EMOTIONS*	9
COLD *icy/cold fear, land of cold and fear, shiver of fear, frozen mask of fear, X be/go cold with fear, X('s face) be frozen in fear*	14
HEAT *heat of fear, fear fuel X, X fuel/spark off fear, X vent fear on Y, fear make X feel warm*	7
LIGHT *bright fear, projection of fear, flicker of fear, X reflect fear, eyes glitter with fear*	6
DARK *shadow of fear, fear darken X, X be overshadowed by fear, eyes (be) dark with fear*	4
HIGH/LOW (INTENSITY) *fear be high among X, fear peak, fear be ascendant, fear rise, X heighten fear*	7
PAIN *agony/convulsion/spasm/throes/throb/tremor of fear, X ache/be tortured with fear*	8
A SHARP OBJECT *prick/shaft of fear, fear cut to X, fear slice through X, X strike fear into Y*	7
AN ORGANISM *growing fear, root of fear, revival of fear, X breed/regenerate fear, X stem from fear, fear stem from X, X blossom into fear*	9
A WILD/CAPTIVE ANIMAL *fear be fierce, fear lurk beneath X, X feed fear, X control fear, X handle/lose control over/unleash fear*	6
A BARRIER *fear barrier, barrier of fear, fear (be) obstacle, fear block X from EVENT*	4
Total	106

l. OPPONENT IN A STRUGGLE *broke loose / He was knocked out*
m. A RAPTURE/HIGH *I was drunk with joy*
n. INSANITY *They were crazy with happiness*
o. A NATURAL FORCE *He was swept off his feet*
(Kövecses 1998: 129)

As before, there are some problems with this set of mappings. First, it is unclear why (11b,c) are posited as separate mappings rather than special cases of (11a). The same is true for (11e,g); it is unclear what the exact difference is between VITALITY and HEALTH; the expression *feel great* could refer to both. Third, the example given for the mapping in (11h) is a simile, not a metaphor; moreover, it seems to refer to the PLEASURABLE PHYSICAL SENSATION mentioned in the next mapping down; again, it is unclear why it is posited as a separate mapping (if it exists at all). Finally, the example given for the mapping in (11i) is itself questionable. *To be tickled pink* seems to refer to health/vitality rather than to a pleasurable sensation, assuming that it refers to the source domain HEALTHY SKIN COLOR. Thus, it seems that we should collapse the mappings in (11e, g) into HAPPINESS IS VITALITY, and that we should take the existence of the mappings in (11h, l) as very provisional.

Before we can investigate the domain of HAPPINESS using MPA, we have to choose a word to represent the domain. The label HAPPINESS suggests that *happiness* may be the right choice, but there are two *a priori* reasons to choose the word *joy* instead. First, the word *joy* is roughly one-and-a-half times more frequent than *happiness* in the BNC. Second, three out of the five examples in (11) that are metaphorical patterns contain the word *joy* (11e, j, m), and the remaining two, (9k, n) also more typically found with the word *joy* than with the word *happiness*.[5] There is an *a posteriori* reason as well: only eight of the mappings are instantiated in the sample for *happiness*, as compared to eleven in the sample for *joy*, which suggests that the mappings in (11) refer to *joy* rather than *happiness*. I will return to this issue and a detailed comparison of the two words in Section 5.1 below; here, I will focus on the word *joy*.

The sample of 1000 hits for the word *joy* yielded 906 metaphorical expressions. Table 3a lists all metaphorical patterns in the sample that manifest one of the mappings in (11) above together with their frequency of occurrence in the sample.

As in the case of the previously discussed emotion concepts, most of the mappings identified via the introspective method are also identified by the MPA. The only exceptions are HAPPINESS IS BEING IN HEAVEN, BEING HAPPY IS BEING AN ANIMAL THAT LIVES WELL, and HAPPINESS IS A PLEASURABLE PHYSICAL SENSATION; note that these are exactly those mappings

---

5. A web search using the search engine *Google* turned up 570 hits for *crazy with joy* vs. 191 for *crazy with happiness*, and 11 hits for *joy break/breaks/breaking/broke/broken loose,* as compared to 5 for *happiness* (one of which was a citation of Kövecses' example).

Table 3a. Metaphorical patterns manifesting HAPPINESS metaphors posited in the literature

HAPPINESS/BEING HAPPY IS	N
UP *X be elated with joy, joy be lifted*	2
BEING OFF THE GROUND *X('s heart) jump/leap for/with joy*	12
BEING IN HEAVEN —	0
LIGHT *sunny joy, glow/radiance of joy, X's face light up/shine with joy, joy shine in/lighten X's face, X's eyes be bright/luminous with joy, X light Y's eye with joy, X radiate joy, X beams with joy, X reflect joy, joy dim, X blot out joy*	18
VITALITY/HEALTH *X's eyes be alive with joy*	1
WARM *melting joy, joy generate warmth, X blush with joy, warm joy*	4
AN ANIMAL THAT LIVES WELL —	0
A PLEASURABLE PHYSICAL SENSATION —	0
FLUID IN A CONTAINER *heart swell with joy, X swell heart with joy, joy pour into heart, X brim over with joy, joy seep from X, overflowing joy*	6
CAPTIVE ANIMAL *X control fear, X unleash joy, joy be unconfined/unrestrained*	4
OPPONENT IN A STRUGGLE *overwhelming joy, X be/feel overcome with joy, X beat/defeat/kill joy*	7
A RAPTURE/HIGH *heady joy, ecstasy of joy*	3
INSANITY *delirious joy*	1
A NATURAL FORCE *flood/surge of joy, joy surge through X, joy sweep over/through X, X be swept away by joy, joy subside*	7
Total	65

whose existence seemed questionable anyway.[6] Conversely, the mappings identified via the introspective method again represent only a small subset of those identified by MPA; all expression in Table 3a taken together

---

6. In fact, it is plausible to say that the mapping HAPPINESS IS A PLEASURABLE PHYSICAL SENSATION is instantiated by the expressions for HAPPINESS IS WARMTH, since warmth is typically a pleasurable sensation.

account for a mere 7.2 percent of all metaphorical expressions found in the sample. Again, a large portion of the missing patterns is made up of event structure metaphors (location: 81 cases or 8.9%, object: 628 cases or 69.31%). However, this leaves 14.6 percent of the metaphorical patterns unaccounted for. The most frequent of these are shown in Table 3b.

Table 3b. More HAPPINESS metaphors identified via metaphorical pattern analysis

HAPPINESS/BEING HAPPY IS	N
HEAT/FIRE *seething joy, flare/sparks of joy, joy be spark, X smother joy, X burn with joy*	6
A LIQUID *effervescent joy, source/spring of joy, flow/river of joy, joy spring from X, X drink joy*	11
A SUBSTANCE IN A CONTAINER (UNDER PRESSURE) *inner joy, X be filled with/full of joy, X contain joy, X fill Y('s) heart with joy, X leave Y empty of joy, X's heart fill with joy, explosion of joy, X explode/burst with joy, joy burst in X's heart, joy burst through X, X erupt in joy*	38
A MIXED/PURE SUBSTANCE *pure/unalloyed joy, mixed joy, mixture of EMOTION and joy, EMOTION combine with joy, X combine EMOTION with joy, EMOTION mingle with X, EMOTION and X be mingled*	19
A DESTROYABLE OBJECT *X break/destroy/mar Y's joy*	7
DISEASE *sick joy, joy be infectuous, joy befall X, X feel sick with joy, X die of joy*	5
AGGRESSIVE ANIMAL BEHAVIOR *fierce/wild/savage joy*	6
AN ORGANISM *growing/short-lived joy, fruit of joy*	7
Total	99

The patterns in Table 3b account for 10.9 percent, bringing the coverage up to 96.36 percent. The remaining 3.6 percent are made up of infrequent mappings like HAPPINESS IS A BALLOON (*bubble of joy*), HAPPINESS IS BLOOD (*joy pulsate through X*), HAPPINESS IS A SHARP OBJECT (*stab of joy*), and INTENSITY OF HAPPINESS IS DEPTH (*deep joy*).

3.4. SADNESS

Kövecses (1998) lists the following thirteen metaphorical mappings for the concept SADNESS:

(12) SADNESS/BEING SAD IS
   a. DOWN — *He brought me down with his remarks*
   b. DARK — *He is in a dark mood*
   c. LACK OF HEAT — *His remarks threw cold water on the party*
   d. LACK OF VITALITY — *This was disheartening news*
   e. FLUID IN A CONTAINER — *I am filled with sorrow*
   f. VIOLENT PHYSICAL FORCE — *That was a terrible blow*
   g. VIOLENT NATURAL FORCE — *Waves of depression came over him*
   h. ILLNESS — *Time heals all sorrows*
   i. INSANITY — *He was insane with grief*
   j. BURDEN — *He staggered under the pain*
   k. LIVING ORGANISM — *He drowned his sorrow in drink*
   l. CAPTIVE ANIMAL — *His feelings of misery got out of hand*
   m. OPPONENT — *He was seized by a fit of depression*
   (Kövecses 1998: 130)

Again, some of the mappings are open to discussion. First, the mapping in (12c) is not licensed by the example: *to throw cold water on something* means to discourage or disillusion someone, not to make someone sad. Second, both the source and the target domain posited for (12d) are questionable: if *disheartening* is taken as literally referring to the removal of the heart (in analogy to *dismember*), then the source domain should be DEATH; at the very least, this could be subsumed under (12h), ILLNESS; however, even so, the mapping does not belong here, since *disheartening* does not mean 'causing sadness', but rather 'causing disappointment or hopelessness', much like *throw cold water on something*. Third, the example in (12g), *X be a blow*, refers to a feeling of shock rather than sadness. Thus, the existence of the mappings in (12c, d, h) must be taken as a working hypothesis at best, given these examples. As a minor point, we might also ask why the source domain in (12g) is characterized as '*violent* natural force', rather than simply 'natural force', as before.

Also as in the case of the preceding mappings, some of the examples are metaphorical patterns, and interestingly, none of them contain the word *sadness*. Instead, they contain related words: *depression* in (12g,m), *sorrow* in (12h, k), *grief* in (12i), and *misery* in (12l). While the emotions these words refer to all share some aspect of SADNESS, they also differ in ways that argue against simply including all of them under this emotion concept. Especially *grief* seems to refer to a much stronger emotion than *sadness*, and moreover, it is typically associated with the loss or death of someone. The question thus arises, which word to take as representative of the domain SADNESS. In terms of frequency and unmarkedness, the only plausible choice is *sadness*; but this means that we may miss some of the mappings associated with related, but not identical emotions.

There are 737 hits for *sadness* in the BNC, and these contain 716 metaphorical patterns. Table 4a shows those patterns instantiating one of the mappings in (12), together with their frequencies of occurrence, normalized to 1000 hits (the actual frequencies are given in parentheses).

Table 4a. Metaphorical patterns manifesting SADNESS metaphors posited in the literature

SADNESS/BEING SAD IS	N
BEING DOWN *sinking feeling of sadness*	1 (1)
DARKNESS *dull/purple sadness, sadness dull EMOTION, X's eye be dim with sadness, sadness cloud X's features*	7 (5)
LACK OF HEAT *dank sadness, X cool from bitterness to sadness, eye grow chill with sadness, sadness manifest as cold feeling*	6 (4)
LACK OF VITALITY/ILLNESS *X suffer sadness, X heal Y of sadness*	6 (4)
FLUID IN A CONTAINER — (but cf. SADNESS IS A FLUID and SAD PERSON IS A CONTAINER as separately occurring metaphors below)	0 (0)
VIOLENT PHYSICAL FORCE —	0 (0)
NATURAL FORCE *rush/wave of sadness, sadness sweep/wash over/through X*	10 (7)
INSANITY —	0 (0)
BURDEN *heavy sadness, burden of sadness, X make sadness heavy, heart be heavy with sadness, sadness weigh heavily in heart, EMOTION outweigh sadness*	10 (7)
LIVING ORGANISM *sadness grow*	1 (1)
CAPTIVE ANIMAL *X control sadness, X release sadness*	3 (2)
OPPONENT *overwhelming sadness, sadness overwhelm/suffocate X, sadness take hold of X, X be overcome with sadness, sadness be overpowering, X confront/counteract/ endure/ward off sadness, sadness close in on X*	21 (15)
Total	65 (45)

With two exceptions, all mappings posited in the literature are identified by MPA. The first of these exceptions is expected: it concerns the source domain VIOLENT PHYSICAL FORCE, whose occurrence in the target domain SADNESS was questionable anyway. The second exception concerns one of the mappings that was posited to account for a metaphorical pattern containing the word *grief*. The fact that this was not found for *sadness* suggests that the there may be a difference between these two words concerning their participation in this mapping. An informal web search confirms this: using the *Google* search engine, I searched all websites with the country suffix *.uk* for the strings [*insane with sadness*] and [*insane with grief*]. The first pattern did not occur at all, the second pattern occurred 22 times. Taking into account the overall frequency of the words *sadness* (n = 79,100) and *grief* (n = 139,000), the expected frequencies are 8 for *sadness* and 14 for *grief*, and the observed distribution, i.e. the fact that *insane with X* occurs with *grief* but not with *sadness* is thus highly significant (Fisher Exact, $p < 0.001$). The question remains, of course, why this difference should exist. I would argue that it has to do with the intensity of the emotions referred to by these two words: the emotion referred to by *sadness* is simply not strong enough to be conceptualized as *insanity*. This is confirmed by a look at the words *anger* and *rage*, which also seem to differ in intensity: using the same criteria as before, I searched for the strings [*insane with anger*] and [*insane with rage*]: the former occurred 18 times, the latter 30 times. Given the base frequencies for each word, the expected frequencies are 29 for *anger* (n = 399,000) and 19 for *rage* (n = 270,000), and the deviance from this, i.e. the fact that *insane with anger* occurred less frequently than expected, confirms the connection of the mapping AN EMOTION IS INSANITY to the intensity of an emotion. Clearly, then, the choice of search word is very important for MPA (cf. Section 5).

Taken together, the metaphorical patterns in Table 4a account for 6.4 percent of all metaphorical patterns occurring with *sadness* in the sample. The majority of unaccounted-for cases consists of manifestations of the event-structure metaphors (object: 470, i.e. 65.64%; location: 33, i.e. 4.6%), but more than a fifth (23.26%) remain unaccounted for even if we ignore these. Table 4b shows the most frequent cases.

The patterns in Table 4b account for 18.3 percent, bringing the coverage to 95.04 percent. The remaining 4.96 percent are made up by minor metaphors like SADNESS IS LIGHT (*glimmer of sadness*), SADNESS IS A SHARP OBJECT (*piercing sadness*), and SADNESS IS HEART/BLOOD (*sadness pulse within X*).

Table 4b. More SADNESS metaphors identified via metaphorical pattern analysis

SADNESS/BEING SAD IS	N
A MIXED/PURE SUBSTANCE *mingled sadness, tinge of sadness, amalgam/combination/mixture of EMOTION and sadness, mixed EMOTION and sadness, EMOTION be mingled/mixed/tinged with sadness, memory be mingled/tinged with sadness, event be(come) tinged with sadness, sadness be mixed/tinged with EMOTION, EMOTION and sadness mix, EMOTION tinge sadness, sadness suffuse event*	59 (42)
DEPTH *deep sadness, sadness be deep, event deepen sadness*	31 (22)
A SUBSTANCE IN A CONTAINER (UNDER PRESSURE) *X include sadness, sadness fill X's heart, X's eye/mind fill with sadness, X('s heart/voice) be full of sadness, X fill up with sadness, X be filled with sadness, X contain/hold sadness, X fill Y with sadness, burst of sadness*	42 (30)
A LIQUID *pool of sadness, source of sadness, undercurrent of sadness, undertow of sadness*	7 (5)
AN AURA *aura of sadness, there be sadness about X*	14 (10)
A SOUND *cadence/note/ring/tone of sadness, notes rent air with sadness, sadness echo EMOTION, voice be strident with sadness*	11 (8)
A WEATHER PHENOMENON *air/fog of sadness, atmosphere become tinged with/change to sadness*	11 (8)
TASTE *sweet sadness, sadness rise to throat*	4 (3)
HEAT *sadness consume X, X ventilate sadness*	4 (3)
Total	173 (131)

3.5. DISGUST

DISGUST is not a frequently discussed emotion concept. It is not mentioned in Kövecses (1998) or his other publications (Kövecses 1989, 2002). The *Master Metaphor List* available via the web site of the UC Berkeley lists only one relevant mapping, DISGUST IS NAUSEA. The BNC contains 604 hits for the noun *disgust*, which occur in 747 metaphorical patterns. Only one of these patterns could be construed as referring to NAUSEA, *X be sick with disgust*; one additional example is found in a simile (*disgust rise like bile in X's throat*). This accounts for 0.13 percent of all mappings. Interestingly, an even larger portion than usual is taken up by patterns instantiating event-structure metaphors (object: 248, i.e. 38.02%;

location: 371, i.e. 49.66%), but this still this leaves 12.18 percent unaccounted for. Table 5 shows all metaphorical patterns which instantiate a mapping occurring more than 3 times per 1000 words (as in the case of *sadness*, the frequencies were normalized, the actual frequencies are given in parentheses.

Table 5. Metaphorical patterns manifesting DISGUST metaphors

DISGUST/BEING DISGUSTED IS	N
A MIXED/PURE SUBSTANCE *pure disgust, combination/mixture of disgust and EMOTION, tinge/trace of disgust, disgust mix/be mingled with EMOTION*	22 (13)
A SUBSTANCE IN A CONTAINER (UNDER PRESSURE) *X fill Y with disgust, disgust fill X, X be full of disgust, X's eyes be filled with disgust, outlet for disgust, disgust build up among X, X burst with disgust, disgust be locked up inside X*	23 (14)
AN OPPONENT *repressed disgust, X fight down/repress/suppress disgust, disgust invade/penetrate X, disgust kill/overwhelm X*	15 (9)
PARALYSIS/A DISEASE *disgust paralyze X, X be stiff/rigid with disgust, X suffer from disgust, X be sick with disgust, X become immune to disgust*	11 (7)
HIGH/LOW (INTENSITY) *high disgust, disgust rise (in X)*	8 (5)
COLD *shiver of disgust, cold disgust, disgust shiver through X*	7 (4)
FOOD *candied disgust, bitter disgust, sour gasp of disgust*	7 (4)
LIQUID *disgust flood through X, disgust spill into X, X secrete disgust*	5 (3)
PAIN *tremor of disgust, pained disgust, X wince at disgust*	5 (3)
AN ORGANISM *growing disgust, root/seed of disgust*	5 (3)
HEAT X fuel disgust	3 (2)
A SHARP OBJECT *disgust be spur, shaft of disgust*	3 (2)
A BALLOON *X inflate with disgust, balloon of disgust*	3 (2)
A HEAVY OBJECT *heavy disgust, X outweigh disgust*	3 (2)
Total	120 (73)

The examples in Table 5 account for 9.77 percent, bringing the coverage to 97.59 percent. The remaining 2.41 percent are made up of infrequent mappings like DISGUST IS BREATH (*X blow disgust through X's teeth*), and INTENSITY IS DEPTH (*disgust deepen, deep disgust*).

3.6. Summary

Metaphorical Pattern Analysis has identified the vast majority of metaphors postulated in the literature on the basis of the introspective approach. Where it has failed to do so, this was in all but two cases due to the fact that the mapping was postulated on the basis of insufficient or misanalyzed evidence; in other words, MPA has proven to be more precise than the traditional method. The one genuine failure concerns the mapping FEAR IS A HEAVY OBJECT (or FEAR IS A BURDEN), which did not manifest itself in the sample, but which was shown to be identifiable in principle via MPA. The other potential failure concerned the mapping SADNESS IS INSANITY, which was shown not to apply to the lexical item *sadness*, but which can be identified given the right search word (in this case, *grief*).

What is more, MPA has identified a large number of mappings not mentioned in the previous literature (in fact, at least as many as *are* mentioned). In terms of coverage, then, MPA is clearly superior to the introspective method. Moreover, the fact that metaphorical patterns are easily quantifiable also allows us to make statements about the relative importance of these mappings, which is the topic of the next section.

4. Are there emotion-specific metaphors?

We are now in a position to begin to address seriously the question whether there are emotion-specific metaphors, i.e. metaphors that are used in the conceptualization of only a subset of human emotions. Note that this is fundamentally a question about language use, i.e., about what is frequent or typical, rather than about the linguistic system, i.e. about what is 'possible'; the limits of what emotion *can* be conceptualized via which target domain are defined by how speakers construe these emotions. In the case of metaphorical patterns, usage data are especially important, since such patterns are essentially grammatical templates providing one or more slots for target domain vocabulary, and there is nothing in the linguistic system that would prevent a speaker from inserting any given word into one of these slots. For example, *seething X* is a pattern that we would typically associate with ANGER, but the sample actually also contains the expression *seething joy*, and we could use it with any of the other emotions investigated above (*seething disgust, seething fear, seething sadness*) and get expressions that may sound somewhat unusual, but are nevertheless straightforwardly interpretable (incidentally, a web search yields hits for all three expressions, although *seething sadness* is very infrequent). In other words, introspective judgments about such patterns can only be judgments about their likelihood of occurrence with particular emotion terms anyway.[7]

Thus, the question whether there are emotion-specific metaphors cannot be meaningfully answered in terms of categorical judgments as to which metaphors *can* occur with which emotion concept, but only in terms of statements as to which metaphors *do* occur with that concept in actual usage. However, the informal web search for *seething X* suggests that, given a large enough corpus, all metaphors will be instantiated for all emotions, so the question which metaphors occur in actual usage can itself not be answered categorically. Instead, it must be answered in terms of statistically significant associations of particular metaphors to particular domains, i.e. we must investigate whether there are metaphors that are significantly more strongly associated with a given emotion than would be expected. Since expected frequencies are calculated on the basis of the overall frequency of a given metaphor across different emotion concepts, it is important to choose a representative sample of emotion concepts. As has become clear above, in the present paper this was attempted by selecting five emotion concepts that are widely agreed upon to be basic emotions. Clearly, this can only be seen as a heuristic, and this must be kept in mind when interpreting the results presented in the following subsections.

In order to identify metaphors that are significantly more or significantly less frequent than expected with a particular emotion concept (i.e., that are attracted to or repelled by this domain), I cross-tabulated the frequencies of all 86 metaphors identified in the sample by the MPA (including the event-structure metaphors) with the five emotion concepts discussed in the preceding section. This cross-table shows that the five emotion terms differ significantly in their association to particular metaphors ($\chi^2 = 2772.91$, df = 340, $p < 0.001$). The specific associations were then identified by determining the contribution that each combination of

---

7. Kövecses' work confirms this implicitly, in that he refers likelihood of occurrence or conventionality throughout his discussion, saying that metaphors are "unlikely to occur" with a particular emotion (Kövecses 1998: 134) or that it "can be imagined" that a particular emotion would make use of a given metaphor but that it "would stretch the ordinary, everyday understanding" of it (ibid.: 135).

an emotion concept and a metaphor makes to the overall chi-square value. The results of this analysis are presented in this section.

4.1. Metaphors significantly associated with ANGER

The most strongly associated metaphor for ANGER is EMOTION IS HEATED LIQUID ($\chi^2 = 50.97$, $p < 0.001$), and several metaphors that belong to the same system are also significantly associated with this emotion concept: EMOTION IS A SUBSTANCE UNDER PRESSURE ($\chi^2 = 22.74$, $p < 0.001$), the more general metaphor EMOTION IS HEAT ($\chi^2 = 15.96$, $p < 0.05$), and the related metaphor EMOTION IS FIRE ($\chi^2 = 38.38$, $p < 0.001$). The other specific metaphor identified by the statistical analysis is ANGER IS EMOTION IS A FIERCE/CAPTIVE ANIMAL ($\chi^2 = 16.85$, $p < 0.05$). This supports the central place that these metaphorical systems have been accorded in the literature on ANGER; note that both metaphors are found with the other four emotion concepts too, but not significantly frequently; their special status with respect to ANGER only becomes apparent through a statistical evaluation of their distribution across emotion concepts.

In addition, there are three very general, event-structure-like metaphors that are significantly associated with ANGER: EMOTION IS AN OBJECT DIRECTED AT SOMEONE ($\chi^2 = 38.12$, $p < 0.01$), as in *X direct/target anger at Y* or *X experience/feel anger at Y*, EMOTION IS POSSESSED OBJECT ($\chi^2 = 22.34$, $p < 0.01$), as in *X's anger* or *X have anger*, and INTENSITY OF EMOTION IS HEIGHT ($\chi^2 = 15.35$, $p < 0.05$), as in *anger rise/drop*, *X get up Y's anger*. Note that INTENSITY OF EMOTION IS HEIGHT is consistent with the EMOTION IS A HEATED LIQUID mapping, since heated liquid in a container will expand and hence its level will rise, and EMOTION IS AN OBJECT DIRECTED AT SOMEONE is consistent with (though not necessarily associated with) the image of a fierce animal attacking its prey.

Of course, there are also metaphors that occur significantly less frequently than expected with ANGER. Most interestingly, the LOCATION event-structure metaphor is among these ($\chi^2 = 20.16$, $p < 0.01$), but also CAUSING ANGER IS TRANSFERRING AN OBJECT ($\chi^2 = 16.77$, $p < 0.05$) and BEING/ACTING IN AN EMOTIONAL STATE IS BEING ACCOMPANIED BY AN EMOTION ($\chi^2 = 30.67$, $p < 0.01$), which are part of the OBJECT event-structure metaphor, and INTENSITY OF EMOTION IS SIZE ($\chi^2 = 15.58$, $p < 0.05$), e.g. *great anger*. While the latter can presumably be accounted for by the strong preference to express the intensity of ANGER via the HEIGHT metaphor, the first three show that there are indeed significant differences between emotion terms concerning event-structure metaphors, and that these can therefore not simply be assumed to apply equally to all emotion concepts.

4.2. Metaphors significantly associated with FEAR

The most strongly associated metaphor for FEAR is EMOTION IS A SUPERIOR ($\chi^2 = 33.47$, $p < 0.001$), followed by an event-strucure-like metaphor, EMOTION IS A FOUNDATION ($\chi^2 = 16.06$, $p < 0.01$), as in *X's actions be* BASED ON *fear, X* BASE *actions* ON *fear*, and FEAR IS A CAUSER ($\chi^2 = 18.82$, $p < 0.05$), as in *fear force X to act*. Since no claims have been made in the literature as to which metaphors are particularly important to FEAR, this is a genuine new insight. It is probably no accident that all three metaphors construe FEAR as an entity that compels the experiencer to act (or not to act) in a particular way. In other words, the most salient aspect of FEAR does not seem to be the experience of the emotion itself, but the consequences of that experience.

There are also two mappings that occur less frequently than expected with FEAR, namely ACTING ON AN EMOTION IS ACTING IN A LOCATION ($\chi^2 = 18.37$, $p < 0.01$), as in *X act* IN *fear* (this is part of the LOCATION model also repelled by ANGER) and EMOTION IS AN OBJECT DIRECTED AT SOMEONE ($\chi^2 = 30.03$, $p < 0.001$), as in *X vent fear* ON *Y*.

4.3. Metaphors significantly associated with HAPPINESS

The most strongly associated metaphor for HAPPINESS is part of the OBJECT event-structure metaphors ignored in Section 3, CAUSING EMOTION IS TRANSFERRING AN OBJECT ($\chi^2 = 142.96$, $p < 0.001$), as in *X bring/give (Y) joy, X provide (Y with) joy, X share X's joy*. This is not significantly attracted by any of the other emotion concepts investigated here, which again stresses the importance of including event-structure metaphors in the investigation. Three other general metaphors are also identified by the statistical analysis, TRYING TO ATTAIN AN EMOTION IS SEARCHING FOR AN OBJECT ($\chi^2 = 34.82$, $p < 0.001$), as in *X find joy (in Y)*, INTENSITY OF EMOTION IS SIZE ($\chi^2 = 17.28$, $p < 0.05$), and INTENSITY OF EMOTION IS QUANTITY ($\chi^2 = 15.56$, $p < 0.05$). Note that these three metaphors are also compatible with the OBJECT model. The first of these is particularly interesting, since it forms part of a PURSUIT-OF-HAPPINESS model which is strongly entrenched in English-speaking cultures (cf. Stefanowitsch 2004, see also further Section 4.1 below).

Among the more specific metaphors discussed in Section 3, only one is significantly associated with HAPPINESS, but it is the one perhaps most expected: EMOTION IS UP/BEING OFF THE GROUND ($\chi^2 = 42.19$, $p < 0.001$). As in the case of ANGER, thus, the analysis has identified what is felt to be the 'most typical' metaphor for this domain.

There are two mappings that are less frequent than expected with HAPPINESS, namely EMOTION IS A LOCATION ($\chi^2 = 39.96$, $p < 0.001$), and ACTING

ON AN EMOTION IS ACTING IN A LOCATION (χ^2 = 31.42, p < 0.001). Note that, again, both of these belong to the LOCATION metaphor, while the significantly associated mappings mostly belong to the OBJECT metaphor.

4.4. Metaphors significantly associated with *SADNESS*

The most strongly associated metaphor for SADNESS is INTENSITY OF EMOTION IS DEPTH (χ^2 = 67.73, p < 0.001), as in *sadness deepen*, *deep sadness*, but INTENSITY OF EMOTION IS SIZE (χ^2 = 29.19, p < 0.001) is also found. What is not identified is the counterpart to HAPPINESS IS BEING UP/OFF THE GROUND, i.e. SADNESS IS BEING DOWN. This was to be expected given that it only occurs once in the sample (cf. Table 4a above). However, it is probably not an accident that SADNESS is the only emotion concept investigated here that is significantly attracted to the INTENSITY OF EMOTION IS DEPTH mapping; note that this way of construing intensity is maximally compatible with EMOTION IS BEING DOWN.

Four of the specific mappings discussed in Section 3.4 above are identified by the statistical analysis: EMOTION IS AN (IM)PURE SUBSTANCE (χ^2 = 35.21, p < 0.001), EMOTION IS AN AURA (χ^2 = 22.6, p < 0.001), EMOTION IS PAIN (χ^2 = 19.01, p < 0.01), and EMOTION IS WEATHER (χ^2 = 16.63, p < 0.05). None of these would have been expected to be central to SADNESS on the basis of the literature. In addition, the mapping BEING/ACTING IN AN EMOTIONAL STATE IS BEING ACCOMPANIED BY AN EMOTION, which is part of the OBJECT metaphor, is significantly attracted (χ^2 = 32.93, p < 0.001).

Metaphors that are significantly less frequent than expected are, again, EMOTION IS A LOCATION (χ^2 = 16.67, p < 0.05), and ACTING ON AN EMOTION IS ACTING IN A LOCATION (χ^2 = 34.30, p < 0.001).

4.5. Metaphors significantly associated with *DISGUST*

None of the specific metaphors discussed in Section 3.5 are significantly associated with DISGUST, including DISGUST IS AN ILLNESS, which might have been expected to be. Instead, the only two mappings that are found significantly more frequently than expected are EMOTION IS LOCATION (χ^2 = 437.14, p < 0.001), and ACTING ON AN EMOTION IS ACTING IN A LOCATION (χ^2 = 298.31, p < 0.001), i.e. the mappings that are less frequent with the other four emotions.

Again, there are metaphors that occur less frequently than expected, namely INTENSITY OF EMOTION IS QUANTITY (χ^2 = 18.49, p < 0.01), INTENSITY OF EMOTION IS SIZE (χ^2 = 17.93, p < 0.05), EMOTION IS AN OBJECT IN A LOCATION (χ^2 = 16.82, p < 0.05), and CAUSING EMOTION IS TRANSFERRING AN OB-

JECT ($\chi^2 = 16.03$, $p < 0.05$). Note that all of these are cases of the OBJECT metaphor. Thus, we see a general pattern found with all emotion terms investigated here that they either attract the OBJECT model and repel the LOCATION model, or vice versa. Moreover, DISGUST is the only emotion investigated here which prefers the LOCATION mapping. This fact is hard to interpret, given that only five emotion concepts were investigated, but it may be related to the degree of control that the experiencer has over the emotion in question: it would make sense if more controllable emotions preferred the OBJECT model (where the emotion is seen as an object that can potentially be manipulated by the expericencer), while emotions that are less easily controllable prefered the LOCATION model (where the emotion is seen as a location surrounding the experiencer on all sides).

4.6. Summary

The analysis has confirmed the importance of metaphors that have been claimed in the literature to play a central part for the emotion concepts in question: the HEATED-LIQUID and the FIERCE-ANIMAL systems for ANGER, the UP/OFF-THE-GROUND system for HAPPINESS, and to some extent the DOWN metaphor for SADNESS. In addition, it has identified central metaphors for those emotion concepts that have been discussed in less detail in the literature, such as the AURA and PAIN metaphors for sadness and the SUPERIOR and FOUNDATION metaphors for FEAR. The only emotion concept for which it has not identified any specific metaphorical mappings is DISGUST, where we might have expected the ILLNESS metaphor to be identified. That this did not happen is due to the fact that this metaphor occurs with all five emotion concepts with a similar relative frequency (ANGER 0.93%, DISGUST 0.94%, FEAR 1.24%, HAPPINESS 0.55%, and SADNESS 0.56%). In all cases, the central metaphors yield insights about the emotion concepts in question if we take them to pick out the most important aspects of the metaphors in question.

Clearly, the relatively exhaustive attempt at listing metaphorical mappings (via metaphorical patterns) presented in Section 3 and the attempt to identify central metaphors presented in this section complement each other. On the one hand, it is important to know what mappings are found with a given emotion concept in a reasonably large corpus, since this gives us a notion of which metaphors are conventionalized in a given culture/ language (although, of course, the lists are never complete). On the other hand, it is just as important to know what source domains are particularly strongly attracted to (or repelled by) a given emotion concept, since this will give us a notion of what distinguishes this emotion concept most clearly from other concepts in the culture/language in question.

5. The lexeme-orientation of metaphorical pattern analysis: synonyms and antonyms

The preceding section has shown that MPA allows us to identify metaphorical mappings strongly associated with a given emotion concepts as compared to others. The procedure rests on the assumption (among other things) that it is possible to choose a representative word to stand for each of the concepts investigated. Thus, the procedure glosses over potential differences between different words referring to the same general emotion concept. This is especially evident in cases where there is no obvious unmarked candidate for a given emotion concept, as perhaps with *anger* and *rage* or *happiness* and *joy*, but it is also true in cases where one candidate is clearly marked, as in the case of *sadness* and *grief*, where the latter refers to a feeling of sadness connected to a loss. In this section, I will look into this issue by contrasting two rough synonyms, *happiness* and *joy* (cf. Section 3.3 above). For the sake of completeness, I will also briefly look at two rough antonyms, *happiness* and *sadness*, although this is not fundamentally different from looking at a whole set of words from the same semantic field, as was done in the preceding section.

5.1. *Happiness* and *joy*

Seventy-five of the 87 metaphors identified in the sample occur with *joy* and/or *happiness*. Each mapping's frequency with these two words was cross-tabulated against the frequency of occurrence of all other mappings and submitted to a Fisher-exact test.[8] As is standard procedure for multiple tests, the levels of significance were corrected by of dividing them by the total number of tests performed, in this case, seventy-five.

Only three mappings reached the corrected levels of significance: TRYING TO ATTAIN AN EMOTION IS SEARCHING FOR AN EMOTION ($p < 1.33\text{E}{-}05$, ***) is significantly associated with *happiness*, and BEING/ACTING IN AN EMOTIONAL STATE IS BEING ACCOMPANIED BY AN EMOTION ($p < 1.33\text{E}{-}05$, ***) and BEING

---

8. Since, unlike in Section 4, only two words are contrasted here for each metaphor, an exact test is preferable (cf. Pedersen 1996, Stefanowitsch and Gries 2003, Gries and Stefanowitsch 2004 for a discussion of why the Fisher exact test is optimally suited to dealing with natural language data).

HAPPY IS BEING UP/OFF THE GROUND ($p < 6.67\text{E}{-}04$, *) are significantly associated with *joy*. Before we turn to these in detail, note that the fact that only 3 out of 75 mappings distinguish between the two words, may seem disappointing if we are interested in subtle semantic differences between near synonyms, but it is actually a desirable result in the more general context of identifying metaphors associated with a given target domain, since it suggests that the results of MPA do not depend too heavily on the particular word chosen to represent a target domain (but cf. below).

Note that two of the three metaphors just mentioned were already identified in Section 4 as being significantly associated with the domain HAPPINESS in general. The fact that within this domain they are associated with different words is thus intriguing, as is the way in which they qualitatively differ for *happiness* and *joy*.

Let us begin by looking at the mapping TRYING TO ATTAIN AN EMOTION IS SEARCHING FOR AN EMOTION. While the mapping does occur with the word *joy*, it does not do so very frequently (16 occurrences per thousand hits; significantly more frequently than with any of the other basic emotion words/concepts investigated in Sections 3 and 4). Moreover it is instantiated by only three patterns, *X find joy (in Y), X recapture joy*, and *new-found joy*. In contrast, the mapping is instantiated more than six times as frequently with *happiness* (110 occurrences per thousand hits), by 28 different patterns. These patterns are shown in (13a–c):

(13) a. TRYING TO ATTAIN HAPPINESS IS SEARCHING/HUNTING FOR SOMETHING
sought-after happiness, unlooked-for happiness, pursuit of happiness, search/quest for happiness, path/route/way to happiness, X chase (after) happiness, X be in search of happiness, X harry after happiness, X look for happiness (in X), X search for happiness, X pursue happiness, X seek happiness, X reach out towards happiness, X snatch at happiness, X stretch out hand for happiness

    b. ATTAINING HAPPINESS IS FINDING/CAPTURING SOMETHING
happiness seem within reach, X attain happiness, X find happiness (in/through/with X), X capture/grab/recapture happiness, X reach happiness

    c. NOT BEING ABLE TO ATTAIN HAPPINESS IS INABILITY TO REACH SOMETHING
X stand in way of happiness, happiness elude X, happiness be irretrievable

Apart from the fact that the mapping is instantiated much more frequently for *happiness* than for *joy* in terms of both types and tokens, there is a crucial qualitative difference between the two words. While the patterns instantiating the mapping with *happiness* refer to different aspects of it (the search itself, the route to be taken, the moment of finding, and the possibility of not finding or not being able to reach the desired thing), *joy* occurs only with the sub-mapping ATTAINING HAPPINESS IS FINDING OR CAPTURING SOMETHING. The motivation for this difference can presumably be found in our (culturally mediated) perception of the role that the two emotions play in our lives: while *happiness* and *joy* refer to similar emotions, HAPPINESS is potentially a less intensely experienced emotional state (see below), and hence potentially a more stable one and one whose attainment is more easily conceptualized as being the responsibility of the experiencer. Thus, it is possible to actively look for HAPPINESS (and hold on to it once it is found), while the more intense, short-lived JOY can only be stumbled upon by chance (see also Stefanowitsch 2004).

The greater intensity of the emotional experience referred to by *joy* is most likely also responsible for the fact that the mapping BEING HAPPY IS BEING UP/OFF THE GROUND is significantly associated with *joy* as compared to *happiness*, if such an difference in intensity in fact exists.

Goddard (1997: 93), summarizing discussions in Wierzbicka (1992, 1996: 215ff.), suggests that it does. Contrasting the English word *happy* with its French and German translation equivalents, *heureux* and *glücklich*, he claims that the latter two refer to a more intense emotional experience than the former, and he uses a metaphor to express this difference:

> Essentially, English *happy* conveys a "weaker," less intense emotion than *glücklich* and *heureux*. Speaking metaphorically, emotions such as *Glück* and *bonheur* FILL A PERSON TO OVERFLOWING, leaving no room for any further desires or wishes (Goddard 1997: 93, emphasis added).

These cross-linguistic claims will not be discussed here (they are discussed in Stefanowitsch 2004), but they are relevant to the comparison between *happiness* and *joy*, since Goddard remarks that English *joy(ful)* is comparable in intensity to *hereux* and *glücklich* (Goddard 1997: 94). This suggests that his general claim also applies to *joy(ful)*. Note that Goddard is not making statements about metaphors associated with the words under discussion; he is simply *using* a metaphor in order to express something about their meaning in general. Still, if his characterization is correct, it could be reflected in the metaphorical system he uses. In the remainder of this subsection, I will briefly investigate this possibility.

The metaphorical system consists of the mappings AN EMOTION IS A LIQUID and AN EMOTION IS A SUBSTANCE IN A CONTAINER. These metaphors are not among those that differ significantly for *joy* and *happiness* in terms of their frequency. However, Goddard's quote suggests a qualitative difference, not a quantitative one: both words should be associated with LIQUID and CONTAINMENT metaphors, but in the case of *joy* there should be a higher proportion of patterns that refer to full or overflowing containers. Table 6 shows all patterns from the sample that instantiate the metaphors in question, divided into two sets: patterns referring to liquids or containment in general, and patterns referring to full or overflowing containers or liquids under pressure or under the influence of a strong force.

As the comparison of the observed frequencies with the expected ones (given in parentheses) shows, FULLNESS/PRESSURE metaphors are indeed more frequent for *joy* and less frequent for *happiness*, and this difference is statistically significant (Fisher exact, $p < 0.01$, **).

The case of LIQUID/CONTAINMENT metaphors shows that at least in some cases, a quantitative comparison of metaphors at the most general level does not suffice to uncover differences in the metaphorical behavior of near synonyms. Instead, it is necessary to take into account the qualitatively different ways in which such general metaphors manifest themselves in specific cases (these differences can then of course also be quantified).

5.2. *Happiness* and *sadness*

The direct comparison of the words *happiness* and *sadness* more or less confirms the results obtained by contrasting all five basic emotion terms in Section 4. Sixty-nine of the 87 metaphors identified in Section 3 occurred with *happiness* and/or with *sadness*. Their frequencies for these two words were submitted to a series of Fisher-exact tests, as in the preceding subsection. Twelve metaphors reached the corrected levels of significance, six of which are associated with *happiness* and six with *sadness*.

The two mappings most strongly associated with *happiness* as compared to *sadness* are the ones that were also identified as most significant by the comparison of all five emotion concepts in Section 4: TRYING TO ATTAIN AN EMOTION IS SEARCHING FOR AN EMOTION ($p < 1.45\text{E}{-}05$, ***), and CAUSING AN EMOTION IS TRANSFERRING AN OBJECT ($p < 1.45\text{E}{-}05$, ***), as well as, two mappings that are related to the latter, namely EMOTIONS ARE POSSESSIONS ($p < 7.25\text{E}{-}04$, *) and THE CAUSE OF AN EMOTION IS THE DEPARTURE POINT OF A MOVING OBJECT ($p < 1.45\text{E}{-}04$, **). In addition, two of the specific mappings discussed in Section 3 were identified: EMOTION IS LIGHT

Table 6. LIQUID metaphors for happiness and joy

	happiness	joy
source of NP$_{emot}$	12	6
NP$_{emot}$ *spring from X*	1	1
X open self to NP$_{emot}$		1
NP$_{emot}$ *pour into heart*		1
inner NP$_{emot}$	1	2
X contain/include/hold NP$_{emot}$	7	1
NP$_{emot}$ *be in X*		2
distillation of NP$_{emot}$	1	
X drink NP$_{emot}$		1
NP$_{emot}$ *evaporate*	1	
X leave X empty of NP$_{emot}$	1	1
TOTAL	23 (16)	16 (23)

FULLNESS, PRESSURE, and BURSTING metaphors	happiness	joy
effervescent/seething NP$_{emot}$		2
pressure of NP$_{emot}$	1	
swell of NP$_{emot}$	1	
heave of NP$_{emot}$	1	
rush of NP$_{emot}$	1	
surge of NP$_{emot}$	2	1
river be NP$_{emot}$		1
flood of NP$_{emot}$		1
NP$_{emot}$ *subside*		1
filled/loaded with/full of NP$_{emot}$	8	15
heart (be) full to bursting with NP$_{emot}$	1	
heart fill/swell with NP$_{emot}$		2
X fill/swell Y('s heart) with NP$_{emot}$	1	6
NP$_{emot}$ *brim in heart*	1	
burst/explosion of NP$_{emot}$	1	1
cold void run over with NP$_{emot}$	1	
NP$_{emot}$ *burst in/through X('s) heart*		2
NP$_{emot}$ *overflow*		1
X brim over with NP$_{emot}$		1
X burst/erupt/explode in/with NP$_{emot}$		6
NP$_{emot}$ *surge/sweep/wash over/through X*	1	3
X be swept away by NP$_{emot}$		1
X pour NP$_{emot}$		1
flow of NP$_{emot}$ *emanate from X*		1
NP$_{emot}$ *seep from X*		1
Total	20 (27)	47 (40)

(p < 1.45E–05, ***), as in *bright/shining happiness, X shine/sparkle with happiness*, and EMOTIONS ARE FRAGILE OBJECTS (p < 7.25E–04, *), as in *X damage/destroy/ruin happiness, X hack happiness to shreds*. The relation of *happiness* to LIGHT, like that of ANGER to HEAT, is presumably an experiential one. Light and darkness are actually physiologically related to happiness and sadness: long periods of darkness can cause so-called *seasonal depression*, which can be treated by exposure to bright light.[9] The relation of *happiness* to FRAGILE OBJECTS is presumably related to the cultural value we place on happiness: happiness is something we are forever trying to attain (cf. the PURSUIT-OF-HAPPINESS model), and once we do, we try to protect it from potential causes of unhappiness. Sadness, in contrast, is not a state we try to attain, and if we enter it through circumstances beyond our control, we try to change this as quickly as possible. Thus, it makes sense that we conceptualize the end of *happiness*, but not that of *sadness*, as the destruction of a fragile object.

Turning to *sadness*, we find that five of the six mappings that are significantly associated with *sadness* as compared to *happiness* were already identified by the comparison of all five emotion concepts in Section 4, and need no further comment: BEING/ACTING IN AN EMOTIONAL STATE IS BEING ACCOMPANIED BY AN EMOTION (p < 1.45E–05, ***), EMOTIONS ARE PURE/MIXED SUBSTANCES (p < 1.45E–05, ***), EMOTION IS PAIN (p < 1.45E–05, ***), INTENSITY OF EMOTION IS DEPTH (p<1.45E–05, ***), and EMOTION IS AN AURA (p < 7.25E–04, *). One mapping, EMOTION IS A MOVING OBJECT DIRECTED AT SOMEONE (p < 7.25E–04, *) was identified in addition; note that it is part of the OBJECT model and thus consistent with our previous results.

In sum, although no major surprises emerged from a direct comparison of the words *happiness* and *sadness* in light of the previous comparison of all five emotion words, the direct comparison did yield some additional detail missed by the general comparison. Two things in particular are worth pointing out. First, in the overall comparison we were dealing with the words *joy* and *sadness*; the fact that a comparison of *happiness* and *sadness* yields such similar results confirms the claim that near synonyms will broadly be associated with the same metaphors (and thus, that it is possi-

---

9. Cf., for example, Ferenczi (1997). The HAPPINESS IS LIGHT metaphor forms a rich, coherent system of metaphorical patterns in the data that often make use of a SUN-AND-CLOUDS/SHADOW imagery, where HAPPINESS IS SUNLIGHT,, as in *shining/unclouded happiness, X beam/shine with happiness, happiness shine from X, happiness beam out in yellow beams*, and A DECREASE IN/ABSENCE OF HAPPINESS IS A SHADOW (CAST BY CLOUDS) *X cloud happiness, X cast a shadow on happiness, clouds make happiness a memory, happiness burst through clouds of sorrow*.

ble to investigate emotion concepts via individual lexical items). Second, even though *happiness* and *sadness* are antonyms, the metaphors they are significantly associated with do not fall into pairs of opposing metaphors. For example, we might expect that if *happiness* is significantly associated with LIGHT, then *sadness* should be significantly associated with DARKNESS, or that if *sadness* is significantly associated with PAIN, then *happiness* should be significantly associated with PHYSICAL WELLBEING. That this is not the case suggests that the emotions referred to by *happiness* and *sadness* are not primarily understood as opposites, but that each of them is conceptualized (and presumably experienced) on its own terms.

5.3. Summary

This brief discussion of how individual lexemes may differ quantitatively or qualitatively in their participation in particular metaphorical mappings has shown at least two things. First, the lexeme-specificity of metaphorical pattern analysis is not a disadvantage in a context where it is the aim of an investigation to uncover mappings associated with entire emotion concepts. Even if we choose just one word to represent such a concept, chances are that we will not miss any major metaphors. Second, the lexeme-specificity of MPA is actually a great advantage where it is the aim of an investigation to uncover subtle differences within a given general emotion concept.

6. Conclusion

This paper has shown that metaphorical pattern analysis is superior to the introspective method often used by researchers working in the conceptual theory of metaphor (and in other frameworks). It outperforms the traditional method in the identification of metaphorical mappings associated with a given target domain, and by allowing strict quantification of the results, it opens up completely new avenues of research.

Of course, this paper has done little more than demonstrate the feasibility of the method. In order to unfold its full potential, the method will have to be systematically applied in a large number of target domains, and hopefully the growing interest in quantitative corpus-based studies will result in such applications. Ultimately, we might even envision a lexical database containing a large number of lexical items and the metaphorical patterns they occur with (analogous to the FrameNet project at the UC

Berkeley), which would allow easy retrieval of all metaphors associated with a particular lexical item (or semantic field) and vice versa.

There are many practical and theoretical uses for the kind of information gained by metaphorical pattern analysis (whether in the form of a database or in the form of small-scale studies of individual target domains). On a descriptive level, MPA may complement lexical semantic approaches to word meaning, for example in the generation of dictionaries. On a theoretical level MPA allows us to address central questions concerning metaphorical mappings, for example: (i) the systematicity and productivity of individual metaphorical mappings; (ii) the universality of metaphorical mappings (MPA can serve as a basis for contrastive studies investigating cross-cultural and cross-linguistic similarities and differences in the metaphorical conceptualization of experience); and (iii) the psychological reality of metaphorical mappings (the results of MPA, esp. the possibility to assess the importance of a given metaphorical mapping for a given target domain, can serve as a basis for generating specific hypotheses concerning the mental representation of such mappings).

Data Sources

BNC   British National Corpus, World Edition.
Src 1 *News 10 Now*: Oswego County bar owners rally against smoking ban. Online at http:// news10now.com/content/all_news/ ?ArID=10946, last access April 2004)
Src 2 www.angelfire.com/tx3/taylez/dlb02.html, last access April 2004.

References

Athanasiadou, Angeliki and Elzbieta Tabaskowska
    1998   *Speaking of emotions. Conceptualization and expression*. Berlin and New York: Mouton de Gruyter.
Black, Max
    1962   Metaphor. In: *Models and metaphors. Studies in Language and Philosophy*, 25–47. Ithaca, NY: Cornell University Press.
    1992 [1979] More about metaphor. In: Andrew Ortony (ed.), *Metaphor and Thought*. Second edition. Cambridge: Cambridge University Press, 20–41.
Ferenczi, Michael A.
    1997   Seasonal depression and light therapy. *Mill Hill Essays*, Vol. 3. London: National Institute for Medical Research.

Gibbs, Raymond
   1994   *The poetics of mind. Figurative Thought, Language, and Understanding*. Cambridge: Cambridge University Press.

Goddard, Cliff
   1997   *Semantic Analysis. A Practical Introduction*. Oxford: Oxford University Press.

Hunston, Susan and Gil Francis
   1999   *Pattern grammar*. Amsterdam: John Benjamins.

Jäkel, Olaf
   1997   *Metaphern in abstrakten Diskurs-Domänen*. Frankfurt a.M.: Lang.

Kövecses, Zoltan
   1986   *Metaphors of Anger, Pride and Love*. Amsterdam and Philadelphia: Benjamins.
   1989   *Speaking of Emotions*. New York: Springer.
   1998   Are there any emotion-specific metaphors? In: Angeliki Athanasiadou and Elzbieta Tabaskowska (eds.), *Speaking of Emotions. Conceptualization and Expression*, 127–151. Berlin and New York: Mouton de Gruyter.
   2002   *Metaphor. A Practical Introduction*. Oxford: Oxford University Press.

Lakoff, George and Mark Johnson
   1980   *Metaphors We Live By*. Chicago and London: The University of Chicago Press.

Lakoff, George
   1987   *Women, Fire, and Dangerous Things*. Chicago: The University of Chicago Press.
   1993   The contemporary theory of metaphor. In: Andrew Ortony (ed.), *Metaphor and Thought*. Second edition, 202–251. Cambridge: Cambridge University Press.

Langacker, Ronald W.
   1987   *Foundations of Cognitive Grammar*. Vol. I: *Theoretical Prerequisites*. Stanford: Stanford University Press.

Niemeier, Susanne and René Dirven (eds.)
   1997   *The Language of Emotions*. Amsterdam and Philadelphia: Benjamins.

Ortony, Andrew and Terence J. Turner
   1990   What's basic about basic emotions? *Psychological Review* 97: 315–331.

Pedersen, Ted
   1996   Fishing for exactness. *Proceedings of the SCSUG 96*, 188–200. Austin, TX.

Sinclair, John
   1991   *Corpus, Concordance, Collocation*. Oxford: Oxford University Press.

Stefanowitsch, Anatol
   2004   Happiness in English and German: A metaphorical-pattern analysis. In: Michel Achard and Suzanne Kemmer (eds.), *Language, Culture, and Mind*, 134–149. Stanford: CSLI.

Stefanowitsch, Anatol and Stefan Gries
   2005   Covarying collexemes. *Corpus Linguistics and Linguistic Theory* 1: 1–46.

Ungerer, Friedrich and Hans-Jörg Schmid
   1996   *An Introduction to Cognitive Linguistics.* London and New York: Longman.
Weinrich, Harald
   1976   *Sprache in Texten.* Stuttgart: Klett.
Wierzbicka, Anna
   1992   Talking about emotions: semantics, culture and cognition. *Cognition and Emotion* 6: 289–319.
   1996   *Semantics. Primes and Universals.* Oxford: Oxford University Press.

The grammar of linguistic metaphors

Alice Deignan

Abstract

Linguistic metaphors are a major source of evidence for conceptual metaphors, yet researchers are often content to rely on intuitively derived examples. This is an oversight, because analyzing metaphors from naturally occurring data may reveal potentially significant patterns not otherwise noticed (Deignan 1999).

Especially in the domain of grammar, the patterns found in naturally occurring data are not necessarily predictable from the theoretical model. For example, it is common for literal and metaphorical meanings of a word to be of different word classes (Deignan 2005).

In this study, the central lexical items from the source domains ANIMALS, MOVEMENT, PLANTS and FIRE were concordanced using a 59 million word section of the Bank of English, and analyzed for differences between literal and metaphorical uses with respect to word class and syntactic patterning. The analysis confirms earlier findings that metaphorical uses of words show differences in their grammatical behavior, or even their word class, when compared to their literal use. In addition, it shows that metaphorical uses of a word commonly appear in distinctive and relatively fixed syntactic patterns.

These findings raise questions about the nature of metaphorical mapping, because they cannot be explained completely by the relatively static view of mapping that is sometimes suggested in discussion of Conceptual Metaphor Theory.

1. Introduction

In recent years, computerised corpora have been used to study linguistic metaphors from a range of perspectives. Some writers have used corpora to compare and contrast the use of metaphors in different genres, notably Charteris-Black (2004, see also Koller, this volume). Cross-linguistic analyses have been carried out into the frequencies and meanings of the different metaphors that are used to discuss the same topic across different languages, for instance in work by Boers and Demecheleer (1997). Unlike these types of work, the corpus studies reported here do not focus on specific genres or topics, but attempt to look at some metaphorical patterns found in a general corpus of English. Rather than considering specific topics, meanings or ideological orientations, this work examines detailed linguistic patterns and contrasts them with the patterns found in literal uses of the same words. These patterns are considered against the backdrop of Conceptual Metaphor Theory. It will be argued that the patterns found in naturally-occurring linguistic metaphors are a type of evidence that has been somewhat neglected to date, but can usefully inform theoretical development.

In this paper, grammatical patterns are described at the macro-level of part of speech, and at a more detailed level of syntactic patterning. It will be shown that there are frequent and possibly regular formal differences between metaphorical and literal uses of the same words, and that many metaphorical uses seem to be restricted grammatically (cf. Deignan 2005, Hanks 2004, this volume, cf. also Hilpert, this volume for similar observations concerning metonymic uses). Implications of this for Conceptual Metaphor Theory are considered. The corpus used is a 59 million-word cross-section of the Bank of English, owned by HarperCollins Publishers, which consists of contemporary, naturally-occurring written and spoken texts, predominantly British English but also including American and Australian English. The principle search tool used is a concordancer, with various tools for refining and selecting from a concordance, supplemented by a program for automatically calculating the most frequent collocates of a search word.

2. Conceptual Metaphor Theory and linguistic metaphors

It is important to reiterate at the outset that Conceptual Metaphor Theory was not developed in order to explain linguistic patterns. The relationship is the other way round; patterns observed in language provide some of the main evidence which led to the development of the theory. Lakoff (1990) writes that three types of evidence persuaded him that metaphor must be central to abstract thought, a tenet which underpins Conceptual Metaphor Theory. They are:

- 'The systematicity in correspondences between linguistic metaphors', such as the numerous words and expressions from the domain of journeys that are used to talk about love;
- 'The use of metaphor to govern reasoning and behaviour based on that reasoning'; and
- 'The possibility for understanding novel extensions in terms of the conventional correspondences'; for instance, a novel journey metaphor can be understood to refer to love by analogy to existing conventional journey metaphors. (1990: 50)

The first type of evidence is very clearly linguistic, and the third is also dependent on language analysis. The first type is the most widely cited in support of Conceptual Metaphor Theory. Numerous other examples of systematicity of linguistic metaphors are cited throughout the key writing. For instance, the first chapter of the seminal *Metaphors We Live By* (Lakoff and Johnson 1980) notes and discusses realisations of the conceptual metaphor ARGUMENT IS WAR, such as

Your claims are *indefensible*;
He *attacked* every weak point in my argument;
His criticisms were *right on target*. (1980: 4)

Many other clusters of linguistic metaphors are discussed throughout *Metaphors We Live By* and in other key writing. Kövecses put a case for the examination of linguistic metaphors in order to detect underlying conceptual metaphors, arguing:

In order to be able to arrive at the metaphors, metonymies and inherent concepts [...] one needs to study the conventionalised linguistic expressions that are related to a given notion. (1991: 30)

Given this importance placed on language as evidence for the theory, it does not seem unreasonable for a descriptive linguist to turn the relationship around: to look to the theory for a possible account of the patterns that he or she observes in naturally-occurring language. This was attempted in the studies described here. It will be shown that Conceptual Metaphor Theory does not seem to provide a complete explanation for aspects of the grammatical behaviour of linguistic metaphors.

3. Research into the grammar of linguistic metaphors

Researchers who use naturally-occurring language data have made some thought-provoking observations about the grammar of metaphors. Cameron studied the use of metaphor in a corpus of educational discourse (2003). She compared the numbers of metaphors in different parts of speech, with unexpected results: for instance, nearly half the metaphors in her data are verbs, but adjectives and adverbs together account for less than 5%. Her findings suggest that A = B metaphors, such as *Man is a wolf*, the type used to illustrate many theoretical studies, are in fact atypical of language in use.

Goatly (1997) also makes some interesting points about metaphor and word class, based on corpora which included literary texts and the Bank of

English, the corpus used for the research described in this paper. In his data, as in Cameron's, metaphors are found in all the major parts of speech, not merely as nouns. Goatly suggests that the usual focus on noun metaphors arises because they are inherently more marked than other parts of speech. The primary function of a noun is to refer, and the use of a referent from a different domain is very noticeable. He gives an example from the literary work of L. P. Hartley, who in the opening line of the novel *The Go-Between* wrote that "The past is a *foreign country*, they do things differently there". It is immediately striking that the phrase *foreign country* cannot be intended in its literal sense. Verbs used metaphorically will be less obvious, and perceiving them depends on the reader or listener noticing an unusual context, which will normally be less striking than an unusual referent. Metaphorical adjectives are identifiable through being used to modify a noun not usually associated with them. Again, this will be less obvious than the unusual referent of a nominal metaphor.

Cameron's and Goatly's studies thus indicate that the focus on nominal examples in much metaphor theory is not representative of the diversity of use in naturally-occurring data. Their arguments suggest that the grammar of metaphor is an area deserving of further detailed investigation.

4. Defining "metaphor"

In the examples discussed above, the literal and metaphorical senses of words are from the same part of speech: literal nouns are used metaphorically as nouns, and so on. However, once concordance data is studied in any amount of detail, another pattern emerges. There are many words that have pairs of meanings, apparently related to each other by metaphor, that are not the same part of speech. *Squirrel* is one such word. Used with its literal meaning, it is a noun, but with its metaphorical meaning it is rarely or never used as a noun; instead it is well-established as a verbal metaphor, in corpus citations such as:

(1) ... as consumers *squirrel away* huge sums for the downpayment on a home.

The verb *to squirrel* is very rarely or never used to refer to the behaviour of squirrels or similar animals, and thus there is no overlap of form between literal and metaphorical meanings.

It could be argued that because such "metaphors" are of a different word class, and are therefore not identical in form to any literal counterpart, they should not be regarded as a true metaphors. They would be considered instead the products of metaphorically-driven language development. This view is not taken here. That is, the verbal use of *squirrel* is regarded as a true metaphor, because the semantic link from this verb to our knowledge of the behaviour of literal squirrels – that they hoard food secretly – seems unarguable.

There are two further reasons for not insisting on identicalness of form between literal and metaphorical uses. Firstly, as will be shown in the next section, there is a very large number of words that behave in the same way as *squirrel*. Secondly, even where a metaphor and its literal counterpart are the same part of speech, when their linguistic behaviour is examined at a greater level of detail they will rarely be found to be formally identical. Sinclair, the pioneering corpus linguist, shows that there are correspondences between form and meaning such that different meanings of a word very often take different grammatical patterns, if not at the level of part of speech, then at a more detailed syntactic level (1991). He uses corpus data to show that the intransitive use of *build*, often followed by the particle *up*, tends to be metaphorical, in citations such as

(2) Problems are *building up*.

In contrast, the non-metaphorical use of *build* is usually transitive, and tends not to be followed by a particle. If metaphors only exist where a literal counterpart is identical in form, the above use of *build up* would be ruled out. This would lead to the exclusion of a very large number of uses that are often considered metaphors, or even all such uses.

5. Metaphor and part of speech

Corpus analyses of metaphorical uses show quickly that the case of *squirrel* is not an isolated one: a large number of literal nouns have metaphorical uses that are a different part of speech. In previous studies (Deignan 2003, 2005), I examined lexis from the source domains of ANIMALS, MOVEMENT and CLEANLINESS AND DIRT, and the metaphorical uses of lexis from each domain. These three source domains were chosen because it was established using thesauri and the corpus that salient lexis in each tends to be different parts of speech. Key words in the source domain of ANIMALS are the names of types of animals, that is, nouns; key words in the source domain of CLEANLINESS are adjectives such as *clean* and *dirty*, and in the domain of MOVEMENT, verbs such as *move, rock* and *shake*.

Concordances of words from these source domains were studied, those which have one or more metaphorical meanings were identified, and the word classes of the literal and metaphorical uses were noted. The results suggested that literal nouns are often adjectives or verbs when used in their metaphorical senses, while literal verbs and adjectives show some, though less marked, grammatical differences in their metaphorical uses. Examples of differences between the literal and metaphorical meanings of animal lexis arc now discussed.

5.1. Metaphors from the source domain of animals

It is generally assumed in the metaphor literature (for example, Searle 1993), and that words for animals are used to describe human characteristics, often negatively evaluated ones. I used thesauri to identify the central lexis from the source domain of animals, and concordanced these to study their metaphorical uses (Deignan 2005). My corpus searches confirmed that animal lexis is used extensively in the target domain of human behaviour, but they also suggested that examples such as *Man is a wolf*, often discussed in the literature, are atypical in other ways.

The corpus also confirmed Cameron and Goatly's findings noted above, showing very few examples of metaphors that equate a person with an animal in a straightforward A = B form. Further, in terms of grammatical form, there was only one example of an animal metaphor where there is no grammatical conversion: *cow* used as a highly derogatory term for a woman. (There is a derived adjective, *cowed*, but its meaning seems very distant from the literal sense of *cow*).

The corpus findings suggested that when a word referring to an animal is used metaphorically to describe human characteristics or behaviour, it often takes the form of a verb in addition to any nominal metaphorical meaning. *Pig, wolf, monkey, rat, fox, bitch* and *dog* can be used as both nouns and verbs with metaphorical meanings, in citations such as:

(3) ... bunch of racist *pigs*.
(4) He had probably *pigged* out in a fast food place.

Although nominal animal metaphors exist, where there is both a noun and a verb metaphor, the noun metaphor is generally much less frequent than the verb. For example, in the concordance for *fox* and inflections, which contains 461 citations (discounting citations of the common English surname *Fox*), the noun metaphor occurs only three times, always following *old*. On the other hand, the verb metaphor is found eighteen times. Citations include:

(5) ... you sly old *fox*.
(6) Experts are going to be completely *foxed* by this one.

For the words *hound, hare, ferret, weasel, squirrel* and *ape*, the only metaphorical use is verbal, there being no noun metaphor in conventional use. Citations include:

(7) O'Connor was the person who *ferreted* out the truth.
(8) He was *hounded* out of his job.

Studies of adjectives from the source domain of cleanliness and dirt, and verbs from the source domain of movement did not show similar patterns. Related metaphorical uses tended to be of the same part of speech as their literal counterparts. However, at a more detailed level, some differences in grammatical patterning were noted. In the next section, another source domain is considered.

5.2. Metaphors from the source domain of plants

To further investigate the behaviour of metaphorical uses of literal nouns, lexis from the source domain of plants was examined. Key lexis includes the nouns *plant, flower, tree* and words for species of and parts of plants, and verbs used to describe growth and cultivation of plants. A number of nouns, such as *tree*, have little or no metaphorical use. Concordances were analysed to determine the main metaphorical meanings of the source domain nouns. A similar pattern to that for the domain of animals was found, although it was less striking and there were some exceptions. Table 1 shows numerical findings for *blossom*.

Table 1. Literal and metaphorical meanings found in corpus citations of *blossom*

	Noun	Verb	Total
Literal	167 (127)	5 (45)	172
Metaphorical	2 (42)	55 (15)	57
Total	169	60	229

Note: Expected frequencies are shown in parentheses; $p < 0.001***$ (Fisher-Yates exact test)

As Table 1 shows, the literal meanings of *blossom* tend to be nominal, in citations such as:

(9) ... sprays of mimosa and almond blossom.

The only metaphorical citations that take a noun form are archaic, and include:

(10) ... having sadly lost his first wife and one daughter in the blossom of her age.

Verb citations include:

(11) Rain begins to fall, peach trees blossom. (Literal), and
(12) Venture capitalists provide the vital infusion of funds to help budding capitalists blossom. (Metaphorical).

The inflections of *blossom* have been analysed separately because, as will be shown in the following section, inflections of the same word sometimes show different sets of meanings. In the case of *blossom*, the tendency for metaphors not to be nouns seems general. The adjectival form, *blossoming*, is also common as a metaphor, appearing 32 times. In some cases it is difficult to distinguish this from the *-ing* form of the verb.

Some other nouns denoting parts of plants, such as *branch* and *stem* are used with metaphorical meanings. Metaphorical *branch* is both nominal and verbal, the verbal use having no literal counterpart. Metaphorical *stem* is always verbal, in citations such as

(13) The fight between the two miners stems from Renison's recent takeover bid.

and has no literal counterpart. *Root* is a very frequent metaphor, and can take noun or verb forms, the verb form being relatively infrequent with a literal meaning.

(14) This fungus can pass from root to root. (Literal, noun)
(15) ... tackling the root causes of poverty and not just its symptoms. (Metaphorical, noun)
(16) The cuttings should be rooted by late September. (Literal, verb)
(17) His own life [was] rooted in the ancient traditions. (Metaphorical, verb)

No counter examples were found, in the form of words that have a stronger tendency to be nominal in their metaphorical uses than literal. Although the pattern is not as overwhelming as for metaphors from the source domain of animals, this study of plant metaphors does suggest a tendency away from nominal uses and towards verbal uses in the target domain.

6. Detailed grammatical form

The corpus investigations into part of speech described above suggested that there might be patterns of interest to be found at a more detailed level, and so in the second part of this investigation into grammatical patterning, detailed syntactic structure was examined. In this section, I report on differences between singular and plural inflections of the words *rock* and *flame*, and then discuss the apparent restrictedness of lexico-grammatical patterns in which some metaphors are found.

6.1. Metaphors in different inflections

An earlier study of the concordances of nominal *rock* and *rocks* showed that there seemed to be differences in evaluative orientation between the singular and plural forms (Deignan 2003, 2005). The singular form *rock* tends to suggest a positive interpretation, in citations such as

(18) ...long regarded in Washington as a rock of stability in a notoriously unpredictable region.
(19) Nothing must undermine the sanctity of human life – the rock on which our society is built.

Plural *rocks* generally refer to negatively viewed events, in citations such as:

(20) A flagship initiative started eight months ago to boost home ownership in Greater London has hit the rocks already
(21) He lived in fear of his own marriage ending up on the rocks.

This difference could be explained with reference to source domain meanings. A single rock may imply a solid physical foundation or support, with Biblical allusions to the parable of houses that are built on different materials. In contrast, the metaphorical expressions that include plural *rocks*, such as *hit the rocks* or *be on the rocks*, seem to be grounded in images of shipwrecks or other disasters, where rocks are dangerous.

Sinclair (1991) and Louw (1993) write of the phenomenon of particular words having positive or negative semantic prosodies, that is, appearing in typically positive or typically negative surroundings and thus taking on a positive or negative shade of meaning. Neither writer makes the point with specific reference to metaphor, although one of Louw's examples, the negative *symptomatic*, is metaphorical. Sinclair and Louw argue that a particular positive or negative interpretation becomes generally associated with a particular word, and Louw claims that breaking the usual prosody can be an indication of insincerity, or a creative expression of irony. The example of *rock* and *rocks* shows that prosodies are found in metaphorical meanings, and also suggests that they can be specific to particular inflections of a word.

To further investigate the semantic prosodies of different inflections, I analysed concordances of some lexis from the source domain of heat. Lakoff (1987) notes the use of heat metaphors to talk about both passion and anger. Both metaphors are found in the concordances for *flame* and *flames*, but appear to be distributed differently, as will be shown. Unsurprisingly, passion or lust metaphors tend to have positive prosodies, while anger metaphors tend to be negative. Other emotions are also connoted by *flame(s)*, including the notion of a very strong belief, religious or otherwise, and a range of negatively viewed emotions such as fanaticism and racism. All citations of the two inflections were studied, and the main metaphorical meanings of each were identified. These were then divided into those that appeared to have positive prosodies and those that appeared to have negative ones. A similar pattern as for *rock/rocks* emerged.

There are 529 nominal citations of singular *flame*, including instances of the simile "drawn like moths to a flame", which was not counted as a metaphor because the meaning of *flame* within the simile is literal. Including these, 346 citations are literal, referring directly to a tongue of literal fire. 13 citations refer to a colour, or modify a colour, such as "flame-orange", and were also considered literal. A further 25 are similar in meaning, being used to refer to vividly coloured hair; 43 citations are in proper names such as the names of rock bands, and 7 are in contexts too obscure to assign to a sense with certainty. The remaining 95 citations are metaphorical. Their main meanings are described and illustrated in Table 2, divided into those with positive prosodies and those with negative.

116 *Alice Deignan*

Table 2. Metaphorical meanings of *flame*

Meaning	Collocates	Examples	Frequency
Lover	time markers: old, new, recent, ex, former	"… she is ditched at the altar after Ross spots his old *flame* Rachel in the congregation." "His relationship with former *flame* Brooke Shields is purely platonic."	57
feelings of love, desire, romance	carry, kindle	"George still carried a *flame* for Kelly." "Phil never lost interest in [his] first love, and given the chance to rekindle that *flame*…"	12
belief, determination	keep	"Gascoigne does his best to keep that *flame* alight." "… keeping the *flame* burning."	11
religion/ human spirit	[flame] of	"… the *flame* of Buddhahood." "… the unquenchable *flame* of the human spirit."	5
other		"… [those] who have had their entrepreneurial *flame* smothered." "… the *flame* of academia that had once burnt so brightly."	5
Total positive			90
Negative	[flame] of	"…a *flame* of suffering." "… the *flame* of complacency." "… fanning the *flame* of racial hatred."	5

It can be seen that in the singular use the vast majority of meanings and citations are positively oriented, and refer to feelings of love and desire, or to strong feelings that have an element of enduring faith or belief. Where *flame* refers to negative feelings or behaviour, it appears in the fixed expression *flame of*, and such citations are relatively infrequent.

There are 642 citations of the plural form, *flames*. 560 of these are literal, 24 are proper names, leaving 58 metaphorical uses, a slightly lower proportion than for the singular form. Table 3 gives the metaphorical meanings that were identified in the concordance, again divided into those that seem to have positive prosodies and those that are negative.

Table 4 gives numbers of positively and negatively evaluating metaphors for each form. More than half of the citations of the plural form of *flames* are negative in prosody, in contrast to the singular form, *flame*. The plural form appears in two metaphors that are not found in the concordance for the singular: *shoot down in flames* and *[crash/be] in flames*. The expression *flames of* is also relatively frequent, and is always negative, occurring in citations that describe fanatical, often violent mob behaviour. When the concordance data are sliced according to metaphorical mean-

Table 3. Metaphorical meanings of *flames*

Meaning	Collocates	Examples	Frequency
lover	old, latest	"I'd watch it when old *flames* try to be friends."	9
love, desire		"… keeping the *flames* of love alive." "… *flames* of passion dimly remembered."	7
passion	fan	"…will the *flames* of passion be fanned?"	5
other, positive		"…the incomparable *flames* of Pele and Eusebio."	3
Total positive			24
be criticised	shot down in	"Weren't this band the band of the month last month? Now they're just shot down in *flames*?"	3
be in a disastrous situation	in flames	"…his future crashing in *flames*."	2
other, negative	[flames] of, fan	flames of speculation/ intolerance/ bigotry/ nationalism	29
Total negative			34

Table 4. Positive and negatively oriented metaphors from singular and plural forms of *flame*.

	Singular *flame*	Plural *flames*	Total
Positive	90 (71)	24 (43)	114
Negative	5 (24)	34 (15)	39
Total	95	58	153

Note: Expected frequencies are shown in parentheses; $p < 0.001$*** (Fisher-Yates exact test)

ing first and inflection second, it can be seen that some expressions occur in both singular and plural inflections, but with a strong tendency to be one or the other. *Flame* meaning "lover" can be plural but tends to be singular, while *flame of* followed by a noun denoting negative feelings can be singular but tends to be plural.

One reason for the different evaluative polarities of the inflections may be that a literal flame is usually under control, and may be symbolic, as, for instance, the Olympic flame. A literal flame may also be of use, as a candle or a burning match. In contrast, literal flames are often undesired, out of control and very dangerous, and may also be the result of the behaviour of angry groups of people.

The concordances of *fire* and *fires* also show that the singular and the plural uses share relatively few metaphors. Singular *fire* appears in a number of fixed expressions, most of which have no plural form, including *playing with fire* and *get on like a house on fire*, as well as metaphors related to the source domain of war rather than temperature such as *[be] under fire*.

These studies suggest that different inflections of the same source domain words may appear in different evaluative patterns in the target domain, or in different conceptual metaphors altogether. In some cases this can be explained by considering the schemata that each individual word form seems likely to evoke. It is not argued that singular forms will always show positive prosodies and plural forms negative, but that there is no reason to expect the singular and plural forms to have the same metaphorical meanings or evaluative orientation. This may well apply to different verbal inflections. For instance preliminary studies have suggested that for some verbs the distribution of meanings across passive and active uses is uneven (Deignan 2003). The findings suggest that individual word forms or lexical phrases are metaphorically mapped, rather than a word family as a whole.

6.2. Lexico-grammatical patterns

A very common finding of concordance analyses of metaphors is that metaphors seem to appear in relatively fixed expressions compared to literal meanings, which seem to be more freely combining (Deignan 1999). These are not restricted to idioms in the classical sense, that is, very fixed, usually semantically opaque strings. This tendency can be seen in the concordance for *flames*, which includes semi-fixed expressions such as *fan the flames* and *shoot down in flames* in citations such as:

(22) The show's presenter has been accused of fanning the flames of bigotry.
(23) I expected to be shot down in flames.

Similar patterns have been evident in other words discussed here; for instance, *rocks* tends to appear with a metaphorical meaning in the expressions *hit the rocks* and *be on the rocks*. Metaphorical *flower* and its inflections are found almost exclusively in the expressions *flower of* and *flowering of*. None of these expressions can be regarded as idioms in the classical sense, of being fixed to a high degree and semantically opaque, features seen in expressions such as *get on like a house on fire*. Nonetheless, these metaphorical uses either do not combine freely with a wide range of other words, and/ or are restricted to particular grammatical patterns or inflections.

7. Implications

Two features have emerged from the data discussed here:
1. Source domain nouns often have metaphorical meanings that are verbs.
2. Metaphorical meaning are sometimes associated with a single inflection, and/ or are found in expressions that are fixed lexically and/ or grammatically.

It is possible that these features have no significance, but this is unconvincing given that they are observed again and again in lexis from many different source domains. Explanations for these features may be of importance for metaphor theory, or may be linked to aspects of language use more generally.

The first observation has interesting implications for Conceptual Metaphor Theory. The corpus data show that nouns from the source domain of plants and animals tend to appear in the target domain as verbs. An explanation can be found in meanings typically expressed by literal and metaphorical expressions. There is a general consensus that source domains tend to be concrete while target domains tend to be abstract (for example, Reddy 1993). This might suggest that many source domains might tend to be focussed around concrete nouns, while target domains might focus on language describing abstract processes and relationships. For instance, nouns describing concrete entities such as *blossom* from the domain of plants do not map obviously onto an entity in the domain of development, but the source domain processes involved in plants growing and being cultivated do. As a result, the verbal form of *blossom* appears much more frequently in the target domain. The mapping from animals onto human characteristics also shows this. The most frequent and salient lexis in the source domain are nouns describing animals, but these are required to describe ways of behaving, hence the logical transformation into verbs.

This seems straightforward in itself but is slightly at odds with Conceptual Metaphor Theory. It is generally held that conceptual metaphors map the source domain onto the target domain so that the correspondences and logical relationships from the source domain are replicated in the target domain. This was described by Lakoff (1990) as the Invariance Hypothesis. The hypothesis postulates mappings as fixed correspondences between source and target domains, recreating the structure of the source domain in the target domain except where this is barred by the inherent structure of the target domain. If linguistic metaphors are realizations of underlying mental structure as held in Conceptual Metaphor

Theory, it can be inferred that the relationships between parts of speech are a linguistic expression of the structure of the source domain. Nouns realize entities, verbs realize processes and actions, and adjectives realize states and attributes. The relationship between nouns, verbs and adjectives within a sentence expresses the perceived relationships between entities, attributes and actions. If structural relationships are recreated by metaphor, one would expect parts of speech to be stable when metaphorically mapped. The corpus data discussed here have shown that this expectation is frequently broken.

The Invariance Hypothesis allows for the inherent structure of the target domain to prevent mappings. Source domain entities that have no correspondence in the target domain structure are dropped from the mapping. However, the corpus data discussed here point to a more dynamic picture of the interaction between source and target domains. In these data, the target domain contributes to the form of the linguistic metaphor, rather than having a structure imposed on it. The linguistic and structural relations between metaphorically used words seem to be the product of input from both source and target domains, a notion that is closer to the idea of Blending (Fauconnier and Turner 2002) than to Conceptual Metaphor Theory.

The second observation, that individual word forms are associated with particular meanings, is consistent with work by Sinclair (for example, 1991; 2004) and other corpus linguists. Sinclair's observation that differences in meaning are accompanied by differences in form was illustrated above with his example of *build*. The implications of this for a grammatical description of English have been explored by Hunston and Francis (2000). They gathered an enormous amount of corpus data to demonstrate that the different meanings of polysemous words have a strong tendency to be realized in distinctive grammatical patterns at a detailed level. Like the previous point, this is potentially in contradiction with the Invariance Hypothesis. If words tend to fall into different syntactic relationships with each other when used metaphorically, it is not clear to what extent a metaphorical set of uses can truly recreate relationships between literal uses of the same words.

This observation also strikes a chord with work by researchers into collocation. In the corpus data described here, it appeared that the metaphorical meanings of words tended to appear in linguistic contexts that were relatively fixed, both syntactically and lexically. Collocation is now understood to be an important force in the formation of all text (for instance, Erman and Warren 2000), whether expressing literal or metaphorical meaning. These analyses of concordance data from a metaphorical perspective would seem to suggest that it is even more significant for non-literal language. As yet there does not seem to be an explanation for this within the work of cognitive linguistics.

8. Theory driven and data-driven approaches

Writing within the Conceptual Metaphor Theory tradition has tended to emphasize the structure of domains, while individual linguistic mappings are often discussed in terms of their role within that structure. This is essentially a top-down approach. The development of Conceptual Metaphor Theory was a much-needed re-emphasis within the field of metaphor studies, which had been focussed for too long on isolated, literary metaphors. However, while this approach apparently provides a useful framework within which to work, it has been argued in this paper that it does not account for detailed patterns found in linguistic metaphor. Taking a top-down approach can allow linguistic patterns to be ignored, possibly at the expense of useful insights. It may be that the balance needs to again be redressed, and that it is time to work more directly with the individual linguistic metaphors from naturally-occurring texts, searching back for theoretical implications, rather than proceeding from theory to find the linguistic examples that are needed in order to support it.

References

Boers, Frank and Murielle Demecheleer
   1997   A few metaphorical models in (Western) economic discourse. In: Wolf-Andreas Liebert, Gisela Redeker and Linda Waugh (eds.), *Discourse and Perspective in Cognitive Linguistics*, 115–129. Amsterdam: John Benjamins.

Cameron, Lynne
   2003   *Metaphor in Educational Discourse.* London: Continuum.

Charteris-Black, Jonathan
   2004   *Corpus Approaches to Critical Metaphor Analysis.* Basingstoke: Palgrave Macmillan.

Deignan, Alice
   1999   Linguistic metaphors and collocation in non-literary corpus data. *Metaphor and Symbol* 14: 19–38.
   2003   Linguistic metaphors, grammar and Conceptual Metaphor Theory: Evidence from the Bank of English. Paper presented at the 8. International Cognitive Linguistics Conference, La Rioja, Spain.

    2005   *Metaphor and Corpus Linguistics.* Amsterdam: John Benjamins.
Erman, Britt and Beatrice Warren
    2000   The open choice principle and the idiom principle. *Text* 20: 29–62.
Fauconnier, Giles and Mark Turner
    2002   *The Way We Think. Conceptual Blending and the mind's hidden complexities.* New York: Basicbooks.
Goatly, Andrew
    1997   *The Language of Metaphors.* London: Routledge.
Hunston, Susan and Gill Francis
    2000   *Pattern Grammar: A corpus-driven approach to the lexical grammar of English.* Amsterdam: John Benjamins.
Kövecses, Zoltán
    1991   Happiness: A definitional effort. *Metaphor and Symbolic Activity* 6: 29–46.
    2002   *Metaphor: A Practical Introduction.* Oxford: Oxford University Press.
Lakoff, George
    1990   The Invariance Hypothesis: Is abstract reasoning based on image-schemas? *Cognitive Linguistics* 1: 39–74
    1987   *Women, Fire and Dangerous Things: What Categories Reveal about the Mind.* Chicago: The University of Chicago Press.
Louw, William
    1993   Irony in the text or insincerity in the writer? The diagnostic potential of semantic prosodies. In: Mona Baker, Gill Francis, and Elena Tognini-Bonelli (eds.), *Text and Technology: In Honour of John Sinclair*, 157–176. Amsterdam: John Benjamins.
Reddy, Michael
    1993   The conduit metaphor: A case of frame conflict in our language about language. In: Andrew Ortony (ed.), *Metaphor and Thought.* Second edition, 164–201. Cambridge: Cambridge University Press.
Searle, John
    1993   Metaphor. In: Andrew Ortony (ed.), *Metaphor and Thought.* Second edition, 83–111. Cambridge: Cambridge University Press.
Sinclair, John
    1991   *Corpus, Concordance, Collocation.* Oxford: Oxford University Press.
    2004   *Trust the Text: Language, Corpus and Discourse.* London: Routledge.

Keeping an eye on the data: Metonymies and their patterns*

Martin Hilpert

Abstract

This paper outlines a corpus-based method for the analysis of metonymic expressions based on a series of quantitative and qualitative analyses.

While an intuitive approach to metonymy successfully identifies lexical items which have metonymic extensions, intuition alone cannot settle the question how these extensions map onto linguistic form. Consider the expression *set all hearts on fire*, which has been claimed to instantiate the conceptual metonymy THE HEART FOR THE PERSON. Intuitively, it is hard to tell whether the quantifier *all* has something to do with the figurative interpretation. In contrast, a corpus-linguistic analysis brings to light that quantified *heart* (*some hearts, a few hearts, many hearts*) is by default interpreted metonymically. This suggests that the figurative extensions of a given lexical item correlate with distinctive patterns. These patterns are solely determinable through analysis of authentic data.

It turns out that in the investigated data, figurative usages made up more that 40% for all body lexemes; more that 65% of the data under investigation is organized in a limited array of patterns. These patterns expose a close correlation of form and meaning. Thus, collocation is a major clue to the interpretation of metonymic expressions. Furthermore, literal and non-literal examples contrast significantly with respect to neighboring word classes.

I draw four conclusions from this pilot study: Metonymy can be analyzed through corpus analysis of source domain lexis. Metonymic expressions tend to be organized in patterns – these patterns trigger a specific metonymy. Metonymic expressions differ from literal expressions with respect to collocation and with respect to colligation.

1. Introduction

Cognitive semantic investigations into metonymy have been largely based on either introspective data or examples taken from dictionaries (e.g. Lakoff 1987, Gibbs 1994). This paper outlines a corpus-based approach to the analysis of metonymy. Along with the methodology, I present a case study in which the metonymic extensions of the English lexeme *eye* are identified through corpus analysis. The analysis shows that

---

* I would like to thank Anatol Stefanowitsch for guiding me to this topic and for many stimulating discussions and Chris Taylor for discussing earlier versions of this paper with me. All remaining errors and inconsistencies are, of course, mine.

the figurative meanings of this lexeme map onto distinct linguistic *patterns* (Hunston and Francis 2000, see also Stefanowitsch, this volume). I argue that such a data-driven approach has a number of advantages over more traditional approaches.

While an intuitive approach to metonymy may identify isolated metonymic extensions of lexical items, intuition alone cannot settle the question how these extensions map onto linguistic form. Consider an example proposed by Niemeier (2000), which instantiates the conceptual metonymy THE HEART FOR THE PERSON.

(1) set all hearts on fire

Intuitively, it is hard to tell why example (1) receives the figurative interpretation it does. A corpus analysis will show that *hearts* preceded by a quantifier (*some hearts, a few hearts, many hearts*) are by default interpreted metonymically. The pattern QUANTIFIER *hearts* invariably triggers the conceptual metonymy THE HEART FOR THE PERSON.[1] The data suggest that the figurative extensions of a given lexical item correlate with fixed or semi-fixed patterns. The description of patterns has a long tradition in Corpus Linguistics (Sinclair 1991), however, its application to issues in Cognitive Linguistics is a more recent development.

Hunston and Francis (2000) define *pattern* as "all words and structures that are regularly associated with a word and contribute to its meaning". I find this definition conceptually close to the notion of *construction*, as proposed by Goldberg (1996: 68):

A construction is [...] a pairing of form with meaning/use such that some aspect of the form or some aspect of the meaning/use is not strictly predictable from the component parts or from other constructions already established to exist in the language.

Goldberg's definition is more general, but more precise at the same time. It is more general, because constructions need not be matters of words; they can exist independently of lexical material. It is more precise, because it involves the idea of non-compositionality; the meaning of the construction must be more than the meaning of its component parts. However, Goldberg's definition does not capture *collocation*, i.e. what

---

1. Note that the metonymy is embedded in the metaphor LOVE IS FIRE (Kövecses 1990:46). I do not propose that (1) is resolved as 'set everybody on fire'. Rather, the pattern resolves to 'make everybody fall in love'.

words are regularly associated with a construction.² Hunston and Francis' idea of a pattern is clearly related to frequency. Thus, I find the two definitions to complement and enrich each other with respect to the subject at hand. In accordance with Goldberg, I view patterns as constructions that mean more than their parts; in accordance with Hunston and Francis, I view patterns as frequently co-occurring strings of lexical items.

Several strains of work relate to the present analysis, while differing in their aims. Work in psycholinguistics (Gibbs 1994, Ortony et al. 1978) and work in computational linguistics (Markert and Hahn 2002, Martin, this volume) has focused on the broader linguistic context of figurative expressions. Martin (this volume) finds, for example, that if a conceptual metaphor has been used in previous discourse, it is likely that lexemes of the source domain will be used metaphorically again. Whereas Martin thus analyzes broad contextual effects, the present analysis stresses the importance of the *microcontext* of figurative expressions. By microcontext I mean both *collocation*, the adjacence of certain lexical items, and *colligation*, the adjacence of certain word classes. A similar approach has been adopted in Markert and Nissim (2002), who analyze the domain of *country names*. One of their findings is that the pattern *provide* COUNTRY *with* triggers the PLACE-FOR-PEOPLE metonymy by default. By contrast, the pattern *in* COUNTRY is always interpreted literally. In addition to Deignan's corpus research into metaphor (1999, this volume), corpus-based research into metonymy has been carried out by Deignan and Potter (2004). They report that many figurative usages of body lexis occur in semi-fixed expressions like for example *one's heart goes out to NP*.

On a more general level, the findings of the present analysis are compatible with the basic tenets of *Construction Grammar* (Fillmore 1988, Fillmore et al. 1988, Goldberg 1995, 1996) and *Cognitive Grammar* (Langacker 1987, 1991, 2002). In both frameworks, speakers' knowledge of language is viewed as a large inventory of form-meaning pairs.³ This inventory accommodates everything from morphemes to patterns of argument-structure, like the *ditransitive construction*. In between these two extremes are larger lexical chunks, such as idioms and semi-fixed expressions. These con-

---

2. A framework for the corpus-based analysis of interdependencies between words and constructions is developed in Stefanowitsch and Gries (2003) and Gries and Stefanowitsch (2004).
3. Both Construction Grammar and Cognitive Grammar are thus incompatible with a modular approach to grammar, in which the lexicon is opposed to modules for syntax, morphology, and phonology.

structions are at the center of the present analysis. A considerable share of the investigated data form patterns that mean more than just the meaning of their parts. In these patterns, the lexeme receives its metonymic extension only by virtue of the construction in which it occurs.

These findings support the claim that most figurative usages are identified through pattern analysis, rather than checking of *selection restrictions*. Pragmatic theories of figurative meaning (e.g. Searle 1979) hold that the literal meaning of an utterance is processed first. If selection restrictions are found to be violated or the utterance is inappropriate in some other way, the figurative meaning is processed in a second step. It seems a reasonable hypothesis to assume that highly entrenched patterns give the hearer enough scaffolding to process the figurative meaning directly.

The remainder of this paper is organized as follows. Section two gives a working definition of metonymy and sets up a typology of metonymic relations. Section three lays out the methodology, which will be applied to a case study of the English body lexeme *eye* in section four. Section five discusses implications of the approach and the case study.

2. Metonymy

In accordance with Lakoff and Johnson (1980), I view metonymy as a phenomenon of indirect reference in which a linguistic sign refers not to its default referent R_i, but to another referent R_j.[4] To set metonymy apart from other kinds of indirect reference such as *metaphor* or *irony*, classical rhetorics defines metonymy as an exchange of names for things that are closely related or belong together. Cognitive Linguistics captures this idea with the term *domain* (Croft 1993). Things that 'belong together' are said to be in the same cognitive domain. People's world knowledge is organized in domains. For example, people have to have knowledge of the domain 'car' to make sense of the following examples:

(2) I got myself a new *set of wheels*.
(3) *The Ford* behind me was honking violantly.
(4) *Ringo* squeezed himself into a tight space.

---

4. Metonymy is not restricted to linguistic signs, though. It is applicable to all kinds of signification processes, be they linguistic, visual, auditory or purely conceptual. See Gibbs (1999).

Items within a domain 'belong together' in different ways. In example (2), a part of the car stands for the car as a whole. In example (3), the brand name stands for the driver. In example (4), the name of the driver stands for the car. The different ways of 'belonging together' are called *contiguity relations*. A common example is PART FOR WHOLE, but there are many more. In cognitive linguistic terminology, metonymy is an *intra-domain mapping* from R_i to R_j. The referents R_i and R_j belong to the same domain, and thus stand in a contiguity relation.

Several typologies of metonymy (Stern 1931, Lakoff and Johnson 1980, Fass 1997, Kövecses and Radden 1998) present lists of contiguity relations. For the present analysis, I follow Seto (1999) in drawing a distinction between two basic types. The first type covers all contiguity relations between an *entity* and its *parts*. Contiguity relations of this kind will be called *E-Metonymies*. The second type includes contiguity relations that obtain between *categories* and *subcategories*. Such contiguity relations will be called *C-Metonymies*.[5] In short, E-Metonymies are 'part-of' relations whereas C-Metonymies are 'kind-of' relations. See Figure 1 for a taxonomy of metonymic relations which are illustrated by examples (5) to (10).

Figure 1. A taxonomy of metonymic relations

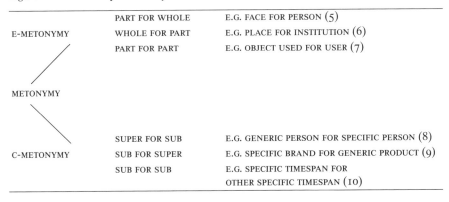

E-Metonymies

(5) We need some new **faces** around here.
(6) **Paris** is introducing longer skirts this season.
(7) **The buses** are on strike.

---

5. Seto (1999) refers to C-Metonymies by the term *synecdoche*. I will not adopt this use.

C-Metonymies
(8) Now that he's been promoted, he thinks he's really **somebody**.
(9) Could you give me some **scotch tape**?
(10) Gimme **a second**.

Although all E-Metonymies can be subsumed under three general types, the contiguity relations instantiating these types display considerable variety. The most straightforward type replaces an entity with a salient subpart of that entity, as in example (5). Also a complex whole may stand for some aspect of that whole, as in example (6). Example (7) evokes the domain of public transportation. A part of this domain, 'the buses', substitutes another, namely 'the bus drivers'. Such *domain-based E-Metonymies* are also exemplified by PART FOR PART relations like INSTRUMENT FOR ACTIVITY or CAUSE FOR EFFECT.

By necessity, C-Metonymies fall into three general types.[6] Relations between categories obtain either between supercategory and subcategory, as in examples (8) and (9), or between subcategories, as in example (10). Here, one shortish timespan stands for another shortish timespan.[7] The coarse definition of C-Metonymy as a 'kind-of' relation presents it as conceptually close to metaphor. C-Metonymies are no metaphors, because the mapping from R_i to R_j takes place within a single domain, never across domain boundaries. Of course there are borderline cases. Consider examples (11) and (12).

(11) Marcus Judge had **kept an eye on** her finances from the beginning.
(12) The drug barons work **hand in glove** with the pharmaceutical industry.

In both examples, the phrases in bold face are interpreted figuratively. Both employ 'kind-of' relations. *Keep an eye on NP* here means 'be attentive to NP', which is a hypernym of 'to watch NP'. *Hand in glove* here means 'accordant', which is a hypernym for the literal interpretation 'physically fitting'. Despite this convergence, there is one crucial difference. Whereas 'watching' and 'being attentive' belong to the same domain, 'physically fitting' and 'accordant' cannot be subsumed under a sin-

---

6. Koch (2001:217) discusses SPECIES-GENUS and SPECIES-SPECIES relations and argues that these cannot be subsumed under PART-WHOLE relations.
7. Classical rhetorics would classify example (10) as a case of *litotes*. Within the present framework, both *litotes* and *exaggeration* (e.g.: *This is gonna take **ages***) are accommodated as C-Metonymies.

gle domain, because 'physically fitting' is concrete and 'accordant' is abstract. Thus, example (11) is a C-Metonymy and example (12) is a metaphor. Metaphors can map concrete states and entities onto abstract ones, C-Metonymies cannot do so.

Another issue is *chaining* of metonymies. It has been observed that metonymies stack on top of each other.[8] A shift in reference from R_i to R_j is pushed further to R_k and beyond. From a diachronic perspective, chaining of metonymies may result in *synchronic polysemy* as well as *diachronic semantic change*. In the former, the intermediate metonymic meanings survive, in the latter, they die out. Consider Figures 2a and 2b, which show two examples from Nerlich and Clarke (2001). Whereas the successive metonymic shifts of *paper* have formed a threefold polysemy, the source sense of *barbecue* has died out.

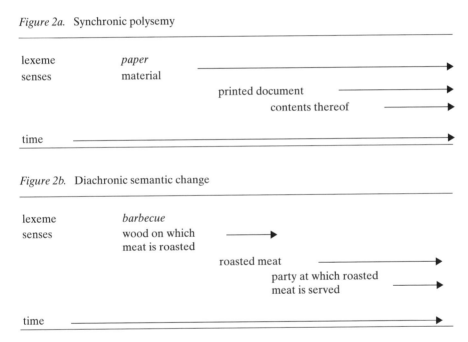

Figure 2a. Synchronic polysemy

Figure 2b. Diachronic semantic change

Corpus analysis reveals the state of synchronic polysemy at the moment of corpus compilation. Diachronic semantic change can be investigated through analysis of different historical corpora (see e.g. Goossens 1995),

---

8. Reddy (1979) must be given credit to have discovered the phenomenon. Accounts of it are in Warren (1992), Nerlich and Clarke (2001) and Ruiz de Mendoza Ibáñez and Díez Velasco (2002).

but the present analysis is restricted to the exploration of synchronic polysemy, as it draws exclusively upon corpus data from the British National Corpus. However, even the analysis of synchronic data yields some insight into chaining of metonymies. Consider examples (13) and (14).

(13) I fear probably not, said he, **keeping an eye on** the tape recorder.
(14) Marcus Judge had **kept an eye on** her finances from the beginning.

Both examples instantiate INSTRUMENT FOR ACTIVITY metonymies, but the targeted activities differ. In example (13), *keep an eye on NP* means 'watch NP'. In example (14), it means 'pay attention to NP'. Finances cannot literally be watched. This could lead the researcher to posit two different metonymies, namely EYE FOR WATCHING and EYE FOR ATTENTION. It is more parsimonious to assume a chained metonymy. The first metonymy, EYE FOR WATCHING, is extended by a second metonymy, namely WATCHING FOR ATTENTION. There are two constraints on positing chained metonymies. The first is that all intermediate steps have to be productive.[9] That is, expressions of both EYE FOR WATCHING and WATCHING FOR ATTENTION must be found in the corpus to lend credibility to the chained metonymy. The second constraint is that each metonymic link must be motivated by a strong experiential basis (Grady 1997). In the presentation of chained metonymies, the first metonymy will be said to *feed* the second. Thus in example (14), EYE FOR WATCHING feeds WATCHING FOR ATTENTION.

3. Methodology

The basic stance of a corpus-based approach to metonymy is that it puts data before theory. It is assumed that observation of large amounts of authentic data is a viable method for language description (Sinclair 1991). Hence, it is assumed that the metonymic language found in the corpus reflects on the linguistic reality of Present Day English.

The present analysis pursues two major aims. The first aim is to explore the metonymies (e.g. INSTRUMENT FOR ACTIVITY, EYE FOR WATCHING) that are found with the lexeme under investigation. Corpus analysis is not only a means to such a qualitative exploration, it also allows for quantification. The metonymies found with a lexeme can be organized in terms of their frequen-

---

9. Otherwise, the researcher could freely assume chained metonymies with extinct intermediate steps.

cy, which shows the entrenchment of a given metonymy. In sum, the first aim is to analyze the nature and entrenchment of metonymic extensions.

The second major aim is to explore the relation of form and meaning in these metonymic extensions. I will show that contiguity relations tend to map onto distinct patterns. These patterns may be fixed or semi-fixed. To illustrate, example (1), in which *hearts* are interpreted as 'people' is an instance of the pattern QUANTIFIER *hearts*. This pattern is semi-fixed, since it only specifies the lexeme *hearts*, while the quantifier may be filled by a range of different lexemes (*some, many, a few*, etc.). An example of a fixed pattern is the pattern *turn a blind eye*, which means 'to disregard'. This pattern has no unfilled slots. Patterns are identified through the analysis of concordance lines. Two kinds of regularities to the left and right of a word are observed. The first one is *collocation*, the adjacency of certain lexical items. The second one is *colligation*, the adjacency of certain word classes. The contribution of these to the meaning of the whole expression is analyzed.

These two tasks touch on several relevant issues in the current discussion of metonymy. For instance, some conceptual metonymies are conventionalized and highly systematic (e.g. EYE FOR WATCHING) whereas other conceptual metonymies seem rather ad hoc (e.g. COMPLETED ACTIVITY FOR AGENT). Example (15) illustrates the latter.

(15) Never invite two **China trips** to the same dinner party.

A corpus study will show what percentage of metonymic expressions employs conventionalized mappings. It will also reveal what percentage of metonymic expressions is accounted for by distinct patterns. Another consideration is that if metonymic language tends to be organized in patterns, this would corroborate psycholinguistic findings that context is a major clue in disambiguating polysemous lexical items (Gibbs 1994).

The procedure of the corpus analysis is organized into six steps. First, the complete concordance is categorized into literal and non-literal examples. Four corpus-based dictionaries have been used for this task.[10]

Second, the non-literal examples are searched for patterns. If a substantial number of concordance lines exhibits patterning, it is investigated whether these examples have not only a similar form, but also a similar meaning. If so, the meaning of the pattern is analyzed in detail, with reference to the conceptual metonymies. Metaphoric mappings are also discussed where they play a role in a metonymic extension.

---

10. COBAL, COBUILD, LDCE, OALD, see reference section for exact references.

Third, the non-patterning examples are analyzed in the same way. Metonymic and metaphoric mappings are explored.

Fourth, patterning and non-patterning examples are contrasted with respect to the distribution of the extensions found. I discuss whether the non-patterning examples contain extensions that are not found within any of the patterns.

Fifth comes the analysis of colligating word classes. The lexical items immediately left and right to the search term are categorized according to word class. This procedure is carried out for both the literal and the figurative concordance. The resulting paradigms are contrasted in order to determine broad structural differences in the immediate contexts of literal and figurative usages. The distribution is checked for significant differences of literal and figurative usages with the *Binomial Test*. It is discussed which patterns cause these significant differences.

Sixth, the relative distribution of all figurative extensions is analyzed.

4. Metonymic extensions of *eye*

This section deals with the metonymic extensions regularly associated with *eye*. The lexeme *eye* has been chosen because body part terms are known as a rich source of figurative meaning (Goossens 1995, Kövecses and Szabó 1996, Niemeier 2000). The primary aim is to establish what extensions are found. A secondary aim is to explore the syntactic and lexical patterns that are associated with the metonymic extensions. To this end, all usages of *eye* were extracted from a balanced 10 million word sample from the BNC.[11] The sample contains 909 usages of *eye* altogether. 443 of these (49%) convey a non-literal sense.

4.1. Figurative patterning expressions with eye

The BNC sample contains 22 patterns with *eye*. In some cases there are subpatterns with minor but distinctive differences.

(A) *keep an eye on NP*. The used dictionaries rephrase this pattern as 'watch carefully or attentively'. This definition underdetermines the meaning of the pattern in two respects.

---

11. The files used in the 10 million-word sample are F71-FYP, F98-FRK, G3U-GYY, H00-HYY, J3M-JYN.

(16) I fear probably not, said he, keeping an eye on the tape recorder trying to get ...
(17) They keep an eye on the youngsters and, with the experience ...
(18) Marcus Judge had kept an eye on her finances from the beginning.

First, the examples convey different aspects. Example (16) is durative, (17) is iterative. To *keep an eye on the youngsters* means 'watching them every now and then', but not all the time. Second, only 11 out of 54 examples have the NP slot filled by a concrete, observable object. 24 examples have it filled by a person or some other animate. The remaining 19 examples feature abstract entities, which cannot be perceived visually.

In the examples that include visual perception, the phrase *keep an eye on* maps onto 'watching'. This instantiates the INSTRUMENT FOR ACTIVITY metonymy EYE FOR WATCHING. In examples like (18), the act of visual perception is only the metonymical source for a more abstract target, namely 'attention'. This shift is achieved via a C-Metonymy. EYE FOR WATCHING feeds WATCHING FOR ATTENTION and thus the two form a chained metonymy. Watching an entity is one way of being attentive to it. Being attentive to finances involves other and more complex types of perception.

A subpattern of (A) shows an even greater affinity to abstract NPs. 6 out of 10 examples of *keep a ADJ eye on NP* involve an abstract NP.[12]

(19) ... and generally keeping a benign eye on things. In return for ...
(20) ... to keep an implacably appraising eye on them, the author ...

Another subpattern, *keep POSS eye on NP*, replaces the article with a possessive pronoun. In this pattern, 5 out of 11 examples feature concrete objects, the others feature abstract objects and animates.

(21) Take another look. Keep your eye on the paper.
(22) ... want the jury always to keep their eye on that what really is the issue ...

(B) *have (got) POSS eye on NP*. No concrete NPs are found with this pattern, which uses another chained metonymy. The first step is the same as

---

12. A question of interest is what the adjectives in this pattern actually modify. The adjectives in question are {appraising, benevolent, benign, careful, clear, close, sharp, wary, watchful}. Whereas some of these semantically modify the target concept 'attention', others like *clear*, *sharp* and *watchful* are problem cases. These adjectives seem to modify the source concept 'eye' or the attentive 'agent'.

before. Again the *eye* stands for 'watching' something via the EYE FOR WATCHING metonymy. The meaning of the pattern is that the subject 'wants the NP'. In the E-Metonymy WATCHING FOR WANTING[13] an activity that is accessible to the observer stands for a non-observable mental state.

(23) The modernizers have got their eye on a bit of the party operation
(24) I've had my eye on it for a little while. [about a cottage]
(25) Charlie had his eye on Sonia. She was a dark, broad-faced girl ...

The examples feature different kinds of 'wanting'. Example (23) conveys that the agent wants to 'do the NP'. In example (24), the agent wants to 'purchase the NP'. Example (25) conveys 'sexual interest' on the part of the agent. Six examples are found in the corpus.

(C) *with an eye on NP*. This pattern displays an ambiguity that corresponds to the stages of the chained metonymies that are at work here. First of all, the pattern denotes 'attention' via 'visual perception'. The metonymic links are analogous to (A). Second, the pattern conveys 'wanting' analogous to (B). Two examples of each type occur in the data.

(26) With an eye on a corner sign reading Park Street ...
(27) ... if you're a policeman on the beat, with an eye on promotion ...

(D) *with an eye to NP*. This pattern means 'with regard to NP'. The basic E-Metonymy is EYE FOR WATCHING. It feeds the E-Metonymy WATCHING FOR CONCERN.[14] 'Concern' as a concept is very close to 'attention', but it entails a caring attitude which is absent from 'attention'. Five examples are found.

(28) ... seems to be designed with an eye to the collective worker ...

A subpattern includes a gerund: *with an eye to V-ing NP* can be rephrased as 'with the intention of V-ing NP'. The basic E-Metonymy is the same as before. It feeds the E-Metonymy WATCHING FOR INTENDING. Again, a mental state is replaced by the activity of watching. The data contains three examples.

---

13. WATCHING FOR WANTING is a domain-based PART FOR PART metonymy, namely BEHAVIOR FOR MENTAL STATE. This metonymy is often encountered in language about emotions.
    (i) Might not St Paul or Thomas Aquinas **raise an eyebrow** at the idea that their views ...
    (ii) "Did you know?" She **bit her lip** till it hurt. "Nick did."
14. Also WATCHING FOR CONCERN is an instantiation of BEHAVIOR FOR MENTAL STATE.

(29) … for pleasure but also with an eye to acquiring property …

(E) *have an (ADJ) eye for NP*. This pattern is ambiguous. It either denotes 'having interest in NP' or 'having good perception of NP'. On the first reading, EYE FOR WATCHING feeds the E-Metonymy WATCHING FOR INTEREST, which again connects a mental state with a contiguous action. There are three examples of this in the data.

(30) … farmers who had only an eye for renewed state intervention.

On the second reading, *eye* stands for 'good perception'. The first metonymic link is EYE FOR VISION. In a second step, the interpretation is generalized to 'good perception' via a SUB FOR SUPER C-Metonymy. Vision is the most reliable human faculty of perception, which licenses the VISION FOR GOOD PERCEPTION metonymy. Besides the five genuine examples of this pattern, there are two subpatterns. *POSS ADJ eye for NP* and *with an eye for NP* occur in two examples each.

(31) She already had an eye for such things. The furniture was a trifle …
(32) … my keen eye for spotting talent, where others see only …
(33) With an eye for contemporary styling, Verity Lambert agreed …

(F) *turn a blind eye to NP*. This pattern means that the subject 'disregards NP'. Most examples have some authority tolerate illegality. Ten examples are found in the data. In contexts where the issue is given, the pattern can be used intransitively. Six examples of *turn a blind eye* are found.

(34) The Waco sheriff habitually turned a blind eye to Koresh's activities.
(35) The sergeant'll turn a blind eye.

A possible line of explanation for this idiom is the KNOWING IS SEEING metaphor (Lakoff et al. 1991). Deliberately averting the eyes maps onto 'self-induced ignorance'. However, I suggest a different analysis. A range of patterns has the *eye* stand for 'attention', in pattern (D) *eye* stands for 'concern'. In this pattern *a blind eye* stands for 'non-attention', that is, 'disregard'. The basic metonymy is EYE FOR WATCHING. It feeds the PART FOR PART E-Metonymy NON-WATCHING FOR DISREGARD. This analysis has the advantage that the 'focusing of attention' (or, for that matter, non-attention) actually is a deliberate activity, whereas 'knowing' is not. The motivations for disregarding something are manifold and thus not part of the semantics of the pattern.

(G) *catch POSS eye.* If something catches someone's eye, it makes her or him 'look' at it and, in a second step, 'be attentive to it'. This can be performed by people, but also by inanimate objects. The conceptual metonymy is EYE FOR WATCHING. As the pattern codes 'attention' in a majority of cases, EYE FOR WATCHING regularly feeds WATCHING FOR ATTENTION. 34 matches are found in the data. 19 of them display possessive pronouns, the remaining 15 have full nominals. A subpattern is *catch the eye of NP.* Four examples are found. Two other subpatterns generalize the atttraction of the subject, they are *catch the eye* and *eye-catching* respectively. Three and two examples are found in the corpus.

(36) A detail on the screen had caught his eye.
(37) ... slowly around the table to catch the eye of those present ...
(38) ... considerations of what catches the eye and how much it will cost
(39) ... crimson flowers which are really eye-catching ...

(H) *in / out of the public eye.* Also this pattern maps the *eye* onto 'attention' via the chained metonymy outlined with patterns (A) and (B). The adjective thus literally modifies 'attention'. The prepositions *in / out of* indicate the relation that applies between some entity and public attention.

(40) ... pleasures were always in the public eye. And he was ready ...
(41) So you wanted to keep out of the public eye, did you?

12 matches are found. Another seven examples, albeit without article and preposition, are found of *Public Eye* denoting a journalistic TV series. This has most probably originated from a pun on *private eye* (see below), since the task of a journalistic serial is to investigate issues of public interest.

(I) *private eye.* This is an idiomatic expression for 'a privately hired detective'. The metonymic motivation, though dead, is straight-forward. *Eye* maps onto 'vision' via the PART FOR PART E-Metonymy EYE FOR VISION.[15] 'Vision' maps onto 'investigation' in a PART FOR WHOLE E-Metonymy. Finally, 'investigation' maps onto 'someone who investigates' via ACTIVITY FOR AGENT. There is just one example in the data, but the expression

---

15. This E-Metonymy is an instantiation of the more general BODY PART FOR FACULTY.
    (i) Before I could consciously turn **my brain** to the matter, it had started.
    (ii) He has a **very good ear for profit** as well. [about a Ferengi]

is well documented in the used dictionaries. 11 matches refer to the satire magazine *Private Eye*. Six more matches refer to the magazine only by *the Eye* with capital E.

(42)   If I was some fucking private eye or something I'd head back out ...
(43)   ... to the satirical magazine Private Eye – and he was partly right

(J) *in POSS mind's eye*. This pattern means 'in POSS imagination' through the EYE FOR VISION metonymy. Even though the mind does not see anything, seeing human beings experience mental imagery as visual perception. 16 examples occur in the data, two more examples replace the possessive pronoun with a definite article.

(44)   ... never seen that scene in your mind's eye, it may well be ...
(45)   ... reconstruct the police post in the mind's eye, a small building, tin-roofed ...

(K) *see eye to eye*. This pattern denotes 'agreement'. The idiom is based on the metaphor OPINIONS ARE VIEWPOINTS.[16] The item *eye* retains its literal meaning in this pattern, the metaphorical meaning emerges only at the phrasal level. People who *see eye to eye* have complementary viewpoints and hence, metaphorically speaking, complementary opinions. Six matches are found.

(46)   But then those two don't see eye to eye about anything these days.

(L) *N to the eye*. Here, the *eye* stands for 'the beholder'. The metonymic link is EYE FOR BEHOLDER, which is a case of the more general BODY PART FOR PERSON metonymy. Three instances are found in the corpus.

(47)   They function as a diversion to the eye, and give an air of elegant business ...

(M) *ADJ to the eye*. This pattern is similar to (L). The metonymic link is EYE FOR BEHOLDER. Two examples occur in the data.

---

16. OPINIONS ARE VIEWPOINTS is a productive conceptual metaphor.
    (i) Try to see it *my way*.
    (ii) Art historians Donna R. Barnes and Peter G. Rose present new *perspectives* on still life scenes.

(48) ... a sweet view – sweet to the eye and the mind.

(N) *to the ADJ eye*. The same metonymic link as in (L) and (M) applies. Four examples come up in the corpus.

(49) ... as lanisticola looked, to the discerning eye, quite different ...

(O) *under the eye of NP*. This pattern means 'under the supervision of NP'. The EYE FOR WATCHING metonymy feeds WATCHING FOR SUPERVISING which instantiates the more general ACT FOR COMPLEX ACT metonymy. 'Watching' is a necessary part of 'supervision', but 'advice' and 'control' are of equal importance. In this mapping, an activity that involves mental states is replaced by a salient body part that is involved in the central part of the activity. Six examples occur in the data. One additional example occurs in a context where the NP is given. The ensuing pattern is *under POSS eye*.

(50) ... worked on model ships under the eye of Uncle Philip ...

(P) *the apple of DET/POSS eye*. In the original metaphor behind this idiom, the *apple* refers to the 'pupil'. Folk wisdom has it that a person's most cherished person or thing can be seen in the pupil. Thus, the metaphor is carried on metonymically. The *pupil* stands for a 'person or thing depicted on it'. The DEPICTION FOR DEPICTED metonymy, which is a PART FOR PART relation, has turned opaque. Five matches are found.

(51) ... whose wife thought him the apple of her eye ...

(Q) *V DET/POSS eye over NP*. The meaning of the expression is 'scanning the NP'. The V slot in this pattern is typically filled by *cast* or *run*. The metonymy is EYE FOR WATCHING. Five examples are found:

(52) ... was casting an eye over blonde girls from Sweden ...

(R) *one eye on NP*. This pattern codes that someone is 'paying attention to NP', albeit not the undivided attention, hence only *one* eye. The same metonymies as in (A)–(C) are at work. Accordingly, the pattern may merge for example with (A), as in example (53). Five examples occur in the data.

(53)   ... simultaneously trying to keep one eye on Deirdre ...

(S) *there BE more to NP than meets the eye.* This is said if one suspects 'more than is readily perceivable'. The *eye* maps onto 'vision' in an EYE FOR VISION metonymy. Since the pattern is used with abstract topics, 'vision' is broadened to 'perception' in the C-Metonymy VISION FOR PERCEPTION (cf. pattern [E]). Three examples are in the data.

(54)   ... something more to this than meets the eye.

(T) *black eye.* In this pattern, the adjective does not indicate the colour of the *eye*, but the darkish colour of 'the surrounding region'. This is a PART FOR PART metonymy. Five examples occur in the corpus.

(55)   I knew the source of Jean-Claude's black eye and bruises.

(U) *NP in POSS eye.* This pattern describes 'facial expression'. The metonymic link is EYE FOR EXPRESSION, a case of INSTRUMENT FOR ACTIVITY. The data contains eight matches. Three further examples run *NP COME into POSS eye.*

(56)   ... said Uncle Albert with a twinkle in his eye.
(57)   A gleam came into his eye.

(V) *eye contact.* The used dictionaries define *contact* as 'a state of touching, meeting or communicating'. 'Watching' is one means of achieving this state The EYE FOR WATCHING metonymy is employed. 46 examples occur in the data.

(58)   She had always associated eye contact with frankness; ...

Table 1 summarizes the observed patterns and their metonymies and metaphors.

140 *Martin Hilpert*

Table 1. The patterns of *eye*

	PATTERN	MEANING	METONYMIC / METAPHORICAL LINKS	TOKENS
(A)	keep an eye on NP	'pay attention to NP'	EYE FOR WATCHING WATCHING FOR ATTENTION	56
	keep a ADJ eye on NP	'pay attention to NP'	EYE FOR WATCHING WATCHING FOR ATTENTION	10
	keep POSS eye on NP	'pay attention to NP'	EYE FOR WATCHING WATCHING FOR ATTENTION	11
(B)	have POSS eye on NP	'want NP'	EYE FOR WATCHING WATCHING FOR WANTING	6
(C)	with an eye on NP	'pay attention to NP'	EYE FOR WATCHING WATCHING FOR ATTENTION	2
		'want NP'	EYE FOR WATCHING WATCHING FOR WANTING	2
(D)	with an eye to NP	'with concern for NP'	EYE FOR WATCHING WATCHING FOR CONCERN	5
	with an eye to V-ing NP	'with the intention of V-ing NP'	EYE FOR WATCHING WATCHING FOR INTENDING	3
(E)	have an eye for NP	'have interest in NP'	EYE FOR WATCHING WATCHING FOR INTEREST	3
		'have good perception of NP'	EYE FOR VISION VISION FOR GOOD PERCEPTION	5
	POSS ADJ eye for NP	'good perception of NP'	EYE FOR VISION VISION FOR GOOD PERCEPTION	2
	with an eye for NP	'good perception of NP'	EYE FOR VISION VISION FOR GOOD PERCEPTION	2
(F)	turn a blind eye to NP	'disregard NP'	EYE FOR WATCHING NONWATCHING FOR DISREGARD	11
	turn a blind eye	'disregard something'	EYE FOR WATCHING NONWATCHING FOR DISREGARD	6
(G)	catch POSS eye	'attract POSS looks'	EYE FOR WATCHING	34
	catch the eye of NP	'attract the looks of NP'	EYE FOR WATCHING	4
	catch the eye	'attract looks'	EYE FOR WATCHING	3
	eye-catching	'attracting looks'	EYE FOR WATCHING	2
(H)	PREP the public eye	'PREP the public attention'	EYE FOR WATCHING WATCHING FOR ATTENTION	12
	Public Eye	'TV series'	—	7

(Table 1 contd.)

	PATTERN	MEANING	METONYMIC / METAPHORICAL LINKS	TOKENS
(I)	*private eye*	'private investigator'	EYE FOR VISION VISION FOR INVESTIGATION ACTIVITY FOR AGENT	1
	Private Eye	'magazine'	—	11
	the Eye	'magazine'	—	6
(J)	*in POSS mind's eye*	'in POSS imagination'	EYE FOR VISION	16
	in the mind's eye	'in the imagination'	EYE FOR VISION	2
(K)	*see eye to eye*	'agree'	OPINIONS ARE VIEWPOINTS	7
(L)	*N to the eye*	'N to the beholder'	EYE FOR BEHOLDER	3
(M)	*ADJ to the eye*	'ADJ to the beholder'	EYE FOR BEHOLDER	2
(N)	*to the ADJ eye*	'to the ADJ beholder'	EYE FOR BEHOLDER	4
(O)	*under the eye of NP*	'under observation of NP'	EYE FOR WATCHING WATCHING FOR SUPERVISING	6
	under POSS eye	'under POSS observation'	EYE FOR WATCHING WATCHING FOR SUPERVISION	1
(P)	*the apple of DET/POSS eye*	'cherished object'	DEPICTION FOR DEPICTED	5
(Q)	*V DET/POSS eye over NP*	'scan NP'	EYE FOR WATCHING	5
(R)	*one eye on NP*	'pay some attention to NP'	EYE FOR WATCHING WATCHING FOR ATTENTION	5
(S)	*there BE more to NP than meets the eye*	'there BE more to NP than is readily perceivable'	EYE FOR VISION VISION FOR PERCEPTION	3
(T)	*black eye*	'discoloured eye region'	PART FOR PART	5
(U)	*NP in POSS eye*	'NP in POSS expression'	EYE FOR EXPRESSION	8
	NP COME into POSS eye	'NP enter POSS expression'	EYE FOR EXPRESSION	3
(V)	*eye contact*	'visual contact'	EYE FOR WATCHING	46

4.2. Non-patterning expressions with *eye*

The patterns discussed in the previous section account for 323 of the 443 examples. That leaves a rest of 120 examples, which equals 27% of the figurative data. Figure 3 contrasts the distribution of senses in the patterning and the non-patterning figurative examples in absolute numbers.

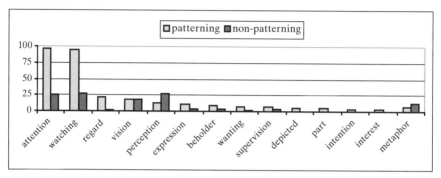

Figure 3. Distribution of figurative senses in patterning and non-patterning expressions with eye

The non-patterning examples do not convey any new senses that are absent from the patterning data. Despite this convergence, the distribution of senses displays some differences. Paramount in the patterning examples are 'attention' and 'watching', which is brought about by the high frequency of the patterns (A) and (V) respectively. Dominant in the non-patterning expressions are the readings 'attention', 'watching' and 'perception'. There are more non-patterning than patterning metaphorical examples. Metaphorical readings often read *eye of NP*. They display different uses of the *NP of NP-construction*.

(59) ... thread that could tower to the silver eye of the moon ...
(60) ... she is, to begin with, the seeing eye of the story ...

Example (59) conveys identity of the two NPs, much as *the state of Texas*. Example (60) codes a participant–event relation between the NPs. A similar example would be *the organizers of the conference*.

4.3. Colligates of literal and figurative usages of *eye*

This section establishes which word classes occur immediately next to *eye* in running text. This will allow us to contrast literal and figurative usages in broader terms. Figures 4a and 4b are based on 466 literal usages and 443 figurative usages of *eye* from the 10 million word BNC sample. The distribution is given in percentages, probability of error is computed with the binomial test.

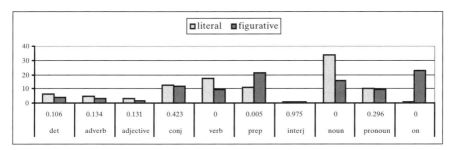

Figure 4a. Distribution of right-side colligates of literal and figurative usages of *eye*

4.3.1. Right-side colligates of literal and figurative usages

Four differences emerge. Literal usages of *eye* significantly more often take verbs and nouns as right-side colligates. The verbs *be* and *have* are responsible for this tendency. With respect to nouns it can be stated that literal *eye* is more often used in compounds (*eye drops*, *eye movements*) than figurative *eye*. The compound *eye contact* accounts for 46 of the 74 examples in which figurative *eye* is followed by a noun, other compounds are rare. As a third differing word class, prepositions encourage figurative interpretation, the preposition *on* particularly so. I list it seperately here, because the structure *eye on* has only very rarely a literal interpretation. Taken together with the other prepositions, figurative *eye* is followed by a preposition in 43.5% of all cases.

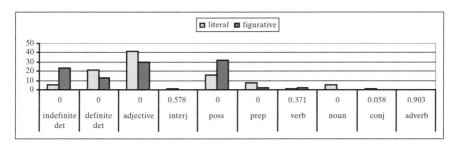

Figure 4b. Distribution of left-side colligates of literal and figurative usages of *eye*

4.3.2. Left-side colligates of literal and figurative usages

The left-side colligates are split into six highly significant and four non-significant classes. Indefinite determiners indicate figurative interpretation (*an eye for design*), conversely definite determiners indicate literal interpretation (*around the eye*). Adjectives modify literal usages of *eye* more often than figurative usages, more frequent than *left* and *right* are in fact technical adjectives like *compound* and *lateral*. Possessives encourage figurative interpretation (*catch her eye*). Prepositions are found significantly more often to the left of literal *eye*, which is due to the preposition *of* (*measurement of eye movements*). Finally, nouns are almost never found to the left of figurative usages of *eye*.

4.4. The senses of *eye*

Thirteen metonymic extensions emerge from the data. Taken together, the first two of these account for 54.6% of the concordance. The first sense maps *eye* onto the activity of 'watching' (*eye contact*), the second maps it onto 'attention' (*keep an eye on him*). The first sense is achieved via the EYE FOR WATCHING metonymy alone, in the second sense EYE FOR WATCHING feeds WATCHING FOR ATTENTION. Either sense accounts for 27.3% of the concordance. *Eye* denotes 'concern' (*with an eye to workers' interests*) via another chained metonymy. Here, EYE FOR WATCHING feeds WATCHING FOR CONCERN. *Eye* refers to the faculty of 'vision' (*a sharp eye*) via the EYE FOR VISION metonymy. The EYE FOR VISION metonymy regularly feeds VISION FOR PERCEPTION which yields the sense of general 'perception' (*my eye for spotting talent*).

Each of the remaining eight senses constitutes less than 2.5% of the overall concordance. *Eye* means facial 'expression' via the EYE FOR EXPRESSION metonymy (*a twinkle in his eye*). *Eye* refers to the 'beholder' via the EYE FOR BEHOLDER metonymy (*pleasant to the eye*). *Eye* triggers the sense of 'wanting' by a chained metonymy. EYE FOR WATCHING feeds WATCHING FOR WANTING (*he had his eye on it*). A body part stands for an activity which stands for a contiguous mental state. *Eye* refers to 'supervision' by a similar chained metonymy. EYE FOR WATCHING feeds WATCHING FOR SUPERVISING (*under the eye of uncle Philip*). The idiom *the apple of my eye* involves a fossilized DEPICTION FOR DEPICTED metonymy. *Eye* refers to its 'surroundings' via a PART FOR PART metonymy (*black eye*). *Eye* also has the meaning of 'intending' via another chained metonymy. EYE FOR WATCHING feeds WATCHING FOR INTENDING (*with an eye to acquiring property*). Similarly, *eye* denotes 'interest'. EYE FOR WATCHING feeds WATCHING FOR INTEREST (*they had an eye for renewed state intervention*). Metaphorical extensions of *eye* rely on metaphors like

THE CENTER IS THE EYE (*the eye of the storm*) or involve the metaphor OPINIONS ARE VIEWPOINTS (*see eye to eye*). See Figure 5 for the distribution of the different senses in absolute numbers.

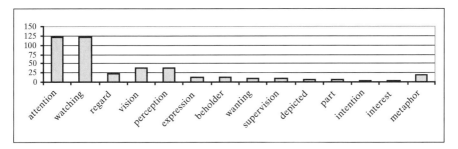

Figure 5. Distribution of senses in figurative expressions with *eye*

Worth discussing is that 49% of the concordance examples display a figurative meaning. This figure matches the finding of Deignan and Potter (2004) that figurative meaning is very common with another English body lexeme, namely *heart*. On a more general level, this underlines the importance of body concepts in human conceptualization (Lakoff and Johnson 1999). If people really conceptualize abstract things in terms of the human body, there should be quantitative evidence for this.

A second issue is that 72.9% of the figurative examples are patterning. This corroborates findings that fixed and semi-fixed expressions are a major part of the lexicon (Barlow 1996, Partington 1998). All metonymic extensions are contained in the patterns, the non-patterning examples do not add to the range of meanings. Many patterns allow for some variety, that is, intervening adjectives or the replacement of a determiner by a possessive pronoun are accommodated. Function words play a decisive role in the discussed patterns. Whereas there are also lexically filled patterns such as *catch the eye*, patterns such as *with an eye to NP* rely on prepositions only. Most patterns feature a preposition to the right of *eye*. This leaves its mark on the right-side colligates. A preposition on the right is an indicator of figurative meaning. The preposition *on* has a special status, since it indicates figurative meaning with a chance of more than 97%. All in all, patterning seems a very robust guide to figurative meaning.

Another topic brought up by the data is chaining of metonymies. All observed chained metonymies have EYE FOR WATCHING at the basis, which has a strong experiential basis and is by far the most entrenched contiguity relation in the data. EYE FOR WATCHING feeds both C-Metonymies (e.g. WATCHING FOR ATTENTION) and E-Metonymies (e.g WATCHING FOR SUPERVISION).

Lastly, very few metaphorical examples (2.7%) are found. This is due to the fact that body parts such as *eye* are first and foremost conceptualized as instruments that map onto contiguous activities. *Eye* thus lends itself easily to conceptual metonymy, but less easily to metaphor.

These findings have important consequences for a cognitive theory of metonymy. Current theory assumes that metonymy is a conceptual tool that enables people to understand non-literal language. Contiguity relations like INSTRUMENT FOR ACTIVITY have the status of memorized problem-solving strategies that are applied when we hear expressions like *under the eye of Uncle Philip*.

On a pragmatic account of metonymy, this expression should be understood in a three-step procedure. First, the expression must be understood literally. Since the literal reading is nonsensical, a fitting metonymy must be chosen in a second step. Third, the metonymy must be applied, so that *eye*, sent through EYE FOR WATCHING and WATCHING FOR ATTENTION, yields 'attention'.

The present analysis suggests a different theory. Since the different metonymic extensions of *eye* occur within fixed or semi-fixed patterns, the microcontext of the lexeme gives hearers enough scaffolding to understand the intended meaning *directly*. That is, the metonymies EYE FOR WATCHING and WATCHING FOR ATTENTION have given rise to the expression *under the eye of NP*, but it seems highly unlikely that hearers re-process them on every occasion.

To be sure, on-line processing of metonymic language occurs. However, it seems to be restricted to unconventionalized, ad hoc cases of metonymy like *Never invite two China trips to the same dinner party*, which are found very rarely in the data. Much more frequent are cases of systematic metonymy. The extensions in the patterns form metonymic networks. For example, the polysemy of *eye* extends first to *watching*, and from there to *wanting, attention, concern*, and so on. The idea that polysemy is motivated along the lines of metaphor and metonymy is one of the basic tenets of Cognitive Linguistics (Lakoff 1987, Sweetser 1990). Work on polysemy in the cognitive tradition has largely focused on metaphor, whereas other approaches have put the role of metonymy center stage in their discussion of systematic polysemy (Nunberg 1995). In the investigated data, systematic extensions vastly outnumber ad hoc metonymies.

The fact that most figurative language is organized in patterns and can be described as systematic polysemy casts doubt onto purely pragmatic theories of metonymy (e.g. Searle 1979). It must be assumed that ad hoc metonymies, as special and comparatively rare cases, are resolved pragmatically, whereas systematic metonymies are resolved via pattern clues.

Metonymic expressions like *under the eye of NP* have entered the lexicon as constructions and are thus a matter of semantics. The present analysis thus suggests a *construction-based* account of metonymy interpretation. Figurative usages of the lexical concepts under investigation get their non-literal meaning only by virtue of their immediate context. These contexts have to be learned, since the meaning of a pattern does not build up from its parts. The meaning of the observed patterns is motivated by the conceptual metonymy, but it is not fully predictable. For example, it is motivated that the expressions *keep an eye on NP* and *have an eye on NP* should refer to 'paying attention'. Being attentive to something regularly involves watching it. However, it is not predictable, why *have an eye on NP* can in some cases refer to 'wanting NP', whereas *keep an eye on NP* can only refer to 'paying attention'.

A construction-based account of metonymy has the advantage that it does not rely on *selection restrictions*. Pragmatic theories of metonymy comprehension assume that hearers compute the literal meaning of the words they hear and resort to a figurative interpretation if a selection restriction is violated.[17] Example (61) illustrates such a case. Ham sandwiches cannot literally wait for their checks. However, some metonymies do not violate selection restrictions. See example (62):

(61) The ham sandwich is waiting for his check.
(62) I didn't see eye to eye with him.

People can literally *see eye to eye*. However, the pattern is never used in this way. Instead of relying on selection restrictions alone, a robust account of metonymy comprehension must take collocation into account.

I hope to have shown that corpus linguistic methodology can be fruitfully applied to the analysis of figurative language. Keeping an eye on the data seems a promising strategy for future research into conceptual metaphor and metonymy.

---

17. This hypothesis, which has been dubbed the *Literal-Meaning-First-Hypothesis*, has come under the severe criticism of psycholinguists (Gibbs 1994) and computational linguists (Hahn and Markert 1997).

References

Barlow, Michael
  1996   Corpora for theory and practice. *International Journal of Corpus Linguistics* 1: 1–37.

BNC
  1995   The British National Corpus (Version 1.0). Oxford University Computing Services for the BNC Consortium. Oxford: Oxford University.

COBAL
  2001   Collins COBUILD English Dictionary for Advanced Learners. Third edition. London: Harper Collins.

COBUILD
  1987   Collins COBUILD English Language Dictionary. London: Collins.

Croft, William
  1993   The role of domains in the interpretation of metaphors and metonymies. *Cognitive Linguistics* 4: 219–256.

Deignan, Alice
  1999   Corpus-based research into metaphor. In Lynne Cameron and Graham Low (eds.), *Researching and Applying Metaphor*, 177–199. Cambridge: Cambridge University Press.

Deignan, Alice and Liz Potter
  2004   A corpus study of metaphors and metonyms in English and Italian. *Journal of Pragmatics* 36: 1231–1252.

Fass, Dan C.
  1997   *Processing Metonymy and Metaphor*. Greenwich CT: Ablex.

Fillmore, Charles J.
  1988   The mechanisms of Construction Grammar. *Proceedings of the Fourteenth Annual Meeting of the Berkeley Linguistics Society*, 35–55.

Fillmore, Charles J., Paul Kay and Catherine O'Connor
  1988   Regularity and idiomaticity in grammatical constructions: The case of Let Alone." *Language* 64: 510–538.

Gibbs, Raymond W.
  1994   *The Poetics of Mind*. Cambridge: Cambridge University Press.
  1999   Speaking and thinking with metonymy. In: Klaus-Uwe Panther and Günter Radden (eds.), *Metonymy in language and thought*, 61–76. Amsterdam: John Benjamins.

Goldberg, Adele E.
  1995   *Constructions: A Construction Grammar Approach to Argument Structure*. Chicago: The University of Chicago Press.
  1996   Construction grammar. In: Keith Brown and Jim Miller (eds.), *Concise Encyclopedia of Syntactic Theories*, 68–71. Oxford: Pergamon.

Goossens, Louis
  1995   From three respectable horses' mouths. Metonymy and conventionalization in a diachronically differentiated database. In: Louis Goossens, Paul Pauwels, Brygida Rudzka-Ostyn, Anne-Marie Simon-Vandenbergen and Johan Vanparys (eds.), *By Word of Mouth: Metaphor, Metonymy and Linguistic Action in a Cognitive Perspective*, 175–204, Amsterdam: John Benjamins.

Grady, Joseph
1997 THEORIES ARE BUILDINGS revisited. *Cognitive Linguistics* 8: 267–290.
Gries, Stefan Th. and Anatol Stefanowitsch
2004 Extending collostructional analysis: a corpus-based perspective on 'alternations'. *International Journal of Corpus Linguistics* 9: 97–129.
Hahn, Udo and Katja Markert
1997 In support of the equal rights movement for literal and figurative language – A parallel search and preferential search model." *Proceedings of the 19th Annual Conference of the Cognitive Science Society*, 609–614.
Hunston, Susan and Gill Francis
2000 *Pattern Grammar*. Amsterdam: John Benjamins.
Koch, Peter
2001 Metonymy. Unity in diversity. *Journal of Historical Pragmatics* 2: 201–244.
Kövecses, Zoltán
1990 *Emotion Concepts*. New York: Springer.
Kövecses, Zoltán and Günter Radden
1998 Metonymy: Developing a cognitive linguistic view. *Cognitive Linguistics* 9: 37–77.
Kövecses, Zoltán and Peter Szabó
1996 Idioms: A view from Cognitive Linguistics. *Applied Linguistics* 17: 326–355.
Lakoff, George
1987 *Women, Fire and Dangerous Things*. Chicago: University of Chicago Press.
Lakoff, George and Mark Johnson
1980 *Metaphors We Live By*. Chicago: The University of Chicago Press.
1999 *Philosophy in the Flesh*. New York: Basic Books.
Lakoff, Georg, Jane Espenson and Alan Schwartz
1991 *Master Metaphor List*. Second edition. Berkeley: University of California at Berkeley.
Langacker, Ronald W.
1987 *Foundations of Cognitive Grammar*. Vol. I. *Theoretical Prerequisites*. Stanford: Stanford University Press.
1991 *Foundations of Cognitive Grammar*. Vol. II. *Descriptive Application*. Stanford: Stanford University Press.
2002 *Concept, Image and Symbol*. Second edition. Berlin and New York: Mouton de Gruyter.
LDCE
1995 Longman Dictionary of Contemporary English. Third edition. Harlow: Longman. [LDCE]
Markert, Katja and Udo Hahn
2002 Understanding metonymies in discourse. *Artificial Intelligence* 135: 145–198.

Markert, Katja and Malvina Nissim
2002   Metonymy resolution as a classification task. Paper presented at the *2002 Conference on Empirical Methods in Natural Language Processing* (EMNLP). Pennsylvania, PA.

Martin, James H.
This volume   A corpus-based analysis of context effects on metaphor comprehension.

Nerlich, Brigitte and David D. Clarke
2001   Serial metonymy: A study of reference-based polysemisation. *Journal of Historical Pragmatics* 2: 245–272.

Niemeier, Susanne
2000   Straight from the heart – metonymic and metaphorical explorations." In: Antonio Barcelona (ed.), *Metaphor and Metonymy at the Crossroads. A Cognitive Perspective*, 195–213. Berlin and New York: Mouton de Gruyter.

Nunberg, Geoffrey D.
1995   Transfers of meaning. *Journal of Semantics* 1: 109–132.

OALD
1989   Oxford Advanced Learner's Dictionary. Fourth edition. Oxford: OUP.

Ortony, Andrew, Diane L. Schallert, Ralph E. Reynolds and Stephen J. Antos
1978   Interpreting metaphors and idioms: Some effects of context on comprehension. *Journal of Verbal Learning and Verbal Behavior* 17: 465–477.

Partington, Alan
1998   *Patterns and Meanings*. Amsterdam: John Benjamins.

Reddy, Michael J.
1979   The Conduit Metaphor: A case of frame conflict in our language about language. In: Andrew Ortony (ed.), *Metaphor and Thought*, 164–201. Cambridge: Cambridge University Press.

Ruiz de Mendoza Ibañez, Francisco J. and Olga I. Dièz Velasco
2002   Patterns of conceptual interaction. In: Ralf Pörings and René Dirven (eds.), *Metaphor and Metonymy in Comparison and Contrast*, 501–546. Berlin & New York: Mouton de Gruyter.

Searle, John R.
1979   Metaphor. In: Andrew Ortony (ed.), *Metaphor and Thought*, 92–123. Cambridge: Cambridge University Press.

Seto, Ken-Ichi
1999   Distinguishing metonymy from synecdoche. In: Klaus-Uwe Panther and Günther Radden (eds.), *Metonymy in Language and Thought*, 255–273. Amsterdam: John Benjamins.

Sinclair, John
1991   *Corpus, Concordance, Collocation*. Oxford: Oxford University Press.

Stefanowitsch, Anatol
This volume   Words and their metaphors: A corpus-based approach.

Stefanowitsch, Anatol and Stefan Th. Gries
2003   Collostructions: investigating the interaction of words and constructions. *International Journal of Corpus Linguistics* 8: 209–243.

Stern, Gustaf
   1965 [1931]   *Meaning and Change of Meaning.* Bloomington: Indiana University Press.
Sweetser, Eve
   1990   *From Etymology to Pragmatics.* Cambridge: Cambridge University Press.
Warren, Beatrice
   1992   *Sense Developments.* Stockholm: Almqvist and Wiksell.

Metonymic proper names: A corpus-based account

Katja Markert and *Malvina Nissim*

Abstract

Many proper names are widely used metonymically. Thus, for example, organisation names can be used for products produced by the organisation, members of an organisation or events associated with the organisation. The treatment of metonymic proper names is crucial for many natural language processing tasks like question answering and anaphora resolution. At the moment, language resources do not contain the necessary information for large-scale metonymy processing.

As a contribution, we describe a general framework for annotating metonymies in domainindependent text that considers the regularity, productivity and underspecification of metonymic usage. We will then concentrate on two fully worked out annotation schemes for location and organisation names and rigorously evaluate these schemes as to their reliability. We also present a gold standard corpus consisting of 4000 annotated occurrences of location and organisation names in the British National Corpus. We use this corpus to examine the distribution of metonymies as well as for experiments in automatic metonymy resolution.

1. Introduction

Metonymy is a form of figurative speech, in which one expression is used to refer to the standard referent of a related one (Lakoff and Johnson 1980).

In Example (1), which is taken from the British National Corpus (BNC, (Burnard 1995)), *Vietnam*, the name of a location, refers to an event (a war) that happened there.[1]

(1) at the time of *Vietnam*, increased spending led to inflation and a trade deficit.

This type of reference shift is very systematic, in that it can occur with any location name, as long as the discourse participants are aware of an event associated with it. For this reason, linguistic studies (Stern 1931, Lakoff and Johnson 1980, Fass 1997) have postulated conventionalised *metonymic patterns* (for example, PLACE-FOR-EVENT) that operate on *semantic*

---

[1]. All examples in this paper are taken from the British National Corpus with the exception of Examples (3), (4), (5), and (31).

classes (here, LOCATION). Simlarly, the usage of *BP* in Example (2) to refer to BP's quotation index is possible for all companies whose index floats in the stock market.

(2) *BP* fell a penny to 307p.

Such regular shifts have also been called *regular polysemy* (Apresjan 1973, Peters and Wilks 2003), or *sense extension* (Copestake and Briscoe 1995). In this paper we will use the term (conventional) metonymy interchangeably with these terms.

Beside such regular shifts, metonymies can also be created on the fly: In Example (3), *seat 19* refers to the person occupying seat 19.[2] We call such occurrences *unconventional* metonymies.

(3) Ask *seat 19* whether he wants to swap.

Apart from being often regular and productive, metonymy is also frequent. For example, Markert and Hahn (2002) found a metonymy in 17% of all utterances in a corpus of 27 German magazine texts; our corpus studies reported in this paper show that about 20% of all occurrences of country names, and about 30% of all occurrences of company names are metonymic. Therefore, metonymy has generated considerable interest in linguistics, lexicography, and in natural language processing (NLP).

Interest in NLP mainly stems from the fact that metonymy resolution can improve many language engineering tasks. Stallard (1993) cited a 27% performance improvement by incorporating metonymy resolution into a question answering system about a limited domain (commercial air flights), which had to understand metonymies such as *Which **wide body jets** serve dinner?* Anaphora resolution, a crucial task in many NLP applications, often depends on metonymy recognition as well (Markert and Hahn 2002, Harabagiu 1998). For example, *he* is anaphoric to *seat 19* in Example (3); also, in Example (4) from the Washington Post (Sunday 28.10.2001), coreference can be established only if *China* and *Beijing* are recognised as metonymies for the government of China.

(4) *China* has agreed to let a United Nations investigator conduct an independent probe into [...] But it was unclear whether *Beijing* would meet past UN demands for unrestricted access to [...]

---

2. Example (3) was actually uttered by a flight attendant on a plane.

Up to now, however, most studies in linguistics and NLP have run into limitations mainly due to the lack of an objective comprehensive characterisation of the phenomenon in real occurring texts. Indeed, the main language resources do not provide sufficient data about metonymy that could serve as a basis for large-scale testing of linguistic theories or NLP algorithms on naturally occurring texts.

In the linguistic tradition, most studies on metonymy, including example lists, are based mainly on linguistic intuition, instead of corpus studies, and are often constucted to make a particular point of interest (Stern 1931, Lakoff and Johnson 1980, Pustejovsky 1995). Therefore, such studies are only illustrated by small sets of especially selected and/or constructed examples, cover only a limited range of what might be encountered in real-world texts and do not necessarily provide an accurate picture of the actual distribution of phenomena. Also, the authors favour giving clear-cut examples, thus obscuring the fact that the literal/metonymic distinction might be hard to make reliably in practice.

Dictionaries necessarily include only conventional metonymic senses, whereas metonymies are open-ended, as Example (3) shows. But even conventional metonymic senses are often not included systematically. So "UK", e.g., has one sense in WordNet (Fellbaum 1998), the country, whereas "United States" has the additional metonymic sense "government of the US", which is clearly available for "UK" as well. Even if literal and metonymic senses are both included they are listed as unrelated entries and the metonymic relationship between them is not expressed. Older versions of WordNet (1.5 and 1.6) integrated some hand-checked cousin rules (similar to metonymic patterns such as ANIMAL-FOR-FOOD) that covered, however, only a small number of polysemic entries. Currently, there are efforts to automatically extract such rules from WordNet (Peters and Wilks 2003, Veale 2004). In addition, most dictionaries do not cover proper names, which can easily be used metonymically, as in Examples (1), (2) and (4) (Stern 1931, Lakoff and Johnson 1980).

Most corpora (the BNC, for example) do not contain any information about word senses. An example of sense-annotated corpora are SEMCOR (Fellbaum 1998) and the SENSEVAL-II and SENSEVAL-III corpora (Hel 2001), whose content words are tagged with their WordNet senses. Unfortunately, the shortcomings of dictionaries regarding metonymies are mirrored in the sense annotation – thus, "United States" is tagged with two distinct senses in SEMCOR, whereas "UK" is always tagged with one sense only. In SENSEVAL-II and SENSEVAL-III metonymic relations are again not annotated explicitly/systematically.

This lack of language resources is the main cause of sparse evaluation of most NLP algorithms dealing with metonymy. Indeed, some of them are evaluated in comparison to constructed examples only (Utiyama et al. 2000, Fass 1997, Hobbs et al. 1993, Pustejovsky 1995), disregarding the range of phenomena in realistic settings. Others (Verspoor 1997, Markert and Hahn 2002, Harabagiu 1998, Stallard 1993) use naturally-occurring data that, however, seem to be analysed according to subjective intuitions of one individual only. These latter approaches seem to take for granted that the comparison data needed for their algorithms (metonymies identified in natural language texts by humans) is easy to generate reliably, which presupposes that humans can easily agree on identification and interpretation of metonymies. Given experiences in sense annotation (Ng and Lee 1996, Jorgensen 1990), this seems unlikely as they show that disciplined efforts with several trained annotators are necessary to arrive at reliably annotated data, as shown in the SENSEVAL excercise (Kilgarriff and Rosenzweig 2000). One might even suspect that the subtle distinctions needed for metonymy annotations are particularly difficult to make reliably. To our knowledge, there are no studies on human agreement in metonymy annotation. The only systematic metonymy annotation we are aware of apart from our own is the one conducted within the ACE project[3], but no agreement figures are reported (see also Section 5).

In this paper we address both the lack of language resources as well as the lack of data on human agreement in annotation studies for metonymies. In particular,
- we present a general annotation framework for metonymies. This framework takes into account both technical desiderata (for example, platform-independence) as well as linguistic properties of metonymies (regularity, productivity and underspecification);
- we present two class-specific annotation schemes (for location and organisation names). We describe a study of organisation names in detail with a focus on the abilities of humans to identify and interpret metonymies as well as the distribution of metonymies in real occurring texts;
- we show that metonymy annotation can be done reliably if detailed guidelines are provided and the annotators are trained;
- using the schemes we built an annotated gold standard corpus that includes 3000 literal/metonymic examples of location names, and

---

3. http://www.itl.nist.gov/iad/894.01/tests/ace/

around a 1000 instances of organisation names, in both cases mirroring as far as possible the original distribution in a corpus of English texts. The rest of the paper is organised as follows. In Section 2 we present a general framework for metonymy annotation, and in Section 3 we present two annotation schemes for location and organisation names. Annotation reliability is rigorously evaluated in several reproducibility experiments described in Section 4, where we also discuss the distribution of readings in our gold standard corpus. In Section 5, we discuss advantages and problems of our work, open issues, and related work.

2. Framework

To ensure scalability and generalisability of metonymy annotation schemes for specific classes, we developed several principles for the construction of metonymy annotation schemes and annotated corpora that take into account linguistic insights and technical requirements.

The corpus should be annotated in a markup language that makes it reusable, platform-independent and easily searchable. We decided to use XML as it is the standard in corpus markup for which searching and editing tools are available.

Principle 1 (Platform-independence): *Encode the corpus in XML.*

To make the corpus useful for many different applications we decided to include texts from as many different domains and genres as possible, hoping to cover a wide variety of metonymies. This is necessary as types and frequencies of metonymies can vary widely from genre to genre (in sports reports the use of a location name for a sports team (*England lose in semifinal*) is extremely frequent). Therefore we used the BNC, a 100 million word corpus that covers many domains and genres.

Principle 2 (Domain and genre): *Include as many different domain and genre types as possible.*

Traditionally, metonymy is seen as operating at the word level, extended to multi-word names as "Republic of Germany" (see e.g. Copestake and Briscoe 1995). Nunberg (1995), however, makes some convincing arguments for metonymy as a phrasal process, but to our knowledge no full account of the interaction of metonymy and phrasal semantics yet exists. Thus, we still attach any annotation to the head noun of the phrase. If the head noun is a multi-word name the annotation encompasses the whole name.[4]

Principle 3 (Annotation extent): *The word level is the unit extent in annotation.*

Because metonymic readings are very systematic, our annotation scheme will take advantage of metonymic patterns in order to express regularities and ease annotation effort. Therefore, we developed general guidelines (specifying extent of annotation units, annotation procedure etc.) and specific guidelines for each semantic class covered (specifying metonymic patterns distinctive to this semantic class). The semantic classes we use are derived from both the metonymy literature and lexical databases like WordNet. Example classes are LOCATION, ANIMAL and ORGANISATION.

Principle 4 (Regularities): *Use semantic classes and metonymic patterns for defining annotation categories.*

The intended referent of a metonymy is rarely as clear as in Example (3). In Example (4), it is clear in context that Chinese officials are involved but the decision-makers cannot be named exactly. Therefore we annotate just the base class of the noun – i.e., its original literal class, in Example (4) LOCATION – and the metonymic pattern used, here PLACE-FOR-PEOPLE, which then implicitly gives the intended class, here PERSON. We annotate both base class and intended class as subsequent reference can refer to either as the examples in (5) show.

(5) a. I bought a *Picasso*. He was a great painter. (not corpus-based)
    b. I bought a *Picasso*. It is a great painting. (not corpus-based)

Principle 5 (Underspecification): *Annotate both base class and metonymic pattern.*

Although the extensive use of metonymic patterns will greatly enhance the coverage of the annotation scheme, there must be at least one category for unconventional metonymies like Example (3).

---

4. The rest of the annotation scheme (e.g indicating the type of metonymy) is to a large degree independent of this decision, so that the annotation extent could be changed to phrasal annotation, if wished in the future.

Principle 6 (Coverage): *Cover conventional and unconventional metonymies.*

Figure 1 shows the basic XML-template for metonymy annotation and Figure 2 an example output for the class LOCATION.

<BASE-CLASS reading=*readingtype* metotype=*metopattern*> annotated-noun </BASE-CLASS> continued-text ...

Figure 1. XML template for metonymy annotation

<LOCATION reading="metonymic" metotype="place-for-people"> China </LOCATION> has agreed ...

Figure 2. XML output of annotation for the class "LOCATION"

3. Annotation scheme for metonymies

Our general framework distinguishes between *literal*, *metonymic* and *mixed* readings for each base class. The overall structure of the annotation scheme is shown in Figure 3:
- *Literal readings* are defined specifically for each base class: for example, they include territorial interpretations for locations.
- *Metonymic readings* cover both metonymies that follow regular metonymic patterns and metonymies that do not (following Principle 6). Most of the regular metonymic patterns are specific to one particular base class (class-specific patterns). Nevertheless, we provide some class-independent metonymic patterns relevant for all base classes as well.
- *Mixed readings* occur when two metonymic patterns or a metonymic pattern and the literal reading are invoked at the same time.[5]

Grounding on Principle 4, this general framework has to be supplemented by specific guidelines/annotation schemes for base classes that undergo regular polysemy as these specify the annotation categories applicable. We conducted two case studies on the base classes LOCATION and ORGANISATION. We developed our class-specific annotation schemes by studying example lists in the literature (Lakoff and Johnson 1980, Stern 1931, Copestake and Briscoe 1995, Fass 1997, among others), and preliminary corpus studies. We discuss the class-specific annotation schemes for

---
5. Mixed readings will be discussed in detail in Section 3.3.

LOCATION and ORGANISATION in Section 3.1 and Section 3.2, and the categories for class-independent metonymic patterns, unconventional metonymic readings, and mixed readings in Section 3.3.

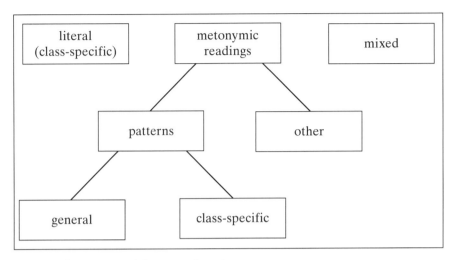

Figure 3. The structure of the annotation scheme

3.1. Annotation scheme for location names

The *literal* reading for location names comprises a locative (see Example (6)) and a political entity interpretation (see Example (7)).

(6) coral coast of *Papua New Guinea*
(7) *Britain's* current account deficit

The locative and the political sense is often distinguished in dictionaries as well as in the ACE annotation scheme (see discussion in Section 5). However, it frequently proved hard to distinguish in our data, as Example (8) illustrates. Here, the unions are both legally affiliated to the state Britain as well as locally situated in the country. Therefore we merged these two readings into one literal reading.

(8) *Britain's* unions

For metonymic readings, we distinguish between the following location-specific patterns.

- PLACE-FOR-PEOPLE: a place stands for any persons/organisations associated with it. Often, the explicit referent is underspecified, as in Example (9), where the reference could be to the government, an organisation or the whole population.

(9) The G-24 group expressed readiness to provide *Albania* with food aid

It is therefore important to assign the right pattern (PLACE-FOR-PEOPLE) at a higher level, and a more specific pattern (*subtype*), if identifiable, at a lower level. Such a hierarchical approach has the great advantage of 'punishing' disagreement only at a later stage and allowing fall-back options for automatic systems. This leads to Principle 7 to be integrated into our general framework.

Principle 7 (Hierarchical structure): *Organise the categories hierarchically.*

We introduce four optional subtypes for the PLACE-FOR-PEOPLE pattern.

CAPITAL-FOR-GOVERNMENT (only for capitals of countries/states) identifies a capital standing for the government of the whole country as *Beijing* in Example (4).

OFF identifies the official administration as in the use of China in Example (4). Additional examples are given in (10) and (11).

(10) EC denunciations of *Israel's* handling of the intifada
(11) *America* did once try to ban alcohol

ORG identifies an organisation (or a set of organisations) associated with the location. This includes sports teams, companies, and others (a list of possible organisations was extracted from WordNet). In Example (12), England identifies a national sports team.[6] In Example (13), France refers to college(s) located in France.

(12) *England* lose in semi-final.
(13) Mr Peter Shuker, the principal, said the college now had links with *France*.

---

6. In British English these metonymies affect subject-verb agreement and might be a problem for automatic parsing.

POP identifies the whole or majority of the population, as in the religious context of Example (14).

(14) The notion that the incarnation was to fulfil the promise to *Israel* and to reconcile the world with God

– PLACE-FOR-EVENT: a location name stands for an event that happened in the location (see also Example (1)). This category is usually illustrated with very clear-cut examples in the literature, but it proved difficult to distinguish from literal readings in practice. (This was also due to its extreme rarity, which did not help in singling out relevant clues). For instance, the occurrence of *Bosnia* in Example (15) clearly refers to the war there, but the occurrence of *Sweden* in Example (16) is less clear-cut. Indeed, the reference (in this particular context) was to a sports event in Sweden, but the literal reading is still true and the metonymic PLACE-FOR-EVENT reading can be obtained by inference. In such cases, we opt for LITERAL, introducing a preference between readings.

(15) you think about some of the crises that are going on in the world from *Bosnia* and so on (PLACE-FOR-EVENT)
(16) he didn't play in *Sweden* (LITERAL)

– PLACE-FOR-PRODUCT: a place stands for a product manufactured in the place, as Bordeaux in Example (17).

(17) a smooth *Bordeaux* that was gutsy enough to cope with our food

3.2. Annotation scheme for organisation names

The LITERAL reading of organisations describes references to the organisation in general, where an organisation is seen as a legal entity, which consists of organisation members that speak with a collective voice, and which has a charter, statute or defined aims. Examples of literal readings include (among others) descriptions of the structure of an organisation (see Example (18)), associations between organisations (see Example (19)) or relations between organisations and products/services they offer (see Example (20)).

(18) *NATO* countries
(19) *Sun* acquired that part of Eastman-Kodak Co's Unix subsidary
(20) *Intel's* Indeo video compression hardware

We distinguish the following organisation-specific patterns:

- ORGANISATION-FOR-MEMBERS: an organisation often stands for its members. This holds especially frequently when a spokesperson or official acts or speaks for the organisation, as in Example (21), but also includes cases where all members of the organisation participate in an action, as in Example (22).

    (21) Last February *NASA* announced [...]
    (22) It's customary to go to work in black or white suits. [...] *Woolworths* wear them

    Similar to PLACE-FOR-PEOPLE metonymies, the concrete referents are often underspecified. A similar hierarchical approach to (optionally) specifying referents can be used. However, we have not included such an extension to the organisation scheme yet.

- ORGANISATION-FOR-FACILITY: organisations can also stand for the facility that houses the organisation or one of its branches, as the following example shows:

    (23) The opening of a *McDonalds* is a major event

    Distinguishing between an organisation or a facility reading in *context* is usually easy. However, the problem lies in the *a priori* assignment of a base class to any given entity. Whenever a facility reading for an organisation base class is encountered, the reading is metonymic, whereas a facility reading for a facility base class is obviously literal. We follow the MUC Named Entity Recognition guidelines (Chinchor 1997) for assigning base classes. For example, hospitals and schools are facilities, whereas companies are organisations. Thus, in Example (24), *Frenchay Hospital*, would be assigned a base class facility with a literal reading.

    (24) A man is recovering in *Frenchay Hospital*, Bristol, after falling from the Severn Bridge.

- ORGANISATION-FOR-PRODUCT: frequently the name of a commercial organisation is used to refer to its products, as in Examples (25–26).

(25) A red light was hung on the *Ford's* tail-gate.

(26) press-men hoisted their notebooks and their *Kodaks*.

- ORGANISATION-FOR-INDEX: an organisation name can be used for an index that indicates its value, for example its stock index, as in Examples (1) and (27).

(27) *Eurotunnel* was the most active stock.

- ORGANISATION-FOR-EVENT: similar to PLACE-FOR-EVENT metonymies, an organisation name can be used to refer to an event associated with the organisation (e.g. a scandal or bankruptcy), as in Example (28).

(28) A remarkable example of back-bench influence on the Prime Minister was seen in the resignation of Leon Brittan from Trade and Industry in the aftermath of *Westland*.[7]

3.3. Class-independent patterns, unconventional metonymic readings, and mixed readings

There are two general metonymic patterns that can be applied to most nouns.

- OBJECT-FOR-NAME: all names can be used as mere signifiers, instead of referring to an object or set of objects. In Example (29), *Guyana* would receive a literal interpretation, whereas *British Guiana* is a mere reference to a previous name of the location. Similary, in Example (30), both *Chevrolet* and *Ford* are used as strings, rather than referring to the companies.

(29) Guyana (formerly *British Guiana*) gained independence

(30) *Chevrolet* is feminine because of its sound (it's a longer word than *Ford*, has an open vowel at the end, connotes Frenchness)

- OBJECT-FOR-REPRESENTATION: a proper noun can refer to a representation (such as a photo or a painting) of the referent of its literal read-

---

7. The Westland affair was an important economic scandal involving the helicopter company Westland in Britain in the 1980s.

ing. Thus *Malta* in Example (31) refers to a drawing of the island when pointing to a map.

(31)   This is *Malta*.

It is not entirely clear whether OBJECT-FOR-REPRESENTATION can be applied to organisation names, because neither a picture of the building, nor of its members or products would be a complete representation of the literal reading of a company as an abstract legal entity. The logo of a company might best be called a representation of the company, but in our current annotation scheme we have not taken this into account.

The category OTHER covers unconventional metonymies (see Principle 6). Since they are open-ended and context-dependent, no specific category indicating the intended class can be introduced. In Example (32), the location name *New Jersey* metonymically refers to the local typical tunes. An example for a metonymy which is not covered by the current patterns for the class ORGANISATION, is given in (33), where *Barclays Bank* stands for an account at the bank. The last example shows that our OTHER category is used for all metonymies that do not fit into one of the prespecified patterns. Rarely, this can include regular patterns for very limited classes, such as bank accounts for all banks. Therefore, it sometimes covers examples which might not be regarded as unconventional language from a linguistic point of view.

(32)   The thing about the record is the influences of the music. The bottom end is very New York/*New Jersey* and the top is very melodic
(33)   funds [...] had been paid into *Barclays Bank*

In addition to literal and metonymic readings, we found examples where two predicates are involved, triggering a different reading each, thus yielding a mixed reading. This occurs very often with *coordinations* and *appositions* as well as with *gerunds*. In Example (34), both a literal (triggered by *arriving in*) and a PLACE-FOR-PEOPLE (with subtype OFF) reading (triggered by *leading critic*) are invoked. Example (35) shows that two metonymic readings can be evoked simultaneously as well, an ORGANISATION-FOR-INDEX reading (triggered by *slipped*) and an ORGANISATION-FOR-MEMBERS reading (triggered by *confirming*).

(34)   they arrived in *Nigeria*, hitherto a leading critic of [...]
(35)   *Barclays* slipped 4p to 351p after confirming 3,000 more job losses.

We therefore introduced the category MIXED to deal with these cases. In our annotation guidelines, we constrain mixed cases to certain syntactic constructions expressed in a dependency grammar framework.

Similar examples have been discussed under the term co-predication in, for example, (Nunberg 1995), but most literature on metonymy does not treat them explicitly.

4. Annotation experiments

In this paper, we describe an annotation excercise for the class ORGANISATION. A similar experiment for the class LOCATION is described in Markert and Nissim (2002b).

4.1. Data

In this experiment we performed sample-based annotation: we extracted text samples containing occurrences of organisation names that were taken from a previously compiled gazetteer (see below). The main advantage of such a procedure is that it allows to collect more data in less time as otherwise one might have to annotate many texts without many names of the desired base class in them.

In order to produce our sampling frame, we collected the 500 company names included in the Fortune500 list.[8] We extended this selection by including, for each company, alternative spelling, acronyms, and abbreviations, resulting in a collection of 528 different names forms our sampling frame *OrgList*.

Using *Gsearch* (Corley et al. 2001), we randomly extracted from the British National Corpus 3700 instances of possible organisation names, allowing any company name in OrgList to occur. All samples include three sentences of context.

Because many organisation names have common noun homographs (for example "Sun" and "Target") our extraction method produced a dataset which also contained many instances that were not company names. These were ignored in the annotation excercise. Overall, only under a third of the extracted occurrences are actual organisation names.

---

8. http://www.fortune.com/fortune/fortune500.

4.2. Method

Annotators. The annotators are the authors of this paper.

Guidelines. The written annotation guidelines consist of general guidelines (containing instructions for annotation extent and readings that are not class-specific) and guidelines for the metonymic patterns specific to the base class ORGANISATION (see also Figure 3).

Identification of readings is driven by *replacement tests* described in the guidelines (e.g. if an occurrence of "BP" can be replaced by "shares of BP", we annotate it as ORGANISATION-FOR-INDEX). The guidelines also contain examples for each category and instructions for ambiguous and underspecified cases.

Reliability Measures. We evaluated the reproducibility of results by using the kappa statistic (K), which measures agreement among a set of annotators making category judgements, correcting for expected chance agreement (Carletta 1996):

$$K = \frac{P(A) - P(E)}{1 - P(E)}$$

where $P(A)$ is the proportion of times the annotators agree, and $P(E)$ is the proportion of times they are expected to agree by chance. Good quality annotation of discourse phenomena normally yields a kappa (K) of about .80.

Tool. The annotation was performed using the MATE annotation tool (Isard et al. 2000), specifically customised for metonymy annotation. The string to be annotated is automatically highlighted. Readings and metonymic patterns can be assigned by simply clicking on specific buttons in the tool.

Training The annotators have been trained by independently annotating 400 samples, which included a total of 125 actual organisation names. All applicable readings and metonymic patterns occurred in the training set. The reliability of the annotation on the training set was measured at $K = .804$ ($N = 125; k = 2$) (where N stands for the number of examples annotated and k for the number of annotators), which is lower than that achieved on the final set (see below). This shows the importance of training for achieving high agreement.

4.3. Results

A summary of the results is given in Table 1.

Table 1. Reliability results for all categories and for each single category.

CLASS	N	P(A)	P(E)	K
ALL	984	.942	.454	.894
LITERAL	984	.957	.538	.908
ORGANISATION-FOR-MEMBERS	984	.971	.678	.911
ORGANISATION-FOR-PRODUCT	984	.987	.870	.898
ORGANISATION-FOR-FACILITY	984	.999	.973	.962
ORGANISATION-FOR-INDEX	984	.999	.987	.923
OBJECT-FOR-NAME	984	1.00	.990	1.00
OTHER	984	.995	.973	.812
MIXED	984	.976	.902	.752

Note: N is the number of annotated instances, P(A) is the observed agreement, P(E) is the expected agreement, and K is the Kappa score.

Reproducibility. We measured reproducibility of the distinction between the categories LITERAL, ORGANISATION-FOR-MEMBERS, ORGANISATION-FOR-PRODUCT, ORGANISATION-FOR-FACILITY, ORGANISATION-FOR-INDEX, OBJECT-FOR-NAME, OTHER, and MIXED. Kappa was measured at .894 ($N = 984; k = 2$), thus showing that the annotation is highly reliable.

Single category reliability. The annotators's experience suggested that some of the categories are harder to assign than others. In order to discover which categories the human judges found difficult to identify, we used Krippendorff's (1980) single category reliability. For a single category, agreement was measured by collapsing all categories but the one of interest into one meta-category and then calculating kappa as usual. We did not measure reliability for the ORGANISATION-FOR-EVENT category because it was assigned only once by the annotators.

All metonymic patterns as well as the literal reading show very high reliability. The lowest agreement is recorded for the mixed reading ($K = .752$), whose annotation proved to be marginally reliable. We believe the reason behind this is the difficulty intrinsic to mixed readings: the annotators have to agree on two different readings triggered by two predicates. This causes two types of problems. Firstly, the annotators might overlook one of the predicates involved. Secondly, even if both predicates are identified by both annotators, they might not agree on the readings they trigger. For example, if one annotator intrepets both predicates as triggering a literal reading, the overall interpretation will be literal, whereas if he interprets one as literal and the other as metonymic, the overall interpretation will be mixed.

The annotation of metonymies of type OTHER is still reliable, although the kappa is lower than that observed for the regular patterns. Indeed, it makes sense to think that unconventional metonymies are harder to distinguish than regular ones.

Gold Standard Corpus. After the annotation, we discussed all cases we had not agreed on, and created a gold standard. In addition to the 984 samples to which both annotators had assigned a reading, we included in the gold standard three cases where one of the annotators had originally not fully understood the context (and had therefore not assigned a reading), but could understand the sample after the joint discussion. All other instances unclear to one or both the annotators were left out. In 20 cases we could not agree on the reading even after discussion. Thus, the gold standard corpus therefore contains 967 annotated instances. The distribution of readings is shown in Figure 4.

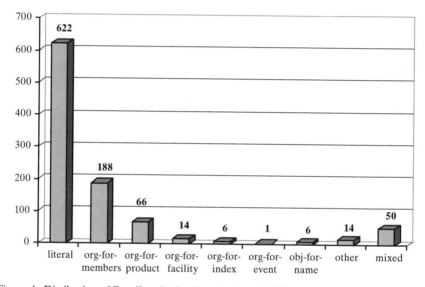

Figure 4. Distibution of Readings in the Organisation Gold Standard Corpus

Literal is overall the most frequent reading (64.3%). Among the metonymic readings, ORGANISATION-FOR-MEMBERS is the most frequent pattern, occurring in 19.4% of all cases, and covering 76% of all metonymies. ORGANISATION-FOR-PRODUCT is the second most common metonymic pattern, occurring in 6.8% of all cases. The categories ORGANISATION-FOR-FACILITY (1.4%), ORGANISATION-FOR-INDEX (0.6%), and OBJECT-FOR-NAME

(0.6%) are rarer than the previous ones, but still represented in the corpus. Only one ORGANISATION-FOR-EVENT metonymy is found in our gold standard corpus. The category OTHER is used only in 1.4% of the cases, thus showing that our regular metonymic patterns have a wide coverage (see also the discussion on following example (31) above). A remarkably high number of mixed readings (5.1%) can also be observed.

Comparison to a study on the LOCATION class. Comparing these results to those obtained in our previous annotation exercise on the class LOCATION (Markert and Nissim 2002b), the following insights can be gained. Firstly, the two annotation exercises yielded a similar degree of reliability ($K = .870$ ($N = 931$; $k = 2$) for locations, and $K = .894$ ($N = 984$; $k = 2$) for organisations), thus showing the validity of our approach and suggesting extensibility to yet other base classes. Secondly, mixed readings appear to be generally difficult to distinguish, with marginal reliability for both classes ($K = .761$ ($N = 931$; $k = 2$) for locations, and $K = .752$ ($N = 984$; $k = 2$) for organisations). Thirdly, although literal readings are the majority both in the location and organisation corpora (79.7% and 64.3%, respectively), organisation names are used metonymically more frequently than location ones, and show more variety in the patterns used.

5. Discussion and related work

Our work fills an important gap in the literature on metonymies. It takes real corpus data into account and presents an annotation scheme for metonymies whose reliability has been extensively tested. By working with real occurring data, we shed light on some points which had been often ignored in the linguistic literature. For example, the pattern ORGANISATION-FOR-INDEX is not listed in the metonymy literature but occurs regularly with company names. In our data it represents 2.1% of all metonymic readings. We also encountered an ORGANISATION-FOR-EVENT reading which is not considered in the literature. In addition, we take mixed readings systematically into account by developing specific guidelines to identify them, and show that they occur quite frequently (5.1%).

With regard to the reliability of our annotation scheme, agreement is exceptionally high. This results from intensive corpus work which also led to detailed guidelines containing many examples, and extensive training on real data both on the LOCATION and ORGANISATION classes. The most similar work to ours is the work conducted within the ACE project which also annotate metonymies in real occurring texts. Also similar is the base-class approach that uses base classes and class-specific metonymic patterns. However, to our knowledge, no agreement data has been published. Therefore it is unclear whether their scheme can be used reliably. In comparison to our scheme, theirs includes a larger number of base classes including both proper and common nouns. On the other hand, though, for each of these classes, they only consider a limited number of metonymic patterns. For example, for the class ORGANISATION, they only annotate ORGANISATION-FOR-FACILITY metonymies.

By randomly extracting examples from a corpus, we mirror as far as possible the real distribution of metonymies and literal readings (for the names in our sampling frame) in the original corpus. In contrast, Marinelli (2004) preselects a small number of names that are likely to be metonymic, such as "Champagne", and "Parkinson". Obviously these especially selected individual names do not reflect the real distribution of metonymic and literal readings in a corpus. No agreement figures are reported.

Our corpus of 3000 annotated location names and the annotation guidelines are available at http://www.ltg.ed.ac.uk/~malvi/mascara. The organisation corpus and respective guidelines will be available from January 2005.

Although we achieved high agreement and high coverage, our corpus work highlighted some difficult issues. In particular, the following problems emerged.

Confusables. Some categories are not easy to distinguish. This holds in particular for LITERAL VS PLACE-FOR-EVENT (for a discussion see Section 3.1 above), LITERAL VS PLACE-FOR-PEOPLE, and LITERAL VS ORGANISATION-FOR-MEMBERS. For the latter, there are cases where it is unclear whether the predicate refers to the company as a whole or to some of its members. Thus, in Example (36), the annotators could not agree whether "being of great importance" should be applied to persons only.

(36) The requirement that wrappers should be sent was of great importance to the *Nestle Co.* [...]

Even in cases which are clear according to our guidelines (see Example (21), where the predicate *announce* triggers an ORGANISATION-FOR-MEMBERS reading in our framework), a different approach might be possible. John Barnden (p.c.), for example, makes the point that such examples can be explained in terms of a metaphoric reading of the predicate which is applicable to the whole company.

Interaction with metaphors. The problem above is exacerbated by the frequent use of metaphorical predicates that cooccur with company names. In Example (37), the interpretation of "arm twisting" affects the choice between a literal or metonymic interpretation of *British Airways*. Ideally, metaphor and metonymy annotation on full text should be combined. However, the complexity of this task exceeds our current efforts.

(37)   Should it twist the arm of *British Airways* [...]

Metonymic chains. In some cases, the referent of the proper name can be identified only via the sequential application of two or more metonymic patterns. This phenomenon is sometimes called *metonymic chain* (Fass 1997). In Example (38), the company name *Daimler* is used to refer to the person driving the car produced by the company.

(38)   As she turned uphill, a dark-red *Daimler* [...] blew its horn at her.

This is therefore a chain consisting of an ORGANISATION-FOR-PRODUCT pattern plus a PRODUCT-FOR-USER pattern. In our scheme such chains are annotated as OTHER.

6. Conclusions and future directions

We have presented a general framework for metonymy annotation that takes linguistic properties of metonymies into account. Within this framework, we have described two fully worked out annotation schemes for the classes LOCATION and ORGANISATION. Their application to a corpus consisting of samples extracted from the British National Corpus allows us to gain insights into the actual distribution of metonymies in real occurring texts, as well as to test the ability of humans to reliably identify metonymies. Currently, our corpus contains a total of 4000 annotated occurrences of location and organisation names.

Our annotation schemes for location and organisation names cover the metonymic patterns presented in the literature and enhance them (i) by introducing explicit guidelines and preference rankings that allow reliable annotation, (ii) by introducing a category MIXED for cases where different readings are invoked simultaneously and (iii) by structuring categories hierarchically. The latter improvement, implemented in the annotation scheme for the class LOCATION, ensures *progressive sense re-*

finement (Resnik and Yarowsky 2000), allowing automatic systems fallback options.

As far as human judgements are concerned, the annotation experiments we have described show very good reproducibility results for our annotation schemes and that training and explicit guidelines allow reliable metonymy annotation (see also Markert and Nissim (2002b)).

In the future, we plan on expanding our annotation schemes in order to cover common nouns as well as other base classes. This would allow us to proceed to full text annotation. We are also interested in combing our approach with other efforts in sense annotation such as SENSEVAL. Using our annotated corpora, we are also working on automatic recognition of metonymies. Initial experiments have shown good results on the class LOCATION (Markert and Nissim 2002a, Nissim and Markert 2003). In the future, we will extend our approach to the class ORGANISATION as well.

References

Apresjan, Juri D.
    1973   Regular polysemy. *Linguistics* 142: 5–32.
Burnard, Lou
    1995   *Users' Reference Guide, British National Corpus.* British National Corpus Consortium, Oxford, England.
Carletta, Jean
    1996   Assessing agreement on classification tasks: The kappa statistic. *Computational Linguistics* 22: 249–254.
Chinchor, Nancy
    1997   MUC-7 Named Entity Task definition. *Proceedings of the 7th Conference on Message Understanding.* Washington, DC.
Copestake, Ann and Ted Briscoe
    1995   Semi-productive polysemy and sense extension. *Journal of Semantics* 12: 15–67.
Corley, Steffan, Martin Corley, Frank Keller, Matthew Crocker and Shari Trewin
    2001   Finding syntactic structure in unparsed corpora: The Gsearch corpus query system. *Computers and the Humanities* 35: 81–94.
Fass, Dan
    1997   *Processing Metaphor and Metonymy.* Ablex, Stanford, CA, 1997.
Fellbaum, Christiane (ed.)
    1998   *WordNet: An Electronic Lexical Database.* MIT Press, Cambridge, MA.
Harabagiu, Sanda
    1998   Deriving metonymic coercions from WordNet. In *Workshop on the Usage of WordNet in Natural Language Processing Systems,* COLING-ACL '98, 142–148, Montreal, Canada.

SENSEVAL-2
  2001	*Second International Workshop on Evaluating Word Sense Disambiguation Systems.* Held as part of ACL-01, Toulouse, France.
Hobbs, Jerry R., Mark E. Stickel, Douglas E. Appelt and Paul Martin
  1993	Interpretation as abduction. *Artificial Intelligence* 63: 69–142.
Isard, Amy, David McKelvie, Andreas Mengel and Morten Baun Moller
  2000	The MATE Workbench – an annotation tool. In: Maria Gavrilidou, Geroge Carayannis, Stella Markantonatou, Stelios Piperdis and Gregory Stainhaouer (eds.), *Proceedings of the 2nd International Conference on Language Resources and Evaluation*. Athens, Greece, 1565–1570.
Jorgensen, Julia
  1990	The psychological reality of word senses. *Journal of Psycholinguistic Research* 19: 167–190.
Kilgarriff, Adam and Joseph Rosenzweig
  2000	English senseval: Report and results. In *Proceedings of the 2nd International Conference on Language Resources and Evaluation*. Athens, Greece.
Krippendorff, Klaus
  1980	*Content Analysis: An Introduction to Its Methodology.* Beverly Hills: Sage Publications.
Lakoff, George and Mark Johnson
  1980	*Metaphors We Live By.* Chicago: The University of Chicago Press.
Marinelli, Rita
  2004	Proper names and polysemy: from a lexicographic experience. *Proceedings of LREC-2004*, 157–160.
Markert, Katja and Udo Hahn
  2002	Understanding metonymies in discourse. *Artificial Intelligence* 135: 145–198.
Markert, Katja and Malvina Nissim
  2002a	Metonymy resolution as a classification task. In *Proceedings of the 2002 Conference on Empirical Methods in Natural Language Processing*, 204–213.
  2002b	Towards a corpus annotated for metonymies: the case of location names. *Proceedings of the 3rd International Conference on Language Resources and Evaluation*, 1385–1392.
Ng, Hwee Tou and Hian Beng Lee
  1996	Integrating multiple knowledge sources to disambiguate word sense: An exemplar-based approach. *Proceedings of the 34th Annual Meeting of the Association for Computational Linguistics*, 40–47.
Nissim, Malvina and Katja Markert
  2003	Syntactic features and word similarity for supervised metonymy resolution. *Proceedings of ACL-03*, 56–63.
Nunberg, Geoffrey
  1995	Transfers of meaning. *Journal of Semantics* 12: 109–132.
Peters, Wim and Yorick Wilks
  2003	Data-driven detection of figurative language use in electronic language resources. *Metaphor and Symbol* 18: 161–174.

Pustejovsky, James
　　1995　　　　The Generative Lexicon. Cambridge, MA: MIT Press.
Resnik, Philip and David Yarowsky
　　2000　　　　Distinguishing systems and distinguishing senses: New evaluation methods for word sense disambiguation. *Natural Language Engineering* 5:113–133.
Stallard, David
　　1993　　　　Two kinds of metonymy. *Proceedings of the 31st Annual Meeting of the Association for Computational Linguistics*, 87–94.
Stern, Gustav
　　1931　　　　*Meaning and Change of Meaning*. Göteborg: Wettergren & Kerbers Förlag.
Utiyama, Masao, Masaki Murata and Hitoshi Isahara
　　2000　　　　A statistical approach to the processing of metonymy. *Proceedings of the 18th International Conference on Computational Linguistics*, 885–891.
Veale, Tony
　　2004　　　　Polysemy and category structure in WordNet: An evidential approach. *Proceedings of LREC- 2004*, 1055–1058.
Verspoor, Cornelia
　　1997　　　　Conventionality-governed logical metonymy. In: Harry Bunt, Lee Kievit, Reinhard Muskens, and Margriet Verlinden (eds.), *Proceedings of the 2nd International Workshop on Computational Semantics*, 300–312.

On groutnolls and nog-heads:
A case study of the interaction between culture and cognition in intelligence metaphors

Kathryn Allan

Abstract

Recent interest in conventional metaphor has focused attention on the impact of cognitive mechanisms on conceptualisation. The emergence of Conceptual Metaphor Theory, and Lakoff and Johnson et al's subsequent development of the Integrated Theory of Primary Metaphor, have been influential in this field, and have led to an increased awareness of the way that the physical affects the mental. In this paper I will argue that whilst it is crucially important to acknowledge the embodied nature of thought, this does not provide an adequate explanation for all types of metaphor. Many of the metaphors pervasive in everyday language are products of their time, and cannot therefore be accounted for without reference to culture.

Here I present a diachronic case study of the link between intelligence and density, expressed in the metaphor STUPIDITY IS CLOSE TEXTURE. The lexical evidence for this metaphor is particularly interesting in the limited number of source concepts from which it is drawn; two thirds of the data are linked with specific physical substances rather than with general, abstract terms for density or thickness. I will examine the motivation for these sources, and explore the possible reasons for the selection of particular substances over others that appear, intuitively, to be equally appropriate. Overall I hope to demonstrate the interaction of cognition and culture in this semantic group.

The data on which I will base my observations is drawn from the *Historical Thesaurus of English* project at the University of Glasgow, which has enabled me to look at the semantics of intelligence in a historical context based on vocabulary from Old English through to Present Day English.

1. Introduction

Though there has been a huge amount of interest in metaphor in recent years, the resulting research has included relatively little in the way of diachronic work. With a few notable exceptions, scholars have tended to concentrate on current examples of metaphor that rely on native speaker intuition, and it is on this kind of data that theories within cognitive linguistics have been based and tested. However, I believe that by examining the origins of metaphors, it is possible to gain new insight into how and why particular mappings are motivated, and the cultural and linguistic influences that can affect the metaphorical process. For this reason I would argue that there is huge potential benefit in marrying modern approaches with historical data (cf. also Koivisto-Alanko and Tissari, this volume).

The data on which this study is centred is taken from the *Historical Thesaurus of English* (*HTE*) project at Glasgow (C. Kay et al., forthcoming), which presents lexical items from Old to Present Day English chronologically and by semantic field. This contains vocabulary grouped by concept far more comprehensively than any previous publication, so it offers new possibilities for historical corpus-based study. Based on the classification presented in *HTE*, I have examined the target concept INTELLIGENCE, focusing on nouns and adjectives, ie expressions for a *clever* or *stupid person*, and *clever* or *stupid*. My analysis starts from an examination of the etymological development of a group of lexical items, to identify earliest meanings and stages in semantic change. This approach renders it unnecessary to draw up any strict guidelines for metaphor until these can be based on evidence – it is very much a data-centred approach, concerned specifically with the origins of and motivations for the way intelligence is conceptualised metaphorically.[1]

The observations presented here are based on a corpus of 1075 *HTE* entries, made up of 464 nouns and 611 adjectives. Just over 11% of the total data dates as far back as OE, and around 40% of the entries are considered current (although a number of these words are archaic, rare or in specialised usage). Although the study is not intended to be quantitative, I have used quantity as a basic indication of the source fields that are particularly productive and therefore characterise our conceptualisation of intelligence. From the corpus, three particularly quantitatively important source concepts have been identified, and these are the SENSES, ANIMALS and DENSITY. It is the last of these, DENSITY, which is discussed here, and it is my intention in this paper to demonstrate that the motivation for this mapping can only be explained by taking account of both cognition and external influences that contribute to the way language develops (see also Allan 2003).

---

1. It should also be pointed out here that I acknowledge the importance of metonymy in the mappings I will go on to describe. However, given the difficulty in distinguishing between metaphor and metonymy (particularly when both are involved, as they are in the DENSITY group), I will use the term 'metaphor' in a very broad sense which includes mappings that could more accurately be described as metonymical.

2. DENSITY as a source concept

Amongst the source concepts that have been recognised to be involved in the way intelligence is conceptualised, DENSITY has received little attention. To a certain extent, this may be because expressions related to the metaphor appear mainly to be associated with low-register colloquial language; until relatively recently this has been studied comparatively little. Recent studies have taken account of spoken language and slang to a greater extent; however, much of this work, and particularly that within the Lakoffian tradition, has been concentrated on a fairly limited set of metaphors which can clearly be shown to be motivated cognitively and experientially, and which underlie the way whole concepts are structured (see for example Boroditsky 2000; Grady 1997). This has allowed room for the thorough investigation and deconstruction of particular mappings in a way that was not previously attempted, and to a large extent the approach has demystified the mapping process by endeavouring to root it in real human experience. Conversely, it has drawn attention away from metaphors that are more culturally conditioned, and which affect conceptualisation on a smaller scale. I would contend that the DENSITY group reflects a metaphor of this kind. Although DENSITY may not now be at the heart of the way INTELLIGENCE is conceptualised, and many of the expressions in the data are either rare or obsolete, it is my impression that it is still highly productive as a means to metaphorize stupidity. This is evidenced by the appearance of recent expressions like *thick as shit* or Scots *thick as mince*.

2.1. The data

All of the entries in the DENSITY group signify stupidity, and a noticeable feature of the data is that there is no symmetrical concept to signify intelligence; in fact, items based on the source concept of loose texture, such as the dialect word *fozy* (with the concrete meaning 'spongy, loose textured'), also signify stupidity. Part of the reason for this may be that density itself is not a symmetrical concept: there is no single word that is commonly used to express the opposite to density without introducing another element of meaning[2], and this may indicate that there is no central antonymous concept.

---

2. The *OED* lists *rarity* with the meaning "Thinness of composition or texture. (Opposed to *density*.)", but points out that this is chiefly used of air; the *NODE* does not include this sense amongst the definitions for the term.

Table 1 shows the number of entries (and percentage of data) in each of the categories I have used, which relate to the substances from which the expressions are derived[3].

Table 1. Entries in each of the categories used

Concept	Entries	% DENSITY data	% Total data
DENSITY	89	100	8.3
WOOD	33	37.1	3.1
GENERAL TERMS	18	20.2	1.7
FOOD	16	18.0	1.5
EARTH	12	13.5	1.1
MISC SUBSTANCES	9	10.1	0.8

As these figures indicate, the interesting thing about the DENSITY group is that the source concepts from which individual entries derive are unexpectedly specific, and there are a very limited number of these. From the data, I have identified three broad groups, WOOD, EARTH and FOOD, and nearly 75% of the entries are connected with one of these. The data for each of the groups is given in tables in the appendix,[4] with the GENERAL group first and the other groups following in order of size.

2.2. Motivation

Because it allows for a range of different processes and connections whilst also acknowledging the conceptual importance of primary metaphor, one theory that provides a helpful framework in which to analyse the DENSITY metaphors is blending theory. In particular, one of the observations made by Fauconnier and Turner (1998) is integral to the way in which this mapping is motivated.

> Even metaphoric mappings that ostensibly look most as if they depend entirely on the construction of metaphoric counterparts can have integration of events as a principal motivation and product. "He digested the book" of course has metaphoric counterparts, such as food and book, but it also projects an integration of events. In

---

3. It should be pointed out that because I have classified compounds and phrases by breaking them into constituent parts, the entry *as thick as (two) plank(s)*, is labelled as 'density-general and wood', and therefore this is included in both the groups GENERAL and WOOD.
4. These include the fields *meaning* (ie CLEVER or STUPID), *word*, *part of speech* (ie noun or adjective), and *date range*. The latter relates to the datings of the first and last supporting quotations given for the expression in the *OED*, and can include *ante* or *circa*; brackets around the final date indicate uncertainty about continued usage after this date, and the symbol > is used to mark an expression as current.

the source, digesting already constitutes an integration of a number of different events. But its counterpart in the target is, independent of the metaphor, a series of discreet events – taking up the book, reading it, parsing its individual sentences, finishing it, thinking about it, understanding it as a whole, and so on. The integrity in the source is projected to the blend so that this array of events in the target acquires a conceptual integration of its events into a unit. On one hand, the metaphor blends conceptual counterparts in the two spaces – eating and reading. On the other hand, the metaphor helps us to integrate some distinct event sequences in the space of reading (Fauconnier and Turner 1998:158).

I believe that this is an important point when considering the DENSITY data. In a similar way to that described here by Fauconnier and Turner for the metaphor "He digested a book", the mapping has two metaphoric 'counterparts': these are a dense substance and intelligence (or rather, stupidity). But the motivation for the metaphor is rooted in "an integration of a number of different events" – it is based on an image, and works almost like a narrative. The idea is presumably that if something is dense in its physical texture, it will be difficult to penetrate, so if a person's mind is dense, ideas and knowledge cannot easily get in or through. A number of common phrases have the same basis: it is natural and conventional to talk about *getting something through one's head* or *skull*, or to say that an idea or theory *won't go in*. Important to this conceptualisation is the idea of impediment to motion, since the density of the mind prevents the passage of ideas, and metaphorically this can also cause a temporary problem, when one has a *mental block*, as opposed to experiencing a *flow of ideas*.

The mapping has a number of entailments, which are dependent on certain other metaphors fundamental to the way the mind is conceptualised. For the mind to have any sort of texture, it must be a physical, bounded entity, and this is a common and well documented mapping; for example, Lakoff and Johnson refer to THE MIND IS AN ENTITY and to 'elaborated', more specific versions of this such as THE MIND IS A MACHINE and THE MIND IS A BRITTLE OBJECT (Lakoff and Johnson 2003: 27–28). For things to get 'through' the mind's boundary and 'inside' it, a container schema must be closely aligned with the mapping. This fits in with other core category groups within the INTELLIGENCE data, including CONTAINER itself, as well as entries relating to grasping – a basic way of accounting for grasp is roughly as a blend of TOUCH and CONTAINER. A primary metaphor related to the container schema is IMPORTANT IS CENTRAL (Grady 1997: 284), and this seems relevant as well. It is clear from this that the metaphorical extension of DENSITY comes out of the same experience of embodiment that has been shown to be at the core of so many other mappings.

3. Specificity

However, although this explains the general mapping for DENSITY, it does not offer any rationale for the high percentage of specific substances in the data, and the question of why terms relating to specific substances rather than to the general property of density should be addressed. The motivation for particular expressions, considered out of the context of a corpus of similar expressions, is relatively opaque. Linking the concept of density itself with INTELLIGENCE would not present the problems of interpretation that specific substances with the same general property can, so that it might seem more logical for the mapping to be restricted to these.

There do seem to be various possible reasons for this. To a certain extent there may be a connection with the point Feyaerts makes about the general mapping between stupidity and a deficient head/brain (Feyaerts 1999). Using a specific substance or entity fits into this 'model' far more neatly and naturally, thereby plugging these metaphors into a more established pattern that can support and strengthen the blend. As well as this, the selection of a specific entity rather than a more general property may be connected to the way in which humans tend to process the world around them and relate concepts to known, familiar sources. A number of scholars have observed that abstract notions tend to be conceptualised in terms of concrete objects, and in general this is the direction that metaphorical mappings tend to follow (see further Saeed 1997: 305–306). Mapping INTELLIGENCE to DENSITY utilises a less abstract source domain, since density is a concept that is used with reference to concrete physical entities, but using a specific, physically apprehensible entity to stand for this concept may be an even better source because of its more concrete nature. This must be affected by the fact that the DENSITY mapping is based (at least in part) on a mental image, ie that of something trying to penetrate the mind. In order to form a mental picture of the property 'density', some substance that has the property of being dense must be involved.

In order to explain the selection of WOOD, EARTH and FOOD as the substances found most commonly, it is crucial to consider the cultural factors that condition the choice of source in any mapping. The subgroups within DENSITY are all related to very common, familiar entities that are part of daily human experience. None are of particularly high value: though wood and food can be important commodities, they tend not to be costly in their crude, uncrafted state and are certainly not perceived as prestigious items of worth. Furthermore, all of the substances involved are of basic rather than complex structure, with uniform consistency, reflected by the fact that most of them are mass nouns or are constituted from mass noun substances. For example, *logs* are countable but are units of *wood*, and have a single texture throughout even though they are discrete bounded items. Similarly, the FOOD group contains entries connected with basic ingredients and substances rather than complex foodstuffs, like *beef-witted* and *suet-brained*.

As the data shows, there are no entries in the DENSITY group pre-dating 1500. This is in direct contrast with data relating to other source concepts for INTELLIGENCE, e.g. VISION, which are well evidenced in OE several centuries earlier. This may well be directly related to problems with written evidence for some areas of vocabulary[5], but without this evidence it seems difficult to determine whether the conceptual link between texture and intelligence had already been widely made by the time the metaphor is recorded. However, it does not seem unlikely that the primary metaphors that underlie the DENSITY mapping were already core to early conceptualisation of the intellect. For example, it is uncontroversial to suggest that the MIND AS CONTAINER metaphor was well-established in Old English, where it is common to talk about things being 'in' mind, and in fact one entry in the data attests this: the OE adjective *idel* also means 'empty'. A number of cognates suggest that this is the earliest sense of the root (see the *OED* entry for *idle*). This would indicate that even if DENSITY was not commonly associated with stupidity, the building blocks for this link were in place.

4. Cognitive 'cohesion'

However, this selection of a particular specific source entity does create a problem in the way the data is interpreted. Whilst density seems like the most obviously relevant property of the source substance for some entries in the data, for others this is more questionable, and this highlights the problems of assessing the basic metaphor involved in any particular mapping. It should be pointed out that the most important aspect of my approach to the data is that it forms part of a corpus, and that the classification

---

5. This corresponds to the lack of early STUPIDITY words in the data as a whole, and may be explained by considering the nature of OE texts. Obviously, manuscripts were extremely expensive, and this affected the type of material that was produced. By nature, and because of the relatively formal register in which they tend to be written, most early texts do not contain much in the way of colourful or creative terminology to describe stupid people.

that I imposed here was reached from an analysis of the data, rather than being theory-based. It is for this reason that I would argue for its validity, even where individual entries require further discussion or justification.

In general though, it seems to me that the idea of cognitive 'cohesion' is helpful here. These entries do seem to me to have a basic property in common, but I acknowledge that the source concepts are not suitable to express lack of intelligence only because they are dense substances. Other properties must also be relevant, and perhaps the combination of properties make them more cognitively 'convincing', especially since metaphorical sources are not selected as a result of conscious reasoning about motivation. Furthermore, it may also be the case that even though a particular item is not originally motivated in the same way as some others that appear similar, it may still be influenced by these and this may even account for its continued usage, at least in part. The importance of folk etymology is by now widely recognised (see for example Rundblad and Kronenfeld 2000); it seems logical that similar mechanisms might lie behind (conscious or subconscious) reasoning about metaphorical mappings.

A high proportion of these entries are from words for pieces of wood – block, log, stock, hulver, chump – but these are almost all more specifically large chunks of wood. As well as carrying the idea of being dense substances, they are also unwieldy, awkwardly-sized, heavy lumps that are uncrafted, and all of this may add to their 'suitability' as sources. In fact, in its notes about etymology, the *OED* suggests that *logger* was "invented as expressing by its sound the notion of something heavy and clumsy". There are entries in the rest of the INTELLIGENCE data that parallel these characteristics, and as well as this largeness and heaviness can correlate with slowness, and SPEED is very important in the way intelligence is conceptualised. Similarly, the idea of formlessness can be found elsewhere in our vocabulary for the mental – we talk about ideas 'taking shape' or 'being shaped' by external influences.

Similarly, in the EARTH category, there are other factors involved in the mappings of both the group and individual entries. Several entries contain the element *mud* – again, mud comes in lumps that lack form and do not hold shape well. Thinking especially of its more liquid form, mud is turbid, so perhaps has a link with the idea of lack of clarity (which fits in with notions of mental clarity). Interestingly, the word *muddle* is derived from *mud* as well.

The FOOD group is perhaps the most problematic in terms of interpretation, particularly since unlike WOOD and EARTH, FOOD is not a basic level category. There are several other entries in the INTELLIGENCE data that are also derived from edible substances which have not been classified in the DENSITY group, and in fact some of these appear to have almost the opposite motivation from the entries in DENSITY. For example, one group is made up of entries derived from liquid or semi-liquid substances, i.e. substances that have the opposite property in terms of physical texture. However, it is not impossible that these strengthen the link between the two concepts despite having 'mutually exclusive' motivation. It is uncontroversial to suggest that, in general, when a link between two concepts has been made that is cognitively 'successful' for speakers, this seems to establish a pathway that attracts other mappings between the same general semantic fields (and, more narrowly, from the same lexical root). At least in part, this can account for the productiveness of certain sources in the DENSITY groups. However, it does not seem unreasonable to propose that this kind of mechanism might be relevant even in cases where motivation differs, especially since the mental processing of metaphors does not appear to involve conscious reasoning (at least in the majority of cases). Using a corpus gives an opportunity to examine data in a wider context, so that it is possible to gain an overview and observe these kinds of patterns.

5. Linguistic 'failures'

As I have pointed out, there would seem to be constraints on the type of entity that can be the source in a mapping, and the substances that appear in the group seems almost without exception to be consistent with these. Almost as interesting as the data that *is* found in the DENSITY group, though, is that which is not – an important question that presents itself here is why certain other dense substances are less successful as sources. Obviously, some are excluded because of other properties they have, which 'override' their potential to be used; an obvious example would be a precious metal like gold. The high value and rarity of gold (and its generally positive associations) are more salient than its density, and because of these it would be extremely unusual for it to be associated with a negative characteristic like stupidity. However, this does not appear to be the case for all other possible sources, and there are a few that would seem to be equally as available and suitable as those that do appear in the data. Stone and low-value metals such as iron and steel seem ideal to be mapped to stupidity, given that they are also reasonably common, high density substances that are used by man in a variety of ways, and yet these do not emerge as established sources.

Stone does appear in the data, but only in two entries (listed within the MISC section): *stone*, which has a single supporting quotation in 1598, and *stunpoll*, which is cited in 1794 and continues into current usage. The *OED* suggests uncertainly that *stunpoll* is derived from a variant of *stone* in compound with *poll*, head, but it should be noted that folk etymology would be likely to associate this with the verb *stun*. There are other items in the data connected to the idea of physical impact – for example, *stupid* itself can be traced back to Latin *stupere* 'to hit, stun' – so that this explanation for the etymology of *stunpoll* is intuitively satisfying. If someone has suffered physical impact to the head, it is likely that their mental faculties are affected negatively, so it is understandable that this can be used to imply a lack of intelligence. This must be a factor in the continued use of this word, and may be more significant than its actual origins. I would speculate that there may be various reasons for the lack of any other stone entries. It may be simply too hard – although substances like wood and lumps of earth are dense, they can be penetrated with effort, whereas stone is a completely different texture, and has no 'give' at all. The same is true of bone, which yields three very recent entries, *bone-headed aj 1903>*, *bonehead n 1908>* and US *ivory dome n 1923>*, and this is also a property of all metals. Correspondingly, there is a difference between being able to comprehend something with difficulty (ie get it 'into one's brain') and being wholly incapable of this; it is perhaps quite different to imply that someone has limited and underused potential to learn compared to no ability at all.

Aside from this, and perhaps more convincingly, there may be an issue about other properties metaphorically associated with any entity. It is uncontroversial to suggest that there are restraints that govern reference, both as regards literal and figurative language. Since any language is a system, a given lexical item cannot support two disparate meanings that might be commonly confused – this would mean that the system was not operating efficiently. In a 1972 work in which he discusses systemic regulation, Samuels observes that "If a form has two meanings – whether as the result of polysemy or homonymy – so incompatible that they cause ambiguity, one of the meanings dies out, or, more rarely, the form itself becomes obsolete" (Samuels 1972: 65). The well-known historical example that he uses to support this is the development of *silly* (< OE *sælig*), from its original meaning *happy* to its current meaning *foolish or stupid*, as shown in Figure 1.

In the thirteenth century this was a highly polysemous term with both positive and negative senses; over the following six centuries all of the meanings with generally positive connotations gradually died out. What is notable about this example is that all of the term's polysemous meanings were concentrated in the same semantic field, human characteristics, and it is because they would have been used in the same context (i.e., to describe people) that they caused confusion and could not be sustained.

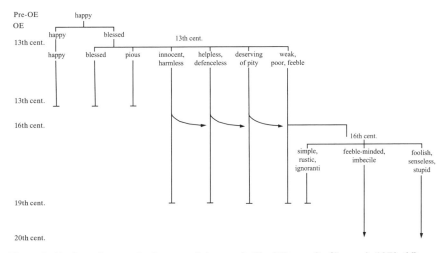

Figure 1. Dating of semantic changes of the word *silly*, OE *gesælig* (Samuels 1972: 66)

It does not seem unreasonable to assume that there may be similar constraints on the source concepts for metaphorical mappings (or at least on widely used mappings that are likely to become conventional). If a concept like wood becomes conventionally associated with the human characteristic stupidity, it may be that (with some qualifications) this precludes its mapping to other targets within the field of human characteristics. Conversely, other substances may not be mapped to stupidity if they are already conventionally associated with other characteristics, and this may be why some substances that appear to be suitable for the mapping do not appear in the data. Stone is commonly and widely used as a source concept for other human characteristics besides stupidity: it can be connected with steadiness and constancy, as when someone is described as a *rock* or *brick*, and equally it can be used to connote cruelty and indifference, as in a *heart of stone* or a *stony expression*. The more common base metals steel and iron, perhaps less familiar substances anyway, seem to have similar constraints. Steel has been used to express the idea of endurance, and this was used by the creators of Superman, who they termed *the man of steel*; it is also the source, like stone, for cruelty or indifference, as in *steely-faced*. Iron tends to be associated with the ability to withstand physical or mental difficulty, as in an *iron stomach* or a *will of iron*. In themselves, these substances fit the motivation that lies behind the DENSITY data; but because language is a system that is rooted in one particular cultural context, they are not available.

6. Conclusion

It is my contention that attempting case studies of particular mappings gives us the opportunity to gain some sense of the complexities involved in metaphor. By using a corpus, it is possible to identify groups of data that may not immediately seem significant or conceptually important, but which can shed light on other recognised mappings, as well as on the mechanics of metaphor in general. A diachronic approach can offer a fresh perspective on the background and influences of specific expressions and the general groups to which these relate; it is possible to identify linguistic 'failures' as well as 'successes', and this may lead to a better understanding of what constrains and motivates individual metaphors, as well as of the metaphorical process itself. I hope, in this paper, to have illustrated a few of the many factors that can be relevant in any mapping, and the way in which cultural and intra-systemic influences can interact with cognitive processes to produce complex and yet cohesive mappings.

References

Allan, Kathryn L.
    2003   An examination of metaphor from Old English to Present Day English, focusing on notions of intelligence/cleverness and stupidity. Ph.D. dissertation, University of Glasgow.

Boroditsky, Lera
    2000   Metaphoric structuring: understanding time through spatial metaphors. In *Cognition* 75: 1–28.

Fauconnier, Gilles and Mark Turner
    1998   Conceptual integration networks. *Cognitive Science* 22: 133–187.

Feyaerts, Kurt
    1999   Metonymic hierarchies: the conceptualization of stupidity in German idiomatic expressions. In: Klaus-Uwe Panther and Günter Radden (eds.), *Metonymy in language and thought*, 309–332. Amsterdam: John Benjamins.

Grady, Joseph E.
    1997   Foundations of meaning: primary metaphors and primary scenes. PhD Thesis, University of California, Berkeley.

Kay, Christian J.
    2000   Metaphors we lived by: pathways between Old and Modern English. In: Jane Roberts and Janet Nelson (eds.) *Essays on Anglo-Saxon and*

Related Themes in Memory of Lynne Grundy, 273–285. London: King's College London.

Kay, Christian J., Jane Roberts, Michael L. Samuels and Irené A.W. Wotherspoon (eds.)
   Forthcoming   *Historical Thesaurus of English*. University of Glasgow.

Lakoff, George and Mark Johnson
   2003   *Metaphors We Live By*. Second edition. Chicago: University of Chicago Press.

Rundblad, Gabriella and David B. Kronenfeld
   2000   Folk-etymology: haphazard perversion or shrewd analogy? In Julie Coleman and Christian J. Kay (eds.) *Lexicology, Semantics and Lexicography*, 19–34. Amsterdam: John Benjamins.

Saeed, John I.
   1997   *Semantics*. Oxford: Blackwell.

Samuels, Michael L.
   1972   *Linguistic Evolution*. London: Cambridge University Press.

Simpson, John and Edmund Weiner (eds.)
   1989   *The Oxford English Dictionary*. Second edition. Oxford: Oxford University Press.

Appendix: Data tables

Table A1. Source domain DENSITY (General)

Meaning	Word	PoS	OE?	a/c1	Date 1	+/–	a/c2	Date 2	–/+	a/c3	Date 3	Curr.
stupid	*gross*	aj			1526	–		1844				
stupid	*grosshead*	n			1580	–		1606				
stupid	*thick(-)skin*	n			1582	–		1893				
stupid	*thick*	aj			1597							>
stupid	*thick-brained*	aj			1619							
stupid	*thickwitted*	aj			1634							>
stupid	*thick-skulled*	aj		a	1653							>
stupid	*thick-skull*	n			1755	–		1894				
stupid	*thick-headed*	aj			1801	–		1891				
stupid	*dense*	aj			1822							>
stupid	*thick-head*	n			1824							>
stupid	*thick*	n			1857							>
stupid	*crass*	aj			1861							>
stupid	*thick-head*	aj			1873	–		1894				
stupid	*thickwit*	n			1904							
stupid	*thickie*	n			1968							>
stupid	*as thick as (two) plank(s)*	aj			1974							>
stupid	*thicko*	n			1976							>

Table A2. Source domain WOOD

Meaning	Word	PoS	OE?	a/c1	Date 1	+/–	a/c2	Date 2	–/+	a/c3	Date 3	Curr.
stupid	blockish	aj			1548	–		1868				
stupid	blockheaded	aj			1549	–		1860				
stupid	blockhead	n			1549							>
stupid	block	n		a	1553	–		1810				
stupid	log-headed	aj			1571	+		1926				>
stupid	wooden	aj		a	1586							>
stupid	loggerhead	n			1588	–		1821	+		1892	
stupid	stock	n			1594							>
stupid	logger-headed	aj			1596	–		1831				
stupid	stockish	aj			1596							>
stupid	block-pate	n			1598							
stupid	blockhead	aj			1606	–		1719				
stupid	stub	n			1644							
stupid	as sad as any mallet	aj			1645							
stupid	timber-headed	aj			1666							
stupid	logger	aj			1675	–		1781	+		1812	
stupid	loggerhead	aj			1684							
stupid	a piece of wood	n			1691							
stupid	hulver-head	n		a	1700							
stupid	chuckle-headed	aj			1764							>
stupid	nog-head	n		c	1800							>
stupid	chuckle-pate	aj			1820							
stupid	stob	n			1825							
stupid	stump	n			1825							>
stupid	log-head	n			1831							
stupid	woodenhead	n			1831							>
stupid	blockheadish	aj			1833	+		1863				
stupid	timber-head	n			1849							
stupid	wooden-headed	aj			1865							
stupid	off his chump	aj			1877							>
stupid	chump	n			1883							>
stupid	nog-headed	aj			1891	–		1893				
stupid	woodentop	n			1983							>

Table A3. Source domain FOOD

Meaning	Word	PoS	OE?	a/c1	Date 1	+/–	a/c2	Date 2	–/+	a/c3	Date 3	Curr.
stupid	grout-head	n			1550	–		1649				
stupid	groutnoll	n			1578	–		1658				
stupid	grout-headed	aj			1578	–		1694	+		1847/78	
stupid	beef-witted	aj			1606							
stupid	beef-brained	aj			1627							
stupid	macaroon	n		a	1631	–	a	1633				
stupid	pudding-headed	aj			1726	–		1867				
stupid	mutton-headed	aj			1768							
stupid	beef-head	n			1775							
stupid	mutton-head	n			1803							>
stupid	beef-headed	aj			1828	+		1900				
stupid	pudding head	n			1851							>
stupid	suet-brained	aj			1921							>
stupid	suet-headed	aj			1937							>
stupid	meat-head	n			1945							>
stupid	meat-headed	aj			1949							>

Table A4. Source domain EARTH

Meaning	Word	PoS	OE?	a/c1	Date 1	+/–	a/c2	Date 2	–/+	a/c3	Date 3	Curr.
stupid	clod-poll/clod pole	n			1601							>
stupid	clod	n			1605							>
stupid	turf	n			1607							
stupid	clod-pate	n			1636	–	a	1679	+	c	1690	
stupid	clod-pated	aj			1638	–		1822				
stupid	muddy-headed	aj			1642	–		1815				
stupid	clod-head	n			1644							
stupid	muddish	aj			1658	+		1829				
stupid	clod-skull	n			1707							
stupid	mud	n			1708	+		1886				
stupid	mud-headed	aj			1793							
stupid	mudhead	n			1882	–		1886				

Table A5. Miscellaneous source domains[6]

Meaning	Word	PoS	OE?	a/c1	Date 1	+/−	a/c2	Date 2	−/+	a/c3	Date 3	Curr.
stupid	clay-brained	aj			1596							
stupid	stone	n			1598							
stupid	leather-headed	aj		a	1668							
stupid	leather-head	n		a	1700							
stupid	stunpoll	n		a	1794							>
stupid	bone-headed	aj			1903							>
stupid	bonehead	n			1908							>
stupid	ivory dome	n			1923							>
stupid	knuckle-head	n			1944							>

---

6. Although these have been grouped separately, it should be pointed out that several of them are not unrelated to items in the previous groups. *Clay-brained* could arguably be classed alongside the EARTH data; similarly, *leather-headed* is semantically close to some of the entries connected with meat, and *knuckle-head* is connected to meat or bone substances.

Sense and sensibility: Rational thought versus emotion in metaphorical language*

Päivi Koivisto-Alanko and *Heli Tissari*

Abstract

Linguists dealing with conceptual metaphors do not seem to agree in their views on the difference between emotion and reason. Some suggest that emotion and reason are conceptually divergent, while others emphasize their functional similarity and co-operation.

On the basis of a range of historical and current corpora, we study metaphorical expressions occurring with the English words *mind, reason, wit, love* and *fear* in order to determine (1) whether metaphors occurring with words for reason (*mind, reason, wit*) and emotion (*love, fear*) can be considered as two internally homogeneous groups; (2) whether these groups behave similarly both in Early Modern English and Present-Day English; and (3) whether and where reason and emotion really diverge from each other.

We show that the conceptual domains of REASON and EMOTION share central, general-level metaphors. Both REASON and EMOTION are found with CONTAINER and PERSONIFICATION metaphors. However, on a more specific level, there are domain-specific metaphors. For example, the metaphor LOVE IS A VALUABLE COMMODITY is very frequent, the metaphor WIT IS A VALUABLE COMMODITY is extremely rare. There are also differences in the actual usage of the shared metaphors; while THE MIND IS A CONTAINER, EMOTIONS ARE FLUIDS IN A CONTAINER, the body. As to the historical comparison, we show that diachronic differences exist. For example, the positive-negative polarity of LOVE and FEAR was different in Early Modern English, where FEAR could also be seen as positive and LOVE had more negative overtones than in Present-Day English. Likewise, the metaphorization of *wit* – a noun which has undergone a significant semantic change from the 14th century to the present – indicates that change in metaphorical structure could be used as one indicator of semantic change. As the modern meaning emerges, INSTRUMENT metaphors increase, as does the VALUABLE COMMODITY metaphor.

Thus, this paper shows that there are both general and domain-specific metaphors, and that subtle changes occur in the latter, that can be traced through time using corpus-linguistic methods.

1. Introduction

Linguists dealing with conceptual metaphors do not seem to agree in their views on the difference between emotion and reason. Quoting

---

* The research reported here was supported by the Academy of Finland Centre of Excellence funding for the Research Unit for Variation and Change in English at the University of Helsinki.

Jäkel (1995), Kövecses (2000: 196) suggests that emotion and reason are conceptually divergent, while Lakoff and Johnson (1999) emphasise their functional similarity and co-operation. Assuming that conceptual metaphors reflect a folk theory of the mind and body (Lakoff 1987: 380–415) and consequently give us valuable information about people's experience of emotion and rational thought, we investigated metaphorical expressions occurring with the English words *fear, love, mind, reason* and *wit* (cf. Koivisto-Alanko 2000, Tissari 2003). Our aim was to see (1) whether metaphors occurring with words for reason (*mind, reason, wit*) and emotion (*fear, love*) can be considered as two internally homogeneous groups; (2) whether these groups behave similarly both in Early Modern (ca. 1500–1700) and Present-Day English; and (3) whether and where rational thought and emotion really diverge from each other. Our study can also be seen as a contribution to the ongoing discussion about the linguistic conceptualisation of thought across languages (Palmer, Goddard and Lee 2003), on which it provides a diachronic and "emotionally intelligent" view.

2. Theoretical background

In this section we give a very concise overview of previous research on metaphors of rational thought and emotion. Metaphors of rational thought and intellection have been studied both by (synchronic) cognitive linguists and etymologically oriented scholars but, like research in the field of emotion, it also relates to psychology, anthropology and cultural studies (e.g. Holland and Quinn 1989 [1987]).

2.1. Cognitive metaphors for rational thought

The sphere of rational thought, stretching from understanding to intellection and beyond, has been described in several works on cognitive metaphors (Lakoff and Johnson 1980, Reddy 1979, Sweetser 1990, Jäkel 1990, cf. also Allan, this volume, for a study on STUPIDITY, the opposite of rational thought).

Lakoff and Johnson (1980, cf. also Johnson 1987) considered UNDERSTANDING IS SEEING the central metaphor for rational thought, since they hold that VISION is experientially the most dominant source domain for metaphorical use. The ontological IDEAS ARE OBJECTS metaphor is also deemed central (cf. Reddy 1979). In the realm of historical linguistics, Eve Sweetser (1990: 32–33) drew attention to the MIND-AS-BODY metaphor where the links VISION IS MANIPULATION and VISION IS INTELLECTION can be found. Olaf Jäkel (1995) has challenged Lakoff and Johnson in claiming that MENTAL ACTIVITY IS MANIPULATION (THE MIND IS A WORKSHOP etc.) is a higher-level metaphor than UNDERSTANDING IS SEEING. Jäkel (1995: 225–226), relying on his extensive corpus and etymological evidence, holds that MENTAL ACTIVITY IS MANIPULATION has a wider range of expressions in language, covers the entire range of mental activities, and is both etymologically and interlinguistically more plausible. The MIND IS A MACHINE metaphor (also recognised by Lakoff and Johnson) is, according to Jäkel, one of its subcategories.

2.2. Cognitive metaphors for emotion

Lakoff and Johnson (1980: 30–32) pointed out that emotions as states are conceptualised as containers (*be in love*). They also listed a number of other metaphors for love, but emotions have been more thoroughly studied by Kövecses (1990, 2000), who is interested in the differences and similarities between them. He suggests that the idea of containment is central to all emotions, which can be conceptualised either as CONTAINERS or as contained by THE BODY (Kövecses 1990: 144–149). There are also other metaphors which apply across a range of emotions. These include: THE EMOTIONS ARE NATURAL FORCES, EMOTION IS FIRE, EMOTION IS AN OPPONENT, AN EMOTION IS AN (INANIMATE) OBJECT, EMOTIONS ARE VALUABLE OBJECTS, EMOTIONS ARE FRAGILE OBJECTS, and AN EMOTION IS A LIVING ORGANISM (PLANT, ANIMAL, PERSON) (Kövecses 1990: 160–167, cf. Stefanowitsch, this volume, for a systematic corpus-based approach to emotion metaphors including a critical appraisal of Kövecses's work).

2.3. Something similar, something different

Despite his suggestion that emotion and reason are conceptually divergent, Kövecses (2000: 35–50, 196) emphasises that metaphors which apply to emotions also apply to other concepts. He says that abstract concepts share "conceptual materials". This is indeed a prerequisite for the whole theory of conceptual metaphors (Lakoff and Johnson 1980, Lakoff and Turner 1989). The real question, which Kövecses's (1990, 2000) studies of emotion also attempt to answer, concerns the topography of conceptual areas: which materials are (not) shared, how and why.

3. Method and data

3.1. Method

We wish to stress that our approach differs from most studies on conceptual metaphor, which have sought major metaphors for the concept studied. We hope to gain a new perspective on cognitive metaphors with a narrower but deeper view. We intend to investigate systematically how the metaphorical use of *fear, love, mind, reason* and *wit* – words central to the concepts of rational thought and emotion – changes in diachrony.

Even though this is a corpus linguistic study, we did not even attempt a true quantitative approach (i.e., we will not present our findings in numbers), but we did take frequency as the main factor defining salience (Geeraerts 1997: 44, Koivisto-Alanko 2000: 47–48). We tried to minimise the role of introspection – inasmuch it is possible in semantics – by choosing five key terms that were retrieved from computerised corpora and analysed in their immediate context. However, we felt that it would hardly have been fitting to give exact figures on data which was by no means unambiguous. Of the difficulties we faced in "pinning down" the metaphors, the two most relevant were overlaps between metaphors and defining the boundary between metaphorical and non-metaphorical usages (e.g. formulaic *by reason of*).[1]

The analysis addresses the role of the actual word studied, not the expression in general. We included in this study only those metaphors containing the words *fear, love, mind, reason* or *wit* that were common to both rational thought and emotion. We first analysed the data for emotion and rational thought separately and established the most frequently used metaphors for each word, choosing for this study only those metaphors that were shared by both domains. This means that we have deliberately left out some central metaphors that did not fit within the scope of this study.

It should be noted that all the words chosen to represent rational thought and emotion in this study are polysemous (cf. Bierwiaczonek 2002: 36–47). Although the different senses of a word do not have an identical metaphorical structure, they still belong to the same category (albeit in separate prototypical clusters), thus also having more in common in terms of metaphorical structure than two unrelated words would (Koivisto-Alanko 2000: 37–40).

---

1. According to Zoltán Kövecses (personal communication), we may have emphasised lower-level metaphors somewhat at the cost of upper-level (more general) ones.

The question of polysemy and metaphorical structure in semantic change – where does metaphor end and separate meaning begin? – would require a study of its own. In this paper the matter is touched upon only in connection with the semantic change in *wit* (for a thorough analysis of *wit* in diachrony, cf. Koivisto-Alanko 2000: 136ff.).

3.2. Data

The data comes from four English language corpora. Two represent Early Modern English, and two Present-Day English. The Early Modern English corpora comprise *The Corpus of Early English Correspondence Sampler*, CEECS (which also contains some Late Middle English), and the Early Modern English period of *The Helsinki Corpus of English Texts*, HC. The Present-Day English data comes from two one-million word corpora representing 1990s American and British English, *The Freiburg-Brown Corpus*, FROWN, and *The Freiburg-LOB Corpus*, FLOB (for more specific information on these corpora, see Kytö 1996; Nurmi 1998; Hundt, Sand & Siemund 1998; and Hundt, Sand & Skandera 1999).

Koivisto-Alanko's data (Table 1) comprised 181 occurrences of the noun *wit*, 1096 of *mind*, and 1124 of *reason*. Both the singular and plural forms of these nouns were searched for. Only nouns were taken into account in the data for rational thought, because the noun and verb *wit* began to diverge in the late 14th century and could not be treated as equal in the same time periods. In practice, there is not much difference, as most of the metaphorical use appears with nouns. Since the *wit* material is less extensive than that of the other words, we have included some illustrative examples from the *British National Corpus* (BNC) and, in one case, from the Late Middle English period of the *Helsinki Corpus*. *Wit* is clearly the rarest of the nouns, while *mind* and *reason* provide about as many examples in toto, but behave differently in the various corpora. *Reason* appears much more seldom in the letter corpus than *mind*.

Table 2, which describes Tissari's data on *love*, occurring 2296 times, and *fear*, 882 times, includes both the noun and verb plus compounds, derivational nouns, adjectives and adverbs, e.g., *lovingly,* and *fearful*. This gives an idea of the relative frequency of the lexemes in terms of their productivity. Table 2 shows that *love* is at least twice as frequent as *fear* in all the corpora, and three times as frequent as *fear* in CEECS. In practice, we noticed that very few metaphors accompany adjectives and adverbs derived from the base *love*, or even the noun *lover* (cf. Tissari 2003: 331). Consequently, the focus of the *fear* analysis was on the verb and noun *fear*.

Table 1. The data on *wit*, *mind* and *reason*.

	WIT	N/10,000	MIND	N/10,000	REASON	N/10,000
CEECS	121	0.5	329	7.3	183	4.1
HC	114	2.1	267	4.8	313	5.7
FROWN	17	0.2	263	2.6	304	3.0
FLOB	129	0.3	237	2.4	324	3.2
Total	181	0.6	1096	3.7	1124	3.7

Table 2. The data on *love* and *fear*.

	LOVE	N/10,000	FEAR	N/10,000
CEECS	792	17.6	255	5.7
HC	498	9.0	211	3.8
FROWN	528	5.3	239	2.4
FLOB	478	4.8	177	1.8
Total	2296	7.7	882	2.9

4. Analysis

Our analysis section begins from the so-called ontological metaphor (Lakoff and Johnson 1980), through which abstract concepts are understood as physical entities. We here regard ENTITY as a supracategory to CONTAINER, INSTRUMENT/TOOL/WEAPON, OBSTACLE and VALUABLE COMMODITY, and associate the COMMODITY metaphor with quantification. We then move on to another ENTITY, THE HUMAN BODY, which is both a source domain for rational thought and THE CONTAINER FOR EMOTIONS. Conceptualising an abstract concept in terms of A HUMAN BODY seems to be close to personification. Last but not least, we deal with FORCE metaphors. We use italics to highlight the metaphorical expressions in our quotes.

4.1. ENTITY

To begin with, it is clear from our data that both reason and emotion are conceptualised as physical ENTITIES, but these cannot always be given a more specific name. Let us take *fear* as an example (see 5.1. for a lengthier discussion of the metaphorical ENTITIES of emotion):

(1) And from the time he had been a small boy, with the terrifying example of his father *to shape his fears*, he had feared nothing half as much as being out of control. (FROWN: L06: 3)

(2) Kemira said the monopolies commission's fears for competition in the UK fertiliser market were *"wholly misplaced"* and that the decision would hurt UK output and jobs. (FLOB: H27: 10)

4.1.1. INSTRUMENT/TOOL/WEAPON

Although the source domains INSTRUMENT, TOOL, and WEAPON might seem clear-cut entities, they can be seen as subcategories of several higher-level metaphors. Here we have chosen to group them under the very general category of ENTITY but, as will be seen, MENTAL ACTIVITY IS MANIPULATION is just as valid. In the *wit* material all sharp objects, whether they be used for work or battle, fall very naturally together as a typical metaphor of the word *wit*:

(3) For I assure you, *there is no such whetstone, to sharpen a good witte* and encourage a will to learninge, as is praise. (HC: ASCH 183)
(4) For wit is *a keen instrument*, and every one can *cut* and *gash* with it, but *to carve* a Beautiful image and to polish it requires great art and dexterity. (HC: TILLOTS II: ii 430)

This metaphor is even more common in PDE (example 5). There it would, of course, fit into the ARGUMENT IS WAR metaphorical structure, but since there is a clear continuity from EModE, with senses denoting superior intelligence, and the later expression of intelligence in speech and writing (what we now call *wit*), we prefer to see the INSTRUMENT/TOOL/WEAPON as applicable to both ARGUMENT IS WAR and MENTAL ACTIVITY IS MANIPULATION.

(5) I *fired fusillades of wit* at their habits ... (FROWN: K11:14)

Mind can be an INSTRUMENT or A WEAPON, but it is quite rare. There are, however, several cases of THE MIND AS SCALES, as in PDE:

(6) And if any one shall *throughly weigh* in his Mind the Force and Energy of the one and of the other, he shall soon find them to be different things ... (HC: BOETHPR 127)

Reason can sometimes be seen as A MEASURE (cf. section 4.3). The most common formula in the Early Modern *reason* data is *by reason (where)of*, which is best analysed as AN INSTRUMENT, but may, in some cases, be A MEASURE as well:

(7) If the maister of the pudding cart before named, would let the filthines of the butcherie tarie so long there vntill it stanke so sore, *by reason of* long continuing in that place, and for lacke of carying out betime ... (HC: TURNER D1V)

In PDE, *by reason of* is obsolete. Instead, there are a great deal of *for this/that reason* and *the reason for this is* – expressions which are quite difficult to classify as metaphorical. In general, metaphorical use of REASON seems to have lessened from EModE to PDE.

Love and *fear* are not usually conceptualised as INSTRUMENTS, but religious contexts, in which *love* and *fear* can serve as INSTRUMENTS of salvation, provide an exception:

(8) *Work out* your own salvation *with fear* and trembling ... (FLOB: D12: 27)

4.1.2. OBSTACLE / WHIP

Fear is often given as the reason why something happens or does not happen. The phrase which tends to be used is *for fear (of)*. On a metaphorical level, FEAR seems to be AN OBSTACLE, or A WHIP, in contrast to any other TOOL:

(9) ... and therfore he wyl chaunge his euyll maners and conditions, and forsake his wyckednes, *for fear* to lose hys prosperitie and riches. (HC: BOETHCO 111)

This is not always indicated through the fixed phrase. To compare:

(10) ... your spontaneity and ease of manner with him will be *inhibited by* your fear of saying the wrong thing or giving him the impression that you are not too bright ... (FLOB: F06: 19)

One might comment that fear creates inhibitions and that there is nothing metaphorical about that, but it is relevant that the verb *inhibit* has the senses "to forbid" and "to hinder" and that these come before the psychological sense (s.v. OED *inhibit* v 1, 2, 3).

4.1.3. Quantification and VALUABLE COMMODITY

In the ideal case, romantic love is mutual and both participants love each other to an equal degree (Kövecses 1986: 93–96, 1988: 56–59). Metaphorical quantification of love is a means of discussing complex issues in a compact way. Quantity tends to be relevant to any relationship, be it ultimately in terms of mutual responsibilities or intensity of emotion. On a larger scale, quantification seems to be one way among others of expressing the metaphor LOVE IS A VALUABLE COMMODITY, which is very frequent in the data.

A further way of understanding the quantification of both *love* and *fear* is the metaphor SIGNIFICANT IS BIG (Lakoff and Johnson 1980: 50). There is nevertheless an important difference between "big love" and "big fear", because the former is usually desirable (example 11), while the latter is not (example 12). It can be interpreted as indicating a serious danger. By contrast, the phrase *without fear* signals safety (example 13).

(11) … you cannot poscibilly *measure my loue*. (CEECS: 1628? BHARLEY 4)
(12) Harry, sayes hee, what is it, that the lesser it is, the *more* it is to be *feared*? The king mused at it; but, to grace the jest better, he answered, he knew not. Will answered, it was a little bridge ouer a deepe riuer; at which hee smyled. (HC: ARMIN 45)
(13) Only thus can Plato drop all qualifications and call Protagoras' doctrine just plain untrue, *without any fear of* the riposte … (FLOB: J52: 2)

In the metaphors for rational thought we can see that *wit* and *reason* are quantifiable whereas *mind* is not. The VALUABLE COMMODITY metaphor is rare for *wit* (example 14) and *reason* (example 15), but its use increases somewhat toward the present. This has mainly to do with a shift in the meaning of *wit* from the domain of intellection toward the PDE meaning of expressing intellect in an entertaining manner (Koivisto-Alanko 2000). *Mind* cannot be considered A VALUABLE COMMODITY in our data.

(14) … thou knowest *I am poore, and haue neyther wealth nor wit*, and what thou lendest to the poore God will pay thee ten fold … (HC: ARMIN 47)
(15) … in the tender wittes be sparkes of voluptuositie: whiche, norished by any occasion or obiecte, encrease often tymes in to so terrible a fire, that *therwith all vertue and reason is consumed*. (HC: ELYOT 23)

4.1.4. CONTAINER

The CONTAINER metaphor is central to both rational thought and emotion. The CONTAINER metaphor is the most frequent for *mind* in our data. There are unspecific metaphors – such as *in my mind*, but also more specialised metaphors. The mind is, especially in the Early Modern material, the home, the mind of somebody, and therefore a safe place, thus constituting a metaphor SANITY IS SAFETY:

(16) ... which others endeavoured to possess him with; so that he was too soon brought to set himself secure, and *fortifie his Mind against that*, by dispossessing it all he could of the belief or apprehensions of Religion. (HC: BURNETROC 15)

The CONTAINER metaphor appears in the *wit* material only in the HOME/ SAFE PLACE – SANITY IS SAFETY context, where a person is sane as long as he is within his wits. The use of the personal pronoun is very common here (example 17). Almost as often as sanity is depicted as staying within the confines of one's wit/s (or mind), loss of sanity can be metaphorically described as letting one's wits run free (example 18). Some of these uses can also be seen as metaphors of CONTROL (cf. section 4.3).

(17) Againe, do you compare those that are *in their right mind*, with such as be mad, or *out of their wits*. (HC: GIFFORD B3V)
(18) Oute! I am madde! *My wyttes be ner goon!* (HC: DIGBY 108)

Sometimes it is not entirely clear whether the *in/out of one's wits* usage, reflecting SANITY IS SAFETY, actually makes use of the CONTAINER metaphor at all. The metaphor is sometimes, by analogy, that of ROPE/TETHER:

(19) For the prince ys *at his wyttes end* at thys time, and a sounde and princely preparacion made for hym this winter wold breake his backe the next yere ... (CEECS: 1586 RDUDLEY 423)

The same usage appears in Present-day English as well; here the interpretation can be either CONTAINER or ROPE/BORDER. The idea, however, is that of safe, limited space, thus CONTROL:

(20) It is not *beyond the wit* of the criminal justice system to find ways of managing these women in the community ... (FLOB: B09:54)

It should be noted that there are some rare cases (only in PDE) where WIT IS A FLUID IN A CONTAINER:

(21)   Your wit *surfaces over and over* like the rush of foam to the rim ... (FROWN: K03:1)

The great majority of the EModE *reason* material especially, appearing in law texts and handbooks, is formulaic, and thus difficult to analyse beyond the very general assumption that the *in reason* use is a CONTAINER metaphor, even though it often cannot be reliably established from the context as separate from PLACE, SPACE or even FLUID (example 22). Most of the formulae are calques, which makes the task even harder (see also section 4.1.1 on the very common *by reason of*).

(22)   And I pray ye, for these things, beleave us pore men that serve, and have best cause to know *what course in reason ys best*. (CEECS: 1586 RDUDLEY 73)

There are, however, some cases in the EModE material where a clearly identifiable CONTAINER metaphor can be spotted. In all these cases, *reason* is a safe, positive place (example 23). There are very few occurrences of the CONTAINER metaphor in the extensive PDE *reason* material. The *in reason* use has disappeared and *within reason* is infrequent.

(23)   For order bindeth together all thynges, soo that what thing *departheth from reson* and order appointed to the wicked, the same thing must nedes fall into some order ... (HC: BOETHCO 111)

The phrases *to be in love, to fall in love*, and even *to be out of love* contribute to the high frequency of the metaphor LOVE IS (A FLUID IN) A CONTAINER, but there are also other ways of suggesting a person's containment in love:

(24)   We *closed each other up in a closet of 'love'* that nearly *smothered* us both. (FROWN: P19: 18)

No analogous phrases exist for *fear*, but the preposition *in* often precedes the noun *fear*. Moreover, other expressions such as the verb *surround* suggest that fear can be experienced as containment:

(25)   Because of the *fear* and stigma that still *surround* mental illness, and the hopeless, helpless feeling that "nothing can be done", a lot of people end up suffering alone. (FROWN: F11: 7)

Containment and quantity may be involved (blended)[2] in the same expression:

(26)   ... the people were *in a greate feare* and dreade ... (HC: FISHER 1, 397)

Interestingly, containment by fear can also be considered positive in the religious context. The data includes many Early Modern examples which rely on the notion that if one fears God, there is little else to fear. Thus FEAR OF GOD becomes A SAFE PLACE. This notion seems to be especially characteristic of young people's education and upbringing. Parents and educators refer to fear of God as the motivation for disciplined and wise behaviour:

(27)   The Lord blless you and *presarue you in His feare*. Deare Ned, be carefull of your self ... (CEECS: 1640 BHARLEY 83)[3]

4.1.5.   BODY

THE MIND IS THE BODY is another central metaphor of rational thought (Sweetser 1990, Lakoff and Johnson 1999: 235 ff.) in our material as well, especially in the historical part. It is divided into two, BODY PART and BODY (whole/undefined) (examples 28 and 29). In PDE, the BODY metaphor is much less frequent.

(28)   Wherby he confoundeth the vertue called temperance, whiche is the moderatrice as well of *all motions of the minde*, called affectes, as of all actis procedyng of man. (HC: ELYOT 149)
(29)   Australia showed them, with *fast hands and minds*. (FLOB: A23:67)

For *wit*, the BODY metaphor is quite rare. The earlier examples (the five wits) are often better categorised as personification (see, however, example 30 where even the metaphor status is admittedly questionable), and there are no examples from the end of the 17th and beginning of the 18th

---

2. There would indeed be much to say on how the metaphors blend into each other, but we deliberately left this discussion out of the present article in order to stay within our spatial limits.
3. Fabiszak (2002: 263–265, 270) calls this metaphor FEAR IS A BOUNDED SPACE in her study of Old English fear metaphors. In addition to this metaphor, she discusses FEAR IS AN OPPONENT, FEAR IS A COMMODITY, and THE BODY IS THE CONTAINER FOR FEAR.

century. In PDE the overlap with personification is also possible (example 31). There are few BODY metaphors in the *reason* material.

(30) The Brayne is either too drye or too moyst, then can it not worke his kinde: for then is the body made colde: then are the spirites of lyfe melted and resolved away: and then foloweth *feebleness of the wittes, and of al other members of the body*, and at the laste death. (HC: VICARY 34)

(31) The safe delivery of their twins was Anne's greatest gift to Shakespeare's future *fertility of wit* ... (FLOB: G08:14)

Example (31) above could also be understood in terms of BIRTH/PROGENERATION (Turner 1996: 52–56).

Kövecses (1990: 144–159) emphasises the role of THE BODY as the metaphorical CONTAINER FOR THE EMOTIONS. More specifically, emotions can be seen as FLUIDS in the body (cf. section 4.1.4). The present data agrees with these suggestions, as well as implying that people situate emotions in the eyes (Lakoff and Johnson 1980: 50, Kövecses 1990: 173):

(32) ... "love *is in the eyes* of the beholder." (FLOB: G G55: 4)[4]

4.2. Personification

We suggest that personification can be separated from the BODY metaphor by the following points: 1) no body part or bodily function is specified, 2) the personified entity is capable of conscious action and 3) the personified entity is demonstrably human. The personified mind has a dual role in metaphors of rational thought, being either the superior, authoritative LEADER, or the subordinate, innocent or irresponsible INFERIOR, often a CHILD. *Following one's own mind* is not always seen as a positive thing, especially in the Early Modern period:

(33) And therfore doughter Margaret, I can in this thynge no further, but lyke as you labour me againe *to folowe your minde* to desire and praye you both againe to leaue of such labour, and with my former answeres to holde your selfe content. (HC: MORELET 509)

---

4. Another example can be found in the *British National Corpus*:
   (32b) As she looked up at him she saw such tenderness, *such deep love in his eyes* that her own filled with tears. (Bowring, *Vets in Opposition* [JYE 4702])

(34) ... one that did his kinde, and the other who *foolishly followed his owne minde* ... (HC: ARMIN 12)

Perhaps because of genre (there are more philosophical and religious texts in the historical material), THE MIND AS AN AUTHORITY is rarer, though it does exist, in PDE. At the other end of the hierarchy the SUBORDINATE/ INNOCENT CHILD metaphor is fairly common in EModE (example 35, see also example 39).

(35) I am persuaded the deuill doth *seduce and bewitch mens mindes*. (HC: GIFFORD B4V)

In PDE the CHILD metaphors are rare, the general personification or THE WORKER being more common:

(36) For really, when she *puts her mind to it*, there is no one better than Mom at finding solutions. (FLOB: K28:8)

Wit has two or three (a change takes place during the period) quite distinct senses in EModE, personification also reflecting this change. The older perceptive "five senses" meaning, which disappeared during EModE, makes use of the WORKER metaphor (example 37). This metaphor is retained in the plural form, although the five wits are replaced by the five senses. At the other end of the hierarchy, though, *wit* is never A LEADER OR A SUPREME AUTHORITY, but rather A LEARNED or ESTEEMED PERSON (example 38).

(37) ... in this place is registred and kept those things that are done and spoken with the senses, and keepeth them in his treasurie vnto the *putting foorth of the fiue or common wittes*. (HC: VICARY 31)
(38) I know not how it comes to pass that some men *have the fortune to be esteemed Wits* onely for jesting out of the common road ... (HC: TILLOTS II: ii 427)

Reason has only one proper personification, that of A JUDGE, or A SUPREME AUTHORITY, an uncontested leader. In a hierarchy, REASON will lead MINDS and WITS:

(39) That *the minde has not been made* obedient to rules and *pliant to reason* when at first it was most tender, most easy to be bowed. (HC: LOCKE 50)

In PDE, personification is less typical but does exist:

(40) ... an organisation with *a voice of reason that continually has to shout* to make itself heard ... (FLOB: B20:39)

The personification of love has a long history. Shakespeare often employs Cupid in his descriptions of romantic love. Note that Cupid is mischievous, and thus a challenging and complex person to face, not simply a positive experience. Shakespeare even calls love a "devil":

(41) Love is a *devil*. (Shakespeare: *Love's Labour's Lost* 1.02.172)

In the present data, self-love appears as A TRICKSTER:

(42) ... *selfe love* is never willingly *unmasked*. (CEECS: 1660S WTHIMELBY 17)

Kövecses (2000: 63, 90) appears to suggest that a persons's "real self" is considered to be hidden under the surface of THE PERSON AS THE CONTAINER, and that this self can be regarded as A TRICKSTER.

More straightforwardly, fear seems nearly always to be an unpleasant acquaintance. Kövecses (1990: 74–78) provides the following source domains for the personification of fear: VICIOUS ENEMY (HUMAN or ANIMAL), TORMENTOR, SUPERNATURAL BEING (GHOST etc.), OPPONENT, and SUPERIOR. There was too little data on *fear* to reasonably distinguish between these, but both the list and the data suggest that personification is not a very clear-cut strategy. How do we know whether A VICIOUS ENEMY is HUMAN or ANIMAL? It may be difficult even to say whether one is dealing with AN ANIMAL or A PLANT in cases where emotions are born and die, etc. (cf. Tissari 2003: 372–373). In the following, fear is something which wakes a person up (AN ALARM CLOCK? A BARKING DOG? A NASTY PERSON? A FORCE?):

(43) Fear *had gotten her fully awake* ... (FROWN: L20: 28)

4.3. FORCE/CONTROL

It has been suggested that the metaphors LOVE IS A PHYSICAL FORCE and LOVE IS A NATURAL FORCE reflect passivity, lack of control, and pleasantness, three central aspects of falling in love (Kövecses 1996: 89). An example is:

(44) She *swept me off my feet.* (Kövecses 1996: 88–90)

A phrase from our EModE data shows that love is not necessarily pleasant:

(45) *the trowbely* [= troubled] *waves of love* (CEECS: 1472? TMULL I, 126)

Besides, the person who loves can be "in control":

(46) Make account, I pray you, of my *firme* frindeship loue and care ... (CEECS: 1587 ELIZABETH1 44)

The metaphors of FEAR in our data agree better with the examples given in previous literature. See, for instance:

(47) Fear *swept over* him. (Kövecses 1990: 78)
(48) Again he felt a *surge of fear.* (FROWN: N21: 23)

However, FEAR can also be A FAVOURABLE FORCE, as in:

(49) ... let Ch: be your north starr, his holy word your card, and *keepe your canvase pregnant with His feare,* and upon my life, you will make a happy voyage. (CEECS: 1639 RHARLEY 212)

In the data for metaphors of rational thought, FORCE is not a central domain. However, if we take metaphors of CONTROL into account here, *mind, wit* and *reason* are all relevant. *Reason* is very often a general, unpersonified AUTHORITY (and/or LAW). This CONTROL metaphor can also be described as a metaphor of FORCE in which REASON is "very much like a force of nature", and "To refuse to reach a natural conclusion is to resist the force of reason" (Lakoff and Johnson 1999: 237, see also 215–216, 236–237):

(50) Therfore let us se what examples of semblable beneuolence we can finde amonge the gentiles, in whom was no vertue inspired, but that only which *natural reason induced.* (HC: ELYOT 152)
(51) ... it is often seen that he is fuller of trouble than if in *the day-light of his reason* he were to contest with a potent enemy ... (HC: JETAYLOR 15)

The AUTHORITY personifications discussed above can also be seen as metaphors of CONTROL. Some of the formulae can be interpreted as REASON IS A MEASURE. There reason sets the limits and without reason there is loss of CONTROL (examples 52 and 53). This metaphor also exists in PDE (example 54).

(52) ... also weryed with *the prolixitie or length of my reason* ... (HC: BOETHCO 112)
(53) ... wher, by collor of these provisions, prises will ryse *without reason* ... (CEECS: 1585 WCECIL 41)
(54) ... that *stands to reason*, now doesn't it? (FLOB: B08: 49)

As mentioned in section 4.1.4, the SANITY IS SAFETY metaphor which we have classified under ENTITY/CONTAINER is also a metaphor of CONTROL. Examples 16 to 20 above underline the borderline between CHAOS and ORDER, SANITY and INSANITY, thus CONTROL and LOSS OF CONTROL. Suffice it to note here that while *mind*, *wit* and *reason* can all be HOMES or SAFE PLACES, only *wit* can also be A BORDER or A ROPE/TETHER, marking the line between the controlled and the chaotic.

5. Discussion

We now compare our results with previous studies and compare metaphors of rational thought with those of emotion. As historical semanticians, we are interested in diachronic variation and, working simultaneously in cognitive and corpus linguistics, it is natural to ask how our corpus method suits the cognitive question.

5.1. Comparison with Lakoff, Jäkel and Kövecses

How do these findings compare with the theories on metaphors of rational thought and emotion that we outlined in section 2? Rational thought provides some divergence. One remarkable point is that the use of the CONTAINER metaphor in our data does not suggest the supremacy of the MIND IS A WORKSHOP metaphor offered by Jäkel (1995). SANITY IS SAFETY (MIND/WIT/REASON IS A SAFE PLACE) is the most representative CONTAINER metaphor for *mind*, *wit* and *reason*. In our data, *wit* is the word which best corresponded to the assumed frequency of the MIND IS A WORKSHOP metaphor, where it was most often a case of the five senses meaning.

This is, in fact, how the workings of the mind and the senses were conceived of in medieval philosophy and it is still reflected in EModE metaphors. The five bodily wits laboured to gather information to be processed by higher intellectual faculties, imagination formed images of the data and reason analysed these images. Intellect was the higher level of reason which was able to perceive theological truths and other things outside ordinary experience (Burnley 1979: 105, Curry 1926: 304). Perhaps the MIND IS A WORKSHOP metaphor can even be traced back to these ideas (cf. Geeraerts and Grondelaers 1995).

It should be remarked that the UNDERSTANDING IS SEEING metaphor (which did not really fall within the scope of this study, since it is not central to emotion) was in fact very rare in our data. It appeared only related to BODY metaphors (with the equating of the mind with the eyes, etc.). This would seem to support Jäkel's idea that MENTAL ACTIVITY IS MANIPULATION is a higher-level metaphor. It should be remembered that the reasons for this may be methodological as well, since it is possible that our keywords were just not sufficiently closely linked to the concept of UNDERSTANDING.[5]

As to the relationship between Kövecses's (1990: 160–167) list of emotion metaphors and the present data, the ENTITY (ontological) metaphor seems to be the most interesting. The reason is that the characteristics of that ENTITY or OBJECT apparently depend on evaluating the emotion as positive or negative. If the emotion is positive, and thus desirable, it is A VALUABLE COMMODITY. If it is negative, it might be labelled GARBAGE, WASTE, WEEDS or whatever people want to get rid of. At least this clearly applies to *love* and *fear*, a typical context for fear being:

(55) People can walk in the streets *without fear* of attack. (FLOB: A36: 89)

Perhaps one should label the opposite of A VALUABLE COMMODITY very simply and generally; for example A NEGATIVE ENTITY. FEAR AS A NEGATIVE ENTITY does not tend to show specific characteristics, unless we include FEAR AS A HUMAN or SUPERNATURAL BEING in this category. The category NEGATIVE ENTITY could also be seen to include FEAR as an OBSTACLE to doing

---

5. We did, however, take a quick look at the noun *understanding* in the Helsinki Corpus Early Modern period. Its use seemed fairly consistent with especially *mind* and *wit*, and no metaphors of seeing were immediately apparent. This raises an interesting point: does it tell something about the conceptual range of a metaphor if it is not used in connection with the actual words denoting the concept?

something or A WHIP. These metaphors reveal something important about the human psyche and certainly existed before psychologists began to talk about inhibitions.

5.2. Investigation of (common) metaphorical ground for rational thought and emotion

Let us take up the questions posed at the beginning: Are there more similarities among the members of the groups of words denoting rational thought and emotion than between these two groups? There certainly are some marked differences. The VALUABLE COMMODITY metaphor is more important with emotion words, only occurring with any frequency with *wit* in the data for rational thought, and even then not in connection with the earlier meanings of perception and less specified cognitive faculties. It was far more normal to view words denoting rational thought as INSTRUMENTS or WEAPONS. The BODY metaphor is applicable to emotions almost solely as THE CONTAINER FOR EMOTIONS, whereas the faculties of rational thought were most often viewed as body parts. LOVE, FEAR, and REASON were all FORCES, but when compared with rational thought, they are on the opposite sides of the FORCE–CONTROL continuum: reason lays down the law and sets measures against which love and fear surge.

On the other hand, the high-level conceptual metaphors of CONTAINER, BODY, personification and FORCE/CONTROL were important in conceptualising both rational thought and emotion. The divergences emerge only on a closer look. In some cases rational thought and emotion can indeed be said to diametrically opposed (Kövecses 2000: 196), as is the case with metaphors of CONTROL where MEASURES set by REASON and TETHERS made of WITS guard the MIND against the wild FORCES of LOVE and FEAR. However, even in the realm of the SANITY IS SAFETY metaphor, which has been shown to be surprisingly central in our data, FEAR OF GOD and SANITY converge as A SAFE PLACE. Moreover, even though REASON and FEAR may be opposing forces, they may sometimes be used for similar purposes, as in example 56, where FEAR is in a position of power much in the way of REASON.

(56)   *Feare* and awe ought to give you the first power over their *mindes*, and *Love* and Freindship in riper years to hold it. (HC: LOCKE 55)

5.3. The diachronic dimension

The diachronic dimension of this study yielded two different (but interconnected) types of change in metaphorical use. Firstly, there is the role of metaphorical usage as an indicator of actual semantic change. The assumption that semantic change also produces a change in the metaphorical use of a word is proved correct by the *wit* data. The change in the meaning of *wit* is reflected by the following: 1) The old "five senses" meaning which disappears during EModE belongs to the MENTAL ACTIVITY IS MANIPULATION sphere (WITS ARE WORKERS) which is less frequent in the PDE material; 2) as intelligence and erudition become more central aspects of the meaning of *wit*, the personification A LEARNED / ESTEEMED PERSON emerges, and 3) as the modern "use of (imaginative) intelligence in the expression of speech and writing" meaning begins to emerge in the Early Modern period – first as "superior intelligence" types of meanings – the INSTRUMENT/TOOL/WEAPON metaphor gains in frequency, as does the VALUABLE COMMODITY metaphor. This shows that cognitive metaphors may provide a tool for minimising the role of intuition (and/or introspection) in historical semantic research. It seems it should be possible to locate and date semantic change by analysing cognitive metaphors in diachrony if the corpus is sufficiently large.

Secondly, cultural change is reflected in cognitive metaphors as well. *Reason* undergoes a culturally significant change in metaphorical structure, though not full-fledged semantic change. Its personifications become much less frequent and its metaphorical use decreases in general. The REASON-AS-AN-AUTHORITY, as well as the weak and childish MINDS, easily led astray, seem to be dependent on genre (in this case, philosophical writings), and thus products of a particular cultural period.

That FEAR is every now and then conceptualised as A VALUABLE COMMODITY rather than A NEGATIVE ENTITY in the Early Modern period seems to be a further cultural change. This suggests that emotions are evaluated differently in different periods. Cultural studies of emotion have also suggested that emotions are understood differently in different societies (Harré 1988). It can even be difficult to say which concepts are emotion concepts and which are not. FEAR OF GOD as A VALUABLE COMMODITY extends from an emotion concept towards a religious concept and a shared value. Note how close the word *value* itself comes to A VALUABLE COMMODITY.

5.4. Methodological observations

It seems that, methodologically speaking, there is a marked difference between considering metaphors of a certain concept and metaphors where the operative word is a certain concept (or representative of a concept). The roles of *fear, love, mind, reason* and *wit* in metaphorical expressions do not always coincide with metaphors of the concepts of rational thought and emotion (see also Stefanowitsch, this volume).

In this comparative study, our method has some clear merits, since we were able to process a large amount of data and retrieve all occurrences of each word. Intuition had no role at this preliminary stage, which would not have been the case if we had both searched for all possible metaphors of rational thought and emotion in all the data. Consequently, we can be fairly certain that we have not missed any metaphors significant for the comparison.

The method proved to be sound from the diachronic point of view as well. It is a reliable and comparatively rapid way of obtaining information on metaphors as indicators of semantic change. Moreover, even though we spotted several differences between the frequencies of even high-level metaphors in our study as compared to the more traditional metaphor studies, the actual metaphors were the same. Therefore, were one to study even longer periods of time with a large corpus, this method of focusing on certain keywords might, in addition to producing valuable results on its own, also provide preliminary information for a study encompassing all possible metaphors for a certain concept (identifying the metaphors typical of each time period, producing possible keywords for advanced searches, etc.).

6. Conclusion

Our study on metaphors occurring with the words *fear*, *love*, *mind*, *reason* and *wit* proved fruitful in several ways. We were able to assess previous research in the same field, to pinpoint similarities and differences between not only metaphors of emotion and rational thought, but also Early Modern and Present-Day English, and to justify our method. Let us say finally that not only is cognitive linguistics applicable to historical studies, but that historical linguistics may have a lot to offer to modern cognitive linguistics. A study such as ours raises several questions regarding method and definitions: at which point in historical development does metaphorical use end and non-metaphorical "new" meaning begin? How well does change in metaphorical structure indicate change in meaning? Could it be used to define larger meaning categories? Finally, where are the boundaries between cultural (thus changeable) and embodied (constant) metaphors?

References

Bierwiaczonek, Boguslaw
   2002   *A Cognitive Study of the Concept of LOVE in English.* Katowice: Wydawnictwo Uniwersytetu Śląskiego.

Burnley, J.D.
   1979   *Chaucer's Language and the Philosophers' Tradition.* Cambridge: D.S. Brewer.

Curry, Walter Clyde
   1960 [1926]   *Chaucer and the Medieval Sciences.* New York: Barnes and Noble.

Fabiszak, Malgorzata
   2002   A semantic analysis of FEAR, GRIEF and ANGER words in Old English. In: Javier E. Díaz Vera (ed.), *A Changing World of Words: Studies in English Historical Lexicography, Lexicology and Semantics,* 255–274. Amsterdam: Rodopi.

Geeraerts, Dirk
   1997   *Diachronic Prototype Semantics: A Contribution to Historical Lexicology.* Oxford: Clarendon Press.

Geeraerts, Dirk and Stefan Grondelaers
   1995   Looking back at anger: Cultural traditions and metaphorical patterns. In: John R. Taylor and Robert E. MacLaury (eds.), *Language and the Cognitive Construal of the World,* 153–179. Berlin: Mouton de Gruyter.

Harré, Rom (ed.)
   1988   *The Social Construction of Emotions.* Oxford: Basil Blackwell.

Holland, Dorothy and Naomi Quinn
   1989 [1987]   *Cultural Models in Language and Thought.* Cambridge: Cambridge University Press.

Hundt, Marianne, Andrea Sand and Rainer Siemund
   1998   *Manual of Information to accompany The Freiburg-LOB Corpus of British English ('FLOB').* Online at <http://khnt.hit.uib.no/icame/manuals/flob/index.htm>.

Hundt, Marianne, Andrea Sand and Paul Skandera
   1999   *Manual of Information to accompany The Freiburg-Brown Corpus of American English ('Frown').* <http://khnt.hit.uib.no/icame/manuals/frown/index.htm>.

Jäkel, Olaf
   1995   The metaphorical concept of mind: 'Mental activity is manipulation'. In: John R. Taylor and Robert E. MacLaury (eds.), *Language and the Cognitive Construal of the World,* 197–229. Berlin and New York: Mouton de Gruyter.

Johnson, Mark
   1987   *The Body in the Mind: The Bodily Basis of Meaning, Imagination, and Reason.* Chicago: The University of Chicago Press.

Koivisto-Alanko, Päivi
   2000   *Abstract Words in Abstract Worlds: Directionality and Prototypical Structure in the Semantic Change in English Nouns of Cognition.* Helsinki: Société Néophilologique.

Kövecses, Zoltán
    2000   *Metaphor and Emotion: Language, Culture, and Body in Human Feeling*. Cambridge: Cambridge University Press.

Kytö, Merja (ed.)
    1996   *Manual to the Diachronic Part of The Helsinki Corpus of English Texts: Coding Conventions and Lists of Source Texts*. Third edition. Helsinki: Department of English, University of Helsinki.

Lakoff, George
    1987   *Women, Fire and Dangerous Things: What Categories Reveal about the Mind*. Chicago: The University of Chicago Press.

Lakoff, George and Mark Johnson
    1980   *Metaphors We Live By*. Chigaco: The University of Chigaco Press.
    1999   *Philosophy in the Flesh: The Embodied Mind and Its Challenge to Western Thought*. New York: Basic Books.

Lakoff, George and Mark Turner
    1989   *More than Cool Reason: A Field Guide to Poetic Metaphor*. Chicago: The University of Chicago Press.

Nurmi, Arja
    1998   *Manual for the Corpus of Early English Correspondence Sampler CEECS*. Helsinki: Department of English, University of Helsinki. On-line at <http://khnt.hit.uib.no/icame/manuals/ceecs/INDEX.HTM>.

Palmer, Gary B., Cliff Goddard and Penny Lee (eds.)
    2003   *Talking about Thinking across Languages*. Special issue of *Cognitive Linguistics* 14(2–3).

Reddy, Michael
    1979   The conduit metaphor – a case of frame conflict in our language about language. In: Andrew Ortony (ed.), *Metaphor and Thought*, 284–324. Cambridge: Cambridge University Press.

Spevack, Marvin
    1970   *A Complete and Systematic Concordance to the Works of Shakespeare*. Vol. 5. Hildesheim: Georg Olms.

Tissari, Heli
    2003   *LOVEscapes: Changes in prototypical senses and cognitive metaphors since 1500*. Helsinki: Société Néophilologique.

Turner, Mark
    1996   *The Literary Mind*. New York and Oxford: Oxford University Press.

A corpus-based analysis of context effects on metaphor comprehension

James H. Martin

Abstract

This article describes our attempts to shed light on the relationship between results from psycholinguistic research on the effects of context on metaphor comprehension and the nature of metaphor as it occurs in naturally occurring text.

The hypothesis underlying this work is that the facilitation and inhibition effects observed in laboratory subjects reflect the patterns of co-occurrence of various kinds of contexts with metaphoric language in the environment.

We take a three part approach to exploring this hypothesis: a rational analysis of the notion of a context effect, an empirical corpus-based effort to fill out that rational analysis, and a reconsideration of the pertinent psycholinguistic results with respect to that analysis. Finally, we present a proposal for a mechanistic model that is in accord with the results of this analysis.

1. Introduction

A wide variety of results from psycholinguistic research over the last several decades have shown that context has a strong effect on the processing of metaphoric language (Gernsbacher et al. 2001, Gerrig and Healy 1983, Gibbs 1984, Gildea and Glucksberg 1983, Glucksberg 1982, Kemper 1989, Inhoff et al. 1984, Keysar 1989, Ortony et al. 1978). These results have been used to both support and refute a bewildering array of computational accounts of metaphor processing (Fass 1991, Fass 1988, Martin 1990, Martin 1992, Martin 1994, Gentner et al. 1988, Gildea and Glucksberg 1983, Russell 1976, Wilks 1978, Hobbs 1979, Carbonell 1981, Indurkhya 1987, Narayanan 1999). Perhaps the most well-known result from this research is that appropriate contexts facilitate the processing of metaphor to the extent that there is no significant timing difference from equivalent literal language. These results has been primarily used to argue against the stage model (Searle 1979) of metaphor processing where the literal meaning of an utterance is first computed, found to be lacking, and then reanalyzed as a metaphor.

Lost in this debate is the fact that a considerable amount of information has been amassed showing how specific *kinds of context* facilitate, fail to facilitate, or actually inhibit the process of metaphor comprehension. These results provide constraints on computational models of metaphor above and beyond basic timing constraints (Gerrig 1989). Specifically, if the presence or absence of a particular type of information has predictable effects on metaphor comprehension, then computational theories of metaphor must show how they can transparently admit such influences.

A second issue that has received little attention is the exact relationship between the psycholinguistic effects observed in the laboratory and the environment of naturally occurring text. Of particular interest is the question of whether these effects are artifacts of a specialized metaphor processing mechanism, or whether they are simply reflections of the way that metaphor naturally occurs in real text. If the latter situation holds then that provides further evidence that the capacity to interpret metaphor is similar to, if not the same as, our ability to process other kinds of language.

The bulk of this article is an attempt to shed further light on these two issues. We are interested in studying the nature of these contextual influences by taking a detailed look out at the environment. More specifically, we are concerned with the relationship between observed patterns of co-occurrence of context and metaphor in naturally occurring text and known psycholinguistic results on these kinds of contexts.

The hypothesis underlying this work is that the facilitation and inhibition effects observed in laboratory subjects reflect the patterns of co-occurrence of these contexts with metaphoric language in the environment. We take a three part approach to exploring this hypothesis: a rational analysis of the notion of a context effect, an empirical corpus-based effort to provide real data for that rational analysis, and a reconsideration of the pertinent psycholinguistic results with respect to the analysis.

2. A minimal rational analysis of context effects on metaphor

We start by taking a step back to consider the effect of context on metaphor comprehension from a rather minimalist rational point of view. By this, we have in mind an account derived from minimal assumptions about cognitive processing, combined with a detailed corpus-based observation of the phenomenon in question. Under this view, the first step in analyzing some phenomenon is to analyze the task and make certain minimal assumptions about the information needed to perform it. The second step is to look to the environment to see how such information is presented in situations where the task presumably has to be addressed. The final step is to juxtapose measures of human performance on appropriate tasks with the analysis of the environment. This can suggest likely hypotheses for computational models and impose constraints on such models.

The analysis presented here is loosely inspired by Anderson's theory of the adaptive nature of human cognition (Anderson 1990, Anderson and Schooler 1991, Oaksford and Chater 1998). The basic notion in this approach is that an efficient language processor can be seen as having molded itself to the regularities in its environment. When faced with a particular language problem, the processor takes action based on an implicit or explicit encoding of these regularities. Such an approach makes the testable claim that observable regularities in the environment will lead to predictions about processor performance under similar conditions.

We begin by defining the task as comprehending a sentence containing a metaphor after having already processed a short span of text. The preceding span of text and the ensuing metaphor will be referred to as the *context* and the *test sentence*, respectively. By comprehension, we have in mind the simple notion commonly used in various chronometric psycholinguistic studies. In these studies, a subject typically reads some context and is then presented with a test sentence. They are told to perform some simple physical task when they feel that they have adequately understood the sentence. In these experiments, the subject is typically not asked to study and deeply appreciate the test sentence. Rather, they are being asked to process the text in a normal automatic fashion. The time taken to perform the physical recognition task is measured and compared across the various conditions of interest.

Having sketched out the task, the next step is to determine the various sources of information needed to perform it. While there is wide disagreement about the mechanisms underlying metaphor comprehension, nearly all current theories postulate that successful metaphor comprehension results in, or involves at some stage, representations involving a *source* concept, a *target* concept and a set of correspondences or associations between them, often referred to as a *ground*.

To make these notions concrete consider the following example extracted from the Wall Street Journal.

(1) Spain Fund *tumbled* 23% in *turbulent* trading, *dragging down* the shares of other so-called country funds.

This example has three instantiations of the NUMERICAL-VALUE-AS-LOCATION metaphor (Hobbs 1979). In this metaphor, the core source concept is the notion of a location in physical space, often an altitude. The target domain is the notion of some abstract state that has an associated numerical value. The ground, or set of structured correspondences, in this case stipulates that the numerical value is to be viewed as a physical location and that a change in value is to be viewed as motion along some dimension.

In our current study, we make the minimal assumption that language that serves to introduce the source or target concepts directly into the context may have an effect on the processing of subsequent metaphors involving these concepts. A further assumption is that text that introduces a metaphor of the same basic type as the test metaphor into the context can be seen as introducing the ground of the metaphor.

Having sketched out the task and its potential information needs, the next step is to analyze the ways that the environment actually presents this information to readers in naturally occurring texts. Specifically, we need to be able to locate and identify specific metaphors in text and to locate their corresponding source, target and metaphorical uses in contexts immediately preceding the metaphor. These various contexts can then be analyzed in terms of how well they *predict the occurrence of the subsequent metaphor*. Specifically, we are interested in whether particular contexts can be seen as making a subsequent metaphor more or less likely. Of course, to be able to assess the predictive value of these contexts, information about the overall frequency of occurrence of these contextual cues and the metaphors themselves needs to be gathered.

The comparison to human performance is based on data from metaphor comprehension experiments measuring the time needed to perform various experimental tasks that shed light on comprehension difficulty. Such experiments have shown that the rate at which sentences are comprehended is affected by the context within which the sentences are presented. Three types of contexts are of interest here:

- Contexts containing literal expressions of the source concepts of the test metaphor
- Contexts containing relevant literal expressions of the target concepts of the test metaphor
- And finally, contexts containing metaphoric expressions with the same basic structure, or ground, as the test metaphor.

The rational account presented here is ultimately based on the juxtaposition of this human performance data with the data gleaned from the environment. The specific hypothesis is that it is the degree to which the various types of context *predict* the future occurrence of a metaphor that determines the degree of facilitation observed in the human performance data. We will refer to this as the *Metaphor Prediction Hypothesis* (MPH).

3. Corpus analysis

There have been large number empirical studies of naturally occurring metaphor in both spoken and written forms. However, none of these studies provide the specific contextual data needed to test the validity of the MPH. Fortunately, various factors gleaned from these studies point towards a way to gather the appropriate information.

The first result comes from exhaustive analyses that have been performed to determine the overall frequency of metaphor and metonymy in a wide variety of texts (Pollio et al. 1990). These studies show that these phenomena appear quite frequently, averaging around 5 uses per 100 words of text. The second result comes from a wide variety of research that indicates that there is a relatively small core set of important conceptual metaphors underlying most of the metaphors actually observed (Talmy 1975, Talmy 1988, Lakoff and Johnson 1980, Lakoff 1987, Lakoff and Turner 1988, Johnson 1987).

Taken together, these considerations indicate that an analysis of a relatively small number of sentences randomly sampled from a coherent corpus would provide useful information. Specifically, by sampling a relatively small amount of text from a coherent collection of text it should be possible to produce an accurate characterization of the important conceptual metaphors that occur in a given collection. In such an analysis metaphors in the sampled text are identified by hand and clustered together based on the conceptual similarity of their source, target and ground components. Such an analysis has been performed on a random sample of sentences from the Wall Street Journal (Martin 1994).

The results from this study provided us with the basis to collect the specific contextual information we require; the collected examples of the more frequently occurring metaphor types give us the means to search for further examples of those specific types *in context*.

3.1. Methodology

The need to gather information specific to particular types of metaphor led us to focus on a small number of conceptual metaphors known to frequent the Wall Street Journal corpus. Based on the sampling and clustering work already completed, it was possible to develop simple and accurate lexical profiles of some of these metaphors. These profiles made it possible to filter large amounts of text for the occurrence of specific metaphor types.

To be concrete, consider the NUMERICAL-VALUE-AS-LOCATION metaphor discussed above. It is the most frequently occurring metaphor in the Wall Street Journal and is used to express a wide range of economic and commercial concepts. By examining the sampled metaphors of this type, we were able to produce two lists of words that provided a lexical profile of this metaphor. The first contained words used to express the source concept of location or change of location. The second list contained words used to express the target concepts of the sampled metaphors. In this case, the source list included words such as *fall, tumble, sink, downhill, slide, drop, top, climb, rise, boost,* and *plunge.* The target list included *recession, inflation, bid, rate, borrow, priced, earnings, trading, price, pay, costs, income,* and *earnings.*

Taken together these two lists provide an extremely crude, but effective, way to find metaphors of a particular type; any sentence containing words from both the source and target list for a particular metaphor type is a candidate for containing the metaphor used to produce the lists. Used separately they can be used to find candidate sentences containing expressions of either the source or target domains of particular metaphors.

Such lists were produced for four metaphors which were known to occur with considerable regularity in the WSJ corpus: NUMERICAL-VALUE-AS-LOCATION, COMMERCIAL-ACTIVITY-AS-CONTAINER, COMMERCIAL-ACTIVITY-AS-PATH-FOLLOWING and COMMERCIAL-ACTIVITY-AS-WAR. Representative examples of each of these metaphors from the WSJ are shown in Table 1.

To broaden the reach of these lists, they were each augmented through the use of a thesaurus, introspection, and further sampling. Next a simple program was written to find example sentences of each type; given a source list, a target list, and a metaphor name, this program tags all sentences in a corpus containing at least one term from each list. An iterative process was used to refine the lists to remove obvious and frequent false positives.

Using this simple approach, it was possible to quickly filter large amounts text from the Wall Street Journal at the sentence level for the metaphors of interest. For the purposes of this study approximately 600 instances of each of the four metaphor types shown in Table 1 were identified. Due to the differing relative frequencies of the metaphors this necessitated examining widely different amounts of text for each metaphor. This ranged from

130,000 words for the NUMERICAL-VALUE-AS-LOCATION metaphor to nearly 2,000,000 for the COMMERCIAL-ACTIVITY-AS-WAR metaphor.

Of course, while this simple technique is extremely effective in this text type it is by no means perfect. Therefore, each sentence tagged was verified by hand to make certain that it actually contained the correct metaphor. It is also highly likely that the approach will miss some metaphors of each type. We believe that this situation is acceptable in the current study as long as we are sure that it will find a large percentage of the metaphors that do occur. Fortunately, one of the findings from our earlier work (Martin 1994) is that each individual metaphor type displays a Zipf-like distribution for the lexical items that are used to express that metaphor. In other words, while these metaphors are wildly productive, a relatively small number of lexical items account for the bulk of metaphor instances.

Table 1. Sample metaphors known to frequent the WSJ

NUMERICAL-VALUE-AS-LOCATION

Barge rates on the Mississippi River *sank* yesterday on speculation that widespread rain this week in the Midwest might temporarily alleviate the situation.

At the same time, an increase of land under cultivation after the drought has *boosted* production of corn, soybeans and other commodities, causing a *fall* in prices that has been only partly *cushioned* by heavy grain buying by the Soviets

COMMERCIAL-ACTIVITY-AS-CONTAINER

Four Brazilian fruit-juice makers are planning to *enter* the Japanese market and to build a huge juice-storage tank complex, a Japanese trading-house official said.

The situation is that the bankruptcy court will *get out of* the shipbuilding business.

COMMERCIAL-ACTIVITY-AS-PATH-FOLLOWING

So *where* does the IMF *go from here*?

Swissair, which signed a marketing agreement with Delta Air Lines early this year, *took the next step* this summer by buying Delta.

COMMERCIAL-ACTIVITY-AS-WAR

While the *two camps* have competed *aggressively* for years, lately the *fight has turned ferocious* – and often damaging to the public.

What triggered the latest *clash* was a *skirmish* over the timing of a New Zealand government bond issue.

Finally, this corpus was tagged with the source and target lists separately to identify all expressions of these concepts in context. The resulting corpus thus contains sentences tagged as containing expressions of the source concepts, target concepts, or metaphors, for each of the four metaphors embedded in their original contexts. This tagged corpus then served as the basis for obtaining the predictive measures needed to test the MPH.

3.2. Results bearing on the MPH

The following sections detail the results of these analyses for each of the three context types, for each of the four metaphors. Specifically, they present the following information.
– Base frequency rates for each of the metaphors.
– Predictiveness of contexts containing literal expressions of the source concept of subsequent test metaphors.
– Predictiveness of contexts containing expressions of concepts that serve as targets for subsequent metaphors.
– Predictiveness of contexts containing a metaphor for subsequent metaphors of the same type.

At this point in the analysis, the notion of context has to be made more concrete. The term context has been used in a wide variety of ways in the psycholinguistics literature. It has been used to refer to everything from clauses preceding a metaphor within a sentence, to multiple paragraph-length preceding texts. Based on an informal examination of this literature, we decided to focus on five sentence context windows. Mapping this directly to the psycholinguistic literature we have contexts consisting of four sentences, followed by a sentence containing a metaphor. However, since we are interested in determining the predictive power of the various types of contexts it is more useful to think of single sentence contexts, followed by a four sentence window. In this framework, the ability of a given kind of context to predict a subsequent metaphor will be estimated as the conditional probability of seeing a metaphor in a subsequent four sentence context given a particular type of contextual cue.

3.2.1. Prior probabilities

To assess the predictive power of the four types of context, the prior probability of finding an instance of one of the four metaphors in a random context had to be measured. These probabilities were estimated by considering the amount of text that had to be searched to gather the approximately 600 instances of each of the four metaphors. The base rate for each metaphor was estimated as the ratio of the number of metaphors found to sentences examined.

Rather than making any independence assumptions, the probability of one or more instances of these metaphors occurring in a random 4 sentence sequence was determined directly by sliding a four sentence window across the tagged texts and counting the number of windows containing at least one instance of the metaphor. Again the probability measure is estimated as the ratio of 4 sentence windows containing a metaphor to the number of windows. Table 2 gives both the individual and 4 sentence window frequencies for each metaphor expressed as probabilities.

Table 2. Base rates for metaphors studied

Metaphor	P(Metaphor)	P(Metaphor in Window)
NUMERICAL-VALUE-AS-LOCATION	.104	.265
COMMERCIAL-ACTIVITY-AS-PATH	.016	.046
COMMERCIAL-ACTIVITY-AS-CONTAINER	.017	.044
COMMERCIAL-ACTIVITY-AS-WAR	.006	.011

It should be noted that the window results reflect a clear tendency on the part of these metaphors to cluster. Specifically, for each metaphor, the number of non-metaphor four sentence windows observed was higher than would be expected if the metaphors were uniformly distributed throughout the text. As a consequence the probability of running into one of these metaphors in a random four sentence span is less than would be expected if they were uniformly distributed across the texts.

These probabilities will be used as a baseline to measure the predictive power of the various contexts for ensuing metaphors. If the probability of seeing a metaphor in the next four sentences, given the current context type, is higher than these base rates, then that evidence should facilitate comprehension. Inhibition should be signaled by a lower than base rate probability given a particular context.

3.2.2. Literal source concept

Our first results concern the predictive power of contexts containing literal expressions of a source concept of the test metaphor. To be more concrete, we are interested in contexts like the following:

(2) Dirk was out climbing mountains all last week.
(3) Back at the office, his chances for promotion had plunged.

The first sentence contains a literal expression of the concept change of location in the vertical direction. The second sentence contains a metaphor where the source concept is from the same conceptual domain. The statistic of interest is the conditional probability of seeing a metaphor in the next four sentences, given that a literal use of the source of that metaphor has already been seen.

To obtain these statistics, the tagged corpus was first examined by hand. Literal uses of the already tagged source terms were marked as such. The probability of encountering a metaphor given a literal source encounter was estimated by computing the ratio of the number of literal source uses followed by a metaphor in a subsequent four sentence context, to the number of literal uses found overall. Table 3 presents the results for each of our four metaphors.

Table 3. Predictive Power of Literal Source Contexts

Metaphor	P(Metaphor|Source)	Change from Base Rate
NUMERICAL-VALUE-AS-LOCATION	.069	.259
COMMERCIAL-ACTIVITY-AS-PATH	.022	.491
COMMERCIAL-ACTIVITY-AS-CONTAINER	.038	.844
COMMERCIAL-ACTIVITY-AS-WAR	< .004	< .418

These results indicate that literal concepts are poor predictors of specific future metaphors with that concept as a source. Each of the four metaphors occurs below its base frequency in contexts containing literal language from their source domain. In the case of the COMMERCIAL-ACTIVITY-AS-WAR metaphor, no contexts containing literal war expressions followed by this metaphor were found after examining all sentences containing literal war expressions extracted from approximately 2,000,000 words of text.

3.2.3. Target concept expressions

The next set of results concern how well expressions involving the target concept of a metaphor predict future expressions of a specific metaphor. Again, to be concrete, we are interested in contexts like the following.

(4) Dirk's opportunities for a promotion had been improving for several months.
(5) With his latest success they skyrocketed.

The first sentence introduces the notion of "opportunity for promotion". The second sentence follows up by metaphorically structuring that notion as a change of altitude. To formalize such situations we are interested in the conditional probability of seeing a specific metaphor given that some expression of the target concept has already been seen.

The following results were computed in a fashion similar to the previous literal source result. The ratio of target uses followed by a metaphor to the number of target uses found overall was computed by scanning the tagged corpus.

Table 4. Predictive power of target contexts

Metaphor	P(Metaphor|Target)	Change from Base Rate
NUMERICAL-VALUE-AS-LOCATION	.677	2.55
COMMERCIAL-ACTIVITY-AS-PATH	.073	1.59
COMMERCIAL-ACTIVITY-AS-CONTAINER	.087	1.95
COMMERCIAL-ACTIVITY-AS-WAR	.031	2.84

As shown in Table 4, these metaphors are more likely to occur in contexts containing expressions of their target concepts. As with the literal source result, the numbers varied from metaphor to metaphor but all displayed some effect of increasing the probability of the metaphor from its base rate.

3.2.4. Metaphoric expressions

Our final result concerns the predictive power of a particular metaphor for subsequent instances of the same metaphor. The following example illustrates this situation.

(6) Dirk's opportunities for promotion had been *falling* for months.
(7) With his latest boondoggle, they really *plummeted*.

The first sentence contains a metaphor that structures the notion of changing opportunity as a change in altitude. The ensuing context follows up with an expression with the same basic metaphorical structure.

Table 5. Predictive power of metaphorical contexts

Metaphor	P(Metaphor|Metaphor)	Change from Base Rate
NUMERICAL-VALUE-AS-LOCATION	.703	2.65
COMMERCIAL-ACTIVITY-AS-PATH	.196	4.29
COMMERCIAL-ACTIVITY-AS-CONTAINER	.267	6.00
COMMERCIAL-ACTIVITY-AS-WAR	.277	25.20

As indicated in Table 5, this predictor is obviously the best from among those studied, with the clearest advantage in the case of the COMMERCIAL-ACTIVITY-AS-WAR metaphor.

4. Psycholinguistic results

Our next task was to take these corpus-based results and juxtapose them with relevant data from the psycholinguistic literature. As might be expected, none of the relevant experiments presented here has results that directly correspond to our predictive measures. Nevertheless, there are results that can with some massaging be readily interpreted as relevant to our measures.

4.1. Literal source contexts

The primary result for the case of literal source contexts comes from a series of studies reported by Inhoff (1984). In these experiments, subjects were first presented with a single context sentence followed by a metaphor test sentence. The three types of context that were investigated correspond nicely to our contexts: a literal source context, a literal target context, and a closely related metaphor context. Reaction times across the three contexts were then compared to assess the relative effects of these contexts.

The major difference between these results and our corpus analysis is that their literal source context was constructed by employing a literal use of the *same word* as is used metaphorically in the test sentence. Our corpus results measured *any* literal use from the same conceptual field as the source of the metaphorical use.

The basic results of this study were that recognition time was shortest with metaphorical contexts, longer with relevant literal target contexts, and much longer still with literal source contexts. These results reflect the same pattern seen in our corpus based study. Specifically, the corpus indicates that when compared to target and metaphor contexts, literal source contexts are the least predictive.

This study was silent on the stronger prediction made by the MPH. The MPH predicts that since literal source texts reduce the likelihood of subsequent metaphors with the same source, they should have an *inhibitory* effect on recognition rates. Gernsbacher et al. (2001) report just such an effect. Contexts involving a literal use from the source domain of a subsequent metaphor suppress the reading time of the metaphor as compared to a baseline context prime.

4.2. Target contexts

The most widely replicated result in the literature on context effects shows that appropriate contexts strongly facilitate the interpretation of relevant metaphors. In these experiments, literal expressions of various concepts serve to facilitate subsequent metaphors involving those same concepts as targets (Ortony et al. 1978, Gerrig and Healy 1983, Inhoff et al. 1984, Kemper 1989). Note that as with the previous literal source result, what the facilitation is with respect to varies from study to study.

As already discussed, one of the results reported in Inhoff et al (1984) shows that target contexts facilitate metaphor comprehension as compared to literal source contexts. In a separate experiment, they also showed that target contexts facilitate subsequent metaphor comprehension as compared to unrelated contexts. The results from Kemper (1989) show a similar pattern for both the literal source and target conditions.

The work reported by Gerrig and Healy (1983) is somewhat different from these other context studies. Rather than manipulate prior sentential context, they manipulated the presentation of material within metaphorical sentences. Consider the following example:

(8) The train followed the parallel ribbons.
(9) The parallel ribbons were followed by the train.

In the active example, the word "train" provides a prior target context within which "parallel ribbons" is interpreted. In the passive example, no such context is available at the point that the referent to "ribbons" is introduced. Their results show that a context providing arrangement of clauses facilitates recognition over the null context clause arrangement.

To summarize, the pattern of results observed in these studies is consistent with the patterns of predictiveness observed in our corpus and is consistent with the MPH. Contexts containing expressions of target concepts of subsequent metaphors facilitate comprehension of those metaphors.

4.3. Metaphorical contexts

Results concerning our final context type, metaphorical contexts, come from both the Inhoff et al (1984) and Kemper (1989) studies. In both cases, contexts were created containing instances of metaphors generated from constructs that correspond to the notion of conventional conceptual metaphors. Materials were prepared so that test sentences containing metaphors were preceded by contexts containing an instance of the same metaphor type.

In these studies, metaphorical contexts displayed the highest degree of facilitation. In both sets of experiments a pattern of facilitation was shown that had source concepts with the least facilitation, followed by target concepts, followed by metaphors with the highest facilitation. As with the results on source and target contexts, these results are in accord with our corpus-based findings.

5. Discussion

This section examines the implications of our corpus-based results from three perspectives that are somewhat broader than the narrow focus taken thus far. We present a discourse oriented discussion of the results, followed by a review of the results along with other known constraints on metaphor processing, and finally a proposal for a mechanistic account that is consistent with these constraints.

5.1. Discourse

If one combines the view of metaphor advanced by Lakoff and Johnson (1980) with more discourse oriented notions of what makes a text coherent, then none of our corpus-based results are particularly surprising. Coherent text tends to be about some topic, or set of topics that display a high degree of semantic overlap and interconnectedness. This notion of coherence combined with the fact that the topics will be metaphorically structured in systematic ways can be used to account for all of our results.

First consider the literal-source expression in context situation. Our results show that these contexts predict that future metaphors with that source are fairly unlikely. The source and target domains of metaphors are by definition about different kinds or types of concepts. It is, therefore, not at all surprising to find that literal expressions of source concepts rarely co-occur with metaphors using that concept as a source. This follows since coherent texts don't typically mix completely disjoint topics within the kind of short spans we looked at in our study.

The results observed for contexts containing expressions of target concepts can be accounted for in a similar fashion. Again, if a coherent text is about some topic then it is likely that if that topic is even partially structured with some metaphor, then that metaphor will eventually occur in the context. Of course, conceptual domains differ both in the degree to which they metaphorically structured and in the number of distinct metaphors used to structure them. These factors will tend to mitigate the predictive power of target language for any particular metaphor.

Finally, consider the observed predictive power of metaphors for future metaphors of the same type. Given a context where a concept has already been introduced and metaphorically structured, one would expect repetitions of that metaphor as long as the discourse continued to focus on relevant aspects of that concept.

5.2. Empirical constraints

The task of turning a high level discourse-oriented account into a plausible mechanism is a non-trivial one. The following section presents a sketch of one such proposal. Before considering that proposal, this section will review the various constraints that we now have for such a model. Among these constraints are ones that have been culled from the psycholinguistic literature and ones that follow the results of our corpus study:
- Total Time Constraint
- Non-Optionality Constraint
- On-Line Constraint
- Differential Behavior Constraint
- Contextual Influence Constraint

The *Total Time Constraint* (Gerrig 1989) states that when supported by appropriate context the time needed to process various kinds of non-literal language does not differ significantly from the time taken to interpret direct literal language. Minimally, this constraint argues that whatever mechanism is proposed for processing metaphoric language it can not have a markedly different time complexity from those mechanisms proposed for literal language processing. However, it does not by itself require that identical processing mechanisms be employed for metaphorical and literal language.

The *Non-Optionality Constraint* (Glucksberg et al. 1982, Keysar 1989) stems from research that shows that possible metaphorical interpretations are activated even in contexts where the literal meaning is both well-formed and preferred by those contexts. These results are based on demonstrations that show parallel metaphorical readings interfering with correct and plausible literal readings resulting in longer processing times on various tasks. These results parallel those in lexical access that show initial activation of all of a words senses followed by a rapid pruning based on local and global context.

The *On-Line Constraint* (Gerrig and Healy 1983) states that metaphorical interpretations, like other interpretations, are constructed in an on-line incremental fashion. Gerrig and Healy's research shows that the order of presentation of material providing evidence for or against a metaphorical reading has strong effects on on-line processing. In effect, they show that subjects display a non-monotonic behavior, where the activation of particular interpretations is continuously updated based on available evidence. This update procedure may result in what they call *truncation*, where an interpretation that had been viable is eliminated when evidence becomes available. In the case of metaphor, they show that placing evidence for a metaphorical interpretation early in the sentence leads to faster reaction times. This arises from an earlier truncation of the parallel literal meaning. When disambiguating information is delayed to later in the sentence reaction times are longer because of interference from the competing interpretations.

It should be noted that these two constraints are really two sides of the same coin. They both point toward a model of processing where parallel interpretations are created and pruned based on currently available evidence. In this regard, they provide further evidence that metaphorical processing is subject to the same kind of constraints observed for literal language.

The *Contextual Influence Constraint* refines the total time constraint by specifying how various *kinds* of contexts can effect the processing time of subsequent metaphors. The basic pattern observed both in experimental settings and our corpus is that prior metaphors of the same type have the strongest effect on subsequent processing, followed by target concepts, and finally literal source concepts. The corpus-based results further predict an inhibitory effect on subsequent metaphor processing. Therefore, any mechanism that is proposed to account for metaphor processing must in some straightforward manner display this pattern.

Finally, the *Differential Behavior Constraint* stems from our results that show that metaphors, like lexical items, display differing frequency and recency patterns. Therefore, while various kinds of context do influence the time needed to process metaphor, the specific amount of facilitation varies with the specific type of metaphor. Like the other constraints, this one is consistent with findings from both the memory and lexical access literatures. Individual memory traces items display idiosyncratic patterns of access based on frequency and recency.

Taken together, these constraints argue for an approach to metaphor that is in large part based on the kind of generic evidential memory access and working memory constraints that have been independently proposed for processing ordinary language.

5.3. A construction based account

There are far too many mechanistic accounts of metaphor processing to assess them all with respect to our list of constraints. Rather than attempt such a survey, we will sketch an instantiation of one position based on work from current research on computational modeling on semantic interpretation and current work on Construction Grammar (Fillmore et al. 1988).

The account presented here is based on three interrelated research efforts: the notion of conventional conceptual metaphors as first articulated by Lakoff and Johnson (1980), direct computational implementations of this notion as in (Martin 1990), and finally more fine-grained, on-line, computational implementations found in Jurafsky (1992) and Jurafsky and Narayanan (1998). These implementations are based in part on a broadened notion of a construction that accounts for frequency based evidential access in a manner that is consistent with the data presented in this article.

In a construction-based account, knowledge of language is equated with knowledge of a large repository of constructions ranging from individual lexical items to rather abstract constructions like the Subject–Predicate Construction. In between, there exist a wide range of constructions encompassing both frozen and productive idioms and more traditional syntactic configurations. At the core of this approach is the idea that individual constructions consist of a structural alignment of specific grammatical, semantic and pragmatic facts about the language. Grammatical constructs are, therefore, coupled directly with their specific semantic and pragmatic content.

Under the accounts given in Jurafsky (1992) and Jurafsky and Narayanan (1998), interpretation is seen as a process of accumulating evidence in an incremental on-line fashion for the instantiation of a construction. Once instantiated, an interpretation is created by combining the particular semantic and pragmatic content of a construction with the corresponding content from other constructions in a working store. Multiple interpretations may be pursued in parallel as long as there is sufficient space in working memory and the individual interpretations are sufficiently well-formed. Pruning of competing interpretations occurs when an interpretation becomes too ill-formed when compared against its competitors in working memory.

Extending these notions to the case of conventional conceptual metaphors is fairly straightforward. Considered as constructions, conventional metaphors consist of a bundle of associations that directly encode the semantic and pragmatic constraints on the source and target concepts that make up the metaphor. In context, the source and target components of a metaphor provide constraints on what can serve as possible evidence for the presence of a given metaphor. In the case of wholly conceptual metaphors this evidence is based on two factors: the presence of concepts placed in working memory by other constructions that match either the source and target parts of the metaphor, and the combined predictive power of these concepts based on statistical information particular to each individual metaphor. Finally, the set of conventional conceptual associations, or ground, provides the semantic and pragmatic constraints by which the intended meaning of the metaphor is constructed from the other conceptual content in working memory.

Note that under this model, the success or failure of a given metaphorical interpretation is not based in any direct way on the well-formedness of a literal interpretation. They are both merely possible candidates created from constructions that have been simultaneously activated by context. Successful interpretations are those that are most well-formed based on the constraints from their constituent constructions, and the degree of support they receive from context.

To summarize, the proposed construction-based framework is based on the following notions.
- An extension of the notion of a construction from traditional form-meaning pairings to conventionalized concept-concept pairings.
- Generic memory access notions such as priming, recency and frequency to control the activation of particular constructions.
- Working memory constraints to constrain the number of possible parallel interpretations.

5.4. Plausibility of the metaphorical construction account

We now move on to consider how such a model might fare in light of the five constraints given above. In keeping with the spirit of the model, our intent is to show that the model is in accord with the constraints because it treats metaphor as a normal part of language processing, making use of generic processing capabilities.

5.4.1. Total-time constraint

Under this model, knowledge of conventional conceptual metaphor is represented within the same type of framework, and is subject to the same kind of processing constraints, as other forms of linguistic knowledge including syntactic, idiomatic, lexical and pragmatic knowledge. The observed processing time for all types of interpretations is simply based on the amount of contextual evidence for the correct combination of constructions. Specifically, metaphorical utterances will be processed quickly and effectively when they provide sufficient evidence for the activation and integration of the appropriate conventional metaphors. This is precisely the same kind of processing required for all other literal and non-literal language.

5.4.2. On-line constraint and non-optionality cConstraint

As discussed above, these two constraints are two sides of the same coin and will be discussed together. Under the framework sketched here, interpretation occurs via the activation and integration of constructions into working memory based on evidence from both within the utterance and prior context. Simultaneous interpretations can be pursued in parallel as long as there is sufficient evidence to activate their constituent constructions and the resulting interpretations are sufficiently well-formed. As more evidence becomes available the well-formedess of any interpretation may drop, causing it to be pruned from working memory. Therefore, metaphorical interpretations may be built up incrementally and eventually survive or be pruned based on the available evidence. The On-Line constraint is satisfied since partial metaphorical interpretations will always be built as long as there is minimal sufficient evidence to activate the required metaphorical constructions. At the same time these partial results can be either confirmed or short-circuited by subsequent evidence as it becomes available on-line.

5.4.3. Differential behavior constraint

In our suggested framework, individual conceptual metaphors are retrieved from long-term memory in the same fashion as other memory traces based on what Anderson (1990) calls their *need probability*. This is simply the probability that a memory trace will be needed given the evidence currently available in the context. In our model, this is achieved by augmenting constructions with two types of frequency information: the overall frequency of individual constructions, and the predictive power of the presence of their parts in context as evidence. The differential behavior of various metaphors arises both from their differing frequencies and the differing ability of their source and target parts to predict future uses.

5.4.4. *Contextual influence*

As with the previous constraints, contextual influences on metaphor are accounted for by assuming that they result from behavior that is a known part of the human memory system. Specifically, constructions are considered to be structured memory traces that are susceptible to all the various priming, recency and frequency effects observed in both the memory literature and the literature on lexical access and access to idioms. In particular, as suggested by Anderson's model, metaphorical constructions can be primed based either on their prior activation or the prior activation of their parts. The degree of activation is simply based on how predictive the evidence is of future uses of the metaphor. Therefore, the observed vast difference in ability of source concepts, target concepts and whole metaphors to predict future metaphors arises directly from the differing patterns of occurrence of these cues in real texts.

6. Conclusions

Our results indicate that the various experimental results concerning the effects of context on metaphor processing are neither artifacts of the laboratory nor artifacts of a special purpose metaphor processing mechanism. Rather, they are reflections of the environment in the language comprehension mechanism. Specifically, the various inhibition and facilitation effects of context on metaphor comprehension are consistent with corpus-based results concerning the predictive value of contextual cues for future metaphors. These results, when combined with converging evidence from other relevant studies, paint a picture of the on-line metaphor comprehension process as a normal part of our cognitive language capacity.

References

Anderson, John R.
    1990   *The Adaptive Character of Thought*. Hillsdale, NJ: Lawrence Erlbaum.
Anderson, John R. and Lael J. Schooler
    1991   Reflections of the environment in memory. *Psychological Science* 2: 396–408.
Carbonell, Jaime
    1981   Invariance hierarchies in metaphor interpretation. *Proceedings of the Third Meeting of the Cognitive Science Society*, 292–295. Hillsdale, NJ: Lawrence Erlbaum.

Fass, Dan
  1988 *Collative Semantics: A Semantics for Natural Language.* PhD dissertation, New Mexico State University, Las Cruces, New Mexico.
  1991 met*: A method for discriminating metaphor and metonymy by computer. *Computational Linguistics* 17: 49–90.

Fillmore, Charles, Paul Kay and Mary O'Connor
  1988 Regularity and idiomaticity in grammatical constructions: The case of *let alone. Language* 64: 510–538.

Gentner, Dedre, Brian Falkenhainer and Janice Skorstad
  1988 Viewing metaphor as analogy. In: David H. Helman (ed.), *Analogical Reasoning,* 171–177. Dordrecht: Kluwer Academic Publishers.

Gernsbacher, Morton Ann, Boaz Keysar, Rachel Robertson and Necia Werner
  2001 The Role of Suppression and Enhancement in Understanding Metaphors. *Journal of Memory and Language* 45: 433–450.

Gerrig, Richard J.
  1989 Empirical constraints on computational theories of metaphor: Comments on Indurkhya. *Cognitive Science* 13: 235–241.

Gerrig, Richard J. and Alice F. Healy
  1983 Dual processes in metaphor understanding: comprehension and appreciation. *Journal of Experimental Psychology: Learning, Memory and Cognition* 9: 667–675.

Gibbs, Raymond W.
  1984 Literal meaning and psychological theory. *Cognitive Science* 8: 275–304.
  1992 Categorization and metaphor understanding. *Psychological Review* 99: 572–577.

Gildea, Patricia and Sam Glucksberg
  1983 On understanding metaphor: The role of context. *Journal of Verbal Learning and Verbal Behavior* 22: 577–590.

Glucksberg, Sam, Patricia Gildea and Howard Bookin
  1982 On understanding nonliteral speech: Can people ignore metaphors?. *Journal of Verbal Learning and Verbal Behavior* 21: 85–98.

Hobbs, Jerry
  1979 Metaphor, metaphor schemata, and selective inferencing. Technical Note 204, San Mateo, CA: SRI.

Indurkhya, Bipin
  1987 Approximate semantic transference: A computational theory of metaphors and analogy. *Cognitive Science* 11: 445–480.

Inhoff, Alber W., Susan D Lima and Patrick J Carrol
  1984 Contextual effects on metaphor comprehension in reading. *Memory and Cognition* 12: 558–567.

Johnson, Mark
  1987 *The Body in the Mind: The Bodily Basis of Meaning, Imagination and Reason.* Chicago: The University of Chicago Press.

Jurafsky, Dan
  1996 A probabilistic model of lexical and syntactic access and disambiguation. *Cognitive Science* 20: 137–194.

Kemper, Susan
 1989 Priming the comprehension of metaphors. *Metaphor and Symbolic Activity* 4: 1–17.
Keysar, Boaz
 1989 On the functional equivalence of literal and metaphorical interpretations in discourse. *Journal of Language and Memory* 28: 375–385.
Lakoff, George
 1987 *Women, Fire and Dangerous Things.* Chicago: The University of Chicago Press.
Lakoff, George and Mark Johnson
 1980 *Metaphors We Live By.* Chicago: The University of Chicago Press.
Lakoff, George and Mark Turner
 1988 *More Than Cool Reason: A Field Guide to Poetic Metaphor.* Chicago: The University of Chicago Press.
Martin, James H.
 1990 *A Computational Model of Metaphor Interpretation.* Cambridge, MA: Academic Press.
 1992 Computer understanding of conventional metaphoric language. *Cognitive Science* 16: 233–270.
 1994 Metabank: A knowledge-base of metaphoric language conventions. *Computational Intelligence* 10: 134–149.
Narayanan, Srini
 1999 Moving right along: A computational model of metaphoric reasoning about events. *Proceedings of the National Conference on Artificial Intelligence*, 121–128. Menlo Park, CA: AAAI Press.
Narayanan, Srini and Dan Jurafsky
 1998 Bayesian models of human sentence processing. *Proceedings of the Cognitive Science Society*, 752–757. Hillsdale, NJ: Lawrence Erlbaum.
Oaksford, Mike and Nicholas Chater
 1998 An introduction to rational models of cognition. In: *Rational Models of Cognition*, 1–17. Oxford: Oxford University Press.
Ortony, Andrew, Diane L. Schallert, Ralph E. Reynolds and Stephen J. Antos
 1978 Interpreting metaphors and idioms: Some effects of context on comprehension. *Journal of Verbal Learning and Verbal Behavior* 17: 465–477.
Pollio, Howard R., Michael K. Smith, and Marilyn R. Pollio
 1990 Figurative language and cognitive psychology. *Language and Cognitive Processes* 5: 141–167.
Russell, Sylvia W.
 1976 Computer understanding of metaphorically used verbs. *American Journal of Computational Linguistics*, Microfiche 44.
Searle, John R.
 1979 Metaphor. In: Andrew Ortony (ed), *Metaphor and Thought*, 92–123. Cambridge University Press.
Talmy, Leonard
 1975 Semantics and syntax of motion. In: John Kimball (ed), *Syntax and Semantics* 4, 181–238. New York: Academic Press.

1988 Force dynamics in language and cognition. *Cognitive Science* 12: 49–100.

Wilks, Yorick
1978 Making preferences more active. *Artificial Intelligence* 11: 197–223.

Of critical importance: Using electronic text corpora to study metaphor in business media discourse

Veronika Koller

Abstract

In this paper, I argue that by relying on broad empirical evidence, corpus linguistics methods represent an opportunity to fortify claims about the socio-cultural and ideological aspects of metaphor usage. In addition, I will show how ascertaining surface patterns of metaphoric expressions in discourse to some extent allows for inferences to be drawn about the conceptual metaphors that discourse is based upon. After outlining the links between metaphor, socio-cultural context and ideology in some more detail and elaborate on why corpus studies are indispensable for a critical approach to metaphor, I present a case study and the specific methods used in it. The empirical analysis demonstrates how a quantitative analysis of metaphoric expressions in business media discourse does more than merely describe the surface and raises questions as to the socio-cultural factors influencing metaphor usage, the ideological work done by selectively employed expressions and the cognitive models that discourse is based upon.

1. Introduction

Cognitive semantics is a field that has so far proved to be surprisingly immune to the spread of corpus linguistics methods. Notwithstanding forays into corpus-based lexical semantics (Stubbs, 2001) and the often arduous sense tagging of corpora (Véronis, 2003), studies in cognitive semantics, especially those on conceptual mappings, are still underrepresented in corpus linguistics when compared to, say, word class studies. This is all the more astonishing as corpus linguistics would be in an ideal position to accommodate the often voiced criticism that cognitive metaphor research following Lakoff and Johnson (1980; Johnson, 1987; Lakoff, 1993) "relies on idealized cases, disconnected from the context of actual use in natural discourse" (Quinn 1991: 91). The fact that this lack of representative, naturally occurring empirical data in cognitive metaphor study still persists in more recent approaches to the subject (Fauconnier and Turner, 2002; Lakoff and Johnson, 1999) further underscores the small impact corpus-based approaches have so far had on investigations into conceptual mappings.

Nevertheless, and despite the obstacles involved,[1] headway has been made in using electronic corpora in metaphor research. To date, corpus analysis has, for instance, been carried out to establish the syntactic and semantic patterns of metaphoric expressions (Deignan, 1999), to identify those expressions as a stylistic device in fictional texts (Heywood, Semino and Short, 2002) or to ascertain pragmatic phenomena accompanying metaphor usage in spoken discourse (Cameron and Deignan, 2003). It is no coincidence that relevant work betrays a particular interest in the cultural context (Deignan, 2003) and ideological function (Charteris-Black, 2004; Musolff, 2003) of metaphor. The observation that "ideological patterns may arise from the application of a particular metaphor and the neglect of alternative ones" (Wolf and Polzenhagen 2003: 268) indeed calls for investigations into metaphor usage in naturally occurring discourse. A corpus puts this discourse at the researcher's fingertips and furthermore guarantees that results are representative – in any case, "as representative as possible of the larger population" (McEnery and Wilson 2001: 80) and certainly more representative than those generated by the analysis of isolated samples or, worse still, introspection alone.

In what follows, I shall argue that by relying on broad empirical evidence, corpus linguistics methods represent an opportunity to fortify claims about the socio-cultural and ideological aspects of metaphor usage. Apart from that, I will also show how ascertaining surface patterns of metaphoric expressions in discourse to some extent allows for inferences to be drawn about the conceptual metaphors that discourse is based upon. To this end, the paper is divided as follows: The next section will outline the links between metaphor, socio-cultural context and ideology in some more detail and elaborate on why corpus studies are indispensable for a critical approach to metaphor. Putting theory into practice, I will next present a case study and the specific methods used in it. That empirical part is intended to demonstrate how a quantitative analysis of metaphoric expressions in business media discourse does more than merely describe the surface. Beyond that, it raises questions as to the socio-cultural factors influencing metaphor usage, the ideological work done by selectively employed expressions and the cognitive models that discourse is based upon. The article finally closes by suggesting further possible fields of research as well as refinements in method.

---

1. These obstacles include misidentifying or overlooking relevant metaphoric expressions, extensive manual reworking and the disproportionate amount of time required for compiling, combining and comparing corpora.

2. Theoretical and methodological considerations

Any corpus-related form of language study necessarily deals with performance rather than competence, with *parole* rather than *langue*, with language-in-use rather than language-as-system. In the context of metaphor, this means that corpus studies rely not so much on theories of embodiment and the universal image schemas they posit (Lakoff and Johnson, 1999), but rather on the oppositional notions brought forth to counter that view of metaphor as a transcultural, ahistoric phenomon. In cognitive semantics' brand of the nature-nurture debate, the (additional) impact cultural models may have on metaphor formation and usage has not gone unnoticed (Boers und Littlemore, 2003; Emanatian, 1999; Gibbs, 1999; Kövecses, 1999; 2000: 67–77). According to this strand in metaphor research, cultural and hence intersubjectively shared schemata "function to interpret experience and guide action in a wide variety of domains including events, institutions, and physical and mental objects" (Gibbs 1999: 153). According to this view of cognition as "distributed" among members of a particular community (Hutchins, 1995), mental models can be imported into, and multiplied in, social structures, rendering even such elementary cognitive models as image schemata part of the socio-cultural context. Gibbs (1999: 153) furthermore points out that perception may itself be determined by cultural factors: Aspects of the physical world deemed important enough to become the material for so-called primary metaphors (Grady, 1997) may vary from culture to culture. Moreover, socio-cultural interpretations of the physical or social phenomena that bring about metaphor can also affect the evaluative connotations of a given metaphor. Finally, at the level of complex metaphors, Deignan (2003) emphasizes that different spheres may be regarded as more or less important in different cultures, making them more or less likely to be drawn upon in metaphor formation.

Beyond that, the formation and usage of higher-level complex metaphors is also influenced by ideologies, i.e. by "representations of ... the world which ... contribute to establishing, maintaining and changing social relations of power, domination and exploitation" (Fairclough 2003: 9). In a socio-cognitive view, ideology has also been defined as "the 'interface' between the cognitive representations and processes underlying discourse and action, on the one hand, and the societal position and interests of social groups, on the other hand" (van Dijk 1995: 18). In this context, metaphor can be used by those social groups to convey and reinforce the ideologically vested conceptual models their discourse is based upon. Indeed, metaphor is central in doing so, as it constructs reality by conceptualising some of its aspects (the target domain) in terms of other aspects (the source domain). Metaphor thereby transports that view of the world held by speakers using the metaphor and hence "may create realities for us, especially social realities" (Lakoff and Johnson 1980: 156). It is important to note that selective metaphor usage will be influenced by the social group and discourse community the speaker identifies with: In-group membership is (re)constructed to a significant degree by drawing on the group's shared cognitive and discursive resources. In the present case, i.e. business media discourse, we are faced with the added complexity that journalists are likely to show a high degree of readership orientation and thus echo and reinforce the conceptual models they perceive in their audience. Hence, metaphoric expressions ascertained in that kind of secondary discourse do not necessarily reveal the metaphors shared by journalists alone.

It is this more socio-culturally oriented critical approach to conceptual metaphor that relies most on a systematic analysis of comprehensive data collections: The claim that cognitive scenarios and image schemata as well as the metaphors they generate are distributed across groups of social actors can only be verified by investigating the language use of a large number of speakers. Likewise, any approach considering socio-cultural aspects requires that its claims be tested against the social world. Relying on introspection, or extrapolating from the analysis of selected sample texts, runs the risk of addressing the idiosyncratic rather than the typical, the individual rather than the socially shared. In particular, corpus linguists have pointed out that introspection, while a valuable starting point, often proves to be misleading when tested against vast amounts of data as those typically provided by large electronic corpora (Stubbs 2001: 72). Investigating the ideological function of metaphor usage likewise requires a broad empirical database: If ideology is theorised to take the form of dominant conceptual models of the world and if these models underlie the discourse of a particular social group, then it stands to reason that ideologies and their linguistic expression should be spread across the respective discourse community, a claim best checked against the large-scale authentic language use of that community.

So what can corpora and corpus linguistics contribute to investigating metaphors as distributed models that are subject to socio-cultural influences and do ideological work? Generally speaking, any corpus-based study of metaphoric expressions relies on collections of machine-readable texts that can be analysed by means of specific software such as WordSmith Tools. These collections can either be compiled by the researcher, who, however, is restricted by rather limited financial and temporal resources. Hence, the size of such corpora typically ranges from 2000 to 200,000 words or tokens (Kennedy 1998: 73–74). The present study is a case in point, using as it does two purpose-built corpora of approximately 160,000 words each. An alternative is provided by corpora compiled and made available – for free or, increasingly, upon payment of a licensing or membership fee – by academic project teams in cooperation with a publisher. These corpora can vary vastly in size; an example of a very large corpus is the 450-million-word Bank of English that was developed at the University of Birmingham and is marketed by Cobuild Collins. Large general corpora are intended to offer a comprehensive representation of a language or language variety and thus not only comprise a multitude of different text genres from a variety of speakers and discourses, but also typically consist of at least one million words. These large corpora are usually analysed with the help of an integrated software package that is tailored to the corpus it comes with.[2]

In terms of method, tackling semantic issues by means of corpus analysis is anything but straightforward. Since metaphor generation or extraction programs are not readily available to end users, corpus research into metaphor necessarily has to begin with attested linguistic expressions. While such a corpus-based approach is in line with post-hoc research focusing on metaphor in text and interaction (Cameron and Low 1999: 79), any concordance program obviously only shows the more or less decontextualised chunk of text the researcher has been looking for. This chunk usually includes a span of, say, five words to the right and to the left of the search word, or node. However comprehensive the list of forms searched for may be, their number can never be exhaustive and some potential metaphoric expressions may well be missed and can only be retrieved by looking at longer stretches of text. Moreover, identifying what counts as an instance of metaphoric usage and deciding on the underlying conceptual metaphor can all too easily run the risk of subjectivism: Indeed, metaphor identification will at least to some extent always rely on "informed intuition" (Deignan 1999: 180). Granted, some metaphoric expressions can be identified quite easily as they only occur in semi-fixed collocational phrases (for example *launch a campaign*, *target audience*; see Deignan 1999: 197)[3] or because their very occurrence in a text with a particular topic suggests meta-

---

2. One of the drawbacks of customised corpus software is obviously the lack of a standard, meaning that corpus analysts regularly have to switch between the different navigations and interfaces of the programs that come with the most common general corpora.
3. Data from the Bank of English sample, subcorpus of media texts.

phoric usage (for example dancing terms in a corpus on corporate restructuring). Nevertheless, subjectivity and random inference of underlying conceptual metaphors invariably loom large. In his approach to validating metaphor research, Low (1999: 64) proposes to look at whether conventional metaphors, both the speaker's and other people's, are extended creatively, whether text producers make explicit that they conceive of a topic in the form of a particular metaphor, whether text producers discuss what semantic features are transferred and, finally, whether text producers challenge others whose use of phrases differs with regard to semantic, especially metaphoric, overtones. Low (2003: 252) further advises to make metaphor identification as explicit as possible, especially in problematic cases where there is no linguistic evidence, in cases of multiple identifications or in those of a conceptual metaphor format digressing from the classic A IS B. His recommendations undoubtedly represent a valuable help in deducing conceptual metaphor from surface-level metaphoric expressions and thus in filtering out idiosyncratic metaphor usage that is not part of the conceptual map informing the discourse. Practically speaking, however, the large amounts of data dealt with in corpus studies are anathema to the idea of meticulously going through the motions of metaphor identification in each and every instance. In the present study, for example, it is obvious that a single researcher cannot, within a reasonable time frame, apply Low's checklist to each of the 1,531 attested occurrences of metaphoric expressions in the two corpora (see next section). In practice, the above criteria are therefore likely to be applied only to those metaphoric expressions which are not accounted for by any pre-defined lexical field and which therefore need testing.

It has already been mentioned that computer-generated results require elaborate manual reworking. Still, there is no doubt that metaphor research can indeed gain from corpus analysis. First, the large amounts of data that make exact metaphor identification such a difficult task on the one hand, on the other hand broaden the empirical basis for testing hypotheses. Even in its simplest form, corpus research ascertaining the frequencies of metaphoric expressions can help draw inferences about the productivity and relevance of conceptual metaphors in discourse. Another benefit is corpus analysis's potential to reveal the use of metaphoric expressions across word classes, an issue neglected all too often in cognitive linguistic theory focusing on NOUN A IS NOUN B type conceptual metaphors. Given the hypothesis that prevailing word classes might point to the nature of underlying cognitive models, Steen (1999: 81) notes that it is indeed vital to "discriminate between types of metaphor embodying specific configurations of metaphor features" and adds that to this end, "corpus research is crucial".

On the other hand, Hodge and Kress ask that "the minimal unit for analysis [be] not a single form or text in isolation, but a reading of a sequence in context, containing prior or later forms in text" (1993: 181). To heed their demand and avoid isolating the results, thus risking to focus on lexical metaphoric expressions at the expense of phrasal and higher-level ones, the attested metaphoric tokens need to be linked back to their textual environment. Recontextualisation on the paragraph level can be done with the help of the WordSmith Tools concordancer used for this study, as the program not only provides the immediate co-text of up to 25 words left and right of the node but can also display maximised co-text of approximately 400 words for single concordance lines.

However, texts typically feature more complex metaphoric chains, which convey the structure of the underlying conceptual map (Koller, 2003) and achieve text cohesion (Goatly 1997: 166). As these are not easily detected by mere automatic co-text expansion, attested metaphoric occurrences can be manually tagged and a second search can be run to uncover how the metaphoric tags that have been searched for are spread across the whole text. The dispersion plot function of the WordSmith Tools concordancing program provides a graphic representation of these spreads. Comparing the graphs for different metaphors yields a specific picture of where metaphors cluster and which metaphors are predominant in each instance. Beyond that, the computer-generated results should be related back to the actual texts to see what role the specific metaphors have within, or in relation to, the respective clusters.

If one regards journalistic texts as implicitly argumentative, metaphor clusters in a text's introduction might indicate an ideational, defining function ("setting the agenda"), clustering in the middle could serve interpersonal, argumentative ends and, finally, clustering towards the end of a text may have another interpersonal, namely persuasive function ("driving a point home"). Should one function prevail in the texts, inferences could be drawn for the respective discourse as a whole as being characterised by, for example, persuasion rather than explanation. This would in turn reveal the text producer's and recipients' primary role in the discourse community and the relations between them. The mostly monologic nature of media discourse (Fairclough 1995: 40) suggests that metaphoric expressions could be predominantly used for persuasive ends.

Finally, quantitative needs to be complemented by qualitative analysis: Samples showing high density should be singled out and analysed to see, for instance, whether metaphoric occurrences are quoted from primary business discourse or originate from secondary business media discourse, whether they are ascribed to an out-group or claimed by an in-group or whether they are attenuated or intensified (Eubanks, 2000). In addition, relations between the cluster metaphors can also be investigated, such as metaphors extending, elaborating, exemplifying, generalising or questioning (Kyratzis, 1997) as well as negating or simply echoing each other. Moreover, combining the functions within metaphoric chains with a functional grammar analysis can also corroborate or modify, if not contradict, assumptions about the nature of underlying metaphoric models. However, since this article focuses on the corpus approach to metaphor, qualitative text analysis will not be dealt with in any further detail. Instead, the following empirical section will outline the quantitative method used in this study and discuss the results it yielded.

3. Example of a corpus-based method: Metaphors in business media discourse

This case study is meant to show how the analysis of purpose-built corpora of machine-readable text can throw light on metaphor as used in business magazines and papers. While aware of the fact that quantitative corpus analysis can only ever be a valuable starting point for claims about the metaphoric features of cognition and discourse, this empirical section will nevertheless take account of the focus of this anthology and present the first part of the analysis only: establishing frequency patterns and word class distribution for metaphorically used lexemes from pre-defined world fields, recontextualising and finally tagging results to ascertain the metaphoric structure of, and metaphor density in, individual texts. I shall first briefly describe the corpora analysed, then elaborate on the details of the method used in their analysis and finally present quantitative results as well as indicate how these raise questions to be followed up in subsequent qualitative analysis.

Instead of trying to tackle the vast field of business media discourse as a whole, this study is limited to print media articles on two specific, albeit central topics of business reporting: marketing as well as mergers and acquisitions (M&A). The two ensuing text corpora represent collections of magazine and newspaper articles on the two topics and were specifically compiled for this study. As such, they bring together texts published in four different business publications (*Business Week [BW]*, *The Economist [EC]*, *Fortune [FO]*, *Financial Times [FT]*) between 1996 and 2001. Each corpus contains approximately 160,000 words (see Table 1). The fact that the corpora include three magazines and a daily newspaper (*Financial Times*) accounts for a notable difference in average article length, since the latter as a format is characterised by short news items usually absent from the former. Accordingly, the *Financial Times* shows the shortest articles by far. To make up for this bias, a larger number of articles was included so that each publication contributes roughly a quarter to the respective corpus.

Table 1. Corpora structure

Publication	Marketing and sales		Mergers and acquisitions	
	Number of articles/words	Average article length	Number of articles/words	Average article length
BW (US)	34/40,946	1204 words	29/42,022	1449 words
EC (UK)	42/39,205	933 words	49/41,363	844 words
FO (US)	36/38,907	1081 words	22/40,765	1853 words
FT (UK)	98/40,518	413 words	64/40,168	628 words
TOTAL	210/159,576		164/164,318	

Generally speaking, the focus of this study is metaphor as it features in the language use of groups, allowing for assumptions about the conceptual system the discourse thus investigated is based upon. In this context, language use is not regarded as a mere derivative of the conceptual system but rather as being in a mutually constitutive relation to it, with ideology as the interface between them. In particular, selectively used or muted metaphors are seen as bearers of ideology as they discursively construct reality from a particular point of view. How then can dominant metaphors be ascertained in the two corpora?

In the present study, the first step in answering this question was to define a lexical field comprising 35 lemmas each from three domains, amounting to 105 lemmas for both marketing and sales as well as mergers and acquisitions.[4] The different domains were posited as central to the discourse in question, as based on anecdotal evidence and previous knowledge of the discourse. (To make sure that the study would not only reveal what I had been looking for, I also defined an alternative lexical field for each discourse which dominant metaphors could be checked against. These were romance for marketing and sales, and dancing – a non-aggressive form of relational movement – for M&A. In what follows, however,

---

4. A short note on terminology seems in order: Contrary to Crystal's use of the term *lemma* (2003), the term is here employed to mean a headword (for example *prey*) which can be split up into several lexemes, including phrasal ones (for example *prey, to prey [up]on*). These lexemes in turn comprise various word forms (for example *preying, preys, preyed*).

these will not be discussed, in order to avoid making this paper unnecessarily complex.) Moreover, it was hypothesised that lemmas would not only show collocational patterns (for example *hostile takeover* and *corporate marriage* co-occurring as instantiations of the WAR and the MATING metaphor, respectively, in texts on mergers and acquisitions) but that lemmas from all three domains would indeed co-occur in texts, thus forming clusters. In the case of marketing and sales, the fields investigated were war, sports and games, and for M&A, the lexical field was that of evolutionary struggle, containing types from the domains of fighting, mating and feeding. It should be noted that the lexical field of war/fighting in each case includes five flexible lemmas which, again drawing on previous knowledge of business media texts, were assumed to be typical of the respective discourse domains. These "wildcards" are *blitz, campaign, cut-throat, field, launch* for marketing and sales, and *defence, hostility, raid, victim, vulnerability* in the case of M&A. As the domains differ vastly in terms of their relevance for, and frequency in, business media discourse, it was, for example, harder to decide on lemmas from the domain of gambling than it was for the domain of war. In this context, thesauri and specific glossaries proved helpful in establishing comparably sized lexical fields.

It soon became clear that the orginal aim of including an equal number of nouns, verbs and adjectives/adverbs in each field could not be met. This is partly due to the fact that with some lemmas, a particular word class is outside the metaphoric spectrum, corroborating Low's observation that sometimes "where two words exist which are ... semantically related but of a different grammatical class, one may have a metaphorical use which is not extended to the other" (1988: 131). Hence, the lexical fields of romance/mating include *consummation* or *to consummate*, since these collocate with *marriage* (external reference data from the Bank of English), but not the adjective *consummate*. Another example is *suitor* as opposed to *to sue*. However, the fields were calibrated and revised to lessen the nominal bias that emerged. What is more, the imbalance was adjusted by calculating relative rather than absolute word class frequencies. Finally, it should be noted that prepositions have been omitted from the lexical fields. Although they undoubtedly play a crucial role for spatial metaphors (e.g., *market entry*), "their noun/verb colligates are too general to yield any imagery or to make manifest any specific schemata" (Goatly 1997: 91). Adjectives/adverbs, however, were included, notwithstanding the fact that they, unless in predicative position, mostly occur in relation to nouns or verbs as well. Yet, not being mere function words they evoke metaphoric models more readily than do prepositions. On a general note, word class distribution plays an important role in metaphor research as "the unit of metaphor [is] independent of any grammatical unit" (Kittay 1987: 24).

Another issue that is bound to rear its ugly head at some point in metaphor research design is that of so-called "dead" metaphors, here defined as expressions the origin and metaphoricity of which is opaque to language users. While instances such as *campaign* – being derived from Latin *campus* or (battle)field – certainly function as metaphoric expressions in the diachronic system of the language, it is arguable whether they can still be regarded as having a metaphoric effect in the synchronic system and hence in language use. To determine this question, one has to look at whether the conceptual mapping that gave rise to the expression is still transparent to text producers and recipients in the discourse community at hand and/or whether discourse participants still perceive a contrast between literal and metaphoric senses (Gibbs and Steen, 2002). For studies not including field research in metaphor processing, a look at the core meanings given in small dictionaries still serves as an indicator of how encroached a metaphoric meaning really is. Taking the case of *campaign* as but one example, the Collins Cobuild English Dictionary, the Concise Oxford Dictionary and the Longman Dictionary of Contemporary English all list the metaphoric meaning first, making it the predominant one. On a scale of transparency, a term such as *campaign* is therefore located, if not at the extreme end of complete opaqueness, then certainly heading that way. Still, the question of how such terms as *campaign*, *launch* or *target* have come to be used in business discourse in the first place is a crucial one. After all, the very dominant presence of such terms from the military domain in business discourse is by no means coincidental. While the lexemes in question are certainly not consciously employed by all speakers in every single instance, their presence is still significant as it ties in perfectly with that of other lemmas from the war domain that are perceived as more metaphoric, for example *blitz* or *troops*. To discard some technical metaphoric expressions (i.e., those restricted to a particular discourse domain) because of their ambiguous status in the synchronic system would therefore clearly impoverish the data.

With the lexical fields thus established,[5] each corpus was searched for the 105 lemmas contained in the fields, accounting for spelling variants (for example, *home run* vs. *home-run* or *homerun*, *maneuver* vs. *manoeuvre*) in doing so. As mentioned above, the software used for the search was the concordancing program included in the WordSmith Tools 3.0

---

5. A list of the lemmas finally included in the respective lexical fields can be found in Tables A1 and A2 in the appendix.

suite. Although the search was lemma-based, the various emerging lexemes were also taken account of: After all, "if only the base form is studied, some metaphorical uses may be missed" (Deignan 1999: 189). The concordance lines were then edited manually to filter out non-metaphoric instances and irrelevant metaphoric occurrences, i.e. those which do not represent realisations of the conceptual metaphors identified. An example of the latter would be *embrace* from the domain of MATING in M&A discourse, which does occur in the corpus as the collocation *to embrace the idea*, but not as a metaphor for corporate mergers.

The present study corroborates Kennedy's observation that corpus analysis "typically provides basic descriptive statistics on the number of ... tokens in the corpus or section of the corpus, the number of different word types and the type-token ratios" (1998: 258). Although the corpora were manually tagged for metaphoric expressions, rendering the results amenable to inferential statistics (Kretzschmar, Meyer and Ingegneri 1997: 174), the function these expressions and their underlying conceptual metaphors have at the textual, interpersonal and, most importantly, ideological level were deemed more important than their statistical significance. Thus, I did not formulate, and seek to validate, hypotheses but rather took descriptive statistics as a starting point for qualitative text analysis, a method which I consider most suitable for addressing questions of the possible socio-cognitive impact of metaphoric expressions in discourse.

The procedure outlined above yielded the following results: First, it listed the absolute frequencies of metaphoric expressions (see Tables A1 and A2) and the two corpora's average metaphor density per 1,000 words (5.3 for marketing and sales and 4.17 for M&A, respectively). Second, it showed the relative frequency of metaphoric expressions across the three domains: Here, it can be seen that metaphors of war and fighting are by far the most frequent in the two corpora, accounting for 64.52 and 72.89 per cent, respectively. Metaphors of sports and mating come in second (23.25 and 20.12 per cent), with those of games and feeding trailing far behind at 12.23 and seven per cent.[6]

Third, the quantitative analysis revealed the relative frequency of metaphoric expressions across word classes and domains: In general, the marketing and sales corpus shows a similar proportion of nominal forms in both

---

6. Due to cross-classification of the lemmas *play, game, shoot, field* and *ball*, the number of tokens for the three domains in the marketing and sales corpus totals 916, thus exceeding the number of 845 metaphoric expressions given in Table A1. Accordingly, the percentages above are calculated on the basis of 916.

the lexical field and with metaphoric expressions (see Table A1). However, verbs are over-represented, increasing in percentage from just under 30 per cent in the lexical fields up to 37.04 per cent in metaphoric usage. Adjectives and adverbs on the other hand are under-represented, with respective proportions being almost halved in metaphoric usage. The M&A corpus records under-representation most notably with verbs, which fall from more than a quarter to under a fifth in metaphoric usage. If we further split up word class representation by looking at the various domains, we can see that adjectives and adverbs are underrepresented across domains and discourses (with the exception of the fighting domain), sometimes significantly so: In the domain of mating, for example, adjectives plummet from just over 20 per cent in the lexical field to less than 6 per cent in metaphoric usage. Nouns on the other hand are overrepresented in almost all domains (except that of sports). This corroborates Goatly's observation that "nouns, referring directly to things, can more directly evoke images than other parts of speech" as "the meaning ... of nouns will ... be conceptualized as bundles of [rather than single] semantic features" (1997: 84).

Beyond that, findings show a varying number of the 35 types from the lexical fields being actually realised as metaphoric expressions in each case: In both corpora, the domain of war or fighting is the one to show the highest percentage of lexical field items to be realised metaphorically, namely as much as 94.29 and 97.14 per cent, respectively. The domains to rank second in terms of frequency of occurrence (i.e., number of metaphoric tokens) also come in second as far as number of lexical field items to be realised (i.e., metaphoric types) is concerned (74.29 per cent for SPORTS and 65.71 per cent for MATING metaphors). Finally, the least frequent metaphors also record the lowest number of different types, with 51.43 per cent being realised from the lexical field of games and less than half of the items from the field of feeding (45.71 per cent). If we divide the number of a metaphor's types by that of its tokens, we arrive at the metaphoric type-token ratio (mTTR), which indicates how varied the corpus is in terms of metaphor: The more metaphoric types, i.e., different metaphoric expressions, there are, the lower the mTTR is and the more metaphoric variation we find in the corpus. Obviously, the mTTR increases in reciprocal proportion to the number of types: In both corpora, the WAR/FIGHTING metaphor is expressed by the highest number of different metaphoric types and thus shows the lowest mTTR (0.05 and 0.07, respectively), while instances of SPORTS and MATING metaphors come in second (mTTR 0.21 and 0.17). Metaphoric expressions of games and feeding show ratios as high as 0.17 and 0.31.

It is also worth looking at the overall mTTR in the two corpora: For marketing and sales, this is 0.09 (on the basis of 845; 0.08 on the basis of 916), while the M&A corpus, which features fewer tokens, shows a ratio of 0.11. These figures obviously correlate with the corpora's overall metaphor density, which was lower for the M&A corpus. However, mTTRs vary widely throughout the respective corpus: As can be seen from Figure 1, the three most frequent types (*campaign, launch, target* and *target, hostility, battle*) show an extremely high number of tokens, accounting for 43.55 (marketing and sales, on the basis of 845; 40.17 on the basis of 916) and 30.76 per cent (M&A) of all metaphoric occurrences, respectively.[7] Numbers fall sharply after that and soon dwindle off to an mTTR of 100, or one token per type. Not only do these figures show that the majority of metaphoric expressions of war is accounted for by only three types, but they also corroborate the relation between the frequency of a metaphoric expression and the opaqueness of its metaphoric nature: The more frequently an expression is used, the less it is recognised as figurative.

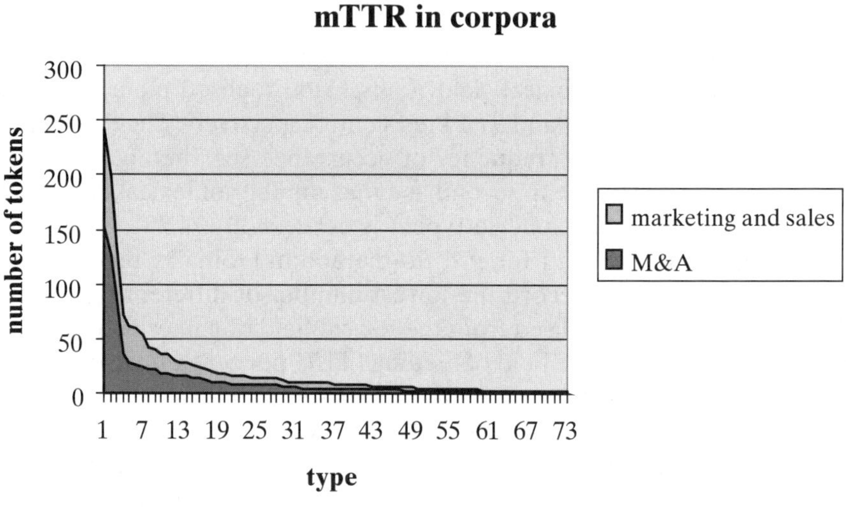

mTTR in corpora

Figure 1. mTTR throughout corpora

---

7. Significantly, the *Financial Times* shows an even higher rate: Here, the three most frequent types account for as much as 70 and just under 50 per cent. This phenomenon is perhaps best explained by the time pressure which determines the specific production conditions of daily newspapers and makes journalists fall back on highly conventional expressions.

The numbers presented above go some way to indicating how active the underlying mental models or parts of them actually are and what relevance journalists ascribe to them. Further, the dominant metaphor of war/fighting can be hypothesised to be cognitively supported by other metaphors in the cluster. Such a dominant metaphor could be both especially vivid as a mental model and particularly relevant to the higher-level socio-cultural ends of the text producer. The most relevant and vivid metaphors can attain the status of a motif (Steen 1999: 95), possibly not only in a particular sample text but in a whole discourse as well (the collocation *hostile take-over* being a case in point). In addition, breaking the quantitative evidence down into word classes suggests whether a particular metaphoric type may be based on a prominent nominal-static, verbal-dynamic or adjectival-descriptive model.

However, the markers of modality are more than justified here: Subsequent qualitative analysis along the lines of functional grammar (Halliday and Matthiessen, 2004) revealed that the sample texts in fact all feature very dynamic movement scenarios. In all word classes, metaphoric expressions for instance tend to combine with progressive aspect and durative/intensive trajectory to convey dynamicity and metaphoric movement (e.g., "some of the biggest names in cyberspace are *stepping up* their Asian operations"; Einhorn 2000: 34). Function clearly overrides form, and it would therefore be misleading to take quantitative word class distribution as unproblematically conveying the nature of basic conceptual models. Instead, word class distribution rather indicates the forms conceptual models take when realised in the form of metaphoric expressions. Nevertheless, deduction of models, even of those that have to be modified later, still provides a first working hypothesis about the schemata possibly prevailing in the group the metaphor producer belongs to. Alternatively, such models could also reflect on the group schemata the writer refers to, that is, businesspeople. In this context, it is important to note that the reader profiles of the four publications not only show that between two thirds (*Business Week* US edition) and a stunning 91 per cent (*The Economist* Europe) of readers are actually men, but also that in terms of education, profession and income, the group written about is largely convergent with the group written for – readers are obviously meant to recognize themselves in the journals and papers.[8] One way in which journalists can facilitate such identification

---

8. As for *Business Week* (US edition), its subscriber profile shows a median age of 48. Just over two thirds of readers hold a university degree, which translates into a quarter of them having a senior management position, with readers' median personal income amounting to

is by taking up the models they perceive in their target audience, either indirectly through quotations or directly, by selective metaphor usage.

These considerations already point to a more macroscopic look at both the discourse and the socio-economic practice the conceptual models help to (re)produce. In the context of business media discourse, this practice is very much determined by a largely masculinised late capitalist framework. The fact that journalists accommodate their discursive strategies to an overwhelmingly male group may well be a reason why the quantitatively most dominant metaphor in both corpora draws on the masculinised domain of war/fighting. The related metaphor BUSINESS IS WAR is ideological in that it constructs an aspect of the world (marketing or M&A) from a particular vantage point, namely as an act of large-scale aggression enacted mostly by men. In a circular fashion, the very prominence of the metaphor, which is reflected in the above figures, will again impact on cognition, entrenching the model in question even further and securing the gendered power relations characterising the social practice that is business.

4. Conclusion and outlook

A number of research questions were not addressed in this article: First, culture-specific aspects of metaphor usage arising from the British or US origin of the texts were not dealt with systematically. This is despite the fact that with some metaphoric expressions, cultural phenomena could well be drawn upon for interpretation. An example is the strikingly higher number of metaphoric expressions from the domain of kingship in the US magazine *Fortune* and its slightly exotic and hence distancing and attenuating effect. For the sake of staying focused, however, such a discus-

---

$84,022 (€68,752) p.a. in 2003 (Business Week, 2004). Data from the same year indicate that the average European *Economist* reader is 45 years of age, and that 93 per cent are university graduates with a median annual personal income of €144,000 at their disposal (The Economist, 2004). The third publication, *Fortune* (European edition), records a median age of 49.4 years for its readers. In terms of education, 83 per cent of international readers are university graduates with a median personal income of $119,400/€97,696 (Fortune, 2004). Finally, the reader profile of the *Financial Times* (global 2003 figures) shows that the average age of its reader is 50, and that 29 per cent of US readers are board level directors. Consequently, their personal income averages £106,280 (€159,168) per year (Financial Times, 2004). While unfortunately no figures were available for education, there is no reason to believe that the FT should differ vastly from the other publications on this parameter.

sion was limited to individual findings. Likewise, the corpora were not systematically analysed for different genres either, to avoid "trading off resolution for scope" (Seidel 1991: 112). Suffice it to point out that the highest percentage in both corpora – between two thirds and three quarters – is accounted for by general articles, followed by reports and surveys in both cases, making up just over 10 per cent. On the other end of the scale, interviews and book reviews hardly feature at all.

Finally, the hardest decision concerning a possible research question was related to the issue of authorship and gender. The corpora had originally been tagged for the authors' gender as this parameter suggests itself to any researcher interested in the ideological aspect of metaphor. When analysing the data on gender and authorship that were yielded by a computer-based search of the relevant tags, however, findings were ambiguous. For example, marketing texts in *Business Week* are overwhelmingly written by women while the situation is reversed in *Fortune*. More importantly, there are considerable obstacles to a serious study of how gender influences metaphor usage in the data. First, there is the high percentage of anonymous articles (30 per cent in the marketing and sales corpus and 39.63 per cent in the mergers and acquisitions corpus), which is mostly accounted for by *The Economist*. In addition, the total of 246 articles marked for authorship altogether matches only 173 different authors, raising questions of idiosyncratic rather than gender-specific metaphor usage. In view of such hurdles, the gender of the authors was eventually not taken into account. Yet, the question remains an intriguing one and future research may well start out from a different set of data clearly marked for the text producers' gender.

Obviously, the method outlined for this study represents but a very basic attempt at addressing cognitive metaphor with the help of electronic corpora and concordancing software, and the analysis could no doubt be refined quite substantially. Additional parameters worth investigating include first and foremost syntactical and collocational patterns. Beyond that, this study has employed corpus analysis in a limited fashion to describe how metaphoric expressions behave in texts, and it would be fascinating to expand the analysis to include probabilities of metaphor occurrence. Such an approach could well be combined with genre analysis to see if particular genres favour particular metaphors.

Generally speaking, when discussing the benefits and drawbacks of using computer-assisted corpus analysis in metaphor research, Kittay's (1987: 9) concern whether "metaphor can be given a computable realization" always lurks in the background, along with Lakoff's caveat that image schemas are by definition not amenable to algorithmic processes (1993: 249) and Eubanks' additional reservation that rule-governed computational models cannot account for the social dimension of metaphor (2000: 132). Nevertheless, Musolff (2003: 349) correctly points out that

> the corpus-based study of metaphor in public discourse can make a significant contribution to cognitive metaphor analysis by providing empirical evidence ... of argumentative trends for their use in a given discourse community.

This study was intended to show that metaphor researchers can, and indeed should, make the best of what computer-aided analysis has to offer. Combining the social and the cognitive in an interdisciplinary fashion is best done by looking at data on a large scale, and corpus analysis is a promising means to this increasingly important end.

References

Boers, Frank, and Jeannette Littlemore (eds.)
    2003   *Cross-cultural Differences in Conceptual Metaphor: Applied Linguistics Perspectives.* Special issue of *Metaphor and Symbol* 18(4).
Business Week
    2004   BW media kit: Business Week International Europe edition. Online at http://mediakit.businessweek.com/a-m-mend.html. Accessed 9 August 2005.
Charteris-Black, Jonathan
    2004   *Corpus Approaches to Critical Metaphor Analysis.* Basingstoke: Palgrave Macmillan.
Cameron, Lynne, and Alice Deignan
    2003   Combining large and small corpora to investigate tuning devices around metaphor in spoken discourse. *Metaphor and Symbol* 18: 149–160.
Cameron, Lynne, and Graham Low
    1999   Metaphor. Language Teaching 32: 77–69.
Collins Cobuild English Dictionary for Advanced Learners
    1995   s.v. "campaign". Second edition. London: Collins.
The Concise Oxford English Dictionary
    1995   s.v. "campaign". 9th ed. Oxford: Oxford University Press.
Crystal, David
    2003   *A Dictionary of Linguistics and Phonetics.* 5th ed. Oxford/Malden, MA: Blackwell. s.v. "lemma".
Deignan, Alice
    1999   Corpus-based research into metaphor. In: Lynne Cameron, and Graham Low (eds.), *Researching and Applying Metaphor,* 177–199. Cambridge: Cambridge University Press.

2003 Metaphorical expressions and culture: An indirect link. In: Frank Boers and Jeannette Littlemore (eds.), *Cross-Cultural Differences in Conceptual Metaphor: Applied Linguistics Perspectives*, 255–271. Special issue of *Metaphor and Symbol* 18 (4).

The Economist
2004 Advertising information. Available from http://printmediakit.economist.com/Reader_profile.9.0.html. Accessed 9 August 2005.

Einhorn, Bruce
2000 Portal combat. *Business Week*, 17 January: 34–35.

Emanatian, Michele
1999 Congruence by degree: On the relation between metaphor and cultural models. In: Raymond W. Gibbs and Gerard Steen (eds.), *Metaphor in Cognitive Linguistics*, 205–218. Amsterdam and Philadelphia: John Benjamins.

Eubanks, Philip
2000 *A War of Words in the Discourse of Trade: The Rhetorical Constitution of Metaphor*. Carbondale, IL: Southern Illinois University Press.

Fairclough, Norman
1995 *Critical Discourse Analysis*. London/New York: Longman.
2003 *Analysing Discourse: Textual Analysis for Social Research*. London/New York: Routledge.

Fauconnier, Gilles and Mark Turner
2002 *The Way We Think: Conceptual Blending and the Mind's Hidden Complexities*. New York: Basic Books.

Financial Times
2004 The global audience. Available from http://www.fttoolkit.co.uk/html/newspaper/global_audience.html. Accessed 9 August 2005.

Fortune
2004 Fortune reader profile. Available from http://www.fortune.com/fortune/mediakit/readerprofile.html. Accessed 9 August 2005.

Gibbs, Raymond W. Jr.
1999 Taking metaphor out of our heads and putting it into the cultural world. In: Raymond W. Gibbs and Gerard Steen (eds.), *Metaphor in Cognitive Linguistics*, 145–166. Amsterdam/Philadelphia: John Benjamins.

Gibbs, Raymond W. Jr., and Gerard Steen
2002 Finding metaphor in language and thought: Metaphor in language as use. Paper presented at the *Conference on Metaphor in Language and Thought*, São Paulo, 21–25 October 2002.

Goatly, Andrew
1997 *The Language of Metaphors*. London: Routledge.

Grady, Joe
1997 Foundations of meaning: Primary metaphors and primary scenes. Ph.D. dissertation, Department of Linguistics, University of California Berkeley.

Halliday, Michael A.K., and Christian M.I.M. Matthiessen

2004 An Introduction to Functional Grammar. Third edition. London: Edward Arnold.

Heywood, John, Elena Semino and Mick Short
2002 Linguistic metaphor identification in two extracts from novels. *Language and Literature* 11: 35–54.

Hodge, Robert and Gunther Kress
1993 *Language as Ideology*. 2nd. ed.. London and New York: Routledge.

Hutchins, Edward
1995 *Cognition in the Wild*. Cambridge, MA: MIT Press.

Johnson, Mark
1987 *The Body in the Mind: The Bodily Basis of Meaning, Imagination, and Reason*. Chicago: University of Chicago Press.

Kennedy, Graeme D.
1998 *An Introduction to Corpus Linguistics*. London and New York: Longman.

Kittay, Eva F.
1987 *Metaphor: Its Cognitive Force and Linguistic Structure*. Oxford: Clarendon Press.

Kövecses, Zoltan
1999 Metaphor: Does it constitute or reflect cultural models? In: Raymond W. Gibbs Jr., and Gerard Steen (eds.), *Metaphor in Cognitive Linguistics*, 167–188. Amsterdam and Philadelphia: John Benjamins.
2002 *Metaphor: A Practical Introduction*. Oxford: Oxford University Press.

Koller, Veronika
2002 "A shotgun wedding": Co-occurrence of war and marriage metaphors in mergers and acquisitions discourse. *Metaphor and Symbol* 17: 179–203.
2003 Metaphor clusters, metaphor chains: Analyzing the multifunctionality of metaphor in text. *Metaphorik.de* 5: 115–134. Available online at http://www.metaphorik.de/05/koller.pdf. Accessed 9 August 2005.

Kretzschmar, William A. Jr., Charles F. Meyer, and Dominique Ingegneri
1997 Use of inferential statistics in corpus studies. In: Magnus Ljung (ed.), *Corpus-based Studies in English*, 167–177. Amsterdam and Atlanta, GA: Rodopi.

Kyratzis, Sakis
1997 Metaphorically Speaking: Sex, Politics and the Greeks. Ph.D. dissertation, Department of Linguistics and English Language, Lancaster University.

Lakoff, George
1993 The contemporary theory of metaphor. In: Andrew Ortony (ed.), *Metaphor and Thought*, Second edition, 202–251. Cambridge: Cambridge University Press.

Lakoff, George and Mark Johnson
1980 *Metaphors We Live By*. Chicago: University of Chicago Press.
1999 *Philosophy in the Flesh: The Embodied Mind and Its Challenge to Western Thought*. New York: Basic Books.

Longman Dictionary of Contemporary English
1995 s.v. "campaign". 3d ed. London/New York: Longman.

Low, Graham
  1988   On teaching metaphor. *Applied Linguistics* 9(2): 125–147.
  1999   Validating metaphor research projects. In *Researching and Applying Metaphor*, Lynne Cameron, and Graham Low (eds.), 48–65. Cambridge: Cambridge University Press.
  2003   Validating metaphoric models in Applied Linguistics. In: Frank Boers, and Jeannette Littlemore (eds.), *Cross-Cultural Differences in Conceptual Metaphor: Applied Linguistics Perspectives*, 239–254. Special issue of *Metaphor and Symbol* 18(4).
McEnery, Tony, and Andrew Wilson
  2001   *Corpus Linguistics*. Second edition. Edinburgh: Edinburgh University Press.
Musolff, Andreas
  2003   Ideological functions of metaphor: The conceptual metaphors of *health* and *illness* in public discourse. In *Cognitive Models in Language and Thought: Ideology, Metaphor and Meanings*, René Dirven, Roslyn Frank, and Martin Pütz (eds.), 327–352. Berlin and New York: Mouton de Gruyter.
Quinn, Naomi
  1991   The cultural basis of metaphor. In: James W. Fernandez (ed.), *Beyond Metaphor: The Theory of Tropes in Anthropology*, 56–93. Stanford: Stanford University Press.
Seidel, John
  1991   Method and madness in the application of computer technology to qualitative data analysis. In Nigel G. Fielding, and Raymond M. Lee (eds.), *Using Computers in Qualitative Research*, 107–116. London and Thousand Oaks, CA: Sage.
Steen, Gerard
  1999   Metaphor and discourse: Towards a linguistic checklist for metaphor analysis. In: Lynne Cameron and Graham Low (eds.), *Researching and Applying Metaphor*, 81–104. Cambridge: Cambridge University Press.
Stubbs, Michael
  2001   *Words and Phrases: Corpus Studies of Lexical Semantics*. Oxford: Blackwell.
van Dijk, Teun A.
  1995   Discourse analysis as ideology analysis. In: Christina Schäffner and Anita L. Wenden (eds.), *Language and Peace*, 17–33. Aldershot: Dartmouth.
Véronis, Jean
  2003   Sense tagging: Does it make sense? In: Andrew Wilson, Paul Rayson and Tony McEnery (eds.), *Corpus Linguistics by the Lune: A Festschrift for Geoffrey Leech*, 273–290. (Lódz Studies in Language 8). Frankfurt a.M.: Peter Lang.
Wolf, Hans-Georg, and Frank Polzenhagen
  2003   Conceptual metaphor as ideological stylistic means: An exemplary analysis. In René Dirven, Roslyn Frank, and Martin Pütz (eds.), *Cognitive Models in Language and Thought: Ideology, Metaphor and Meanings*, 247–275. Berlin/New York: Mouton de Gruyter.

Appendix

Note: Tables A1 and A2 are to be read as follows: Zero value (0) indicates that instances were looked for but not found in the corpus. A dash indicates that the corpus was not scanned for a particular lemma. Abbreviations are taken from the Bank of English tag set: NN = singular noun, NNS = plural noun; VB = verb base form, VBD = past tense, VBG = -ING form, VBN = past participle, VBZ = 3rd person singular present; JJ = adjective, RB = adverb. An asterisk (*) indicates the percentage of word classes in the respective lexical fields.

Of critical importance 259

Table A1. Metaphoric expressions in marketing and sales corpus

LEMMA	LEXEME	TOTAL	PUBLICATION				WORD CLASS		
			BW	EC	FO	FT	Noun (56.18%*)	Verb (29.90%*)	Adjective/adverb (13.92%*)
CAMPAIGN	campaign/campaigners, to campaign	152	39	18	22	73	99NN, 51NNS/1NNS	1VBZ	–
LAUNCH	launch, to launch, pre-/post-launch	127	36	26	12	53	33NN, 5NNS	20VB, 21VBD, 15VBG, 27VBN, 4VBZ	2JJ
TARGET	target, to target	89	28	18	11	32	27NN, 11NNS	15VB, 13VBG, 19VBN, 4VBZ	–
PLAY	play/player, to (out)play, playful	36	13	3	16	4	4NN/1NN, 14NNS	8VB, 5VBG, 3VBN, 1VBZ	0
BATTLE	battle/-field/-ground, to battle, embattled	28	10	4	11	3	18NN, 1NNS/0/3NN	1VB, 2VBG, 1VBZ	2JJ
WAR	war/warfare/warrior, warlike/warring	26	15	4	6	1	11NN, 10NNS/2NN/1NN, 1NNS	–	1JJ
FIGHT	fight/-er, to fight	24	7	4	8	5	7NN/1NNS	3VB, 10VBG, 2VBN, 1VBZ	–
GAME	gambler/game, to gamble	21	8	1	9	3	17NN, 3NNS/0	1VBG	–
SURVIVAL	survival/survivor, to survive	21	10	4	3	4	4NN/1NNS	12VB, 2VBG, 2VBN	–
BET	bet, to bet	18	7	4	6	1	10NN	2VB, 6VBG	–
JUMP	jump, to jump	18	11	0	4	3	1NN	8VB, 5VBD, 3VBG, 1VBN	–
ARMS	arms (weapons)/armor/army, to arm	16	3	4	6	3	3NNS/0/2NN, 2NNS	1VBG, 8VBN	–
GOAL	goal	16	8	1	4	3	12NN, 4NNS	–	–
KILLER	killer/killing, to kill	15	3	3	8	1	5NN/1NN	3VB, 3VBG, 2VBD, 1VBN	–
FAST	fast	14	6	3	2	3	–	–	3JJ, 11RB
FAIRNESS	fairness, un/fair	13	1	4	7	1	1NN	–	12JJ

Continued on next page.

Table A1 continued

LEMMA	LEXEME	TOTAL PUBLICATION					WORD CLASS		
			BW	EC	FO	FT	Noun (56.18%*)	Verb (29.90%*)	Adjective/adverb (13.92%*)
BLITZ	blitz, to blitz	12	7	2	2	1	7NN, 1NNS	1VB, 1VBD, 2VBN	–
RUN	run/runner, to run, runaway	10	1	2	5	2	2NN, 1NNS/1NNS	1VB, 2VBG, 1VN	2JJ
RACE	race, to race, racy	9	5	1	1	2	7NN	1VBN, 1VBZ	0
SPEED	speed, to speed, speedy	9	5	3	1	0	3NN	5VB, 1VBG	0
CATCH	catch, to catch	8	5	1	1	1	1NN	4VB, 1VBD, 2VBG	–
FIERCE	fierce	8	4	0	1	3	–	–	7JJ, 1RB
THROW	throw, to throw	8	0	2	5	1	1NN	3VB, 2VBG, 2VBN	–
BOMB	bomb/-shell, to bomb/bombard	7	2	2	1	2	1NN/0	1VB, 1VBG/3VBN, 1VBZ	–
SCORE	score, to score	7	3	1	1	2	1NNS	2VB, 2VBD, 1VBN, 1VBZ	–
SHOOT	shootout/ shot/-gun, to shoot	7	2	2	2	1	0/4NN, 1NNS/0	1VB, 1VBN	–
TIRE	to tire, tired/tireless/ tiresome	7	1	2	3	1	–	2VB	1JJ/1JJ/3JJ
TRENCH	trench, to en/retrench	7	4	0	3	0	1NN	5VBN/1VBG	–
FIELD	field, to field	5	2	0	2	1	4NN	1VBD	–
FRONT	front	5	1	1	0	3	5NN	–	–
STAKES	stakes	5	1	3	1	0	5NNS	–	–
ASSAULT	assault, to assault	4	2	1	1	0	3NN	1VBG	–
BRUISE	bruise, to bruise	4	2	1	1	0	1NNS	3VBG	–
CHAMPION	champion, to champion	4	0	3	0	1	1NN	1VB, 1VBG, 1VBN	–
CHIP	chip	4	2	1	0	1	3NN, 1NNS	–	–
HEAD-TO-HEAD	head-to-head	4	1	1	1	1	–	–	1JJ, 3RB
PUNCH	punch, to punch	4	2	0	2	0	4NN	0	–

Continued on next page.

Table A1 continued

LEMMA	LEXEME	TOTAL	PUBLICATION				WORD CLASS		
			BW	EC	FO	FT	Noun (56.18%*)	Verb (29.90%*)	Adjective/adverb (13.92%*)
RIP	rip-off, to rip off	4	0	0	1	3	1NN	2VB, 1VBN	–
TRUMP	trump, to trump	4	2	0	2	0	2NN	2VB	–
VETERAN	veteran	4	1	1	2	0	2NN, 2NNS	–	–
ATTACK	attack, to attack	3	1	1	0	1	1NN, 1NNS	1VBD	–
CARD	card	3	1	1	1	0	1NN, 2NNS	–	–
ENEMY	enemy, inimical	3	0	1	1	1	1NN, 2NNS	–	0
GUARD	to guard	3	1	1	0	1	–	1VB, 2VBN	–
KICK	kick-off, to kick off	3	2	0	0	1	1NN	1VB, 1VBD	–
LUCK	luck, lucky	3	0	0	2	1	0	–	3JJ
PACK	pack	3	1	1	1	0	3NN	–	–
TURF	turf	3	0	2	1	0	3NN	–	–
BALL	ball	2	1	0	1	0	2NN	–	–
BANKROLL	bankroll, to bankroll	2	1	1	0	0	0	1VB, 1VBG	–
BLOOD	blood, to bleed, bloody	2	1	0	1	0	1NN	0	1JJ
CASUALTY	casualty	2	0	1	0	1	1NN, 1NNS	–	–
COMBAT	combat, to combat, combative	2	1	0	1	0	2NN	0	0
GAMBIT	gambit	2	2	0	0	0	2NN	–	–
HAND	hand	2	1	1	0	0	1NN, 1NNS	–	–
MANEUVER	maneuver (manoeuvre), to maneuver (manoeuvre)	2	1	0	1	0	2NN	0	–
SURRENDER	surrender, to surrender	2	0	1	1	0	0	1VB, 1VBN	–
TROOPS	troops	2	1	1	0	0	2NNS	–	–

Continued on next page.

Table A1 continued

LEMMA	LEXEME	TOTAL	PUBLICATION				WORD CLASS		
			BW	EC	FO	FT	Noun (56.18%*)	Verb (29.90%*)	Adjective/adverb (13.92%*)
VICTORY	victory, victorious	2	0	0	2	0	2NN	–	0
WEAPON	weapon/-ry	2	1	0	1	0	2NN/0	–	–
BACKFIRE	to backfire	1	0	0	0	1	–	1VB	–
BRUTALITY	brutality; brutal	1	0	0	1	0	0	–	1JJ
CHEAT	cheat, to cheat	1	0	0	1	0	1NN	0	–
CONQUEROR	conqueror/conquest, to conquer	1	0	1	0	0	0/1NN	0	–
CUT-THROAT	cut-throat	1	0	1	0	0	–	–	1JJ
DEFEAT	defeat, to defeat	1	1	0	0	0	0	1VBD	–
ENDGAME	endgame	1	1	0	0	0	1NN	–	–
JACKPOT	jackpot	1	0	0	1	0	1NN	–	–
LEAGUE	league	1	0	0	0	1	1NN	–	–
OPENING	opening	1	1	0	0	0	1NN	–	–
PAWN	pawn	1	1	0	0	0	1NNS	–	–
POKER	poker, to poker, pokerfaced	1	0	0	1	0	0	0	1RB
TIME-OUT	time-out	1	1	0	0	0	1NN	–	–
TOTAL		845 100%	281 33.25%	145 17.16%	192 22.72%	227 26.86%	475 56.21%	313 37.04%	57 6.75%

Note: No relevant metaphoric occurrences of *ace, to beleaguer, blank, breathless, casino, checkmate, chess, coach/to coach, to deal, die/to dice, to double down, draw/to draw, to dribble, foul/to foul/ foul, full house, grand slam, joker, lottery, match, pass/to pass, piker, pole position, raffle/to raffle, red/yellow card, roulette, to shuffle, soldier/soldierly, volley, winning/losing streak*

Table A2. Metaphoric expressions in mergers and acquisitions corpus

LEMMA	LEXEME	TOTAL	PUBLICATION				WORD CLASS		
			BW	EC	FO	FT	Noun (52.43%*)	Verb (26.70%*)	Adjective/adverb (20.87%*)
TARGET	target, to target	91	24	10	5	52	56NN, 25NNS	1VB, 2VBG, 5VBN, 2VBZ	–
HOSTILITY	hostility, hostile	71	14	27	5	25	8NN, 1NNS	–	62JJ
BATTLE	battle/-field/-ground, to battle, embattled	49	25	12	7	5	38NN, 7NNS/1NN/2NN	1VBG	0
WAR	war/warfare/warrior, to war, warlike	36	16	5	8	7	23NN, 10NNS/2NN/1NN	0	0
DEFENCE	defence/defense, to defend, defensive	34	9	13	0	12	10NN, 4NNS/0, 1NNS	4VB, 1VBD, 4VBG, 1VBN,	9JJ
MARRIAGE	marriage, to marry	34	10	16	3	5	27NN, 3NNS	2VB, 1VBD, 1VBG	–
FIGHT	fight/-er, to fight	30	5	10	10	5	12NN, 2NNS/0NN	5VB, 2VBD, 7VBG, 1VBN, 1VBZ	–
RELATION-SHIP	relationship	20	7	5	3	5	14NN, 6NNS	–	–
PREDATOR	predator, predatory	18	4	9	0	5	7NN, 10NNS	–	1JJ
RAID	raid/raider, to raid	18	12	1	3	2	2NN, 1NNS/4NN, 10NNS	1VBG	–
SURVIVAL	survival/survivor, to survive	17	4	6	3	4	2NN/5NN	7VB, 1VBG, 1VBN, 1VBZ	–
VULNERA-BILITY	vulnerability, vulnerable	14	4	7	0	3	0	–	14JJ
ATTACK	attack, to attack	12	5	3	2	2	2NN, 1NNS	3VB, 2VBD, 2VBG, 2VBN	–
VICTORY	victory, victorious	12	2	5	4	1	11NN, 1NNS	–	0
SUITOR	suitor	11	6	2	0	3	8NN, 3NNS	–	–

Continued on next page.

Table A2 continued

LEMMA	LEXEME	TOTAL	PUBLICATION				WORD CLASS		
			BW	EC	FO	FT	Noun (52.43%*)	Verb (26.70%*)	Adjective/adverb (20.87%*)
SHOOT	shootout/shot/-gun, to shoot	10	4	1	5	0	2NN/3NN/1NN	2VB, 2VBZ	–
COURT	court/-ship, to court, courtly	9	1	3	3	2	2NN/2NN, 3NNS	0	2JJ
DIGESTION	(in)digestion, to digest, digestible	9	2	1	2	4	1NN	2VB, 5VBG, 1VBN	0
FIERCE	fierce	9	1	3	4	1	–	–	6JJ, 3RB
GOBBLE	to gobble	8	1	4	2	1	–	3VB, 1VBD, 2VBG, 2VBN	–
TROOPS	troops	8	6	0	2	0	8NNS	–	–
BED	bed-fellow	7	0	6	0	1	6NN/1NNS	–	–
DEFEAT	defeat, to defeat	7	2	4	0	1	3NN	1VB, 1VBG, 2VBN	–
KILLER	killer/killing, to kill	7	1	1	5	0	2NN/0	4VB, 1VBG	–
PREY	prey, to prey on	7	2	1	1	3	7NN	0	–
SWALLOW	to swallow	7	3	2	2	0	–	3VB, 1VBD, 3VBN	–
ARMS	arms (body part)	6	1	4	1	0	1NN, 5NNS	–	–
ARMS	arms (weapons)/armor/army, to arm	6	0	3	3	0	4NN	1VBG, 1VBN	–
BRUISE	bruise, to bruise	6	3	1	2	0	1NNS	4VBG, 1VBN	–
AFFAIR	affair	5	2	3	0	0	1NN, 4NNS	–	–
ASSAULT	assault, to assault	5	1	0	0	4	5NN	0	–
BLOOD	blood, to bleed, bloody	5	0	2	0	3	5NN	0	0
DESIRE	desire, to desire, desirable	5	0	1	1	3	3NN	0	2JJ
ENEMY	enemy, inimical	5	0	2	1	2	4NN, 1NNS	–	0
LOVE	love/lover, to love, lovable	5	1	2	2	0	5NN	–	0

Continued on next page.

Table A2 continued

LEMMA	LEXEME	TOTAL	PUBLICATION				WORD CLASS		
			BW	EC	FO	FT	Noun (52.43%*)	Verb (26.70%*)	Adjective/adverb (20.87%*)
SEX	sex, sexy/sexual	5	2	1	2	0	1NN	–	4JJ/0
APPETITE	appetite/-izer	4	1	1	1	1	3NN, 1NNS	–	0
BRUTALITY	brutality, brutal	4	2	1	0	1	0	–	4JJ
COMBAT	combat, to combat, combative	4	2	0	1	1	1NN	2VB	1JJ
VETERAN	veteran	4	2	0	2	0	1NN, 3NNS	–	–
VICTIM	victim	4	0	2	1	1	2NN, 2NNS	–	–
WOOER	wooer, to woo	4	2	0	2	0	0	3VB, 1VBN	–
ALTAR	altar	3	1	2	0	0	3NN	0	–
DIVORCE	divorce	3	1	2	0	0	3NN	–	–
FLIRT	flirt/-ation, to flirt, flirtatious/flirty	3	0	3	0	0	2NN	1VBG	0/0
FRONT	front	3	0	0	3	0	1NN, 2NNS	–	–
GREED	greed, greedy	3	0	3	0	0	2NN	–	1RB
KISS	kiss, to kiss	3	0	0	3	0	3NNS	0	–
MATE	mate, to mate	3	1	2	0	0	2NN	1VBG	–
BELEA- GUER	to beleaguer	2	0	1	1	0	–	2VBN	–
CONSUM- MATION	consummation, to consummate	2	1	1	0	0	0	1VB, 1VBN	–
DALLIANCE	dalliance, to dally	2	0	2	0	0	1NN	1VBG	–
HUNGER	hunger, to hunger, hungry	2	0	0	1	1	0	0	2JJ
LUST	lust, to lust, lustful	2	1	1	0	0	1NN	1VBZ	0

Continued on next page.

Table A2 continued

LEXEME		TOTAL PUBLICATION					WORD CLASS		
LEMMA	LEXEME		BW	EC	FO	FT	Noun (52.43%*)	Verb (26.70%*)	Adjective/adverb (20.87%*)
MANEUVER	maneuver (manoeuvre), to maneuver (manoeuvre)	2	1	0	1	0	1NN	1VBG	–
NUPTIALS	nuptials, nuptial	2	0	1	0	1	2NNS	–	0
SURRENDER	surrender, to surrender	2	0	1	0	1	1NN	1VBD	–
WEDDING	wedding, to wed	2	1	1	0	0	1NNS	1VBN	–
AFFECTION	affection, affectionate	1	0	1	0	0	1NNS	–	0
BITE	bite, to bite	1	0	0	0	1	1NN	0	–
BOMB	bomb/-shell, to bomb/bombard	1	1	0	0	0	0/1NN	0	–
CASUALTY	casualty	1	0	0	1	0	1NNS	–	–
CONQUEROR	conqueror/conquest, to conquer	1	0	0	0	1	0/1NN	0	–
DEVOUR	to devour	1	0	0	0	1	–	1VBN	–
FOOD	feeder/food, to feed	1	1	0	0	0	0	1VB	–
GULP	gulp, to gulp	1	1	0	0	0	1NN	0	–
JUICY	juicy	1	0	1	0	0	–	–	1JJ
NIBBLE	nibble, to nibble	1	0	0	0	1	1NN	0	–
PALATABLE	palatable	1	1	0	0	0	–	–	1JJ
ROMANCE	romance, romantic	1	0	1	0	0	1NN	–	0
SOLDIER	soldier, soldierly	1	1	0	0	0	1NNS	–	0
SPIT	to spit out	1	1	0	0	0	–	1VBG	–
WEAPON	weapon/-ry	1	0	0	1	0	1NN/0	–	–
TOTAL		686 100%	202 29.45%	203 29.59%	109 15.89%	172 25.07%	449 65.45%	124 18.08%	113 16.47%

Note: No relevant metaphoric occurrences of to backfire, bride/-groom/bridal, chew, course, delicious, diet/to diet/dietary, dinner/to dine, dish, eat/(un)eatable, (in)edible, embrace/to embrace, faithful, feast/feast, fiancé(e), glutton(-y)/gluttonous, to gorge, helping, honeymoon, husband, infatuation/infatuated, maiden (n.), meal, morsel, nourishment/to nourish, passion/passionate, rape/to rape, ravenous, (in)satiable, spouse, starvation/to starve, taste/tasting/to taste/tasty, wife. **Note**: The inclusion of the lemma rape in a lexical field of mating will perhaps strike the reader as odd. The decision to include it was based on the hypothesis that FIGHTING and MATING metaphors in M&A discourse might combine into metaphoric expressions of rape, an assumption that eventually proved wrong (Koller, 2002).

Metaphors, motifs and similes across discourse types: Corpus-Assisted Discourse Studies (CADS) at work*

Alan Partington

Abstract

In earlier studies, I developed a corpus-based methodology for investigating the behavior of systematic metaphors in written business discourse and in spoken news and political discourses. I contended that by uncovering the network of systematic metaphors used in a particular discourse, it was possible for an analyst to hypothesize how actors in an institutional setting (purport to) see their world and their own behavior in it. In the first part of this paper I intend to report on further developments in this area inspired by this approach. Issues of particular interest are: the choice/design/tailoring of corpora, including background or 'comparison' corpora, the use of clusters, how metaphors are used in argumentative texts and, how, in such discourse types, they are invariably used with the overarching function of expressing *evaluation*.

The second part uses corpus study in the hope of throwing light on some of the historical controversies surrounding metaphor and simile, including how they relate to each other, their truth-value and how they differ from non-metaphorical similarity-identity statements. Here too all the evidence shows how metaphor is used, not simply to describe the world, but to make claims about it, to construe it in ways convenient to the speaker/writer.

The strategic and evaluative use of metaphor and what this can tell us about the users and the discourse context are questions of evident interest to discourse analysts. The use of corpora for describing features of discourse, particularly of interaction, that is, the rhetorical aspects of texts, is in its infancy. The studies described in this paper are, then, meant as contributions to the nascent interdisciplinary field of Corpus-Assisted Discourse Analysis (CADS).

1. Introduction

The initial premise to this article is that the techniques of Corpus Linguistics can assist the study of features of discourse, defined as the processes of interaction between speakers or between authors and readers. As regards the use of metaphor, corpus techniques can be productive in two ways. They can help reveal recurrent patterns of metaphorical usage which reflect the systematic behaviour and attitudes of the users. They

---

* The author would like to thank Prof Alison Duguid for her many invaluable comments and suggestions during the preparation of this paper. Hers is the idea of the implied sharing of distinctive features as the foundations of the metaphorical process.

can provide information both about the linguistic-grammatical systems that users employ and the discourse context they are working in. Here we concentrate on political-institutional contexts.

Secondly, corpora quite simply make available large amounts of authentic data. Pre-corpus studies of metaphor have been predominantly qualitative in nature. Qualitative discourse study typically takes a small data set, a single text or a relatively small sample of discourse and examines this in considerable depth. However, too many of these studies have been distinguished by a predilection for inventing suitable examples which, from the point of view of modern data-based linguistics, constitutes an unwarranted intrusion of the analyst into the data field; it introduces an unnecessary degree of confusion of the observer with what is being observed. Complementing the qualitative with a more quantitative approach, as embodied in Corpus Linguistics, not only allows a greater distance to be preserved between observer and data but also enables a far greater amount of data to be contemplated. In addition, it can identify promising areas for qualitative forms of analysis to investigate.

At this moment in linguistic history, then, there are two principal (and principled) ways of employing corpora in the study of metaphor. Firstly, to uncover the particular (sets of) metaphors contained in and which characterize a particular discourse type – we might call them dominant metaphors – as a preliminary to studying how they reflect the ideology of the participants in that discourse type or how these actors employ them to their own ends. This will occupy our attention in the next section. Secondly, corpus techniques can function as a means to examine, to verify or otherwise, the various and often conflicting statements about the nature of metaphor made before such methodologies were available, to subject them to the kind of scrutiny today made possible by commanding large amounts of authentic and contextualized data. Far from abandoning or discrediting the merits of qualitative research, this approach instead implies marrying them to the quantitative methods of research, principally frequency analysis and concordancing. We will see how this might be done in section three.

2. Detective work: uncovering metaphor sets and what they mean

2.1. Metaphor and discourse type

In Partington (1998), among other things, I mused on two related issues. Firstly on how pre-corpus scholars had paid very little attention to the question of how metaphors might differ in different forms of discourse.

Secondly, on the profound intellectual influence that Biber and his co-workers, their emphasis that language consists of innumerable registers and their pioneering of ways of *comparing* language varieties, has had on Corpus Linguistics. Corpus techniques can be used, I argued, to study what I called genre-specific metaphor, that is, the particularities in the way metaphor behaved in differing genres or discourse types. I went on to compare the language contained in a corpus of business journalism (actually a subcorpus of a heterogeneric four-million word newspaper corpus) with other kinds of newspaper texts in the attempt to discover the particular metaphors used in that discourse type. The first step was to discover what the principal vocabulary differences were between business texts and other newspaper texts, since these differences might provide some insight into the question of which metaphors were more frequent in this sector. Several *keyword* lists were prepared using the homonymous program in *WordSmith Tools*, as the business texts were compared to and contrasted with news, sports and arts/magazine texts. These lists were then perused closely and items which appeared in more than one keyword list or which seemed to fall into some sort of semantic set were then concordanced. A number of systematic experiential metaphors were unearthed, namely UP-DOWN, AHEAD-BEHIND and HARD-SOFT, and their particular uses in context were found to be interestingly complex. Other recurring metaphors in business journalism included BUSINESS IS A RACE (especially A HORSE RACE), A BUSINESS TAKE-OVER IS A HUNT and COMPANIES ARE PERSONS, MACHINES or ANIMALS.

2.2. Comparing corpora and designing comparison corpora

In some sense, all work with corpora is properly comparative. Even when a single corpus is employed, it is used to test the data it contains against another body of data. This may consist of the researcher's intuitions, or the data found in reference works such as dictionaries and grammars, or it may comprise statements made by previous authors in the field. Corpus-assisted studies of register, genre or discourse type are of course by definition comparative: it is only possible to both uncover and evaluate the particular features of a discourse type by comparing it with others.

One important aspect of the methodology of such research then is the design of comparison corpora. Each piece of research may pose its own problems and different researchers have adopted various solutions, depending on the particular nature of the research question. As Sperberg-McQueen points out:

> There is no consensus in the community as to the procedures to be followed in corpus design (balanced, opportunistic, statistically sophisticated and defiantly naive approaches all struggle with each other for acceptance) [...] (Sperberg-McQueen, cit. Bell 1996)

The corpus used in Partington (1998) was an elementary form of what Haarman et al (2002) call a *modularized* corpus. It had been specifically designed to contain five subsections or modules of equal size (800,000 words each of home news, foreign news, business, arts, and sports reporting) and it was thus a simple task to compare any single subsection to any other or any one to all the others combined. Modularization not only allows the corpus core to be compiled in a systematic manner and facilitates comparison between segments, it also means that it can grow and be added to in a controlled fashion. Another relatively straightforward procedure is to compare the behaviour of the relevant linguistic items in a single discourse type (or *monogeneric*) corpus with its behaviour in one of the large *heterogeneric* corpora which are commercially available, such as the BNC or the Bank of English. On other occasions, however, as we shall see below, it becomes appropriate to adopt more complex procedures and to edit, tailor or compile a corpus for special purposes.

2.3. Some recent Italian research into political metaphor

Much of the work conducted in Italy since 1998 has concentrated on political language, mainly because a nucleus of linguists here, including myself, work in Political Science faculties and are increasingly interested in the use of corpus techniques to conduct discourse analysis, including the unearthing of particular ideological metaphors and motifs in the language of political figures and institutions. They tend to focus on research questions of three types (where X is a political figure or institution and Y is a political objective):

(i) How does X achieve Y with language?'
(ii) What does this tell us about X?
(iii) Comparative studies: how do $X1$ and $X2$ differ in their use of language? Does this tell us anything about their different principles and objectives?

Garzone and Santulli (2004) contains two case studies, firstly, a study of September 11th rhetoric as contained in British press editorials and leading articles, and secondly a study of Silvio Berlusconi's election speeches.

Word lists were prepared using *WordSmith Tools* and promising items were concordanced. The two most frequent lexical words in these speeches were *Italia* and *stato* (state). Analysis of the collocates of the latter showed how Mr Berlusconi provides two distinct interpretations of the concept. When it is in the hands of the left-wing parties, the cooccurring items, a good number of which are metaphorical, are highly unfavourable, for example *autoritario, burocratico, invasivo, moloch, padrone, stato-partito* (authoritarian, invasive, moloch, bossy, a party-state). Once treated to his party's cure, on the other hand, the state becomes *amico, civile, di diritto, liberale, moderno* (friend, civilised, lawful, liberal, modern). The third most frequent word, *libertà* (liberty) is itself frequently transformed into a metaphor in many expressions of the type *libertà di lavoro, di mercato, di impresa* (freedom of work / market / enterprise). It is a value unattached to any particular individual: rarely are we told *whose* liberty is being debated. Note how these descriptions are strongly evaluative, defining a thing or event as either favourable or unfavourable. I am using evaluation in the sense described by Hunston: 'the indication that something is good or bad' (2004: 157). As we shall see throughout this paper, metaphor and simile in all their various forms share this function: to evaluate events, people and their behaviour.

The other study focuses on the early responses of the British press to the events of September 11th, as evinced in leading and comment articles of four national dailies, the *Daily Telegraph,* the *Guardian,* the *Independent* and *The Times,* in their issues from the days immediately after the attacks (11th to 18th September). The first stage was the compilation of the object corpus. A total of 102 articles, around 150,000 words, were downloaded from the Web pages of the four newspapers and kept in separate sub-corpora. The next move was the creation of a comparison corpus of a similar size, containing leading articles and editorials from the same dailies published in the corresponding week of 2002. Frequency lists were then made by means of the *WordList* tool, both for the whole corpus and the four sub-corpora. These lists were then compared both 'by hand' and by feeding them into the *WordSmith Keywords* program. The resulting keywords lists were studied for interesting items, especially those which seemed to group together into semantic sets. A number of ideological motifs were uncovered in this way. The most frequent word in the 2001 corpus was *world* e.g. *an attack on the whole civilised world, convinced the world is its enemy, aggrieved people around the world, the world will never be the same,* where the existence of a single, unified response to the September 11th attack by the whole of a 'civilised world' is emphasised. The items *war* and *enemy* are very frequent, the former having two senses; that this attack was an *act of war* and thet there is a need to *declare war* on terrorism, whilst the enemy is *shadowy, unseen* and *ghostlike*, its menace somehow thus enhanced. Various items expressed the 'inconceivability' of the events: *inconceivable, unimaginable, unthinkable*, while others were related to the difficulty to describe what had happened: *inexpressible, indescribable, unspeakable*.

Vaghi and Venuti (2004) describe a research project into metaphors of the Euro, involving the compiling and editing of a corpus consisting of articles dealing with the Euro currency. The articles were retrieved from the websites of the *Economist*, the *Financial Times*, the *Guardian* and *The Times* between July 1, 2001 and June 30, 2002 (six months before and after the launch) and a sample of a hundred articles was selected from each paper to create four sub-corpora of around 60,000 words each.

WordSmith Tools frequency lists indicated the terms *entry, joining, membership* and *launch* among the most common content words. According to the authors, *entry* describes the event by creating an opposition between what is inside the EMU as opposed to what remains outside in a way that is very similar to what Lakoff and Johnson (1980: 29–32) describe as 'Container Metaphors'. Various 'container' prepositions, for example, *in, inside, into, out, outside* and *within* were also found in the lists. Both *joining* and *launch*, on the other hand, can be viewed, the authors claim, as expressions of the metaphor THE EURO IS A MECHANICAL OBJECT. An alternative reading is that these expressions – *entry, join, membership* – result from a single conceptual metaphor THE EURO IS A CLUB, a cultural metaphor rather than a Lakoffian experiential one (Duguid, personal communication). In any case, the differing use of these terms proved to be a useful diagnostic for the papers' stances on the issue. For example, the *Guardian*, which generally viewed the EMU favourably, used the term *join** in a neutral fashion, mainly to describe an event going on between two entities without assigning any specific connotation. A significantly favourable evaluation was instead achieved through the use of *launch**, since the term highlights the celebratory aspect of the event. *The Times*, on the other hand, which was strongly against the EMU, had the tendency to attach unfavourable connotations to these items. *Launch** is used relatively rarely, *join** more frequently, and the participants focussed upon are generally those doing the launching or who are desirous of joining, doubts and aspersions usually being expressed about their motives:

(1) Whether Mr Blair tries to stick to economics or admits that the main reasons for **joining** the euro are really political and diplomatic, his

personal honesty will now be irrevocably impugned if a referendum is called.

These terms were worthy of study because, although they all relate to actual or possible membership of the EMU, each one highlights only certain aspects of the issue. Some writers on metaphor emphasize its power to *defamiliarize*, defined as 'the unsettling and querying of the reader's familiar perceptions by the use of linguistic devices such as metaphor, which interrogate habitual codings of experience', which allows a reader/hearer to: '[...] see through and around the conventional grids of meaning' (Fowler 1991: 31). But to do so it has to be both new and in some way contrary to the reader's expectations, whole belief-patterns even. Many other writers point out the converse ability of repeated, conventional metaphors to *familiarize*. Metaphor 'selects, emphasizes, suppresses and organizes' the entity it purports to describe (Bayley 1985: 121). Schön, pessimistically even talks of the 'cognitive myopia' it can induce by (unwittingly or not) overemphasizing certain aspects of reality and disregarding others (1993: 137–163).

On the basis, then, of Partington (1998), Garzone and Santulli (2004) and Vaghi and Venuti (2004) we can begin to outline a standard methodology for using corpus techniques to study these types of research questions:

Step 1: Design, unearth, stumble upon the research question
Step 2: Choose, compile or edit an appropriate corpus
Step 3: Choose, compile or edit an appropriate **reference** corpus/corpora
Step 4: Make frequency lists and run a **Keywords** comparison of the corpora
Step 5: Determine the existence of **sets** of key items
Step 6: **Concordance** interesting key items (with varying quantities of co-text)

2.4. Metaphors and motifs at the White House

Partington (2003: 198–211) considers some of the metaphors and motifs used in the press briefings held at the White House. It begins by noting the quite remarkable variety of metaphors which have been employed by commentators to describe these events:

They are 'a political *chess game*' (Reaves White), in which 'both sides view everything the other side does as a *mere tactic*' (Kamiya). Alternatively, they are 'rhetorical *combat*' (Kurtz), a '*war zone*' in which 'combatants with a multitude of agendas [...] prepared for battle' (Reaves White). They are 'a *wrestling match*' and a *duel* or 'face-off' (Reaves White) but also 'a weird formulaic *dance*' (Kamiya).

The White House spokesperson (or 'podium') is:

a *soldier* under 'hostile media fire [...] on the front lines for Clinton on nearly every major battle (Baker and Kurtz) but also a *sailor* who must 'navigate the treacherous waters of the daily briefings' (CNN allpolitics) and is frequently found 'desperately scrambling and bailing to keep a torrent of scandals from sinking the battered ship of state' (Jurkowitz). He is both a *pugilist* who has 'bobbed and weaved and jabbed [...] his way through all manner of Clinton scandals' but also a *street thug* who 'beats up on reporters' (Kurtz).

While the reporters are:

wild animals, the 'rat-' or 'wolf-pack' [...] which 'fights over morsels' (Warren). They too can be *boxers* out to 'pummel' the spokesman who has 'to stand at the podium and take whatever abuse the fourth estate wanted to dish out' (Kurtz) [...] At the same time, however, they are 'a lot of dupes' (Irvine and Kincaid) and 'the White House reporter is not much more than a well-compensated stenographer' (Warren).

An initial corpus (*Dems* for 'Democrats') of 48 complete briefings, 250,000 words of text, dating from the final years of the Clinton administration, was created by downloading the transcriptions from the White House library web-site.

For the purposes of comparison, a couple of other corpora of political or newspaper language were created. The first was a corpus, also of 250,000 words, of political interviews (named *INTS*) which were downloaded from the BBC and ITV websites, since American networks were less generous or diligent in making their material generally available. The second was *USPR* (for *US press*), a collection of about 380,000 words of American written journalism. A third corpus was of non-political speech, namely the *WSC*, the Wellington (New Zealand) spoken corpus, a one-million word collection of spoken texts of a variety of genres from the early 1990s. None of these corpora by themselves was a perfect comparison corpus since each of them introduced maverick variables into the equation but it was hoped that the use of multiple comparisons would reduce their influence. In any case, they were the best I could contrive at the time.

Finally, from 2000 onwards, I began to collect batches of White House briefings every six months as they were produced by the new Republican incumbents; these are entitled *Rep0, Rep1, Rep(n)*, while the entire accumulation is *Reps*. This turned the nature of the White House briefings collection from what Sinclair (1982) calls a sample corpus into a monitor corpus. It enabled me both to compare the uses of language by the Democrat podiums with that of their Republican counterparts and also to keep watch over any new linguistic habits, including favoured metaphors, which might creep into (and out of) this discourse type. This research project is still in its infancy.

The first stage was the production and study of the keyword lists of the kind already described for previous research. Interesting items were concordanced but were also often clustered. Clusters are simply sequences or strings of words (for *WordSmith* from two to a maximum of eight items) which occur 'with a particular frequency fixed by the inquirer in the set of texts being examined. They are 'a kind of extended collocation' (Partington and Morley 2004). *WordSmith Tools* allows the user to cluster items in three ways, either from the Concordance programme by clicking directly on the cluster menu option, or cluster lists can be prepared from *WordList* (by activating and specifying cluster length in the *settings* menu option) and finally Key-cluster lists can be compiled by comparing cluster lists. These latter become efficient when very large corpora are being examined. Clusters are an intriguing phenomenon in themselves. Partington and Morley (2004) suggest they 'constitute "missing links" on the chain or cline from the linguistic morass to the abstraction we call grammar' and their study will 'tell us a great deal about how speakers go about the construction of discourse'. Biber has studied a somewhat similar phenomenon which he calls 'lexical bundles' (Biber and Conrad 1999; Biber et al 1999: 990–1024). Bundles 'usually do not represent a complete structural unit', but neither do they occur, as it were, 'by accident', since they very often have 'important grammatical correlates' (Biber and Conrad 1999: 182). More relevant to this study, they also frequently have 'meaning correlates' in that they reveal typical ways of saying things and therefore typical author/speaker messages. The following section illustrates this with examples.

2.5. Orientational metaphors in political briefings

It was apparent from the keyword lists that a good number of prepositions or adverbial particles are relatively frequent in briefings compared to other genres, including *on*, *forward*, *forwards*, *to*, and *towards*. In Partington (1998) it was argued that the presence of certain prepositions and adverbs can be indicative of metaphors specific to a certain discourse type and the data observed here support that view.

Lakoff and Johnson discuss at length what they term 'orientational metaphors', which are based on movement in space, and frequently involve prepositions or adverbial particles. For Lakoff and Johnson they are important because they 'arise from the fact that we have bodies of the sort we have and that function as they do in our physical environment' (1980: 14). They are the leading proof for these authors that metaphors are the result of experience and are therefore basic, natural features of thought and action. They include UP-DOWN, IN-OUT and FRONT-BACK metaphors. *Forward* and *toward(s)* are expressive of the latter, of front or forward movement.

The most frequent lexical collocates of *forward* and *toward(s)* in the briefings texts are forms of the verb *move*, of which *move* and *moving* are both themselves in the keyword lists. The most frequent four-word clusters of *move* confirms the close association:

Table 1. Cluster *move*

N	cluster MOVE (4)	Freq.
1	as we move forward	9
2	to move forward with	7
3	continue to move forward	4
4	going to move forward	4
5	move forward with this	4
6	how we move forward	3
7	in the right direction	3
8	that we can move	3
9	to continue to move	3
10	to try to move	3
11	try to move the	3
12	we can move forward	3
13	we move forward in	3
14	we need to move	3

The briefings clearly contain a systematic metaphor concerning moving forward which seems to be of the type PROGRESS IS FORWARD MOTION, with the variation MOVING FORWARD IS NECESSARY. Obviously these metaphors are not restricted to this genre, but these briefings are dominated by them. The administration must at all times be seen to be making *progress*, to be moving or *headed* in *the right direction* (see cluster 7 above), on whatever issue is under discussion. The press sees immobility as stagnation, as culpable lethargy and so the administration must project itself as being in a state of perpetual motion. The centrality of the metaphor to these briefings is brought still further home if we compare the first ten clusters of *move* found in *INTS*:

Table 2. Cluster *move*

N	cluster MOVE (4)	Freq.
1	*move on to the*	8
2	*let me move on*	7
3	*me move on to*	5
4	*to move on to*	4
5	*we'll move on to*	4
6	*let's move on to*	3
7	*and we've got to*	2
8	*I want to move*	2
9	*let me move onto*	2
10	*let's move to now*	2

Move is thus an interviewer's discourse management item in these texts and refers to movement on to another topic.

So much forward motion will often (though by no means always, since it is a good thing in itself) have an aim, a destination. The items *objective(s)* and *goals* as well as *reach* are all in the keyword lists. Note how these metaphors have some sort of evaluative function.

And if FORWARD MOTION is necessary and a good thing in this discourse type, then what is bad? Going *backwards* of course (my emphasis):

(2) MR MCCURRY: And we don't want to go *backwards*.
(3) MR LOCKHART: [...] some critics are saying that the administration is *back-pedaling* for not inviting the Reverend Jesse Jackson to the event yesterday.

And even going slow, slowing down, is to be avoided, just as any obstacle which *bogs down* the forward momentum:

(4) MR LOCKHART: [...] and we shouldn't let it get *bogged down* in trying to have another debate, because that inevitably will *slow down* this process.

The obstacle here, interestingly, is 'debate'.

Another orientational metaphor which is important in these briefings, especially their diplomatic aspect, is that of CLOSENESS-DISTANCE, in which CLOSE IS COOPERATIVE and has a favourable evaluation. A *close ally* is expected to be reliable. *Close ties*, whatever brings people *closer together*, and especially events which cause others to move *closer* to 'our position', are all evaluated as favourable. Whether or not the reverse holds, that is, whether distance is something bad, rather depends on the situation.

When Republicans are found *backing away* or even *backsliding away* from an agreement or commitment, distance is clearly undesirable, as it is when diplomatic positions *move apart*. But 'keeping the guns *away* from criminals', 'to take *away* the tools of these atrocities' are very desirable. Whether *to walk away* is appraised as good or bad depends on what is being walked away from: consider *trouble* and *responsibilities*.

2.6. Tracking language metaphor and thought over time

A brief mention was given above to ongoing research comparing and contrasting the Democratic and Republican briefings language and an examination of the keywords and cluster lists revealed some interesting initial observations. In both sets of texts many of the motifs and metaphors are repeated, for example, all the podiums stress how clear they or their clients' words are – using the conventional metaphor CLARITY IS INTELLIGIBILITY. Both sides are very keen on the *strong(ly)* – *strength* metaphor (or set of metaphors) these items collocate frequently with *economy, economically, growth*, with *commitment, support, supporter, relations / relationship*, with *words, speak, statement*. Both of these – clarity and strength – are, of course, archetypally evaluative, they impart a highly favourable sense to the metaphor they take part in.

The Republican podium (Mr Ari Fleischer) refers explicitly to *the President* much more frequently: it is the most key keyword in *Reps* and seven out of the top 20 key 3- and 4-word clusters contain this item. He prefers to adopt or claim the participant role of – in Levinson's (1988) terms – simple *relayer* or *spokesman* and de-stresses any role as *responsible* or *principle* of the message. He strives to portray his President as strong-minded, intelligent, and ever-present in the political debate.

In the early *Rep0* briefings, the podium often employs metaphors which include the word *sensitive* – *information* or *issues* or *discussions* are *sensitive*, this is a *sensitive time / moment / stage* – generally in the rather optimistic attempt to avoid answering a question. Since the journalists are rarely deterred, the word and the metaphors more or less disappear in later Republican briefings.

In the briefings during and immediately after September 11th, *Rep1*, we find metaphors such as *harboring* terrorists/terrorism, to *foster* terrorism,[1]

---

1. Corpus evidence revealed that *harbour* as a verb generally displays an unfavourable evaluation (collocating with *grudge, anxiety, bacteria*) whereas, interestingly, *foster* as a verb has a largely favourable evaluation (collocating with *civic pride, strong global growth, great new Irish plays*) though with occasional exceptions (*confusion*).

and worldwide *network* of terror[2] – all, of course, highly evaluatively unfavourable. Other intriguing key items included *shoulder*, invariably in the expression *shoulder-to-shoulder with* (*the United States, the American Arab community* etc), which kept company with *solidarity*. At first sight the items *share* and *sharing* would seem to belong to this group, but the concordance showed it to be overwhelmingly involved in a metaphorical concept of *sharing information* and is indicative of the press's preoccupation that the administration was not releasing sufficient *intelligence* on the attacks, that too much was *classified* (both keywords). Among the negative keywords (those appearing considerably less frequently in this period) we find *forward, objectives, decision*. The MOVING FORWARD metaphor discussed above all but vanishes, reflecting perhaps a disorientation and lack of optimism during this time. Predictably *hope* and *laughter* also disappear.[3]

Beyond the concordance, of course, more qualitative types of research are given their rein. Selected segments of briefings may need to be read to discover why the administration feels certain issues are *sensitive* or how it intends to stand *shoulder to shoulder with the Arab American community* and why it feels the need to say so. Quantitative corpus analysis does nothing if not arouse the researcher's curiosity to delve deeper using qualitative means.

2.7. A typology of corpus comparison

Earlier we spoke of the importance in CADS of comparing discourse types through comparing corpora. On the basis of these pieces of research we can now begin to construct a typology of ways of doing so (DT indicates 'discourse type' and t indicates time):

Types of comparison
Simple: DT(a) – DT(b)
Serial: DT(a) – DT(b), DT(c) ... DT(n)
Multiple: DT(a) – DT(b + c ... n)
Monitor / Diachronic: DT(ta) – DT(tb) – DT(tc) ... DT(tn)

A simple comparison entails comparing language from one source with that from another, for example, a set of articles on the Euro from the

---
2. In the plural – *networks* – or as a modifier, for example, *network executives*, the item tends to refer to television stations. There was much debate after September 11th over whether or not it was responsible for them to broadcast messages from Osama bin Laden.
3. Bouts of laughter are indicated minimally in the transcripts as (Laughter).

Guardian with one from the *Times*, whereas a serial comparison would entail measuring the *Guardian* articles first against the *Times*, then against the *Economist*, then against the *Independent*, and so on. A multiple comparison would involve comparing the *Guardian* sets against a corpus containing the *Times*, the *Economist*, the *Independent*, and so on, all grouped together. Those studies which employ the BNC or the Bank of English as the background or reference corpus are of this ilk. Finally, a monitor or diachronic comparison implies comparing discourse from one source with discourse from the same source at a different period of time, similar to the process we saw in the preceding section. These forms of comparison may well need to be combined, the most appropriate combination depending, of course, on the precise nature of the research question.

3. Return to the past: Simile and the *like*

3.1. Dictionaries and gold mines

A second major way of using corpora to study metaphor is in revisiting, testing, verifying what previous authors have had to say. Probably the most influential and wide-ranging collection of modern but pre-corpora thinking on metaphor is *Metaphor and Thought* (Ortony 1993a), which includes contributions by such luminaries as Black, Miller, Searle, Fraser, George Lakoff and Gibbs, among many others. It looks at metaphor from diverse perspectives, including those of semantics, language studies, cognitive psychology and education. It treats such arguments as the structure and function of metaphor, literal and metaphorical meaning, metaphor and learning, and even the metaphors of medieval alchemy.

Some attention is given to the relationship between metaphor and simile, though not as much as might be expected. Still less regard is paid to the nature of simile itself. Most authors who think about them at all see similes as performing overt similarity or comparison statements, and leave the question at that. In stark contrast, there is much acerbic controversy as to whether metaphors do the same or not and in consequence about the precise way they relate to simile. The least dismissive of similes is Miller who sees them as relating very closely indeed to metaphor and containing all the same mysteries:

> similes can pose all the apperceptive problems that metaphors can [...] when Eliot writes, for example, "the evening is spread out against the sky like a patient etherized upon a table," it challenges us to search for the similarity in our experience of

evenings and etherized patients – and may well affect the way we see an evening sky thereafter.[4] (Miller 1993: 375)

For the Corpus Linguist, however, given that, by definition, they contain an overt lexical sign, similes would seem to be a most convenient path into the study of the field of figurative language. Miller lists a number of these simile signals: *like, is like, acts like, looks like, as, is as* Adj *as,*[5] *resembles, reminds me of, is the same as, is similar to* and *the same way* (1993: 371). To these we might add: *seems like, sounds like, (is) more like, gives the impression of / that, not unlike* and even, perhaps, *unlike*. All of these items can, of course, be concordanced.

Ortony (1993b) too suspects that the study of simile may offer rewards. He contemplates the question: how do similes differ from other similarity or comparison statements? None of the lexical signals listed above necessarily introduce similes; they can be used to perform all kinds of explicit comparisons. Ortony considers the two sentences and makes a number of points about them:

[1]   Encyclopedias are like dictionaries
[2]   Encyclopedias are like gold-mines (Ortony 1993b: 346)

His first argument, he declares, 'pertains to the intuitions of ordinary people, as opposed to those of the theoreticians, who are so prone to ignore them' (1993b: 347). If one asks the person-in-the-street 'Are encyclopedias really like gold mines?' one never gets a straightforward answer in the affirmative, Ortony claims, whereas to the question 'Are encyclopedias really like dictionaries?', instead, 'very often one does'. 'This must mean that people do not believe that (2) is true [...] by contrast they normally believe that (1) is true' (Ortony 1993b: 347).

---

4. *Apperception* is a term borrowed from Herbart (1898) and indicates the mental processes required when new things are learned by being related to things already known.
5. Many authors note how the grounds of comparison between the two terms in a metaphor are generally implicit and ambiguous. The formula *as...as*, however, would appear to have the very function of making the grounds explicit. Consider these examples (the grounds are in italics):

    Giggs [...] looked **as** *relaxed and natural on the park* **as** a dog chasing a piece of paper in the wind (Papers)
    Bowie's track 'Some Are' [...] feels **as** *lost and cold* **as** a burnt-out space probe (Papers)

    See also section 3.3 on the cataphoric, suspense-creating conceit similes, whose grounds require overt subsequent exposition.

Secondly, Ortony makes the argument that 'similes such as (2) are much more likely to be found in conjunction with hedges such as "sort of", "kind of", "in a way" and so on' (Ortony 1993b: 347).

Both these claims can be subjected to corpus examination. The corpora employed in this research include: a four-million word newspaper corpus, a large newspaper corpus (100 million words of *Times*, *Telegraph* and *Guardian* texts dating from 1993) called *Papers*, *Dems* and *Reps*, and *Plum*, a 500,000-word collection, downloaded from the Gutenberg Project website, of the early works of P.G. Wodehouse, who has often been lauded for his accomplished use of simile.

To investigate Ortony's ideas on what people think encyopedias are 'really like', the phrase *really like* was concordanced in the four-million word newspaper corpus and invariably appeared with some expression of question or doubt or correction, for example (occurrences of *I'd really like* and so on were, of course, ignored):

(5) Not that the Saudi Arabian embassy is **really like** that [...]
(6) If the world was **really like** that, then each individual today would have only one parent
(7) Meanwhile Little Bill takes a similarly debunking line with W.W. Beauchamp [...] telling him what the Old West was **really like**.
(8) [...] so that future generations will know what they were **really like** to look at and live in.

The phrase *really like* is highly contrastive and is used to focus on differences. One suspects, therefore, that in any question of the form 'Are x really like y?', *really like* will be interpreted as 'the same as', 'exactly equivalent to' and the hearer will search for all possible distinctions between the two entities. Contrary to Ortony's speculation about the intuition of 'ordinary people', a likely reply to 'Are encyclopedias *really like* dictionaries?' would be 'no'. The answer that any question of this type would receive surely depends entirely on the speaker's emotional commitment to the similarity, not to the degree of 'metaphorhood' of the statement.

As for the second assertion: are type (2) statements really more likely to be hedged by *sort of* and *kind of* than type (1)? I concordanced these items in both *Reps* and the four-million word corpus. In the first of these, the two hedges appear with far greater frequency in non-metaphorical environments:

(9) [...] you'll recall, there was a very specific warning given to Saddam Hussein that if he used, chemical, biological weapons the response

Metaphors, motifs and similes across discourse types 283

may also [be] with a weapon of mass destruction or some **kind of** proportionate response.

(10) do you see a need for an interim **sort of** international administration [...]

The phrase is also often used as a politeness hedge to lighten the weight of a request:

(11) My only other question was **sort of** a follow-up on Kelly Wallace's question.
(12) Actually, **kind of** following up on that [...]

It is especially a signal that the speaker is using language rather vaguely because for some reason they are unable to be more precise at this particular moment:

(13) [...] and of course the FAA is **sort of** putting out a directive for tighter security standards
(14) Because the surplus is **sort of** a momentary thing, it comes and goes
(15) [...] and some other reports that there was going to be evidence in a couple of days and that it would be put out before you moved militarily and that **kind of** thing.

The speakers in the above episodes would prefer to have been more explicit and more comprehensible but in spontaneous questioning about complex issues time restraints often get the better of them. The hedges *sort of* and *kind of* help speakers save face by implying that they recognize their language leaves something to be desired but they could do better if only they had more time.

The few metaphors that are found tend to be discourse-type specific, that is, particular to politics or journalism:

(16) is the administration saying that it would be better for Israel to reduce the size or close down some of the settlements, and also to retreat to some **kind of** fortress Israel?
(17) Ari, what **sort of** end game does the President have in mind for the government of Afghanistan?

Both *fortress* used to premodify a place and *end game* are common in reporting politics. In *Papers* we find *fortress Europe* (57 occurrences), fortress *France* and *Germany* (4 each), *fortress Asia* (3). Interestingly there are only single occurrences of fortress *England* and *Britain*, whilst *fortress Wapping*, the metaphorical stronghold of Mr Rupert Murdoch's News International, merits five (all in different newspaper articles). As regards *end game*, in Partington (2003) I commented on the presence of game and especially game-of-chess metaphors in political briefings talk. They were found quite frequently in journalists' moves (as (17) above) but, interestingly, not in the podium's, who perhaps wishes to avoid giving the impression of seeing political events and relations in strategic terms (and risking being seen as devious).

The concordances of *sort of* and *kind of* in newspaper corpora has a completely different story to tell. They were found proportionally far more frequently in metaphorical statements than they were in the briefings texts. This result, however, tells us more about the nature of the two types of discourse than about the hedges themselves. Newspapers texts are written and have relatively more relaxed time constraints in their production than spontaneous speech. In addition, some types of newspaper writing (notably the so-called comment and magazine types) display considerable novelty and variety of expression. As a result they exhibit what we might call a much higher general *figurative density* than the briefings. The higher proportion of figurative uses of our hedges is most probably a simple reflection of this overall density.

It was difficult to give precise proportions of metaphorical as compared to non-metaphorical uses of these items since, in both briefings and newspaper discourse, a very large number of the collocates of these hedges appeared to be neither entirely metaphorical nor wholly non-metaphorical but were either indeterminate or seemed to exist somewhere between the two poles, as the following:

(18) How does he now *sort of* **program** or **sequence** some of these other items on his agenda?

Does the speaker intend the *program* or *sequence* to be taken as metaphorical usage or not? Similarly:

(19) I mean does he see any more federal needs in such a way, a *sort of* **federalizing** security at the nation's airports?

The coinage of the item *federalizing* is a metaphorical extension, it is just *not very* metaphorical.

(20) Did you view that as a general statement or did you see any *kind of* **cues** for specific actions that he was trying to broadcast?

Is *cues* metaphorical or non-metaphorical language? Again, what did the speaker intend?

That the distinction between metaphorical or non-metaphorical language is a continuum rather than a dichotomy is, of course, hardly a novel finding. Goatly (1997: 38–9) lists no less than five different clines running between the two, the most interesting perhaps being *approximate similarity* versus *distant similarity* (consider *a pike is a kind of fish* [literal], *a sock is a kind of glove* [weakly metaphorical], *a kidney is a sort of sewer* [metaphorical]) and *conventionality-unconventionality* (roughly equivalent to *dead*, *inactive* and *novel* or *lively* metaphorical usage). These are observer-oriented categorizations of textual *product*. As discourse analysts, by appealing to the complementary notion of text as *process*, we can add the speaker-oriented concept of intentionality to Goatly's list. In other words, judging from the above examples, whether or not the speaker intended a piece of discourse to be metaphorical should be counted as one of the criteria for determining its degree of 'metaphoricality'.

Ortony's general claim was, if we recall, that we were much more likely to find these hedges in metaphorical than non-metaphorical statements. We have found them in metaphorical, non-metaphorical phrases and all stages between. Nevertheless, the balance of evidence gives some comfort to his claim. We have noted how speakers in the spontaneous briefings use *kind of* and *sort of* to indicate they are using language more loosely than they would wish. One way of using language 'loosely' (Sperber and Wilson 1995[2]) is to speak figuratively; speakers seem to use *sort of* and *kind of* along with a metaphor to indicate an inability to be wholly precise because they are grappling with a complex concept or difficult language. Evidence that this is happening is provided by the fact that speakers often use these hedges when making several stabs at what they wish to say:

(21) in the past Presidents have tried to **kind of** smooth the way between the FBI and the CIA, to make them work closely together, to overcome all the turf battles that exist there

often, as here, moving from a more general or looser description of a state or event to a more detailed one, although the movement is by no means necessarily from the metaphorical to the non, as the following example demonstrates:

(22) How concerned is the President that in defending ourselves we could ignite a **kind of** religious conflict, a holy war?

Compare also examples (18) and (19).
  Finally, the only occurrence of *kind of* with *like* was found in *Dems* and is especially tentative:

(23) MR. LOCKHART: [...] Sometimes, these very large numbers draw – it's kind of **like** pictures, you get drawn to them. (Laughter.)

The speaker indicates that he is aware there is considerable distance between the entities being compared, but note that the expression does not introduce a simile, only a simple (i.e. non-figurative) comparison.
  Ortony's final assertion is not linguistic but logical. Comparison statements of type (1) – *Encyclopedias are like dictionaries* – are true, whereas those of type (2) – *Encyclopedias are like gold mines* – that is, similes, are false. The latter must be the case, he argues, otherwise – were we to accept that 'encyclopedias resemble gold mines' as true – we would have to accept 'the belief that to some degree, and in some respect or respects, everything is like everything else' (1993: 347). Thus encyclopedias could also, if one wished, *be like* 'ice cream, infinity, and anything else you care to think of'. Moreover 'if all similarity statements are true by virtue of the fact that everything is like everything else, then there is no possibility of a similarity statement ever being false'. And since statements which are necessarily true are tautologies, and since tautologies convey no new information, and since most similarity statements self-evidently *do* convey new information, therefore some similarity statements, i.e. similes, must be false.
  There seems to be more than a hint of circularity or question-begging at least in this. Ortony seems to have established that the difference between the two types of statements is that the first are literally true, the second not, but this was surely his starting point. We might also raise the objections, firstly, that tautologies in real world discourse generally convey plenty of new information[6] and, secondly, that whether 'everything is like everything else' in some respect (or, rather, everything can be *made* or *construed* to be like everything else for the sake of argument) is the

---

6. Even seemingly tired and trite ones like 'boys will be boys'. There were 15 occurrences of the expression in *Papers* each expressing a different meaning in context, including the enigmatic 'boys will be boys, and so, it seems, will girls'. There were also two occurrences of the equally intriguing 'boys will be girls'.

mootest of points (and see the point below on 'conceit' metaphor). Ortony's analytical arguments would be incomprehensible to some of his fellow researchers into metaphor. Miller, for one, believes that a 'statement' of the form 'A is like B' is true in the sense that 'the author has observed a resemblance between A and B'. He cites other authors who note how comparison statements are used to make a proposal (Loewenberg 1975) or a claim (Fraser 1993).

A statement of the kind 'encyclopedias are like gold mines' is, of course, the expression of an opinion and opinions are not well handled by truth-based logical semantics. Similes like these have the *form* of a similarity statement but their function is to convey a point of view, a way of seeing the world, a personal argument. However, it must be noted, the same is true of type (1) statements. In order to tell the difference between the two types and to discover what is special about simile-type similarity statements, recourse to corpus evidence may well be helpful.

3.2. Concordancing *like*

Much of the confusion about similarity statements, one feels, may result from the miscellaneous possible meanings and uses of the link expression. Since it is by far the most common, we will concentrate attention on *like*. Although it is also the most frequently mentioned of these signals in the literature, seldom has it been rigorously studied in authentic discourse in context.

In the *Dems* corpus, *like* occurs 187 times in some sort of comparison role. Only a small proportion seem to be what we would classify as out-and-out type (2) figurative use (the subject of conversation here is Mr Milosevic when he was President of the Federal Republic of Yugoslavia):

(24) […] and both President Clinton and Gore have both calling him a junior league Hitler. How do you reconcile that? And secondly, if he does sign a peace agreement, how do you treat him when he comes to the bargaining table, **like** a head of state, or **like** a junior league Hitler?

There were several others, however, which were semi-figurative in nature:

(25) Mike, you say that there is a will on both sides to get this done, but it seems more **like** a test of wills. I mean, if –
MR. MCCURRY: **Like** a good negotiation.

What is most striking about these episodes is how the similarity statements are so clearly the central elements in a rhetorical argument, in both cases arguments which counter or test the podium's case or the administration's previous presentation of a particular contention. In the first example, both Mr Clinton and Mr Gore had used a metaphor of the type *Milosevic is a junior league Hitler* to blacken the man's name. The journalist here throws this description back in the podium's face in the form of a similarity statement using *treat like* in order to argue that the administration might find itself hoist with its own rhetorical petard.

In the second, the journalist once again picks up and reformulates the administration's language – this time the podium's own – and makes a kind of relexicalization pun, converting *will* to *test of wills*, reversing the picture from a favourable to an unfavourable one for the government. Note how the questioner achieves this by using a standard similarity signal *more like*, which has a powerfully contrastive function.[7] The podium's response – 'like a good negotation' – is another reformulation and another similarity statement which re-evaluates the matter favourably.

From these examples it seems clear that, in this discourse type at least, similes are not employed simply as descriptions but to make claims and to counter others' claims about states of affairs in the worlds of the participants, in other words, they can be tactically very effective in competitive debate. As further proof (the context is wrangling among the opposition majority in the Senate):

(26) MR. LOCKHART: I think anyone who can step in and gain control of this process would be welcome.
Q Well, which is it? – in the past, you would complain about how Gingrich was kind of operating Henry Hyde **like** a puppet on a string, and that he was actually exercising –
MR. LOCKHART: No, I think –
Q – too much control. Which do you prefer?

The questioner is again making use of the administration's own, if not actual words, certainly opinion in demeaning Mr Hyde by comparing him with a 'puppet on a string'. 'You would complain' about too much control,

---

7. This can be verified in any corpus of a reasonable size. The four-million word corpus produced 85 occurrences of *more like* of which around three quarters were contrastive: *more like a threat than a promise* being a typical example.

now you're complaining about lack of control: 'which do you prefer?' The sarcasm at the administration's expense is plain.

What is particularly striking about the three examples we have observed is how highly evaluative are the similes employed. Individuals are likened to a minor version of Hitler (24) or to a witless puppet (26), whilst a process is turned into a struggle (25): all three intensely negative evaluations. We have already noted in section 2 above how very many political metaphors have this function. Unfortunately much of the pre-corpus literature on metaphor in general entirely ignores this vital aspect. Lakoff (1993), for instance, while tracing his cognitive theory of metaphor (and castigating all previous views on the subject along the way), seems unaware that virtually all of his (invented) examples are likely to be evaluative when used in context e.g. *we're at a standstill, the end is in sight, he savoured the victory*. Is evaluation not part of cognitive reasoning? He treats a political example when discussing the relationship of metaphor to proverbs, showing how *blind blames the ditch* maps onto the demise of US politician Gary Hart:

> Blind man = Gary Hart
> Falling into a ditch = falling into disgrace
> Blaming the ditch = blaming the reporters who reported his misdemeanours.

However, again, he fails to underscore the evaluative message of such proverbial use – the whole point of the exercise – which is to attack Hart by depicting him as doubly degenerate. He not only commits the original misdemeanour but also incarnates the kind of flawed man envisaged by the proverb.[8]

Searle (1993) notes how similes are generally hyperbolic, implicitly recognizing a function – that of emphatic evaluation – beyond simple descriptive comparison. If we combine an analysis of Searle's and Lakoff's exam-

---

8. The irony is that Lakoff's own political postings on the Web show just how aware he is of how competing arguments are conducted through metaphors. 'Metaphors can kill' he reminds us. However, although highly thought-provoking, the paucity of reference to real life instances of language use in these postings makes it difficult for us to evaluate how widespread and influential are the various metaphors he lists. Which of them really dominate government thinking? For example, he mentions the War is a Game metaphor, which undoubtedly exists, but the evidence from both *Dems* and *Reps* is that, whilst the press occasionally employ it, the administration podiums do not (they might think in such terms, of course, but we have no proof). These postings can be found by entering *Lakoff* and *metaphor* in any Web search engine.

ples, it becomes evident that very many conventional similes and metaphors are based largely on conventional evaluative connotation, that is, whether a thing is good or bad. Taking some of Searle's examples: *bitter irony* or a *thorny problem* depend on BITTER IS BAD, THORNS ARE BAD, whilst a *sweet disposition* relies on SWEET IS GOOD. Lakoff explains Searle's *Sally is (like) a block of ice* as AFFECTION IS WARMTH, but this in turn depends upon WARMTH IS GOOD. To cite a political example, '[...] we are *a shining city* on a hill' (Mr. Cuomo in Bayley 1985: 114) evokes, of course, LIGHT IS GOOD.

Another conspicuous difference of emphasis in the literature regards the internal relationship between the source (or vehicle) and the target (or tenor) in a simile. Most descriptions of simile stress the similarity between the two. Black (1993), for instance, talks of an explicit projection of the qualities of the one onto the other (Lakoff (1993) and Gentner and Jeziorski (1993) talk of *mapping*). Miller, however, points out that 'it is an understatement to say that the mechanism of transference is not well understood...', and that 'in similes, the grounds for the comparison are not obvious' (1993: 375). Of the pre-corpus authorities, Miller is the keenest to stress the importance of context in metaphor / simile interpretation: 'in "A woman without a man is like a fish without a bicycle," it helps to know that the author is a proponent of women's liberation and to recognize the rejected allusion to a fish out of water' (1993: 372). Finally, he concludes that 'a simile is a comparison statement involving two *unlike* things' (1993: 373, my emphasis). Many normal dictionaries include 'unlikeness' in their definition of the word.[9] Richards (1936) had meant something similar in talking of the tension between topic and vehicle.

We might go a little further and suggest that in both metaphor and simile two fundamentally unlike entities are juxtaposed with the implication that they nevertheless have some small set of *salient features* in common. If the grounds of the similarity is made plain then these salient features are listed explicitly, if not, it is the task of the listener/reader to work them out through the normal methods of conversational implicature (Grice 1975). Encyclopedias and gold-mines perhaps share the feature of 'containing treasures'. If the reader looks at the series of metaphors at the start of section 2.4, in those describing briefings the sources and target share a salient feature of 'conflict' or 'antagonism' but also of 'agreeing to take part in a joint activity'. In the metaphors comparing the podium to

---

9. For instance: '**simile**: a figure of speech in which two unlike things are explicitly compared, as in "she is like a rose"': *Webster's Encyclopedic Unabridged Dictionary of the English Language.*

soldier, sailor or boxer the sources and target all share 'violence' or 'danger', whilst in those comparing the journalists to animals they share 'hunting as a pack' and 'intent on survival'. It must be stressed of course that these are all *claims* on the part of the metaphor makers; there is no proof that target and source share these features, but the argument is made each time that the target possesses some of the features which supposedly characterize the source. That such arguments are covert, embedded and non-rational (in the senses that they are unsupported by evidence and also difficult to challenge logically) makes metaphors highly effective and explains why they are so frequent in the construction of argument.

These certainly seem more profitable avenues of thought than regarding the relationship as simply 'false', but the concept *unlike* is nothing if not vague (presumably, if any two entities can be seen as alike for the sake of argument, any two different entities can equally – by definition, in fact – be considered unlike). What precisely is the nature and degree of the unlikeness of the two arguments? Once again, can corpus research throw light on these debates?

Our original question remains, however: what makes similes different from other similarity statements? We have looked at the few similes in the concordance of *like* from *Dems*: in order to answer the question it is necessary to analyse the other uses of this word.

It is, of course, used to indicate 'similar to', but even this sense is far from straightforward. One of the most frequent forms is *like* in combination with *look*, *sound*, *act* etc. meaning 'give the impression (rightly or wrongly)', for example *he's nodding like he understands*, which is often used (in this discourse type) to ask whether an impression corresponds to the truth:

(27)   Q Joe, it sounds **like** you're saying some thought is being given to sending someone back to Belgrade. Is that true?

Like also often appears in combination with *anything / something like that / this*, for example:

(28)   Q Does the President have any plans to go to Europe – go to Brussels or even go to Aviano or anything to review the troops, or anything **like** that?
(29)   Q But he didn't use the word "intend" or "no plans" or anything **like** that.

meaning 'a thing similar to one of the things I am mentioning'. It indicates an inability on the part of the speaker to be more precise and is usually an implied request (at least in this discourse type) for the hearer to help out. If *something like* is followed by a number, it indicates 'approximately':

(30) MR. LOCKHART: We have what can only be described as a dire humanitarian situation in Sierra Leone now. There are something **like** 150,000 people homeless and another – over the last – in the last short time, something **like** 700,000 people who are internally displaced.

Closely related to *anything / something like this* is a form (*in*) *cases / instances /issues / meetings, agreements* etc *like this* meaning 'belonging to the set that this example also belongs to'. In reality the nature of the set is unspecified, it is actually being defined only by its inclusion of the member(s) in question. Sometimes we again find a list:

(31) and also the call that's come from the President and the Secretary of the Treasury for countries **like** Japan and countries in the European Union to do more on stimulating domestic growth
(32) But in the long run, for this to be truly effective as a global regime, we're going to have to have countries **like** China and Russia participating.

sometimes a single entity with *for example*:

(33) Q When you say it would be a NATO force, you mean a NATO-led force. But is it possible that others could be added to that force, **like** Russians, for example?

But to what extent are these similarity statements? The entities here seem to be nominated less as examples, more for themselves; not 'countries like China and Russia' but 'China and Russia'. The form is a similarity statement but the essence seems to be a hedged form of identity statement.
  This is even clearer in the following:

(34) Q What do you think about efforts from third parties – what do you think about efforts from third parties, **like** Ukraine, for example, to try to intervene, to find some sort of diplomatic way out?

where it was Ukraine and nobody else who launched the proposal in question. And it is entirely apparent in the combination *a ... like this*:

(35) as Commander-in-Chief is he not angry at the timing of a leak **like** this, where some military leaders appear to be undermining his authority as Commander-in-Chief?

In many other contexts, *like* quite explicitly means 'the same as', 'identical to' rather than 'similar':

(36) Q And what about from what you all see? I mean, you're watching it **like** everybody else.
(37) MR. LOCKHART: [...] If we keep going **like** this, I'm going to have a lot of free time on my hand.
(38) MR. LOCKHART: **Like** I said, I think it's impossible to predict with any certainty.

The word *like*, then, can be used to indicate either resemblance or identity and indeed is often ambiguous in casual communication. There would seem to be a psychological tendency to conflate resemblance and identity – if one thing resembles another it is the same as the other. This may well have repercussions for the study of simile and metaphor. A simile such as *John is like a pig* is usually taken to be a similarity statement whereas *John is a pig* would seem to be an identity statement. In practice, however, people may generally feel them to be very closely related.

3.3. Gathering some loose ends

Has any light been shed, either by design or by serendipitous accident, on the nature of similes or on the various controversies over metaphor by our combining-contrasting of expert opinion and corpus evidence? It has, first of all, emphasized that the distinction between metaphorical and non-metaphorical language is not polar but a cline; some comparison statements we found were felt to be less metaphorical than other fully-blown ones but still not entirely non-metaphorical. In addition, the comparison of data from more than one corpus brought home how some discourse types are more dense in metaphor than others.

As for the relationship between simile and metaphor, evidence was uncovered that similarity and identity are felt to be so closely linked that in normal circumstances users often fail to make a distinction. Simile and metaphor are probably also normally felt to be equally closely linked.

The data also confirmed that similes (and metaphors) are generally used to express – over and above a statement of similarity – opinions, claims, personal arguments and as such are not susceptible to judgements on their truth. Closely related is the finding that, whatever else they communicate, they are generally evaluative in function. Searle's example from Shakespeare, *Juliet is the sun*, probably does not mean she is extremely large and gaseous, probably does imply that the speaker, Romeo, could not live without her, but definitely does mean that Juliet is evaluated a thoroughly *good thing*. The failure to properly appreciate the evaluative function of metaphor in pre-corpus studies is partly a product of a disregard of contextual forces, in particular, what speakers/writers are trying to *do* with metaphor. It may well be that in natural communication, simple description for its own sake is less common than is generally thought. Instead, it frequently takes place prior to and in the service of evaluation, but only in taking account of the wider context does this become apparent.

The evaluative potential of simile and metaphor means they have two evident functions in the language of politics. Since they present an argument they are part of the language of persuasion. But in other circumstances, for example, during electoral campaigning, they are used more simply to communicate to an audience shared values (or evaluations). Bayley (1985) provides us with a few examples – *America is a door, America is a promise, America is like a shining city* – which the speakers use to indicate that he or she is a certain type of person who evaluates key issues (country, family, foreigners) in a way that squares with the audience's view of the world. We might call them *right noises* political metaphors.[10]

This leads us back to our initial question, that is, what is it that distinguishes Ortony's type (1) and type (2) statements? Ortony argues that the difference is one of truth, Miller would say it is one of likeness, with type (2) statements yoking unlike entities (with the implication, we have added, that they nevertheless share some salient feature(s)). One kind of simile certainly does perform the task of juxtaposing the unlike, what we might call the *conceit simile*. Consider this extended literary example:

---

10. Problems can arise though when audiences are several and heterogeneous. President Bush's famous call for a *crusade* against bin Laden may have gone down well with his electorate but was appreciated less in the Muslim world, as a journalist points out in *Reps*:
'[...] the President used the word crusade last Sunday which has caused some consternation in a lot of Muslim countries. Can you explain his usage of that word, given the connotation to Muslims?'

(39) Love has entered me like a disease, so stealthily I have not seen its approach nor heard its footsteps. My mind recognises the folly of it and yet I still boil and burn with it, precisely as with a fever. To whom or what shall I turn in order to be cured? (Tremain 1989: 160–161)

The distance between source (disease) and target (love) is purposefully dissonant (though perhaps also a touch hackneyed) and the author has to work (and make the receiver work) to connect the two. It is a striking evaluative statement in that it maps a bad thing onto what is generally taken as a good one – a prosodic switch – and, in fact, in the episode in question, the narrator's passion has landed him in a tricky situation.

Such conceit metaphors are clearly quasi-oxymora (or 'indirect' oxymora [Gibbs 1993: 269–270]). True oxymora, like *a cruel kindness* or *a kind cruelty*, worry Miller, who asks whether they are metaphors and adds 'if so, they provide a special challenge for the comparison views of metaphor' since 'they seem to express contrasts not comparisons' (1993: 392). But we can extrapolate from our discussion of conceits / quasi-oxymora to account for true oxymora. Just as *this love is like a disease* implies that 'this love has some of the properties of a disease', *a cruel kindness* surely denotes 'this kindness has some properties of cruelty' (euthanasia?) whilst *a kind cruelty* assumes 'this cruelty has some properties of kindness' (as in not sparing the rod?). By contrast, the class-inclusion view of metaphor (e.g. Glucksberg and Keysar 1990) is going to have real problems with oxymoron: 'this kindness belongs to the category of cruel acts' appears a nonsense.

The similes in the spontaneous political talk we have noted also display both this hackneyed quality and this distance between source and target. The following are from *Reps*:

(40) These are the cat-and-mouse games that Iraq has played to a masterpiece. They have played the world like a fiddle before [...]
(41) You know, sometimes people make outlandish statements, hoping that they can, like flypaper, draw other people down to their level

The distance is, first of all, conceptual – propaganda is compared to playing an instrument, drawing people down is compared to catching unwary flies, Milosevic to a baseball-playing Hitler, a politician to a puppet. Miller does not define what he means by the *unlike*-ness of the two elements. We might hazard a rule-of-thumb: the two terms belong to different categories in the sense that it is not easy to find a superordinate term that includes both. But the difference between the two in the above political examples is also linguistic. Most of the similes in these briefings harness plain, everyday language *fiddle, flypaper* – and thus simple homespun all-American philosophy – onto the speaker's thought. And then, following on Searle's intuition, so many of the comparisons in the similes we have looked at here have an element of the hyperbolic, of exaggeration: *gold mines, Hitler, shining city* and so on.

We begin thus to see why some similes can appear 'more simile' more figurative than others. The following examples are all from *Plum*. The splendid:

(42) depression fell from him like a garment

yokes two very disparate conceptual entities: the falling of a tangible object with the lifting of an intangible mood. The following:

(43) The stationmaster's whiskers are of a Victorian bushiness and give the impression of having been grown under glass
(44) Fillmore seemed to expand like an India rubber ball that has been sat on

introduce discordant vocabulary from gardening and children's discourse to the juxtaposition of man and object, whereas:

(45) Roderick Spode. Big chap with a small moustache and the sort of eye that can open an oyster at sixty paces

has more than an element of exaggeration, but:

(46) When reminded of that house of horror I still quiver like an aspen

while still a simile, feels much less figurative than the others. There is a touch of hyperbole but no register play and there seems to be little cognitive difference between the man's trembling and that of a poplar, largely perhaps because we are fairly used to the comparison of people and trees: *heart of oak, the willowy Amanda* (from *Papers*), and so on. Familiarity automatically reduces the cognitive distance of a juxtaposition.

We can now see that the relation between ordinary comparison statements (Ortony's statement type (1)) and similes (type (2)), is complex, a combination of elements. First of all, the difference is a cline rather than a clear-cut, all-or nothing distinction. Secondly, there is generally a greater distance between the two terms in type (2) statements and this distance may be conceptual, linguistic or rhetorical, or a blending of these. Finally, they are also more likely to be used evaluatively to argue that some event is propitious or unwelcome, that some idea is virtuous or pernicious or that some person is behaving well or badly.

One last question remains: has this study provided any input to the debate on the relationship between metaphor and simile? Returning to example (39), there is an easy interplay between simile and metaphor, the natural moving back and forth from one to the other; evidence to support Miller's ('old-fashioned' he calls it) belief in the interrelation of the two phenomena. Others argue differently, for instance, that the metaphor *Sally is a block of ice* is more covert than the simile *Sally is like a block of ice*, but the concordance evidence seems to indicate that the language and language users frequently conflate *like* as identity and *like* as similarity, and thus any distinction between such phrases in practice tends to vanish. However, the distinction may still be recoverable and useful to users on occasion, as we shall see below.

Still others note that 'the most obvious semantic difference between simile and metaphor is that all similes are true and most metaphors are false ... the earth is like a floor, but it is not a floor' (Davidson 1978: 39). We have already seen how Ortony instead argues that similes are false. In any case, such statements belong to truth semantics; as discourse analysts, we have argued that both should be treated as claims or arguments, valid in their own terms and invested with emotional commitment that makes them 'true' for the speaker.

Bayley, instead, reports the argument that metaphors are 'argumentatively stronger' because they are less easily challenged than similes:

> Whereas simile is open to direct rebuttal:
> – The economy is like a mighty engine
> – No, it's not
>
> metaphor is not; a complex circumlocution would be necessary to deny its aptness:
> – The mighty engine of this nation is revved up
> – Do you mean to suggest that the economy is a mighty engine? If you do, I must disagree (Bayley 1985: 119)

As it stands, the argument is unsatisfactory. The simile *The economy is like a mighty engine* is no more nor less open to challenge than the corresponding metaphor *The economy is a mighty engine*, to which 'No it's not' is equally available as a response. What is true, however, is that *the mighty engine of the nation is revved up* is an *embedded* metaphor, the metaphor is inserted within a nominal phrase serving as the theme of the sentence rather than being set on its own as rheme in *The economy is a mighty engine*. But a simile can equally be embedded and be just as laborious to prise out, for example:

(47)   As a rule, you see, I'm not lugged into Family Rows. On the occasions when Aunt is calling to Aunt **like** mastodons bellowing across primeval swamps... the clan has a tendency to ignore me. (Plum)

would have to be challenged along the following lines:

–   Do you mean to suggest that Aunts bellow like mastodons? If you do, I must disagree

If simile were really argumentatively weaker than metaphor, one wonders why Robert Burns failed to eliminate the *like* of his *my love is like a red red rose...* (quoted by Miller) to stand a better chance of winning over the young lady in his thoughts. He chose to employ a simile for reasons we shall discuss below.

This confusion over the argumentative strengths of these figures arises, one feels, because introspective, data-poor conjecture about these matters has been symptomatic of pre-corpora discussions, inevitably so. Searle, Miller, Ortony and others all tend predominantly to cite or invent examples containing a copula verb, whilst Lakoff and Johnson's entire formulation of metaphorical structure – X IS Y – depends on the copular relation. Thus the question of embedded versus non-embedded figures has seldom been considered.

For the discourse analyst the question itself is probably inappropriate. Instead of speculating on the abstract differences between similes and metaphors, we need to ask: what are the conditions which either force or encourage a speaker or writer to choose to use one rather than the other? Looking back over some of our examples, these conditions appear to be both structural and rhetorical. The sentence *Love has entered me like a disease* is clearly end-weighted. The simile is an adverbial phrase in sentence final position, which allows the writer to give more emphasis to the figure than would have been the case in *The disease of love has entered me*. There is a far greater element of surprise – which is the whole point of a conceit.

Another rhetorical opportunity that similes seem to offer is the possibility to expand the comparison. We have already seen this in example (39) where the narrator elaborates on why his love is like a disease. We might compare the following:

(48)   Life is like some crazy machine that is always going either too slow or too fast. From the cradle to the grave we alternate between the Sargasso Sea and the rapids--forever either becalmed or storm-tossed. (Plum)

Thus similes, especially the conceit type, frequently introduce a particular argumentative structure when the speaker wishes to make more explicit and detailed reference to the grounds of comparison. Speakers frequently employ them for cataphoric, suspense-creating effect; first the surprising enigmatic simile is produced, then the exegesis. Let me tell you why life is like a crazy machine; let me tell you how my love is like a rose or like a disease. As we mentioned above, the overtness, the *self-consciousness* of the comparison in simile can be recovered by users for effect.

Finally and most obviously, conventional similes – *play x like a fiddle* – or metaphors – *the king of the beasts* – are quite simply learned in their particular form and are more likely to get used in it over again. Though not necessarily. Creative users can invent 'cross-overs' like, say, *fiddle-playing on the world*.

4.   Conclusion

Much of mainstream Corpus Linguistics gives the impression of believing corpus use to be a Good Thing in itself. In the business of building modern grammars and dictionary this is certainly the case, given the need to block out contamination from old-fashioned, hidebound approaches and philosophies. Many other kinds of research, the Biber canon of register studies a foremost instance, would simply not be conceivable without corpora.

But in Corpus-Assisted Discourse Studies, corpus techniques are strictly functional to the overall task in hand. As the researches included in this article show, they take their place alongside more qualitative, in-depth procedures including intuition, introspection and immersion in a text. Even sheer speculation at times can be fruitful, if open to subsequent verification. To use a folk simile, the CADS linguist, like the pork butcher, uses all that s/he can, discards nought but the squeal. An example of the fertility of the serendipitous and promiscuous interplay of CADS is the following. While compiling the *Plum* corpus from the Gutenberg Project site, I allowed myself to become distracted into reading *Three Men and a Maid*, an early Wodehouse tale I had never come across before. I was struck by the number and variety of similes employed in the first two chapters alone. But my attention was arrested by a particular passage:

(49) I've had a wonderful time. Everybody's treated me like a rich uncle. I've been in Detroit, you know, and they practically gave me the city and asked me if I'd like another to take home in my pocket. Never saw anything like it. *I might have been the missing heir.* I think America's the greatest invention on record.

The extract is clearly rich in simile (*treated me like a rich uncle*) and metaphor (*they practically gave me the city…*) and so on. *Practically*, when concordanced, proved very frequently to perform the function of introducing a hyperbolic metaphor (*we're practically castaways on a desert island* among many more). But the most remarkable phrase was *I might have been the missing heir* which, it struck me, we might easily paraphrase in a more canonical simile form as 'I was like the missing heir'. So I decided to concordance *might have been* and *Plum* supplied many examples including the following:

(50) but so thickly did it bristle with obstacles that it might have been a mile of No Man's Land.
(51) Most of the time I might have been eating sawdust for all the good it did me.
(52) Angela might have been hewn from the living rock
(53) For all the authority I had over him, I might have been the potted plant against which he was leaning.

The grounds of the simile (that is, *why* X *might have been* Y) are generally either explicit or easily recoverable in the cotext: the *obstacles* make the area like *a mile of No Man's Land*, Angela's rock-like state, we discover, is in her silence at dinner, I am like a potted plant in having no authority, and so on. The key-cluster lists showed that *might have been* is very frequent in Wodehouse's prose, more than three times as common as in the other corpora examined (nine times more common than in the spoken corpora).

If *might* plus perfect aspect lends itself to simile, I was curious about the behaviour of *might be*. The phrase has many functions but there turned out to be a most intriguing form of concessive use:

(54) He might be a child in wordly matters [...] but if the King did not know the difference between home-grown domestic and frozen imported foreign [...]
(55) He might be a pretty minus quantity in a drawing room or at a dance but in a bunker or out in the open with a clee, Eunice felt, you'd be surprised.
(56) He might be a pain in the neck to the family, but he did know how to stop a dog fight.

The concessive expressions here are clearly figurative but they are not similes; they are not 'X is like Y'. Instead they can be paraphrased as 'admittedly, he is a child in worldly affairs' 'we concede he is a pretty minus quantity at a dance' and so on. They are identity rather than similarity statements; in other words they are metaphors.

This would seem to offer us a fresh way of looking at the distinction between metaphor and simile, wherever one exists. The difference between perfect and non-perfect aspect, as between past and present tense, as has frequently been noted, is one of distance, remoteness from the speaker or narrator. This remoteness may be in time (i.e. the past) or it may be in possibility or factuality (*if I had a hammer* implies I don't have one), or it may be social distance (*Could* you pass me the salt), and see Morley (1998: 89–93) on the journalistic use of the past for signalling the *reporting* of others' words or opinions. When any distinction is relevant, the comparison effected by a simile is meant, then, to be somehow more remote than that effected by a metaphor. This greater remoteness is usually signalled lexically (X is *like* Y, it is similar to Y, but X is not the same as Y) but can also be signalled grammatically as in the examples in this section, via verbal aspect.

It is only fitting that we end this paper with a few metaphors and similes of our own. We have said that corpus techniques are one set of procedures among many. But as the two studies above testify, they do occupy a special place in the CADS armoury. They are like a magic window through which we can see language differently and often more deeply into its bones. And the CADS researcher is like a picaresque adventurer: s/he knows from where s/he sets off, may know roughly where s/he wants to end up, but all sorts of wonderful discoveries can lie in wait along the way.

References

Bayley, Paul
   1985   Live oratory in the television age: the language of formal speeches. In: Giuseppe Ragazzini, Donna Miler and Paul Bayley (eds.), *Campaign Language*, 77–174. Bologna: CLUEB.

Bell, Cathryn
   1996   Tutorial: Concordances and Corpora. Online at <http: www.georgetown.edu/cball/corpora/tutorial.html>

Biber, Douglas and Conrad, Susan
   1999   Lexical bundles in conversation and academic prose. In: Hilde Hasselgård and Signe Oksefjell (eds.) *Out of Corpora*, 181–190. Amsterdam: Rodopi.

Biber, Douglas, Stig Johansson, Geoffrey Leech, Susan Conrad and Edward Finegan
   1999   *Longman Grammar of Spoken and Written English*. London: Longman.

Black, Max
   1993   More about metaphor. In: Andrew Ortony (ed.), *Metaphor and Thought*. Second edition, 19–41. Cambridge: Cambridge University Press.

Davidson, Donald
   1978   What metaphors mean. *Critical Inquiry* 5: 31–47.

Fowler, Roger
   1991   *Language and Ideology in the Press*. London: Routledge.

Fraser, Bruce
   1993   The interpretation of novel metaphors. In: Andrew Ortony (ed.), *Metaphor and Thought*. Second edition, 329–341. Cambridge: Cambridge University Press.

Garzone, Guiliana and Francesca Santulli
   2004   What can Corpus Linguistics do for Critical Discourse Analysis? In: Alan Partington, John Morley and Louann Haarman (eds), *Corpora and Discourse*, 351–368. Bern: Peter Lang.

Gentner, Dedre and Michael Jeziorski
   1993   The shift from metaphor to analogy in Western science. In: Andrew Ortony (ed.), *Metaphor and Thought*. Second edition, 447–480. Cambridge: Cambridge University Press.

Gibbs, Raymond
   1993   Process and products in making sense of tropes. In: Andrew Ortony (ed.), *Metaphor and Thought*. Second edition, 252–276. *Metaphor and Thought*. Cambridge: Cambridge University Press.

Glucksberg, Sam and Boaz Keysar
   1990   Understanding metaphorical comparisons. Beyond similarity. *Psychological Review* 97: 3–18.

Grice, Herbert
   1975   Logic and conversation. In Peter Cole and Jerry Morgan (eds), *Syntax and Semantics 3: Speech Acts*, 41–58. New York: Academic Press.

Haarman, Louann, John Morley and Alan Partington
   2002   *Habeas Corpus*: Methodological reflections on the creation and use of a specialized corpus. In: Cesare Gagliardi (ed.), *Quantity and Quality in English Linguistic Research: Some Issues*, 55–119. Pescara: Libreria dell'Universita Editrice.

Herbart, Johann
   1898   Letters and lectures on education. (Translated by H. Flekin and E. Felkin). London: Sonneschein.

Lakoff, George
   1993   Contemporary theory of metaphor. In: Andrew Ortony (ed.), *Metaphor and Thought*. Second edition, 202–251. Cambridge: Cambridge University Press.

Lakoff, George and Mark Johnson
   1980   *Metaphors We Live By*. Chicago: The University of Chicago Press.

Levinson, Stephen
   1988   Putting linguistics on a proper footing: Explorations in Goffman's concepts of participation. In: Paul Drew and Anthony Wootton (eds.), *Erving Goffman: Exploring the Interaction Order,* 161–227. Cambridge: Polity Press.

Loewenberg, Ina
   1975   Identifying metaphors. *Foundations of Language* 12: 315–338.

Miller, George
   1993   Images and models, similes and metaphors. In: Andrew Ortony (ed.), *Metaphor and Thought*. Second edition. Cambridge: Cambridge University Press, 357–400.

Morley, John
   1998   *Truth to Tell*. Bologna: CLUEB.

Ortony, Andrew (Ed.)
   1993   *Metaphor and Thought*. Second edition. Cambridge: Cambridge University Press.
   1993   Similarity in similes and metaphors. In: Andrew Ortony (ed.), *Metaphor and Thought*. Second edition, 342–356. Cambridge: Cambridge University Press.

Partington, Alan
   1998   *Patterns and Meanings*, Amsterdam and Philadelphia: John Benjamins.
   2003   *The Linguistics of Political Argument: Spin-doctor and the Wolf-pack at the White House.* London: Routledge.

Partington, Alan and John Morley
   2004   At the heart of ideology: Word and cluster/bundle frequency in political debate. In: Barbara Lewandowska-Tomaszczyk (ed.), *Practical Applications in Language and Computers*, 179–192. Frankfurt: Peter Lang.

Partington, Alan, John Morley and Louann Haarman
   2004   *Corpora and Discourse*. Bern: Peter Lang.

Richards, Ivor A.
   1936   *The Philosophy of Rhetoric*. London: Oxford University Press.

Rigotti, Francesca
   1992   Il potere e le sue metafore, Bologna: Feltrinelli

Searle, John
   1993   Metaphor. In: Andrew Ortony (ed.), *Metaphor and Thought*. Second edition, 83–111. Cambridge: Cambridge University Press.

Semino, Elena and Michela Masci
   1996   Politics is football: metaphor in the discourse of Silvio Berlusconi in Italy. *Discourse and Society* 7: 243–270.

Schön, Donald
   1993   Generative metaphor: A perspective on problem-setting in social policy. In: Andrew Ortony (ed.), *Metaphor and Thought*. Second edition, 137–163. Cambridge: Cambridge University Press.

Sinclair, John
   1982   Reflections on computer corpora in English language research. In: Stig Johansson (ed.), *Computer Corpora in English Language Research*, 1–6. Bergen: Norwegian Computing Centre for the Humanities.

Sperber, Dan and Deirdre Wilson
   1995   *Relevance*. Second edition. Oxford: Blackwell.

Tremain, Rose
   1989   *Restoration*. London: Sceptre.

Vaghi, Francesca and Marco Venuti
   2004   Metaphor and the Euro. In: Alan Partington, John Morley and Louann Haarman (eds.), 369–381. *Corpora and Discourse*. Bern: Peter Lang.

Webster's Encyclopedic Unabridged Dictionary of the English Language
   1989   New York: Portland House.

Author index

Allan, K.   6, 9–10, 176, 190
Anderson, J.R.   216, 232–233
Apresjan, J.D.   153
Athanasiadou, A.   70
Austin, J.   38

Ballmer, T.   39
Barlow, M.   145
Barnden, J.A.   5, 11–12, 170
Barnden, M.A.   5
Bayley, P.   273, 290, 294, 297
Biber, D.   269, 275, 299
Bierwiaczonek, B.   194
Black, M.   18–20, 24, 63, 280, 290
Boers, F.   37, 106, 239
Boroditsky, L.   177
Brennenstuhl, W.   39
Briscoe, T.   153, 156, 158
Buchlovsky, P.   11–12
Burnley, J.D.   208

Cameron, L.   9, 37, 48, 59, 108–109, 111, 238, 241
Carbonell, J.   214
Carletta, J.   166
Castellón, I.   5
Charteris-Black, J.   9–10, 106, 238
Chater, N.   216
Chinchor, N.   162
Chun, L.   10
Chung, S.F.   10
Church, K.   19
Clarke, D.D.   129
Conrad, S.   275
Copestake, A.   153, 156, 158
Crisp, P.   11
Croft, W.   126
Crystal, D.   245
Curry, W.C.   208

Davidson, D.   18, 297

Deignan, A.   2–3, 7–10, 17, 37, 59, 106–107, 110–111, 114, 118, 125, 145, 238–239, 241, 248
Demecheleer, M.   106
Díez Velasco, O.I.   129
Dirven, R.   70
Duguid, A.   267, 272

Einhorn, B.   251
Emanatian, M.   239
Ennis, T.   10
Erman, B.   120
Eubanks, P.   244, 254

Fabiszak, M.   202
Fairclough, N.   239, 243
Fass, D.   127, 155, 158, 214
Fauconnier, G.   120, 178–179, 237
Fellbaum, C.   154
Fellows, L.   11–12
Ferenczi, M.   101
Ferguson, F.J.   5
Feyaerts, K.   180
Fillmore, C.J.   19, 125, 230
Fowler, R.   273
Francis, G.   120, 124–125
Fraser, B.   280, 287

Garzone, G.   270, 273
Geeraerts, D.   194, 208
Gentner, D.   214, 290
Gernsbacher, M.A.   214, 225
Gerrig, R.J.   214–215, 226, 228
Gibbs, R.W.   71, 123, 125–126, 131, 214, 239, 247, 280, 295
Gildea, P.   214
Glasbey, S.R.   5, 11–12
Glucksberg, S.   36, 214, 228, 295
Goatly, A.   4–5, 9, 108–109, 111, 243, 246, 249, 285
Goddard, C.   98, 192
Goldberg, A.E.   124–125

Goossens, L. 129, 132
Grady, J.E. 37, 46–53, 55, 57–58, 130, 177, 179, 239
Grice, H.P. 290
Gries, S.T. 66, 96, 125
Grondelaers, S. 208

Haarman, L. 270
Hahn, U. 125, 153, 155
Halliday, M.A.K. 251
Hanks, P. 2–3, 6, 8–10, 17, 19, 25, 107
Harabagiu, S. 153, 155
Harré, R. 210
Healy, A.F. 214, 226, 228
Heywood, J. 37, 238
Hilpert, M. 2–3, 6–8, 107
Hobbs, J.R. 155, 214, 216
Hodge, R. 243
Holland, D. 192
Hundt, M. 195
Hunston, S. 120, 124–125, 271

Indurkhya, B. 214
Ingegneri, D. 248
Inhoff, A. 214, 225–226

Jäkel, O. 2, 9, 192–193, 207
Jeziorski, M. 290
Johnson, M. 1, 19, 36–37, 40–42, 44–45, 63–66, 108, 126–127, 145, 152, 154, 158, 179, 192–193, 196, 199, 202–203, 206, 218, 227, 230, 237, 239–240, 272, 275–276, 298
Jorgensen, J. 155
Jurafsky, D. 230

Kay, C. 176
Kemper, S. 226
Kennedy, G. 241, 248
Keysar, B. 214, 228, 295
Kilgarriff, A. 28, 155
Kittay, E.F. 247, 253
Koch, P. 128
Koivisto-Alanko, P. 3, 7, 9–10, 176, 192, 194–195
Koller, V. 2–3, 8–9, 106, 243

Kövecses, Z. 41, 46, 57, 70–73, 78, 84, 88, 91, 108, 124, 127, 132, 192–193, 199, 203, 205–206, 208–209, 239
Kress, G. 243
Kretzschmar, W.A. 248
Krippendorff, K. 167
Kyratzis, S. 244
Kytö, M. 195

Lakoff, G. 1, 3, 9, 19, 36–37, 41–42, 44–45, 63–66, 71, 73, 75, 77, 107–108, 119, 123, 126–127, 135, 145–146, 152, 154, 158, 179, 192–193, 196, 199, 202–203, 206, 218, 227, 230, 237, 239–240, 253, 272, 275–276, 280, 289–290, 298
Langacker, R.W. 69, 125
Lee, M. 155, 192
Leech, G. 38
Levinson, S. 278
Littlemore, J. 239
Loewenberg, I. 287
Low, G. 37, 59, 241–242, 246

Marinelli, R. 170
Markert, K. 2, 7–8, 11, 125, 153, 155, 165, 172
Martin, J.H. 4, 9, 214, 218, 230
Masci, M. 2, 9
Matthiessen, C.M. 251
McEnery, T. 238
Meyer, C.F. 248
Miller, G. 280–281, 290, 295, 298
Musolff, A. 9, 238, 254

Narayanan, S. 214, 230
Nerlich, B. 129
Ng, H. 155
Niemeier, S. 70, 124, 132
Nissim, M. 2, 7–8, 11, 125, 165, 172
Nunberg, G. 146, 156, 165
Nurmi, A. 195

Oaksford, M. 216
Ortony, A. 36, 71, 125, 214, 226, 280–282, 285–286

Palmer, G.B. 192

Partington, A.   2, 6, 9, 145, 268, 270, 273, 275, 284
Pedersen, T.   96
Peters, W.   37, 153–154
Pollio, H.R.   218
Polzenhagen, F.   238
Potter, L.   125, 145
Pustejovsky, J.   19, 29, 154–155

Quinn, N.   192, 237

Radden, G.   127
Reddy, M.   36–37, 45–51, 56, 119, 129, 192
Resnik, P.   172
Richards, I.A.   290
Ritchie, D.   37, 41, 44
Rosenzweig, J.   155
Ruiz de Mendoza Ibáñez, F.J.   129
Russell, S.W.   214

Saeed, J.I.   180
Samuels, M.L.   184–185
Sand, A.   195
Santulli, F.   270, 273
Schmid, H.J.   71
Schooler, L.J.   216
Searle, J.R.   38, 126, 146, 214, 280, 289
Seidel, J.   253
Semino, E.   2, 5–7, 9, 11, 37–40, 56, 58–59, 238
Seto, K.I.   127
Short, M.   38–39, 58, 238
Siemund, R.   195
Sinclair, J.   25, 28, 110, 115, 124, 130, 274
Skandera, P.   195
Sperber, D.   36, 285
Sperberg–McQueen   269
Stallard, D.   155
Steen, G.   11, 37, 247, 251

Stefanowitsch, A.   3–4, 6–7, 10, 20, 64, 66, 69, 93, 96, 98, 123, 125, 193, 211
Stern, G.   127, 154, 158
Stubbs, M.   237, 240
Sweetser, E.   146, 192, 202
Szabó, P.   132

Tabaskowska, E.   70
Talmy, L.   218
Taylor, J.R.   46
Tissari, H.   3, 7, 9–10, 176, 192, 195
Trausan-Matu, S.   11
Tremain, R.   295
Tugwell, D.   28
Turner, M.   1, 120, 178–179, 193, 203, 218, 237
Turner, T.J.   71

Ungerer, F.   71
Utiyama, M.   155

Vaghi, F.   272–273
van Dijk, T.A.   239
Veale, T.   154
Venuti, M.   272–273
Véronis, J.   237
Verspoor, C.   155

Wallington, A.   5, 11–12
Warren, B.   120
Weinrich, H   63
Wierzbicka, A.   98
Wilks, Y.   37, 153–154, 214
Wilson, A.   238
Wilson, D.   36, 285
Wolf, H.G.   238
Wynne, M.   38

Yarowsky, D.   172

Subject index

activation   18–20, 27, 228–233
annotation   1, 2, 4–6, 10–13, 15–16, 36, 38, 59, 152, 154–159, 164–173
– annotation scheme   5, 10–11, 15, 38, 152, 155–159, 161–162, 164, 169–172
– automatic annotation   2, 4
– manual annotation   2, 4, 10, 38, 238, 242–243, 248
– semantic annotation   2, 154–155
antonymy   7, 65, 70, 96, 102, 177
attitude   40, 58, 134, 267

basic sense   19, 21, 39–40, 43, 48, 54, 57
blending   120, 122, 178–180, 202, 297

CADS   15, 267, 269, 279, 299–301
coherence   101, 218, 227
cohesion   181–182, 186, 243
colligation   8, 123, 125, 131–132, 142–145, 246
collocation   20, 28–29, 31, 35, 104, 107, 116–117, 120–125, 131, 147, 150, 241, 246, 248, 251, 253, 271, 275–278, 284
comparison statements   280–281, 287, 290, 293, 296, 299, 301
comprehension   15, 50, 147, 150, 154, 176, 184, 214–217, 219, 221–223, 225, 226, 233–235, 283, 287
computational linguistics   125, 147, 214–215, 234
computational model   215–216, 230, 254
concordance   2, 35–36, 38–40, 42–44, 49–53, 55–57, 80, 104, 106, 107, 109, 111–112, 114–118, 121–122, 131–132, 144–145, 241, 243, 247–248, 253, 268–269, 271, 273, 275, 279, 281–282, 284, 287–279, 300
connotation   115, 163, 184–185, 239, 272, 290, 294
construction   17, 20, 23, 48, 124–126, 142, 147, 165, 230–233
context   8–9, 19, 67, 120, 125, 146–147, 161, 180, 214–215, 217–218, 220–229, 231–233, 237–238, 243–244, 268–269, 294, 300
conventionality   8, 10–11, 17–20, 26–28, 36, 40–41, 46, 48–49, 54, 59, 68, 95, 107–108, 112, 131, 146, 148, 152–154, 157–159, 163–164, 168, 174–175, 179, 185, 226, 230–232, 235, 242, 250, 273, 278, 285, 290, 299
corpus comparison   269, 271, 274, 267, 278–280
Corpus-Assisted Discourse Studies   *see* CADS
critical approach   237–238
culture   9, 10, 41, 93, 95–96, 98, 101, 103, 175, 177, 180, 192, 210–211, 237–240, 251–252, 272

data retrieval   1–6, 11, 23, 38, 64, 107, 111, 131, 156, 195, 211, 219–220, 241–242, 247, 253
degrees of metaphoricity   6, 11, 17, 22, 24, 30, 282, 285
diachrony   9, 17–18, 129, 175–176, 184, 186, 191–192, 194–195, 204, 207, 209–210, 211, 247, 279–280
discourse   9, 24, 37, 59, 125, 227, 237–240, 242–248, 251–252, 267–270, 275, 279–280, 284–286
dispersion   243

embodiment   175, 179, 211, 239, 242
evaluation   114, 116–118, 155–156, 239, 267, 271, 277–279, 288–290, 294–295
experientiality   41, 44, 46, 49, 52, 77, 101, 130, 145, 177, 192, 269, 272
exploitation   21, 24–26
extraction   *see* data retrieval

facilitation   214–215, 217, 222, 225–227, 229, 233, 251
fixed expressions   1, 106, 116–120, 125, 131, 145–146, 198

Subject index 309

frequency   7, 9, 21–22, 29, 37, 56, 63, 65, 68, 71, 73, 78, 80, 82, 84, 86–87, 89, 90–99, 106–107, 113, 119, 125, 130, 153, 156, 194–195, 199–200, 202, 207, 209–211, 217–219, 221, 223, 229–233, 242, 244, 246, 248–250, 268–269, 271–272, 275, 282, 284

genre   8–9, 27, 38, 40, 106, 156, 204, 210, 241, 253, 269, 274–276
grammar   8, 106–108, 110, 118, 112, 114, 120

ideology   9, 106, 237–240, 245, 248, 252–253, 268, 270–271
inflection   8, 112–115, 117–119, 120
inhibition   214–215, 222, 225, 229, 233
intertextuality   9, 24
introspection   6–10, 12, 58, 63–65, 70, 72–73, 75, 79–80, 82–83, 90–91, 102, 123, 194, 210, 219, 238, 240, 268, 298–299
intuition   10, 106, 123–124, 154–155, 175, 211, 241, 269, 281–282, 296
Invariance Hypothesis   119–120

keywords   2, 3, 209, 211, 269, 271, 273, 275–279

lexeme specificity   69–72, 96, 102
lexical field   246–247, 249, 258
lexical semantics   63, 75, 103

manual post-editing   4
metaphor
 – dead metaphor   247, 285
 – noun metaphor   111–112, 114
 – primary metaphor   37, 46–47, 50, 53, 55, 57, 178–179, 239
 – verb metaphor   111–112
metaphor cluster   108, 218, 222, 243–244, 246, 251, 267, 275–276, 278
Metaphor Prediction Hypothesis   218, 225–226
metaphoric chain   243–244
metaphor density   244, 248, 284
metaphorical pattern analysis   *see* MPA
metaphorical patterns   3–4, 18, 37, 48, 56, 66–67, 69, 73, 80, 82, 85, 87–88, 90, 102

metonymy
 – C-metonymy   127–129, 133, 135, 139, 145
 – chained metonymy   129, 130, 133–134, 136, 144–145
 – E-metonymy   127–128, 134–136, 145
metonymic patterns   152, 154, 157–159
motivation   50, 68, 98, 146–147, 177, 175, 178–180, 182, 186
MPA   65–66, 69–70, 73, 76–77, 79, 81–82, 84, 87–88, 90–91, 96–97, 102–103
mTTR   249–250

Narrator's Representation of Speech Acts   *see* NRSA
negative   114, 279
norms   17
NRSA   36, 38–40, 43–45, 49–53, 55–56

part of speech   *see* word class
pattern   32, 36–37, 56, 87–88, 106–107, 112, 114, 118, 121, 123–126, 131–140, 142, 145–147, 160, 237–238, 253
polysemy   120, 129–131, 146, 153–154, 158, 184, 193, 195
predictiveness   221–224, 226, 228, 232–233
priming   231, 233
probability   221–224, 232, 253
processing   8–9, 126, 146, 152–153, 214–216, 227–229, 231–233
productivity   103, 152–153, 155, 176, 195
proper name   152–153, 155–157, 159, 161
prosody   115
prototype   17, 31, 38, 42, 194
psycholinguistics   125, 131, 147, 214–215, 221, 225, 228

qualitative analysis   97–99, 102, 123, 130, 243–244, 248, 251, 268, 279
quantitative analysis   12, 19, 28–29, 40, 63–64, 66, 69–70, 90–94, 99, 102, 116, 123, 130, 143, 176, 178, 194, 199, 223, 237–238, 243–244, 248, 251–252, 268, 279

reasoning   107, 182–183, 287
recency   229, 231, 233
recognition   216, 226

reference corpus   273, 280
register   21, 177, 181, 269, 296, 299
reliability   11, 152, 156, 166–167, 169
resonance   18, 20–22, 24, 26–29, 31–32
retrieval   *see* data retrieval

salience   10, 20, 22, 44, 93, 110, 119, 128, 138, 183, 194, 290, 294
sampling   80, 165, 170, 218–219
searching   *see* data retrieval
semantic change   14, 129, 176, 185, 191, 195, 210–211
semantic field   5, 96, 103, 176, 183, 185
semantic prosody   114–116, 118
semi-fixed expressions   118, 124–125, 131, 145–146, 241, 287
sense annotation   *see* annotation, semantic
similarity   280–282, 286–288, 291–293, 297
simile   82, 88, 115, 267, 271, 280–282, 286–291, 293–294, 296–301; *see also* comparison statement

statistics   *see* quantitative analysis
stereotype   17, 20
structural metaphors   41
synonymy   28, 65, 70–72, 96–97, 99, 101
syntax   *see* grammar
systematicity   7, 103, 107–108, 146

tagging   1, 38–39, 154, 219–220, 222–224, 237, 243–244, 248, 253–254, 258
text type   38, 40, 220
Theory of Norms and Exploitations   19
token   27, 98, 140–141, 241, 243, 249–250
translation equivalents   69, 98
type   98, 249–250
type-token ratio   8, 248–249

universality   71, 103, 239
usage   17, 29, 90–91, 152, 176, 178, 182, 184, 239

word class   8, 106–110, 112, 120, 125, 131–132, 143, 246, 248, 251

Index of domains and mappings

absence 101
absence of happiness as shadow 101
acceptability 72
acceptable behavior 72
accessibility 47, 50
accessible to awareness 50–52
accessible to awareness as in front 52
accessible to awareness as out 50–52
accessible to awareness as up 50–52
accessible to awareness as visible 52
accessible to consideration 52
accessible to consideration as in front 52
accessible to consideration as visible 52
accessible to perception 50–51
accessible to perception as up 50–51
accompaniment 92, 94, 96, 101
achieving a purpose 46–47
achieving a purpose as acquiring a desired object 46–47
acquiring a desired object 46–47
acquisition 46–47
act/acting/activity 9, 92–94, 96, 101, 128, 130–131, 133, 136, 138–139, 146, 193, 197, 208, 210
act for complex act 138
acting in an emotional state as being accompanied by an emotion 92, 94, 96, 101
acting on an emotion as acting in a location 93–94
activity for agent 131, 136
adoration 67
affair 264
affection 266, 290
affection as warmth 290
agent 131, 136
aggressive animal behavior 71, 74, 84
aggressiveness 71, 72, 74, 84
ahead 269
ahead-behind 269
alarm clock 205

altar 265
America 294
America as door 294
America as promise 294
America is like a shining city 294
anger 70–74, 76–77, 90, 92–93, 95
anger as balloon 78
anger as blood 78
anger as darkness 77
anger as fierce animal 77
anger as fire 63–64, 75, 77
anger as gorge 77
anger as hardness 78
anger as heat 75, 101
anger as hot liquid in a container 75, 77, 92
anger as light 77
anger as liquid 75–77
anger as mixed substance 77
anger as natural force 75
anger as object 75
anger as physical annoyance 72
anger as plant 77
anger as pure substance 77
anger as sleeping organism 77
anger as substance 75
animal 71, 74, 77, 80, 82–83, 85–86, 92, 95, 110, 157, 193, 205, 269
animal that lives well 80, 82–83
animated behavior 72
antagonistic communication 6, 37, 44, 55–56
antagonistic communication as physical conflict 6, 37, 44, 55–56
appetite 265
argument 6, 40–42, 44, 48, 55, 65, 67, 108, 197
argument as missile 67
argument as war 6, 40–42, 44, 48, 55, 65, 108, 197
armed physical conflict 40
arms 259, 264

312 *Index of domains and mappings*

assault   260, 264
assistance   57
assistance as support   57
attack   261, 263
attaining happiness as capturing something   97–98
attaining happiness as finding something   97–98
attention   130, 133, 136, 144–146
aura   88, 94–95, 101
authority   204, 206–207, 210
awareness   50–52

back   276
back-front   276
backfire   262
bad   290
ball   261
balloon   78, 84, 89
bankroll   261
barking dog   205
barrier   81
base   93
battle   259, 263
becoming accessible as emerging   47, 50–51
bed   264
behavior   72
behind   269
beholder   137
being angry as being a functioning machine   73
being down   86, 94
being happy as being an animal that lives well   82
being happy as being off the ground   80, 83, 96, 98
being happy as being up   80, 83, 96, 98
being in heaven   80, 83
beleaguer   265
bet   259
birth   203
bite   266
bitter   290
bitter as bad   290
blitz   260
block of ice   297

blood   78, 84, 87, 261, 264
blossom   112–113, 119
body   51, 192–193, 196, 202–203, 209
body as container   51, 202
body as a container for fear   202
body part for person   137
body part   137
bomb   260, 266
border   200, 207
boundary   202
bounded space   202
bruise   260, 264
brutality   262, 265
burden   71, 74, 78–79, 85–86, 90
bursting   100
business   252, 269
business as race   269
business as war   252
business takeover as hunt   269

campaign   259
capital   160
capital for government   160
captive animal   80–81, 83, 85–86, 92
capture   80–81, 83, 85–86, 92, 97–98
card   261
casualty   261, 266
catch   260
cause   73, 92–94, 99, 128
cause for effect   128
cause of an emotion as departure point of a moving object   99
causing an emotion as transferring an object   93–94, 99
causing anger as trespassing   73
center   145
center as eye   145
centrality   179
champion   260
chaos   207
cheat   262
child   203
chip   260
city   294
clarity   278
clarity as intelligibility   278
cleanliness   110–111

Index of domains and mappings

cleverness 178
close as cooperative 277
close texture 175
closeness 277
cloud 101
club 272
coldness 76, 81, 89
combat 261, 265
commercial activity 219–220, 222–224
commercial activity as container 219–220, 222–224
commercial activity as path following 219–220
commercial activity as path 222–224
commercial activity as war 219–220, 222–224
commodity 196, 199, 202, 208–210
communication 45
communication as sending 45
company 269
company as person 269
completed activity for agent 131
concern 134, 144
conduit 45–49, 55
conflict 6, 37, 40, 44, 55–56
conqueror 262, 266
consideration 52–54
considering as looking at 52
constituent 46–47
constituent as contents 46–47
container 45, 69, 71, 74–81, 83–86, 88–89, 92, 99, 179, 181, 193, 196, 200–203, 205, 207, 209, 219–220, 222–224
contents 46–47, 50
control 200, 206–207, 209
consummation 265
cooperation 277
court 264
cow 111
cut-throat 262

dalliance 265
dark 81, 85
darkness 7, 76–77, 86, 102
decrease in happiness as shadow 101
defeat 262, 264
defense 263

density 177–181, 183, 186–187
departure point 99
depicted 138, 144
depiction 138, 144
depiction for depicted 138, 144
depth 84, 88, 90, 94, 101
desert 22, 31
desire 67, 264
destroyable object 84
devour 266
digestion 264
dirt 110
discussion 67
discussion as war 67
disease 76, 84, 89
disgust 71, 88, 94–95
disgust as illness 94
disgust as nausea 88
disregard 135
distance 277
divorce 265
dog 205
door 294
down 77, 85, 95, 269, 276
down-up 276

earth 178, 180, 182, 189
economy 9
effect 128
emergence 47, 50–51, 57
emotion 69, 77, 92–94, 96–97, 99, 101, 193, 196, 203, 209
emotion as inanimate object 193
emotion as aura 94, 101
emotion as being down 94
emotion as being off the ground 93
emotion as being up 93
emotion as fire 92, 193
emotion as foundation 93
emotion as fragile object 101, 193
emotion as heat 92
emotion as heated liquid 92
emotion as impure substance 94
emotion as light 99
emotion as liquid 69, 99
emotion as living organism 193
emotion as location 93–94

emotion as mixed substance   101
emotion as moving object directed at someone   101
emotion as natural force   193
emotion as object   92–94, 193
emotion as object directed at someone   92–93
emotion as object in a location   94
emotion as opponent   193
emotion as pain   94, 101
emotion as possessed object   92
emotion as possession   99
emotion as pure substance   94, 101
emotion as substance in a container   99
emotion as substance under pressure   92
emotion as superior   93
emotion as valuable object   193
enabling consideration as pointing   53
enabling consideration as providing a visual representation   54
enabling   53–54
enabling knowledge as pointing   53
enabling knowledge as providing a visual representation   54
endgame   262
enemy   78, 79, 205, 261, 264
energy   47, 49
entity   196, 179, 207–208
esteemed person   204, 210
Euro   272
Euro as club   272
Euro as mechanical object   272
event   152, 161, 163, 167, 169, 170
existence   53
existence as visibility   53
expression   139
eye   130–131, 133–139, 144–146
eye for beholder   137
eye for expression   139
eye for vision   135–136, 144
eye for watching   130–131, 133–136, 138–139, 144–146

facility   162, 167–168
fairness   259
fast   259

fear   70–71, 78–81, 90, 93, 95, 196, 198, 202, 206, 208–209
fear as bounded space   202
fear as burden   79, 90
fear as causer   93
fear as commodity   202
fear as enemy   78
fear as heavy object   80, 90
fear as incomplete object   78–79
fear as opponent   202
fear as opponent in struggle   78
fear as sleeping organism   80
fear as tormentor   78
fear as vicious enemy   78
fear of god   202, 209
ferret   112
field   260
fierce animal   77, 95
fierceness   77, 95, 260, 264
fight   259, 263
finding   97–98
fire   63–64, 71, 74–75, 77, 84, 92, 124, 193
flame   115–116
flirt   265
flow   25
fluid   *see* liquid
food   89, 178, 180–182, 189, 266
force   25, 71, 74–75, 78–79, 81, 83, 85–86, 196, 205–206, 209
forward motion   276–277, 279
foundation   93, 95
fragile object   101, 193
fragility   101, 193
front   52, 260, 265, 276
front-back   276
fullness   99–100
functioning machine   73–74
functioning   74

gambit   261
game   259
garbage   208
general terms   178
ghost   205
goal   259
gobble   264
god   202, 209

Index of domains and mappings 315

goodness   290
gorge   76–77
government   160
greed   265
guard   261
gulp   266

head-to-head   260
happiness   7, 70–71, 77, 80, 82–84, 88, 93, 95–99, 101
happiness as balloon   84
happiness as being in heaven   82
happiness as being off the ground   94
happiness as being up   94
happiness as blood   84
happiness as light   101
happiness as pleasurable physical sensation   82–83
happiness as sharp object   84
happiness as vitality   82
happiness as warmth   83
hard   78, 269
hard-soft   269
health   80, 82–83
healthy skin color   82
heart   87, 123–124
heart for person   123–124
heat   71, 74–77, 81, 84–86, 88–89, 92, 95, 101
heaven   82
heaviness   80, 89–90
heavy object   89
height   77, 81, 83, 92
home   200, 207
hostility   263
hot liquid   71, 74–75, 77, 92, 95
hounded   112
human   205, 208
hunger   265
hunt   97, 269

idea   45, 68, 192
idea as object   45, 192
illness   78–79, 85–86, 94–95
importance   179
important as central   179
impure substance   94

in   276
inability   97
inability to attain happiness as inability to reach something   97
inanimate object   193
incomplete object   78–79
incompleteness   78–79
inconvenience   72
index   164, 166–168
inferiority   203
information   47, 50
information as contents   47, 50
innocent child   204
in-out   276
insanity   71, 74, 79, 81, 83, 85–86, 90, 207
instrument   128, 130, 133, 139, 146, 196–197, 209–210
instrument for activity   128, 130, 133, 139, 146
intellection   193
intelligence   177, 179–182
intelligibility   278
intensity   76–77, 84, 89, 90, 92–94, 101
intensity as depth   90
intensity of anger as height   77
intensity of emotion as depth   94, 101
intensity of emotion as height   92
intensity of emotion as quantity   93–94
intensity of emotion as size   93–94
intensity of happiness as depth   84
intention   134, 144
interest   135, 144

jackpot   262
judge   204
juicy   266
Juliet   294
Juliet as sun   294
jump   259
jungle   30

kick   261
killer   259, 264
kiss   265
knowing as seeing   52, 55
knowledge   53–54

lack   85–86
lack of heat   85–86
lack of vitality   85–86
launch   259
law   206
leader   203–204
league   262
learned person   204, 210
learning   47
learning as acquiring   47
less   77
less as down   77
light   7, 68, 76–77, 80–81, 83, 87, 99, 101–102
linguistic expression   45
linguistic expression as container   45
liquid   69, 71, 74–78, 79–81, 83–86, 88–89, 92, 95, 99–100, 201, 203
liquid in container   79–80, 83, 85–86, 201
living organism   193
location   25, 92–95, 153, 157–159, 165, 169, 171–172, 219–220, 222–224; see also place
looking at   52
loss of control   207
love   66–67, 71, 124, 196, 199, 201, 205, 209, 264
love as liquid in container   201
love as fire   124
love as natural force   205
love as physical force   205
love as valuable commodity   199
love as war   66
luck   261
lust   67, 71, 265

machine   74, 179, 193, 269
man   108, 111
man as wolf   108, 111
maneuver   261, 266
manipulation   193, 197, 208, 210
marriage   263
mating   246, 265
meaning   45
meaning as object   45
measure   197, 207
mechanical object   272

member   162, 164, 167–168, 170
mental activity   9, 193, 197, 208, 210
mental activity as manipulation   193, 197, 208, 210
mind   179, 181, 192–193, 196–197, 204, 207–208, 210
mind as authority   204
mind as body   192
mind as brittle object   179
mind as container   181
mind as entity   179
mind as machine   179
mind as machine   193
mind as scales   197
mind as workshop   193, 207–208
missile   67
mix   76, 77, 81, 84, 88–89, 101
money   68
more   77
more as up   77
movement   56–57, 99, 110–111, 276–277
moving forward as necessary   276
moving object   99, 101
moving object directed at someone   101

name   163, 167–168
nasty person   205
natural force   71, 74–75, 78–79, 81, 83, 85–86, 193, 205
nausea   88
necessity   276
negative emotion as darkness   77
negative entity   208, 210
nibble   266
non-watching   135
non-watching for disregard   135
numerical value   219–220, 222–224
numerical value as location   219–220, 222–224
nuptials   266

oasis   28–29
object   45–47, 69, 75–76, 78–81, 84, 89, 90, 92–95, 99, 101, 163–164, 167–168, 179, 192–193, 272
object directed at someone   92–93
object for name   163, 167–168

Index of domains and mappings   317

object for representation   163–164
object in a location   94
obstacle   196, 198, 208
off the ground   80, 83, 93–96, 98
opening   262
opinion   137, 145
opinion as viewpoint   137, 145
opponent   71, 74, 78–79, 81, 83, 85–86, 89, 193, 202, 205
opponent in a struggle   78, 81, 83
order   207
organ   69
organ as container   69
organism   69, 76–77, 80–81, 84–86, 89, 193
organization   157–159, 162–168, 169–172
organization for event   163, 167, 169
organization for facility   162, 167–168
organization for index   164, 166–168
organization for members   162, 164, 167–168, 170
organization for product   162, 167, 171
orgasm   21
orgy   21
out   50–52, 276
out-in   276

pack   261
pain   74, 81, 89, 94–95, 101–102
palatable   266
paralysis   89
part   127, 135–136, 139–138, 144
part for part   127, 135–136, 139–138, 144
part for whole   127, 136
path   222–224
path-following   219–220
pawn   262
people   125, 157, 160, 162, 164, 170
perceptibility   50
perceptible as out   50
perception   135, 139, 144
person   123–124, 137, 157, 193, 204–205, 269
physical annoyance   71–72, 74
physical conflict   6, 37, 40, 44, 55–57
physical force   85–86, 205

physical pressure   56–57
physical proximity   57
physical sensation   80, 82–83
physical support   56–57
physical wellbeing   102
pig   111
place   125, 152, 157, 160–164, 170, 201; *see also* location
place for event   152, 161, 163, 170
place for people   125, 157, 160, 162, 164, 170
place for product   161
plant   76–77, 193, 205
play   259
pleasurable physical sensation   80, 82–83
pleasure   80, 82–83
pointing   53
poker   262
politics   9
positive emotion as light   77
possessed object   92
possession   47, 99
predator   263
pressure   81, 84, 88–89, 92, 99–100
prey   264
pride   71
product   161–162, 167, 171
product for user   171
progeneration   203
progress   276
progress as forward motion   276
promise   294
providing   54
punch   260
pure substance   76–77, 84, 88–89, 94, 101
purpose   46–47
pursuit of happiness   93, 101

quantity   93–94

race   260, 269
raid   263
rapture   81, 83
reason   196, 198, 204, 206–207, 209–210
reason as authority   210
reason as measure   207

reason as safe place   207
relationship   263
representation   163–164
rip   261
RM   47, 49, 51
RM as possession   47
rock   114
romance   266
root   113
rope   200, 207
run   260

sadness   7, 71, 84–87, 90, 94–95, 99
sadness as being down   94
sadness as blood   87
sadness as heart   87
sadness as insanity   90
sadness as light   87
sadness as sharp object   87
safe place   200, 202, 207, 209
safety   200, 207, 209
Sally as block of ice   297
Sally is like a block of ice   297
sanity   200, 207, 209
sanity as safety   200, 207, 209
scales   197
score   260
sea   18, 23–25, 30, 32–34
searching   93, 96–97, 99
seeing   52, 55, 57
sending   45
sex   265
sexual desire   71
shadow   101
shame   71
sharp object   76, 81, 87, 89
sharpness   76, 81, 84, 89
shoot   260, 264
size   93–94
skin color   82
sleep   76–77, 80
sleeping organism   76–77, 80
society   18
society as sea   18
soft   269
soldier   266
sound   88

space   201–202
speed   182, 260
spit   266
squirrel   109–110
stakes   260
stem   113
storm   17, 19
struggle   74, 78, 81, 83
stupidity   175, 178, 192
stupidity as close texture   175
subordinate   127, 204
subordinate for subordinate   127
subordinate for superordinate   127
substance   75–77, 81, 84, 88–89, 92, 94, 99, 101, 178
substance in container   81, 84, 88–89, 99
substance under pressure   92
suitor   263
sun   101, 294
superior   72, 74, 78–79, 93, 95, 205
supernatural being   78–79, 205, 208
superordinate   127
superordinate for subordinate   127
supervising   138, 144
supervision   145
support   57
supreme authority   204
surprise   71
surrender   261, 266
survival   259, 263
sweet as good   290
swallow   264
sweetness   290

takeover   269
target   259, 263
taste   88
tether   200, 207, 209
thorn   290
thorn as bad   290
throw   260
time-out   262
tire   260
tool   196–198, 210
tormentor   78, 205
torrent   30
touch   179

Index of domains and mappings   319

transfer   47, 49, 57, 92–94, 99
transmission of energy   47, 49
transmission of energy as transfer   47, 49
trench   260
trespassing   71
trickster   205
troops   261, 264
trump   261
trying to attain an emotion as searching for an emotion   96–97, 99
trying to attain an emotion as searching for an object   93
trying to attain happiness as hunting for something   97
trying to attain happiness as searching for something   97
turf   261

unacceptable behavior   72
understanding   52, 192–193, 208
up   50–52, 77, 94, 80, 83, 93, 95, 96, 98, 269, 276
up-down   269, 276
user   171

valuable commodity   208
valuable object   193
value   193, 196, 199, 208–210
veteran   261, 265
vicious enemy   78, 205
viciousness   78, 205
victim   265
victory   262–263
viewpoints   137, 145
violence   85–86
violent natural force   85
violent physical force   85–86
visibility   52–53, 57
vision   54, 135–136, 139, 144, 181, 193
vision as intellection   193

vision as manipulation   193
vision for good perception   135
vision for perception   139, 144
visual representation   54
vitality   80, 82–83, 85–86
vulnerability   263

wanting   134, 144
war   6, 40–42, 44, 48, 55, 65–67, 108, 197, 219–220, 222–224, 246, 252, 259, 263
warmth   80, 83, 290
warmth as good   290
waste   208
watching   130–131, 133–136, 138–139, 144–146
watching for attention   130, 133, 136, 144–146
watching for concern   134, 144
watching for intending   134, 144
watching for interest   135, 144
watching for supervising   138, 144
watching for supervision   145
watching for wanting   134, 144
weapon   196–197, 209–210, 262, 266
weather   88, 94
wedding   266
weed   208
weight   79
whip   198, 209
whole   127
whole for part   127
wide expanse   25
wild animal   81
wit   196, 201, 204, 207, 210
wit as liquid in a container   201
wit as worker   210
wolf   108, 111
wood   178, 180, 182, 188
wooer   265
workers   210
workshop   193, 207–208